Critical Leisure

Copyright © 2017 by Ariel Samuel Ackrum

All rights reserved.
No part of this publication may be reproduced, distributed, or transmitted in any form or by any means, including photocopying, recording, or other electronic or mechanical methods, without the prior written permission of the publisher, except in the case of brief quotations embodied in critical reviews and certain other noncommercial uses, such as research or private study, permitted by copyright law. For permission requests, email publisher at the address listed below.

Simulacradelic Press
Atlanta, GA
simulacradelicpress@gmail.com
www.simulacradelic.com

Cover & Design by Seth Stubbs
Edited by Seth Stubbs

Library of Congress Control Number: 2017964214
ISBN-13: 978-0-9993980-0-5 (PBK)
eISBN-13: 978-0-9993980-1-2
1. Poetry 2. Philosophy

First Edition

10 9 8 7 6 5 4 3 2 1

Printed in the United States of America

CRITICAL LEISURE

THE POETRY OF SIMULATION

POEMS, 2010-2015

THE ONE-VOLUME EDITION

ARIEL SAMUEL ACKRUM

For my twin.

No ideologies were harmed in the making of this book, for unhinged doors can neither open nor close.

Contents

Book I

Preface: To the Consumer   3

Volume I: Spunctum

1. In loving memory   13
2. My own private network   13
3. a day   14
4. An hour of student email in my pocket   15
5. two women   16
6. Leaving Las Vegas   19
7. "It's a man!" – The Riddle of Technology   20
8. High schooling   24
9. an accusation is not an understanding   24
10. worshippers   28
11. Equipment   29
12. Ambiguous timing   30
13. Movie Theater Exit   30
14. Reprobation   32
15. Mayday, or my day with Marilyn   33
16. Such a thing as   34
17. ento-mate   35
18. Chill Economy   36
19. Chill Economy Cont.   37
20. The Gymnast   37
21. Cheetos fingers   38

22.	this is a game for Us	39
23.	commune of bachelors	39
24.	I always met them, leaving	42
25.	Movie version of a poem about a poem made into a movie	43
26.	Child Judges	44
27.	*on a nice day*	44
28.	It's not forward, but not only new	45
29.	almost another raw-dog poem	46
30.	*certain about certainty*	48
31.	Acidification of Oceanic Feelings	49
32.	Auto-complete searches are pretentious poems	50
33.	*Stephán, asst. mngr.*	51
34.	Revenge of the Mud People	52
35.	gumball-amount-estimating Holocaust machine	53
36.	Where do they all come from?	56
37.	God's egg-beaters	57
38.	boyfriend for a night	59
39.	A note I left someone on a refrigerator somewhere	60
40.	how I lose credibility	61
41.	you over-think things or you stand under them	64
42.	The last poem I'll ever write	66
43.	self-assured self-erasure	67
44.	encapsulation at a distance	68
45.	Loose Lips of Lovers	69
46.	electromancer	72
47.	the models before the runway show	73
48.	dating=restaurants=jobs	76
49.	new delays	78
50.	porn industry	79
51.	closed captioning provided by Christmás. Live más.	79
52.	Daytime TV psychology	81
53.	the dresser	83
54.	vociferous hallucinations	84
55.	stop revolving	85
56.	the demand for poetry, poetry's deferral	86
57.	Carpe diem poem for the brain dead	88

58.	Mistaken Success Ethics	89
59.	"Follow the light with your eyes," said the policeman	91
60.	Door to door thief asking to borrow butter	94
61.	I am not the Kafka of the iPhone generation, but whatever	96
62.	Only my life have I written on an iPhone, never a poem	98
63.	Exegesis exceeds Jesus	100
64.	National Poiesis Party	102
65.	Ripcord of daily rip-off calendars	104
66.	I am better than you because I am better than me also	105
67.	CA Hon. ES	106
68.	Broadway for Christ-bone	107
69.	Thorazine Fanzine	110
70.	KT, Try Standing	112
71.	STARBUCKS, variety, and freedom	122
72.	The red, the white, and the blue	122
73.	Things Bukowski taught and did not merely teach me	123
74.	the webcam girl next door	125
75.	A scene from Family Guy but sadder	126
76.	zero emissions worse than thought experiments?	127
77.	'You better redneckonize'	127
78.	pre-emptive text poetry	128
79.	Katy Parity	129
80.	Katy Parity II	130
81.	Katy Parity III	131
82.	Iron(¬man)ic strategies	133
83.	Holography	134
84.	The In-Betweeners	134
85.	Perspectival ___	137
86.	The Mouth Also Eats	138
87.	No Former-Marine-Lovers!	139
88.	still young and like me	140
89.	the former granite capital of the world	142
90.	the primacy of melancholy	143
91.	kill fast boredom	144
92.	the folding of events and info like time and space will take you back	146

93. dawning on Eve	147
94. we gush redundancies	148
95. carrion	150
96. I wrote this for a girl to seduce her and read it to mine when it got bad.	152
97. CRACK	153
98. Reductio ad Worrisome	154
99. Unintentional Competition	157
100. the gymNazium	158
101. The Renaissance man who does everything half-ass	160
102. le chat noir, le trou noir, la boite noire, le trou du cul noir	161
103. a metaphysical reality	162
104. a seductive ugliness	162
105. new-age old age	163
106. Mudlarking in my living room	164
107. New Years is a man-god leisuring atop a mound…	165
108. The Screen-Effect of the Object	167

Volume II: Flavoring

109. the Lovers	175
110. The Scene	175
111. Instant Stardom	176
112. origami thought	177
113. Meth Ode	178
114. Try ills and tribe elations	179
115. Excellence, Human	180
116. the value of the intellect	183
117. tech support	185
118. the 69 position	187
119. pinch me, piñata	188
120. fear of the dark	188
121. backup drive	189
122. the one and the many	190
123. Met Ru Paul; I tan	190
124. Now	191
125. Textbook Rioting	191
126. the feeling of being lied to	195

127. vacancies for vacationers	195
128. (Total) Field (Vision) Trips	196
129. D, none of the above; E, all the above	196
130. Lindsey Low Han	198
131. Mapping the Unconscious	199
132. Dr. Jekyll skinning my hide	202
133. Primitive Pop Culture	203
134. There are other ways to win, but just playing is one of them	205
135. No complainandum. No explanandum.	207
136. Hope floats, but so do dead bodies	208
137. Authentically a machine	209
138. Don't personify the magic away to avoid a void	210
139. Transience. Pass it on.	213
140. Mayan doomsday/book of Manu	215
141. Blown	216
142. iDeals: new update available	217
143. Plug-in scent	218
144. The one down on the end	218
145. Stiffs get to the bottom of things	220
146. the writer I am	221
147. Anabolic Kleenex	222
148. The basement of the Vietnamese restaurant and of my resolve	224
149. The bleached asshole of capitalism	225
150. the good life mmmmm mmmmm good	226
151. Suet stains in the Highlands	227
152. TXT#hostage	229
153. Life, questionable slut that she is	231
154. Jesus moonwalking on water for viewers like you	232
155. Fast-Casual Tie Events	233
156. The sex of Rhianna, the sex of Martha Stewart	237
157. your days of plenty are numbered	239
158. Title does not suffice, it titillates	239
159. 'the destiny of a theory'	240
160. "Evian is naïve spelled backwards," said Janeanne Garofalo	241
161. Pisces is a riot	244
162. 195 the playboy character of the world	245

163.	No Thanks – a poem for a frenemy	246
164.	Castigate me cavities/Identitus	247
165.	the Superman isn't real, and he's Protean	250
166.	Sub-division Sandwiches	251
167.	twat-latch feasts and the NEW GIFT EXCHANGE	253
168.	Occupy Nature	255
169.	Real world: Mongol edition	255
170.	pacifier laced with LSD	256
171.	the politics of the remainder will make you laugh	258

Book II

Volume III: Speed Reading

172.	Faux-Pretentious Intelligentsia vs. Poetry That Really *'Kills It'*	267
173.	A POV poem about an eye turned in no particular direction	269
174.	the hotels are communities at last	269
175.	defecate the sugar-water of consciousness	271
176.	disaster socialism	272
177.	nights of the living dead	273
178.	rim jobs	274
179.	the anesthetics of banality	276
180.	post-modern chicks in a metamodern world	277
181.	Baroque suppleness	280
182.	the monogram of The Look	281
183.	suicide warnings through text message	283
184.	Pandering, or the Inconstant Constancy	286
185.	Theirselfies (from the English *Themselves*)	288
186.	13 years after the millennium 'failed' to take place	290
187.	vigilante castration	293
188.	Pan's Optic-Con (like Comic-Con)	294
189.	a more fate *I*	297
190.	cookie jar TV	301
191.	founded on a loss	303
192.	To the quirky characters they play, I love (am annoyed by) you all…	304

193. burn fat by cutting out depth	305
194. All that is left is human	306
195. most guidos	307
196. "if I'm not comfortable then I'm not having fun," said Taylor Lautner	308
197. obesity in nursing	309
198. secrets are anticipated	310
199. magazine attention	312
200. retard strength	314
201. The revolution will not be tweeted about	316
202. The Give and take. Or apophenia in practice.	318
203. Love is a hotline, make a B line	327
204. ladies' night dubstep curry	328
205. "Keep Rollin'," said Fred Durst	333
206. précis time	334
207. After Playland	336

Volume IV: Tr@nsf®@t

208. Autumn	345
209. You called me one of those literary theorist guys…	345
210. Trash-cam Lid	348
211. 'What does Chuck Klosterman *not* write about?'	348
212. Poverty is a slimming diet…	350
213. The remnants of a poem I wrote about Iraq, having never been there	353
214. Pit of Balls/Parisian Occupation of Texas	355
215. *This is the life I chose*	358
216. Unjustly cared-for songwriter	360
217. The One, Part II	362
218. Three O(D)'s	365
219. Jarry-rigged	366
220. incoming outrage against outrageous income	367
221. life crisis or something	373
222. Tao Lin is a little bit weirder than I am	375
223. force-feeding optional	376
224. Kim KarDasein is a hot lil' Cummodity	377

225. what the hell kind of show is this?	378
226. we already live forever	379
227. Akrasia	381
228. The cornices of limits	382
229. Tattooed and pierced Christians	383
230. Shel Silverstein Died in Key West, Florida	385
231. imposter syndrome	386
232. Ego depletion	387
233. Give Nature privacy	388
234. Denouncing-nunnery	390
235. raspy poetry	394
236. Animal Planet is strangely Human	394
237. Bump in the Night/The bubbly girl on Train 9	395
238. Inner Tube	397
239. trick or treat, an inclusive disjunction	398
240. The fetish of lovemaking (*or love production*)	399
241. We are all a psychologist's wet dream	401
242. The elephants broke free	402
243. Whiskey poetry or suicide	402
244. Harsh lighting	404

Book III

Volume V: Free Advertising

245. an end to mourning, to mania, to melancholia, to another me	413
246. The Dentist	420
247. Moving Target	422
248. fetishes	426
249. when I shit in winter, I point the heater towards me	428
250. Light-writing in caves	429
251. her salience	430
252. befits the muse	434
253. falling asleep second	439
254. The diabolism of the mirror	440
255. teen mom	442
256. Merry xxxmas	442

257. 'if babies ruled the world, there would be peace on earth.'	443
258. the fat lady sings in auto-tune	444
259. Now and then	445
260. Spelunking	446
261. I never saw her outside Gainesville, GA	446
262. The main attractions of vacations are tourists	447
263. Muham-club-med	449
264. arcade-goers are better off gamblers, prisoners are better off cheaters	450
265. ultrathin condoms	451
266. They fatally groom you for it	453
267. The Cure	456
268. we are all flat screens on which our lives play out for others	462

Volume VI:
Love_Is_An_Anonymous_Cyberbully

269. Singled Out – the underscore and space	467
270. I(E)dentity (or IED entity)	467
271. Bulimia et cetera	470
272. Famous Last Words	470
273. Famous Last Words Cont.	474
274. Suicide	477
275. Campsite, me	480
276. her candlelit viscera	481
277. the soul escapes as an odor	483
278. Subscription-based 'experience' economy	486
279. depth of field	487
280. Immaterial Shit	491
281. almost everything	492
282. flowery language	496
283. motion blur	497
284. "You're not going to like it when I get super tan pre-Paris," she said	499
285. the voice-over monologue at the end of the movie	500
286. Pathos? Sounds Mexican.	502

287. leave the screen of wealth behind, blessed Capricorn	503
288. '50s America Today	504
289. @n@rchy	505
290. Head-scratching contra head-shrinking	507
291. new management	509
292. the cigarette	509
293. the singular plural	510
294. "My struggle," a personal brand	511
295. X Acto (ex-acted) knife	515
296. urgency and forbearance	516
297. The tablet	518
298. dónde está?	520
299. Ellipsis	523
300. Lubricate it with a smile	523
301. melancholia	526
302. sequester me with your skirting fancies	526
303. the togetherness of mixed media	527
304. our strabismic pauses	530
305. Contraria (formerly Utopia)	531
306. A night on the town	532
307. black diamond cross-section of my expressionless face	532
308. the rape of the lock(ed heart)	533
309. the streetwalker	539
310. She is a terror	539
311. etiology of panic	544
312. alcohol on psychiatrics	546
313. Today is just a show for now	546
314. The way she and Saint Nick love me	548
315. phishing for compliments	551
316. Morning breath	551
317. Severed nerve of death	552
318. dirty dancing	552
319. Ode on the Avalon Shopping Center/Neighborhood	554
320. stationery magic	559
321. compensation, a sensation	561
322. clean me with your sandpaper tongue, Leo	562
323. her plastic network of love: arranged a(r)mour, aimless love	563
324. Her needless love	565

325. Startup company	570
326. a transition, Love	572
327. One genius and talented millions	574
328. snapchat	578
329. There Is No Natural High	581
330. the rapid pelvic thrust of anality	582
331. fetish-conscious fetishizers	583
332. I prefer the dead to you, hero	585
333. Born second	587
334. The light in the oven	589
335. font	589
336. On agon, off agon – le cirque de logique	590
337. Youth, get a Life	593
338. save a troll, ride a toll-road	596
339. If I don't disappear	598
340. Poetry is no longer itself	600
341. "Be together, not the same," said the marketer	604
342. Blistery night	605
343. a tree, you can't move me	608
344. Burnout	609
345. under the hood of the vagina	609
346. Slim-picking	610
347. the Dada, doubling and annulling the phoneme	613
348. scrying	614
349. how to make it in this economy	615
350. A language	617
351. The sacrifice of plasticity or the plasticity of sacrifice	618
352. Let us be satellites without love	620
353. My 'goal'	621
354. I am also disgusted by my morals	622
355. Tres Equis Especial and the Most Uninteresting Man in the World	623
356. first impressions	625
357. The beauty of appearances	628
358. Beauty is secretive	628
359. Slippery when wet, she was	630
360. Indifference, hatred, seduction	635
361. Don't take my word for it	636
362. The leap is not a fall	637

363. reification through anti-reification 638
364. Baby, you are a K-hole (from what I
    understand) 638
365. Lorem Ipsum 639
366. Jerking off 640
367. I hate hating myself and wanting to die
    makes me want to die 641
368. Mao Mix for House Cats 642
369. Incompatibility 644
370. Trauma, what dreams are made of 647
371. narcissistic withdrawal 650
372. Endless material for theory 650
373. The paparazzo poet 652
374. Is there a from death, not an out of death? 654
375. To whom is what is given up given 657

BOOK I

When poetry is everywhere simulated, and thus no longer of interest, what becomes fascinating is a poetic disappearance into simulation—and the deleterious amount of leisure required for the pretense of the latter process.

Preface

To the Consumer

The naïve, propitious, seductive worm—
nagging bot fly, 666 microchip—
thereupon was a gnawing at the Will…
ready-made, aching, monolithic coo.

From end-credit screens we gather fructose
to nurse our diabetic Geist, ingest
glucose syrup as the crops have toxins
that rid appearances of syphilis whores.

Dream of virulence in our haute, trained brains
to project ourselves indefatigably,
and from the fissures of our complicity
a touchscreen Fugue *states* and *compliments* us.

O simulacra deliver us from
the evil spirits of yester and fore,
exorcize historicity. Le malhuer?
J'adore! Criminal past! Virtual saint!

God is dead, but Satan left us before!
That anti-remorse proves its opposites:
"Internalize terror. I'll be your mirror.
Phantom omen, amen dull overture."

Critical Leisure, Book I

God's name—erectile dysfunction of poems.
Catchy brand of Isis— "History: a gif."
Ready-had sex. All-holes-filled beauties.
Signs wobble, pulsate… /cunt-meat/ will senesce.

Beauty-queen. Little miss erection there
flashed into the image-feedback.
Conversations sparked: "…complicit
to the demons' cause, tattooed above her clit."

We roll our eyes. The same thing happened
last week. Nothing exciting ever *occurs*.
We slip on our data-suits, tickled.
Moved by filthy plumpers, we *browse* Fate.

If only we could exorcize ourselves
to some languid Happy Island rehab—
slurp up all the pity and penitence
like actresses in Bukkake films.

Satan's smirk is never exchangeable
for tears that lubricate our masturbation,
but what's preferable to Satan's honesty:
Lucifer's sudden disappearance.

Our penetration into the gene
rivals only the cameras' of the cunt.
Forced orgasm, obligatory bliss
is more devilish than bleeding AIDS!

Excess equivalent to nothingness.
Growth hormones that undo virility.
Find then no trending human condition,
advertising little cum-sluts explore.

Indifference is *positively* next
in our evolution and reproduction.
Replace shadows with blushing cadavers.
New wounded! *Responsibility dispelled!*

Preface

Ennui, you once or twice carved our flesh
when we would masturbate 'til blisters burst.
Now, we huff female rags of Information
'til her wah-wah wicks our *erections*.

O Poets of Eternity behold!
No film series could model the bane
of flexibility and obsolescence—
the Hipster's "Fuck art for our sake."

O the data processors we became!
No more gaze! The end of the sign befalls!
We fell once, the contagious hex ensued:
Sin! Fell twice: out of reality hurled!

So long Satan. Even we're below You.
Death is even beyond us. Not us, Her!
Mephisto's evil-genius alludes
still—his most evil deed: transparency.

Our stupefaction, though still incomplete,
cries "All is simulacra. All is sign!"—
hyper-skeptics amongst flows and relays.
All roads Westward lead; neurons loosen, bend.

O glorious identity! For *that*, any
old rubbish will do! Scour the networks,
upload! The singular accident 'shows through'.
Anomie! The metastasizing queue!

The stage already extended into
auditoriums where mirrors distort
infinite light caught in the object's beam.
Anamorphosis! Perception! Delight!

Generous evil, nihilistic Good.
O Oedipus who murders his own clone.
Then Narcissus who makes love to his.

Critical Leisure, Book I

O bestial Orpheus, silence me
like the anthropomorphic God to Man.

One-hundred-thousand dying monarchs
bellow inside me, "Sit on your arse!"
Instead, I'm entitled a victim's riches,
that I beckon "More! More misfortune, please!"

A thousand little accidents to claim
to summon some scoffing objective cause—
suppressant t'exercise emotional absence
and conjure up an answer, a project.

No 'Through the Monitor' like the looking glass.
So long spectacle—dilettantish term!
Modal operation: 'O hyperreal…
O criminal gene—anagrammatize!'

Satan that thinks me, *ex nihilo* saint!
A *lonely* Samarkand befell to *me*.
Beyond relevance—wager even chance.
Evil-genius unfold! Much to wallow in.

The scenic God: *ab nihilo* mystic.
From Lilith's boudoir, phonetic moans!
There materialize linguistic fools
that fossilize on God's performance.

Mere relevance: doubly doltish twin.
And will to truth: a twofold avatar
with whom Atlas smokes his hookah.
Evil's axial hypostasis: Good.

De-regulation on all fronts t'counter
th'hermetic remorse of the death o' God—
histrionicist of our supplantation.
O genius, by which machine in your stead?

If ersatz, strabismus, stultifaction

Preface

have not yet spoken our pluperfect draft—
the prosaic bulb of our blinking fate—
it's only that our knelling is extant.

VOLUME I
SPUNCTUM

*If critics find no art
in the following section,
that's because none remains.
Neither do the poems themselves
have stakes as simulacra. On
this I stake everything, for
in it I 'have' a share.*

Spunctum

1. In loving memory

In the end, the crowd is pushed back
and calmed as if in front of a nightclub—
the World's Night club
(a night concealed by the light of the metro-area)—
by polite bouncers,
ones with useless muscles that are insurance agents by day.
They are the PR execs of the boundary between happening and dull,
the latter concept being that of Reality
for these night owls of Minerva.

The program that they issue at his funeral—
the funeral always about the guilt
morality
and redemption
of those who still haven't croaked from such illnesses,
the still-visible crowd,
a still-plowable market unlike the demographic of the dead
(the written beyond measure)—
is made of tan construction paper:
the costly deconstructed bedding for gerbils
unsafe for the ones who will eat it.

He looks like he is enjoying death.
His smile is more smiley than mine.

2. My own private network

It's hard being nothing/everything/*something*
in one go.

Though I've got wood, let me tell You—
it is a wood/plastic composite.

It is all a Rushed arousal.
I am tugged in all directions
and all my contradictions gather all in a hurry
beneath the canopy of a homepage.

3. a day

The sound of your spouse sucking cocktails
down their windpipe
the sound of your spouse clipping their toe nails
in the next room
the sound of the garage door opening and all the animals going
insane
the sound of fat people walking in jeans, khakis
or wind breakers
the sound of old people eating creamed corn
the sound of a cat playing with grocery bags
the sound of a dog digging in its bed
the sound of a whistling septum
the sound of the shower running—with no one in it
the sound of the computer breathing its hot breath
warming the planet and my loins
the sound of old high-heels with the bottoms worn off
the sound of a touchdown, a deflection, an injury
the sound of the invasive screen
as the advertisements Mayflower closer to shallow
the sound of cereal boxes violently opened
the sound of the house settling
the sound of forks and knives against plates

Spunctum

the sound of the recliner reclining
like a mechanical bull
the sound of the keyboard
and ak-47s with the serial numbers scratched off
the sound of serial numbers scratched off
like lottery tickets with no winnings.

4. An hour of student email in my pocket

Student credit card.
"University president personally asks
that you fill out a survey,"
says his secretary.
Colloquium series.
Call for papers.
Upcoming conference.
Casting Call.
New internships available.
Jobs available.
Campus jobs.
Free résumé help.
Practice test.
Sack lunch round table discussion.
Philosopher's guild film series.
Student credit card.
40% off;
60% off with promo code;
20% off for this weekend only.
Campus jobs.
New internship available.
CIA recruiters.
Calling All Public Policy Majors!

Critical Leisure, Book I, Volume I

Book Cheap Flights…
Concerts in your area.
New E-Harmony matches.
Local singles!
Want to fuck hot, local singles?!

You carry your attachment in constant reach,
taking it to bed with you like an orifice.

We are all choking on each other's coupons
invitations
and best wishes—
advertisements—*not* the ill will of yesteryear.

    5. two women

The first, I saw her at an Amish restaurant somewhere in SC.
The nicest building in the whole town was a KFC/Taco Bell,
nicer than the city hall/hospital.
She was serving from behind the island of delicious food fit for
slaves.
I watched her struggle to stand
to get out of an old Dodge Neon
and float—her cane did most of the walking—
into the back of the little eatery.
She must've been 100 years old.

Most of the muscle in her face had turned to mush—
a representation of her insides.
But the worst part was that her lip was tucked into her dentures
so it really appeared like part of her face was missing,
even though the tucking-in of the lip was *more* disturbing.

Spunctum

I expected one of the other workers to have put a spell on her
to either age her or keep her alive
(as if a walking corpse, hungry but without teeth).
Her skull looked on too tight and it made her eyes bulge out.
They looked more like balls than eyes.
Then she faced me.
It was penetrating like people imagine experiences of possessions.
Real visceral, like I just swallowed something too big—
maybe a million flies like The Green Mile
or a billion demons or their ancestors, germs.

At the table, someone said "Isn't she a real inspiration?"
"Who?" asked others with intrigue.
"That old lady working up there!"
"Jesus Christ," I thought,
"this shit heap can't be acceptable to these fucking idiots,
let alone be a worthwhile goal, can it?"

The food was delicious.

The second, I met her in West Hollywood.
She worked at American Apparel,
and when I went in there with her brother to meet her
all the boys working there whistled at me.
She said "They were all like 'Who's *that*??!'"
Her voice was the sweetest.
I'll bet she could get whatever she wanted from a man.
She had training with daddy.
And you can't live in West Hollywood on a minimum wage
income,
now can you?

Every time we went out, daddy paid for us.

He even paid for the waitress at the 5* sushi restaurant in Beverly Hills
to eat some sushi with us.
But she wanted the waitress to eat the head of the shellfish.
I didn't complain but was embarrassed.

She got us many edibles and good strands of marijuana.
And she made me sandwiches when I didn't even ask.

She quit American Apparel.
Now nanny's part time.
Lives a better life than me from many—if not all—perspectives
and sometimes just to relax and re-energize
takes time off from the city of angels
to return home to the best family on earth.

She has followers, admirers and 'best friends' everywhere
when it comes to men.

She will probably (if she's smart) marry a doctor,
lawyer
or athlete.
She is cute,
a tease
and as companions, go one of the best ones you're going to find
if that's what you're into.
I could see her snagging a millionaire.
She's going to if she wants him to match her Standard of Living.
But with her daddy's money, she doesn't *have* to do shit.

Sometimes I think about how I could trick her
into falling for me,
but I know that would ruin her life,
so I just let her be and entertain the thought of her.

Spunctum

6. Leaving Las Vegas

Under a perennial kernel of truth, we kiss.
And just like the mistletoe it is parasitic.
Unfortunately, we fashion our idea of bliss
incriminating another (our imagined critic).

Without needing to be asked we spill our guts
and having emptied ourselves hope to unwind.
As soon as we're about to cum the scene cuts
and pressed into the lens we go partially-blind.

Rhythm is the real fancied without hyperbole,
and if language is the law verse is the loop-hole—
the officer that didn't show up for the hearing
or mentor that in one throw became the pupil.

If Life were a blonde she'd have black roots.
When she left my sight I'd say "Leave my sight!"
My last words weren't "All her points are moot"
only if "more meaning" wasn't my slogan for delight.

You'll decide to be Open—and on principle only—
but find principles as always already judgments.
Last spurned exotically you'll try out the homely
and, sacrifice unacknowledged, risk repugnance.

One jealous memory like a badgering spouse
will go through every single one of your things.
Suspecting another end that you might be about,
wherever you'll move away it'll attach stings.

7. "It's a man!" – The Riddle of Technology

My mother was a forensic investigator of animal feces.
The news correspondent
was a stomach dissolving the words of the expert, not an echo—
since there are no echoes from TV to TV.
The chain of command was the large intestine.
The masses were the small intestines.
The crowds were the villi—
many a villain (from the perspective of the whole).
In the small intestines, the shit sat and simmered
if the anchormen didn't do their jobs, so it was foretold.
The studying of the living out of the context of Life.
The form through which I write—
I have no control over it.
Neither is it a *duty*.
It may have come from Vietnam or Germany or Hollywood Squares—
from Anywhere, the primordial accidental Elsewhere.

The technology—the future perfect—
is not produced by the imaginary of the past.
We have reabsorbed an imagination that's at least as old as Plato—
more recently the '50s.
Descartes was an Imagineer,
so creative that he manufactured Doubt—
a doubt that he had to imagine b/c he couldn't find it in reality—
the Meditations scroll through space
like the soporific prefaces to Star Wars
…and science was founded this way.
The meal isn't so appetizing
when the locals tell you the bowl is made of the shit of blind creatures—
there is no delocalized sonoric meaning.

Spunctum

A homebody with a hyperactive imagination constructed, incognito,
a Sphinx that will outlast whole civilizations
with their securities & secret services & surveillance.
The Pentagon is afraid of people who can make nukes or something
out of paperclips and gum.
A little unknown writes a 2-pg. paper
turning Justified True Belief on its head
like a cow in a meat locker—
that beef is aged and corned.

Descartes in his jammies,
stroking his mustache and grinning metonymously.
Satan in the Garden hissing,
coiled around the test-tube tree, refrigerating it—
when the apple doesn't fall too far from it
except through Luck unfurnishable by the lab.
Warhol eyeballing the critics in the gallery
sifting through his paintings
like hillbilly 49ers pricing gold, saying "Can you believe this shit??!"
showing that it is possible to be a machine and live more than most—inherited from the cogito.
Morrison becoming a Barbie doll and child-king
and getting fat like an Indian on the rez.
Lebron winning the dunk contest during summer break.
Tiger, the Harvard grad having to go to sex rehab to save his career.
The hyena, the demon,
the woman,
the jester, the philosopher—
these things laugh more often than you,

Critical Leisure, Book I, Volume I

and they wouldn't even need a self if they ended up as one.
If your depression makes you 'more human',
they even one-up you in that,
but you won't catch them talking about it.
Without effort and with failed plans
these tricksters haunt epochs with riddles
(the original form of the joke)
and they don't even care because they aren't political.
Neither are we.

They are too selfish for that. I have made them so.
They even have the right to inebriation due to their extras.
Their genius is just leftovers after much waste,
a spot they missed when cleaning house…
sometimes they impregnate with pre-cum.
"Today, I think I'll destabilize the world
with my stability."
They make scientists nervous because—let's face it—
pretty things are terrifying
to those with a *sense* of rank,
even if that rank is illusory.
A single sentence from their thought
ignores volumes of data
from countless libraries
filled with noisy crowds.
The silence required in the library
is due to the noisiness of their spirits.
They are better off in the computer,
next to Big Bird and Leonard Cohen.
These creatures are annoying objects—
a computer that can drive church-going folk to monkey business
when talking to it doesn't work
and they get progressively more aggressive towards it.
They are accidents.

Spunctum

History is rubbernecking.

These hideous strangers, these monstrous vermin
represent natural downers—*endowment*—to the productive.
They beg the questions:
how could something invisible carry so much weight.
How could something carry so much force that doesn't work?
How could something without a politics
influence *us*?
Nature's little un-aborted accidents
don't need to compete over our souls like gods did.
They speed up the game—
pace-cars that exit the track once the wreckage has been removed,
allowing the race to finish
and the crowd to discharge.

One owes nothing to them,
but *nothing cannot be given.*
If they direct the future, it's not due to their desire but to our lack.
They aren't responsible
for their ghost being hunted by political readers,
scried upon by giggling teen witches.
They lived or didn't.

Foucault missed the joke,
and of course you can have him in your politics.
I just don't trust people who wrote more books than I have time for
and I usually lose interest
when people make an effort to show that they care
w/ paragraphs riddled with revolutionary enthusiasm.

8. High schooling

It was shit,
total shit,
but you could still play patty cake on a girl's behind
and she would turn around
and say "Hehe stooooooooppp ittt…"
while poking it out just a little more,
or push your lover into the fountain,
kick a trashcan over while talking about fucking
or watch the mothers shield their children
in the neighborhoods as you drove by.

Now they shield their stand-ins
from their honesty.

You are a stranger everywhere you go
and you never meet yourself.
That is how seduction continues.

9. an accusation is not an understanding

I think I'm (redundantly) 'pretty good looking'.

Very good looking structurally
but not the best (because of acne, height, x^{n+1}).

There are many I look at and think
"Wow, what a handsome person.
Ariel, are *you* that handsome??! How handsome are you *really*?
You know that you're handsome, but where do you fall on the scale?

Spunctum

And *how wide or big is the scale.*
How much room is there to move?"
At times, I look like shit (when I am looking)
and at times I am beautiful, moreover.

For assurance, I recall what the women,
the good looking (credible) ones, called me.
All those names: Anthony Perkins,
Superman,
Patrick Bateman
(those are the ones I recall at the moment—*I wonder why?*).

But it's hard to tell where you stand
only if you aren't standing on your own two feet.
Taking compliments from beautiful women
could have driven people more into meaning than I am
to their demises.
But me?
I even questioned myself
when the woman all the other men wanted
wanted me
or at the very least got mushy over me
and brought me up when I wasn't even around.
I also didn't care, instantly.

I often found that blowing such an opportunity
'on purpose'
felt more satisfying than attaining someone.

Of course, it *could have* only been
a little sister teasing her older brother/my friend.

But it happened so often from such diverse sources
that even on the terms of morality and its science

the sample population expressed neutrality.
So, my vanity…
if that is my malice, do not blame *me* for it.
Blame the flatterers,
women and men who perhaps even out of spite
complimented me as if I were a god,
their complement.

Bukowski knew he was ugly
and everyone applauded him.
And he *was* exuberant in his ugliness, wasn't he?
For some reason, it's not the same
if you know you're "incredibly handsome"
because people say it.
Though if that's indecent,
I am also dashing in that ugliness
to some extent
for some people.

It usually takes someone reckless to approach me,
I have been told.
I usually won't talk to you
because I am content with masturbating at home,
for my impulsivity is counter-balanced by laziness
that may come off as anxiety—
but those who have met me have never thought me anxious;
even when I've said I am, they've been suspicious.

My unconcern has often been made into *a matter*,
my distance into lack of care,
my lack of sociality into anti-sociality.

When I called myself anxious—when I supposedly lied—
I noticed that I sparked a curiosity unmatched by other approaches.

Spunctum

It is almost as if they've perceived an honest lie,
a natural contradiction
(and how that is different than an artificial one, I don't know)
a little crossword of emotion
before the words have made it into the public subconscious.

Two people used to collide
in the realms of their imaginations
when one person would touch the other first
when they arced off one another
and changed directions.
That was the magnetic hypothesis.

Out of 10,000 people who share your fantasy
and get off on your image while you get off on theirs
unbeknownst to yet considered by the both of you,
these little terminal connections
that occur across the world in subway trains
on campuses
at the bank
in the supermarket checkout line
on aircraft carriers parked in the Mediterranean
at stop lights
online
and sometimes even in your own home
if both of you are famous enough
to have an image that extends beyond meeting.
These unspoken, unmentionable regularities and micro-murders
have their way into your world.

The best possible reality is predicated
on a billion little, forgettable contributories
infringing on the forces that carry you—
Rushes.

They are periods of bliss.
They aren't even periods.
They are good for you
because you never knew what to do with them in the first place.
You couldn't use them
when you were wondering if you were good looking
or if your friend treated you the right way
or what your professor really meant
when she looked at you that way
or why your girlfriend really left
or if you should've or could've.

Keep them in mind by ignoring them.

If they won't save your life
they'll keep you unoccupied.
Hey remember that redhead
who sounded like an orgasm on the other side of the glory-hole
every time she said "Hey welcome to Blossom Tree?"
She won't make you happy either.
And that is part of her good.
And perhaps when a familiar
left me for someone of an *apparently* opposing nature
she was doing it *out of good will*...

I have learned to laugh at my irrelevance to myself.

10. Worshippers

They put you on a pedestal
and then you want to jump off,

away from them.

They put you on a pedestal
and themselves with you.
And when you jump off,
because they are up there too
they feel superior to you in the demise.
Because they are still up there
and no longer must follow.

They *need* the height
and are base because of it.

11. Equipment

The catalogue of equipment
is 300 pages
and none of the pieces in it will make the next issue.
And who has the money to buy the equipment
or the time to look through a catalogue
or the naïveté to weigh buying or not buying?

Even dating websites
like casinos for the rich that are designed for them to win
lack reviews of the applicants.

I'd say "Fuck hobbyists"
but I'm pretty sure they don't know how to screw
without equipment.

Light bulbs flash in the brain *without* installation.

12. Ambiguous timing

It was almost that Seduction up-ahead all along
pulled a never-ending tear on an endless scroll
both showing itself and leaking that what is 'wrong'
in a world is worldly, not this or that former role.

In the East things turned toward each other bow
like bridges closing to allow a promised passage.
In the west we hasten geological processes to avow
with dead eyes wincing from our present mass-age.

A beautiful woman is—as a wince—an authority.
But not a moral authority as in corporations.
Seduction as unrelatedness abolishes sorority—
Meaning felt as a phantom, a tip of amputations.

A poem writes a woman but not instrumentalized.
Though She since Isis is a screen on which appears
what is to be said from that nullity in the mental lives
that must be turned-over like records. In arrears

what occurs shuffles hot and cold undercurrents.
Through you nervous woman the current charges.
And vented—unaware and without endurance—
you peek above declining seas inactive to escort barges.

13. Movie Theater Exit

The ropes hold the crowd
like zip-ties gathering the wrists of a bum on PCP.
At any given time, you don't know whether to hate

Spunctum

sympathize
ridicule
or ignore (all equally valid reactive attitudes).
[...]
The world the earth the tulips in the meadow
the dirty sand kicked up in the stream like a sudden breakout,
a constituency of the Inner.

Perception is already reality TV (Cf. the phenomenologists)
with its staged vantage and its 'natural' script.
All domains—dominating—congregate
and conspire against the understood,
instead of *striving* for *dominance* in theory.
The way all governments conspire against their citizens.

The war film has sold out.
I notice as I hear a woman say it,
pushing her way out of the way she, We came in.

Some people walk right past the handicap girl tearing tickets.
She notices that they don't notice her
(I notice the flutter of her eye—
a sign that falls from her eyelashes as soft evidence).
No *admittance* of our awareness of others' going-by us.
The awareness is its own con-summation (the sum of lies).

I could have walked right in had I not noticed her.
Having already noticed her, I courteously hand her my ticket in.
After saying thanks, I notice she'd ignored me.

On my way out of the theater,
a Hispanic girl—alone, dressed hip-like—holds the door for me,
but I am far away.
Obliged I pick up my pace.

She waits kindly.
I am on Tramadol, a narcotic for dogs, but she doesn't know that.
When I grab the door to hold it for those trailing,
the girl vanishes into the Skittle-colored lobby.
I notice that the door was propped opened all along.

All our lives we walk through doors—
themselves always-already ajar—
thinking someone is being kind to us.
We and the other have false consciousnesses
but have not lost our consciences.

We make this theater exit from existence
day by day.

14. Reprobation

In war, it was thought there is again community
when a shrinking existence could finally pounce
and the locals together capitalize on their impunity
even if they increase their earnings only by an ounce.

Poets were sometimes read as business consultants
by radicals who privileged what they called rupture.
Forgetting exhaustion that accompanies indulgence,
thinking they stopped time they only one-upped her.

Historical conversation hits its wall at spring breakers.
And if there is a future the poet will have little say in it.
Having never been to see the Place of the Makers
the infants voice the Visual as mute display units.

Spunctum

Could trauma of a failed break leave those returned
radicalized enough to tell of the Home as the Foreign.
Or would the break in its failure as such reaffirm
the False as the homeliest place to be ignored in?

Ignorance perhaps can only be accomplished in thought.
And there blooms an anachronistic honesty of illusion.
The break produced within homesickness as an ought
without priority, a prying reappraisal of intrusion.

15. Mayday, or my day with Marilyn

We suffer!
But what is worse is while the kids sit in the cafeterias without lunches
we continue to pity Marilyn Monroe.

A by-gone suffering—
while it is—is not wholly a human suffering.
A human suffering is not profitable, but it can *turn* a profit (into a loss)
or open a parenthesis,
not an antithesis.

But profiting,
when it has lost its whole humanity—
its very possibility residing in its former re-uptake (its umbrella)—
it proffers.

A misunderstood suffering has lost its humanity
and has only become humanitarian.

Misunderstanding is profound, confounded, dumbfounded
suffering.

But who cares about Marilyn Monroe (monetarily robust)?
It is sad, yes. But a story? No.
It is a waste of your sadness. Worse, a utilization of it.

Who cares about past suffering?
Jews Christians publishers producers directors curators
coordinators
and biographers,
not human beings.

Jesus was misunderstood!
But does solidarity across the spiritual realm
really alleviate your felt isolation?

Truly, I am not a Marxist.
But until suffering takes precedence over the celebrity tragedy reel,
we will all watch the Biography Channel alone.

16. Such a thing as

You were a screen on which my poems would debut
but poems were more than at-hand documentaries—
a woman with whom being-there beat ciphering through
and me there who could never proctor mentally.

The world was so full of those stupid apt little phrases
that to those unbareable witnesses (Fun)ction displayed.
There is one of them that to me still amazes
saying classily "Attention is something that must be *paid*."

Spunctum

We are born unnaturally from an impervious debt.
One that is generated with us—ours—not one inherited.
Only through our abolition as such are we then let
into even a world that favors unlikely the merited.

In poetry so far as I could tell there was never a norm.
Over-production and scarcity were skeptically play-fighting
and critical dispensation, Irregularity was the old dorm
in which Poets could ask "Is there such a thing as writing?"

To those who must be informed of what is right
at the suggestion of a past-present boatman who docks
Poets are but a Seductive orator, an oarsman who—uptight—
here ropes ocean to shore, there a departure unlocks.

17. ento-mate

The most intimate and insignificant life-events occur together
and cannot occur without the mediation of technology
(pessimism).

Car takes girl on date. Girl does not take care.
Pandora chooses anniversary song.
Bluetooth reminders about why I'm doing this.
Glove compartment holds box.
Box keeps ring in it.
Then love…after 5 lines of technology, not 5 obstacles.
And this is technically just a 'poem' written on a PC
as an inevitable ode on this.

18. Chill Economy

She skirted across the dining room in her 2-inch wedges
that seemed incapable of prying her heels from the floor
kind of like those electric toy cars
magnetically kept on track.
Her dress did not allow *too much* leg movement
as she inched like a lil' Geisha from her hostess stand.
She could've walked better
with a giant tumor protruding from only one shoulder.
She would've killed me
had she been a zombie and had I been playing Resident Evil.

In the restaurant, there is a second floor
with windows overlooking the dining room.
I thought maybe people paid extra
to peer down from the window at us ants at this 5* restaurant.
But already on the showroom floor
the people pass by like lil' pop-up ads.
You are the desktop underneath them all.

Morality is tirelessly a pop-up blocker.
It is a pop-up
that says it's a virus protection program but is a Trojan.

There are many people around me right now
but I'm writing this as if there were not.
I'm practically giving them away for free.
I am different than a master.

ATTENTION IS UNFAIR
NO MATTER WHAT *WAY* YOU LOOK AT IT.

19. Chill Economy Cont.

In Ukraine,
they do not see shout-out they receive during Oscar.
You buy attitude with Cadillac.
It not come standard but with upgrade—
indeed, with technology package.

20. The Gymnast

She stands at the edge of the mat,
matted like the blonde beast at the edge of a world engulfed in flames:
the accursed share of Logoi (value pluralism).

The cruel gestures of her lineaments do not move
like a desert
like the horizon
or a screen/monitor.
Yet when a smile is called for it comes like daybreak
but surer.

Even if the world was created 5 minutes ago, it doesn't matter:
truth is dancer performed live.

In fact, there is *absolutely no truth* to the contorted grace of her body
because if there were, there would never be a stuck landing.

There is no reality to the gymnast,
but there is sacrifice faith Gift—
uncertainty yet no absolute knowledge of a lack,

a certain boundary, a weakness like a theory.
And only by the ambiguity
of the matrix of her irresponsible talent—
the point of her death—
does she become capable
of the mastery over appearances and body.

When there is the possibility of an endless circulation of debt
through the non-aesthetics—the sheer machination—of the
Ceremony
a short,
brutal,
tactile woman
becomes terrifying
where the ecstasy of her adherence to nothing that is the rule
becomes irrespectively pluperfect.

I suspect this was the effect of the Olympiad on the Greeks…
if we can still speak of suspicion or effect.
I doubt the Greeks did, but who knows
(Plato was not Greek in *that* way—
whatever that means).

21. Cheetos fingers

Later in life—a lifer—
I don't want to be a bitter old man who says of love:
"When you eat processed cheese crackers,
they leave a cheesy residue on your fingers, do they not?
And when all the crackers are gone,
you lick your fingertips one by one."

Spunctum

Beware a love that is flavored air
that *cannot* go stale
that you can consume and consume until death comes apart
and never get full—
one that is fatal not artful,
beginning and ending on the same term.
I say 'beware' to tempt you.
Or not, you'll never know.

22. this is a game for Us

The moon, our anonymous voyeur in the day sky—
our springy nail clipping, an adjunct body gone-by.
Drawn, the tides obscured in her voids pour
like jet fuel into right-angled clouds. A twofold war,
the Blue shades the surgical nurse before it tapers.

Squeezed like internal organs by liars' body shapers,
the moon rebounds and like a stone drink-coaster
soaks up the day, masterwoman behind the boaster.

23. commune of bachelors

I lacked motivation when I felt like I didn't belong to anyone.
It was only when I felt received that I could give in the first place.
Otherwise, the gift itself was a vulgar gift
an anticipatory gift
a transaction.
I would have been a creditor out of envy.
First, I had to receive myself through several No's.

Critical Leisure, Book I, Volume I

I wasn't a queer. I wasn't a communist.
I wasn't an anarchist. I wasn't a bro.

It wasn't depression
lack of sleep
bipolarity
mania
schizophrenia
sociopathy
anxiety
ADHD
acid reflux
IBS
constipation
diarrhea
ASPD
psychosis
or alienation.
I tried these articulations on, but they all shrank.

My condition lacked the potency for solidarity.
A negativity that ran out of viable excuses and accusations.

Many don't know what it's like
to be born during the commercial break
between two feature presentations.
If anything, they *get* it,
but getting is not yet knowing.

You said you've been sad lately. I have too.
But I could smell the perfume on your unwashed body
when you got into my car.
That made me happy even if I didn't acknowledge it.

Spunctum

The little punk village
was emblazoned with the freedom to sleep in on Sunday afternoon.

We had breakfast.
And when we were smoking your cigarettes,
I swabbed that clump of mascara from your eyelid.
People looked at us strangely when I opened the door for you.
I chose to think they were jealous
like they knew the secret of *us*—
the thing, *us*, about which *we* didn't even speak.

To keep that secret what it was—even to ourselves—
we were hostile to one another.
People witnessing us would think we hated each other.
Sometimes I thought that too.
But also, we were both so intelligent and good looking
Both nearly unthinkable.
You were assertive.
I was passive—and you were infected by me.
I thought I loved you, but I couldn't tell you that.
You were fucking multiple men and one woman.
They were all latently or manifestly homosexual.
You probably thought I wasn't sensitive enough,
but I would have shut up enough
to let you look at me as we made love.
I would've laid in bed all day with you.
Sensitivity usually amounts to its easily dispossessed neighbor.

You took me to the anarchist headquarters.
It reminded me of Teenage Mutant Ninja Turtles 1.
I imagined disaffected youths nolleying off the entry ramp
and playing hacked arcade games.
You brought me back to the intelligence room
where you were about to have your anarchist meeting.

I was glad there were no thumbtacks
on the map of Atlanta pinned to the wall.
I wanted to fuck you on the black picnic table
where you were to soon convene.
But you looked too beautiful, so I just stared at you.
I didn't tell you I love you.
You hugged me before I left for the first time.
We've known one another for a year.
You almost looked happy.

I made sure I did too.

24. I always met them, leaving

The silver-lining as of mirrors is a dated metaphor
if seeing one's Destiny as one's Property is the For.
Without the lining set behind there is but a Crystal.
And without reflection we are sidearm of the pistol.

From all of Life how could I ever myself untangle
and orient myself at the Other without an angle?
The angler is we found what in the Depth glows
that as an appendage stays when the being grows.

As far as our concerns go no step avoids its blocks.
Having to go always around we have our future written.
The pace of our Care obstructed always makes stops
and inattentive leaves its timely surfboards shark-bitten.

25. Movie version of a poem about a poem made into a movie

Look down the center cavity of the concrete spire.
You may feel the neural tickle of too much
because seeing everything all at once,
you ignore the details of each.

Descend the stairs to a previous sphere
where those elders competed in intellectual eating contests,
dining on the weenies of the Frankfurt School.
You will find you lack the concepts to think it.

Don't descend.
You will find
that while you hold the handy concepts on the tip of your tongue
they don't match the newspeak required as password
to the current floor.

There are no fire exists for Logos
The spiraling cadaver of the useless flights
humors you *in its offering of humor.*
Instead of its joke-telling, it's their humor itself that's funny.

Look down the center cavity of the stairwell.
You may feel the inadequacy of husbandry.
Is it a family you're going home to?
Or just useless faces, useless differences stone-cold,
alit by the television
like faces dimmed by flashlights
telling the ghost story of their contents?

The return of poetry
will come in the 'as seen on TV' packaging

*of its impossibility of being produced,
aka, made into a movie.*

26. Child Judges

Of those we know who are endlessly waiting
there are but at least the two regular types.
One waits for future occurrence, ends up hating
the other who waits for the present hypes

to forget of themselves so that the present ends.
The one dreams. The other does interpretive work.
Always what we find vulgar what fresh depends
on what is for one Attraction, for the other an irk.

It is not Misfortune but Necessity that peeps up-out
around which the ones who are waiting will clamor.
The gopher without a shadow or body never dug out
that they philosophize giddily with a rubber hammer.

27. *on a nice day*

I'm standing in a bacchanalia and potlatch of decaying pears.
The wasps and yellow jackets are disinterested in me
and in nothing else.
They are scathing,
probably fucking multiple partners
and pigging out
like whores parachuting heroin in Xerxes' mobile bathhouse.

Spunctum

The chain-link fence is an Ubuesque wall,
barring the dogs of the neighboring trailer park from my dog.
She really wants to romp with those mutts like her,
but they're ghettoized.
She and them can only lick one another through the woven
octagons—

that is the honey comb of our individuation.

28. It's not forward, but not only new

Like Faust whose attention the Devil compels
over thought their hearts *promote* abnormal swells.
They cannot propose themselves not abstruse—
these creatures so easily constantly seduced.

From over-production in the realm of theory
in this crisis, what is produced is hyper-really
not the result of the agony of historical actors.
Instead it is the insipience—of nervous factors.

In this what is gained outweighs what is lost
and what was a blanket becomes a permafrost.
The two hearts stumbling over their words
flutter and, in flight, jumble into partitive curds:

a pair whose energies in their unpreparedness
cause them to knock one another like marbles.
A destiny double-crossed. That which in aridness
either splits its shell or remains forever its larval.

In this world of a constant shift in *both* senses

we work. It changes us. Goods passed up on pretenses
confront us as nerves. And to make matters worse
we shake out loud like a sobering drunk's coin purse.

This shaking is the opening of a cut: a future look
into the past. But as a folding not unlike a book.
While the presence of the dual relation can unhinge
a hitherto locked option—that Way is on the fringe.

When they meet at a joint puncture. *That* is the Charm.
While many ignore the collusion or split poets alarm
with an oversupply of words, a pretended commercial
that with such imperfection moves another as inertial.

29. almost another raw-dog poem

When the bishop has a b-ball goal in his disappearing edge pool
and you engage "Colonoscopy for Dummies"
and the dog lays on the hardwood next to its temperpedic bed
and the interior XP is the XP of nothing
and the credit score is the only thing that is free
and the only way to eradicate disease
is cease history and eliminate all humans
and the Gospel comes in an email from
"donotreply@donotreply.net"
and the poetry is described as "raw, real, and true"
in the comments section
and irony is inaudible but might sound like stirred macaroni
because it is like fingerplay with semiotics…
when the man cave allows the men to accessorize
and God speaks in Ed Hardy t-shirts

Spunctum

and the women make their screennames "She' mad but she' magic"
and Jung
acid
cyberpunk
ecstasy
and the hypertext
are presupposed by G. W. F. Hegel
and the movie follows the incident more quickly than consciousness…
when the water slide descends below sea level
and the government shut-down doesn't increase Crime
and the soul is the inner cameraman
and the US gov. snatches foreigners off their own streets
and the local Russian singles
BBW singles
ebony singles
teen singles
and cheating spouses
are only a click away—
much farther away than the orgasm,
itself *played out* like tap and click…
when plastic surgery is discarded for holographic facial re-imaging
and CGI replaces makeup
and all our natural desires are *exposed*
for their preserving artifice
and paradigm shifts occur
at the institute-of-university-college.edu.gov.blogspot
and the cops are all bachelor party strippers…

insurrection will blow beyond stupidity
and stupidity will float along the draft for *a time*—
such is human history.

The feathered suspension of the latter
is sign of a healthy seduction of the former.

30. *certain about certainty*

The heart shakes the body like a nearby T Rex.
The confusion visibly drowns you
like a waterslide shitting you the consumer
back into the water park panic.

There are people who most often quote movies
writers
standup comics
and when you are at a loss YOU are the alien.

It is unclear who are worse:
the inhabitants of Celebration, FL
or the everyday millions
going to a job they hate
to a movie they hate
to a household they resent
to a friend's house
whose speech fills the room
like the Atlantic filling and rupturing the innards of the Titanic.

Everywhere they run for finish lines
wear events t-shirts
buy 50 calibers at flea markets
donate to canned food drives
hunt for deals
unable to deal with their freedom
the freedom of others

Spunctum

the freedom of volcanoes children women aliens
as their brains bug & monitor their bodies from a comfortable
nowhere,
auditing themselves until the future seems 110% sure
and life .01% livable.

It is when everything seems to be in the bag
that the bag fills with vomit
as the altitude sharply declines.

31. Acidification of Oceanic Feelings

The world's autobiographic writing,
the mirror juncture of the Occident
draws instantaneous synonymy.
Here dawns Us, a poetic computer.

O Cruel Theater! Disastrous drip-feed!
All the ingrates/relevance-deprived pedants
in unison broadcast in frothy whine
"We are the world! Not another should die!"
(Actors who play 'themselves' behind the scenes.)

I imagine a maleficent God
become an admirable deity.
Smokes his water-pipe with old Mephisto.
Scoffs at all the voluntary servants.

True Beauty! An ascetic and junkie!
The monocular lickspittle's labor.
In one terminal maudlin convulsion
they'd bore their Others to solely exist

how algal blooms vanquish the living sea.

32. Autocomplete searches are pretentious poems

Sandmen of bacteria, a scanter prison.
Thaumaturgical tragedians of mannerism
sweat gestural inflations of their awareness
through computational pores in facial bareness.
Is what they made on Paint
above the reductionist Subject ranked?
Now thought of as nothing but a host a vessel a vector a prism.
Meta-eternity—*the Infinite Game*
—oppositional requisition.
Not spatio-differentially!
Kiss thy enemy on the cheek!
      Love Thy Tasty Morsels ALL THE SAME!
Pudenda of Metaphysics: techno-geeks.
      Also, *the Definite, Indefatigable Game*—the transparent parity.
Technopoly of cultural authorization.
Autocratic fraternization of *the Singularity!*
Theosophy of technique.
Childlike switchboard of the RULES OF THE GAMING.
      Learn to cheat.
Receive ossification indistinguishable from the buzz of playing.
A manner of naming.
Beyond religious technique!
Global data-pads buffering.
In a bit—a *nihilism lacking both nothing and suffering.*

WTF? SRSLY?

Spunctum

33. *Stephán, asst. mngr.*

He was a cyclist and shaved his head
arms
legs
because it made him more aerodynamic for a hobby.

Probably shaved his pecker because it was made more functional
and made him fuck better.

Probably shaved his butthole so he could shit at breakneck speeds
while reading a pamphlet titled "How to Beat Death"
and so far, he calculated he had bought himself an extra 2047
hours
of beautiful life
on this beautiful earth.
Would probably remove all his organs
if it turned out it was unhealthy to have them.

He frequented the B-Ball courts.
Carried a 2-liter jug of supra-distilled water
extracted from angels put on High in the microwave.
Wore magnetic tape on his triceps that attracted him to himself
and on his calves to balance his Lifeforce.

There are parrots that live to be 120 years old
that drink their own urine mixed with fluorine
and eat pellets of Styrofoam
that would mock him as he quotes Herbert Spencer.

When he called me into the office,
he told me until I reach his level, I'm to show no signs of hostility
and no attitude.

On the one hand,
even parrots taxidermized by callouses and tumors
have dispositional attitudes on things.
On the other,
crazy cannot be learned as a skill.
But I hadn't the heart or the hostile respect
to give him that "bit."

34. Revenge of the Mud People

I'll open my mouth to trap all the mosquitoes of Lethe
and incubate the larvae of a new stupidity—
be the humus for a blank obsidian aestheticism
to rise out of Reason's noxious slumberous mud.

If I'm inundated by sharecroppers of misfortune,
to shed the psychoanalytic mask of my old age
I'll patent the very archetype of my salesman existence—
sit by the financing machines to collect my *accursed stock*.

When I endorse all the miniaturized models
I internalize each meaning and repress each action,
redirected to the wing of significant other creation
by the sexually usurious intern of citations exchange.

After they graph the historical undulation
to simulate the something that can be vocalized
I'll never again taste the material illusion—
the specious brandy that always *drinks us*.

I'll forage a shelter of crud drawn from Styx—
a refuge from all the happy monsoons.

Spunctum

They are throwing dubstep festivals in the rainforest
that will be metabolized up to my perspective
as if they were figments of Tantalus.

In a séance I hope for dead musicians or politicians
to exhale all the bored misery of the 'authentic' sentiment.
Of wishful misfits and dead brands I form my tribe.
We dance by the bon-fire of our discarded traits.

35. *gumball-amount-estimating Holocaust machine*

There is something else
something I cannot say
something I cannot say to a coworker or my mother
or a woman, a professor
or to you the reader.

There is something else
something that the word neither covers nor uncovers
but about which it merely speaks

and my thoughts being in words
something my thoughts miss and fulfill.

There is always something else
or nothing else
but the latter implies a reality
and there is something other than reality.

There is something else always
something I forgot or wasn't important
or will remember later when it's pointless to discuss.

Something else is leftover...
The Else that is elsewhere but not merely elsewhere
to elsewhere —
something other than a chain of events
something the Martians did not leave behind
something other than a Big Bang
or the Last Judgment
or man on the moon
or the picker in the fields
or the child up the chimney
or Jesus on the water or up your ass

...something other than a college degree
or a table of content
or dictionary appendix
or a liver—
watching but not merely watching
there yet not merely there

...something other than an intention
or an aspiration, truth or story
a belief
a desire
a thought
a look
or nothing.

...something to a feminist other than inclusion
to a Nazi other than a Jew
to a woman other than a man
to Crips other than Bloods...
and to one thing other than another.

Spunctum

…something to a message other than content
to an experience other than language
to a television other than vision
to a mission other than a modus vivendi
operandi
tollens
ponens
and to an argument other than agreement or disagreement.

Something puts one foot in front of the other,
laughing unbeknownst to you
to Napoleon
to Dolmancé or Madame Saint-Ange or to Einstein.

Nietzsche Socrates Rimbaud Céline Baudrillard Picasso Mozart
Marx Goethe Freud
or the girl dancing in fragmented darkness to Beyoncé for
mullah—
they are probably closer to something
only because they know how to put periods at the ends of
sentences
and how to call it quits or to die well:
mad
hungover
snobbish…
even their deaths mock us…

There is more to say—
too much to say—
about hairdos
predictive power
or the color of shit
than there is about something else.

And there is ALWAYS *something* else remaining.

36. Where do they all come from?

The people in a studio audience
the people posting on Facebook prayer pages
the people who visit Times Square
the people smooching on a Jumbo-Tron
the people with glass cabinets full of keepsakes
the people who purchase vacationing guides
the people who write Ask Abby and wait a week for a response
suspended
cryogenized
speckled
or dial suicide hotlines and see the light
the people who anticipate birthdays
or those who read exposés
on the inconvenience of general purpose gift-cards
the people who go to small claims court
or those who scroll up and down their call list or reread text
messages
the people who perform at half time shows
the people who ride zip-lines into Amazonia
the people who do not own a TV with a tele-pride.

They are the people who will rehabilitate the mentally retarded
only insofar as they will be employable
at movie theaters, food courts and the mall.

Youth cultures are dank foot-soldiers.
Aren't their undeveloped wills to power cute?

They are desperate
innocent
charming
but no more than mosquitos
scattering anthills high on their pheromone crack
or mice sapped by peckerwoods
like a soldier's celebrity death on a pop network
with a tiptoeing, hardened grace.

The animals though—like trashcans—
can at least default on dignity
if they are generally useful or at the very least in view.

37. God's egg-beaters

She wears blush, but she blushes
as she says when I mention Bukowski
"She's mad but she's magic."
It's tragic for him that this time was made for me
but she sees more than minuses and pluses.

"She wears blush, but she blushes"—
I mean what other turn of phrase
could one-up Bukowski and amaze…
to engender the seduction of her touches.

She wears blush, but she blushes
and the Form appears when the spirit wanes.
More into simulacra than outright Truth claims—
for *the confines for a mime are luscious.*

She wears blush, but she blushes.

Critical Leisure, Book I, Volume I

Her understanding is less a sponge than a layered trifle.
The relief from everyone thinking Blake was nuts is
at least we wake to Kelly and Michael.

She wears blush, but she blushes.
The concert tickets I hear are steep.
When experience goes Molly gives the Spirit rushes
so drape the dental dam like a blanket on the beach.

She wears blush, but she blushes
and I tuck her bra back into her shirt.
I don't think she's a bitch when she makes her fusses
and the brevity of our time together is never curt.

She wears blush, but she blushes
as the law grads talk of fantasy football trades
who may have no access to the glades
of even the mock trial of her kind of Justice.

She wears blush, but she blushes
and if one cannot be wrong one can't be right.
The threat of loss makes the capricious condition such as
possessing her is a time-wasting flight.

She wears blush, but she blushes
as she says when I mention Bukowski
"She's mad but she's magic."
What's unexclusive to her and appealing to me
is that I write her as already-dead time still gushes.

38. boyfriend for a night

Life is a gift with no giver.
But I could see myself emanating from you—
received
given
thrown back at me like a pendulum,
an Archimedean pointlessness woozy like a Kodiak
tranq'ed from the superior elevation of a helicopter,
the shot considering a double velocity,
a downstream flood that is more devastating
and has a higher lag time.

We are tagged animals
undergoing trauma just to be discovered and watched.
You didn't monitor me.
Your back was turned
and you looked to the side as my hands massaged it
like a handful of eels gnawing on a whale carcass
that had fallen to the ocean floor.
Your nerves lit up like New York before a black out
and you said "That feels really good."
You're better than a conservationist who makes artifacts of auras,
just a woman but better.

I saw in you my own reproduction (not my mirror image).
I could have never been an original,
more an aboriginal of a double inheritance.
First does not mean novel.

I could see my soul leak out of my body
like a stain scrubbed out of a lush carpet.
I felt surprisingly whole without it.
An opportunity for selflessness is not a dreadful thing.

It is more a sure thing than a self with its desires and its lack.
One earns the right to make promises.
I refuse to work, but I make an effort to still need to give.

You sense the good ones
on your capacity to *sleep* next to them,
not on how hard you want to fuck them.
To be next to them, not inside them.
Scientists do not understand this.
Surgeons do not do face to face encounters.
Touch is reserved for magicians.
But it is a metaphor for all things in this world.
Metaphors, of course, are worthless today.

39. A note I left someone on a refrigerator somewhere

If a picture is worth a thousand words
then on-screen poems—light writings—
are pettier and more absurd
than imaginary creature sightings.

If a picture is worth a thousand words
then the Internet as the Big Picture
is a Form that can all but undergird
a mode of writing produced by light fixtures.

If a picture is worth a thousand words
then that explains to at least some degree
why twenty-somethings form little art herds
and attempt to make Inner and Outer agree.

If a picture is worth a thousand words

then you might wonder why I'm writing.
And why does Insta have appetites curbed
that flake off like painted sidings?

If a picture is worth a thousand words
then it's no surprise that images tire us.
How in their intensity they go unheard
is debatable for the logos that inspire us.

If a picture is worth a thousand words
you might wonder how I'm unmoved by Joyce
when I look at his eye patch and say "Word!"
but don't care about techniques he employs.

If a picture is worth a thousand words
then the Che Guevara t-shirts *really are* abuzz.
And it's no surprise that McLuhan observes
that pages will bore without electronic fuzz.

If a picture is worth a thousand words
some asshole collected brain-scan photos
and made them into an installation that 'occurred'
and necessitated its viewers' use of Rohtos.

40. how I lose credibility

They usually ask what my sign is and say
"I knew you were a Pisces, you're like THE EPITOME of a Pisces!"
They aren't wrong.
I'm slippery like a fish
but satisfied enough to thwart caution.

Critical Leisure, Book I, Volume I

Without peripheral vision—for being so attendant to the immediate—
I often get hooked
or tricked and killed.
Gutted and deboned: the only way I am edible.
I am curiously high in mercury,
water-insoluble
and ironically used in measurement, he he.

They usually say
"You look like Clarke Kent"
or "Superman"
or "Joe Jonas"
or "Patrick Bateman."
They aren't wrong.
My look, much better than Bukowski,
not as pretty-faced as Verlaine or Rimbaud,
not as intelligent-looking as the Romantics or T.S. Eliot,
not a scientist like Goethe,
not as Pagan or regal or lizard-like as Jim Morrison,
less tough and manly than Hemmingway.
Caught between the punk and the soldier
the insatiable and the generous
the figures of Mars and Neptune
the gods of agriculture and those of industry
the rural man of work and the soft-handed, ivory-tower city-slicker
the cowboy and the bull
the mustang and the mini-horse
the folk nomad and the auditorium filler
Death and the Empress
the Joker and the Knight,
ad infinitum.

"Dapper Dan."

Spunctum

"Woody Allen."
A "soap opera star."
A "writer."
These familiar place-holders are useful in thinking me—the powerless.
They anticipate I'm a school of fish
that in its constructed form resembles a larger fish
and otherwise dissolves when the fish get horny or nervous.
Do not think this has anything to do with Christ.
But it doesn't not have anything to do with Him, either.

Was it a piece of luck that I—
as amalgamated
undecidable
soulless and giddy as Mickey Mouse,
so far from human but too its real reflection in an animal
a shape
a person
a liquid
or the communication between these spheres—
could have as previously stated abomination
aroused such mistrust amongst my fellow humans
I *necessarily* learned to stand on my own?
Too normal for the weird
too punk for the yuppie
too masculine for the queer
too lazy for the productive
too conscious for the authentic
too reclusive for the superficial
too talkative for the modest
and vice versa.
Arrogant always either in my quietness or my conversation.

And moreover, I talk about myself in my poetry.

But who knows themselves who hasn't told of themselves,
who hasn't a creative streak?

Such a streak looks like skid marks on cheap white underwear to most,
but kill whitey.

41. you over-think things, or you stand under them

You said there must be poor people so there can be rich people
and spelled too "2"
and said that your iPhone 5 was your most prized possession
but that you didn't even have the iPhone 5s.
The packaging of your chap-stick was produced in 7 countries.
You liked Atlanta
cross-fit
restaurants
and wine.
But you had grape vodka
and said it was made by prisoners.
Your roommate got it for free because she is a drink promoter.
You ate two whole rolls of sushi with the fish cooked
and some Teddy Grams
and Kroger-brand Ginger gummies.
It seemed like you would eat the whole time I was there,
animal-like,
when errands replace eating on your day off.
And your eyes fluttered from your phone to the TV.
You looked at me like I was a distraction
and I asked if you wanted me to leave.
"I told you I'm boring."

Spunctum

You shrugged before looking up the dress code for your work.
I looked at you and thought you were insane.
You were a manager at Nordstrom
(which heightened my suspicion)
specifically of the plus-size department.
Your roommate's dog shit and pissed on your roommate's carpet.
I offered to clean it up
and you wouldn't let me,
so we chilled with shit in the next room.
The couch pillows separated us.
You weren't getting enough sleep.
"Doesn't watching 'Ted Bundy: Unseen Moments'
get you in the mood."
You didn't understand or hear what I said.
I didn't want to repeat it.
I thought about Videodrome.
You were like the girl in Repulsion.
You have never seen that.
Roman Polanski gets more attention than I do.
But you let me drive home
after drinking all your grape-flavored purple vodka
and half that bottle of shiraz.
Shiraz was our only common concern—
definitely not each other.
It was a human matter, sort of.
I couldn't tell you I was created by a mental breakdown,
that my spiritual existence developed with and through a deep cut,
an accidentally severe cut—
one that severed nerves and bled without agony.
That was when they called me a Stoic.
And I wouldn't have fucked you any harder
than your job
your sex
your desire

production
or technology.
You had to wake up at 6 AM to get there at 7:30 AM
to prepare for your 8 o'clock meeting.

AND THERE IS NO UNDERSTANDING B/W US.

42. The last poem *I'll* ever write

And then without the Real to compare her to
I see in her Italian models from a by-gone 35.
I 'swipe' her. A sign vows that the thing ensues.
But at objectivity will the image let her arrive?

Standing lying pausing the diurnal drone asks
for a constant disruption that can prompt willing—
technical thinking involved in seeing one's task
as worthless without the break or the thrilling.

We meet with energy captivating film audiences
and long to be an exhilarating re-runnable fiction.
Our depressions spur from amplified visual senses
that *inform* all loving planning and diction.

Even on a technical apparatus I see her in a stola.
And the hi-definition colors are her suffibulum.
My thumb re-energized by an American yoga
pivots on the interruption of a projected humdrum.

It could be generations of wine in her veins.
Remove some molecules and Libera may emerge…
entangling the Earth and the human World she came

Spunctum

as being-together and *took place* (didn't merely occur).

For it not to fall into ruin as of its initial conditions
or to promise an inevitable return to the 'swipe'
it must endanger culture for the abandon of type.
But to be needn't call for the Available's remission.

Anna. Even her name is germane. The disyllabic!
How grace spirits itself away with recursion.
How you undergo experience but never have it.
Marine fossils in mountains exalt Depth's reversion.

43. self-assured self-erasure

The skeptic refrains from revealing
and reproaching aporia
instead reworking re-appropriating
receiving and re-gifting it.

Plato used reason like a condom and
for fear of seductive voids
used the superficial abysses of his
thought and a good State.

Oracle's tripod hovering above the pit
seduced the love-fallen
to their deaths into a ravine that smelled
they say like rotten pussy.

Plato assessed the character of the poets
via their representative Homer
and decided that poetry couldn't be trusted

because fat Plato DANCED!

I'm going to drop out with one credit to go.
Good for nothing. Not even poetry.
"On the *side* of Evil." Like destitute Pyrrho
who lived *alone with his sister.*

Between identities moved his convalescence.
And people accused him of simulation.
Skeptical even of himself he lived like a peasant
and refused to lift a finger forever.

Rifts between matter and consciousness
opened and lost its discontinuity
and history the aggregate gave the dictates
of guppies in modern States.

44. encapsulation at a distance

Our bees look desperate
like junkies surviving to do nothing.
Our birds look nervous
like they are in the Panopticon.
They fear a death that's 360 degrees but invisible.
Our ants are much lazier than those in Africa.
It is the difference between a miniature and the 'real' thing.
When the lowest common denominator is reached—
the atom
the toy
the nano-
the microbe
the number 1

Spunctum

the I—
the actual life-size whole thing becomes useless nostalgia.

The nature shows
can show me Africa Nova Scotia the continental divide
the Matter Horn Ole Faithful Canada the Alps
or I'll pay $1,000,000 to climb Mount Everest
or take an unconventional cruise through an ice sheet
or I can visit the National Parks
or hike Appalachia
or become a survivalist or a nudist
but I have played the Oregon Trail on Windows '98
(and that was the primal scene of the internet)
and I've seen Honey Boo Boo—
the fat, metamorphosed thumb of Zeus.
Possibly Medusa would be petrified by super slow-mo.

The world itself is Area 51:
a subterranean simulation factory.

45. Loose Lips of Lovers

Don't celebrate *(calibrate the cell of)* St. Valentine's holy day
and your relationship is over,
predicated on the gods in its own 'unique' way.
Not having one another to grasp,
our souls to keep,
we produce a relationship to get at a sphere beyond paddy cake.

Even if you say you don't want anything,
it means that you want something.
And that nothing something is more than just nothing

as The Nothing.
Is wanting nothing not also a desire?
Being without desire means habitually having too much,
an over-production,
and that doesn't always mean having a desire to have less.
But we do not have one another.
Circumvented, we must produce a relationship through impression
like soldiers
because only drill instructors can make *us* lovers.

"What do you want to do tonight?"— "I don't know…"
You are testing me. A sleeper-cell alright.
And you will break my heart when set from blend to blow.
When you find out I'm not a very good consumer by a breath
you will stop texting me mid-sentence
when I say "Until capitalism ceases, nothing is left,"
while productive forces dissolve one another to increase.

It makes one wonder if there has ever been consent.
Have you ever met someone you didn't slightly invent?
[…]
They set up shop and in doing so set themselves up
and when I wasn't buying,
they set me merely loose never free
just to misremember me.
Because feelings are speculative, they prefer actions,
but the experiences are fetters
to the bare reality of the unexpressed feelings.
Without even a brute Yes congealing,
they have excommunicated the action.
Wanting displays of affection (what in the past they could have read*)*,
they get dinners instead.
Where losers would have given them action through their desire,

Spunctum

they get aimless winners instead.

Filmmakers novelists and song-writers—
even the pessimistic ones—
present love creeping in here or there for nail-biters
between whole persons who,
presupposing each, do not lack their others.
They still use the logic
according to which if these affairs weren't so already-available
we couldn't reenact them.

I wish to avoid this quirky, alternative love
detached from the feeling of its own ambiguity as a goal.
It is a passionate break from the everyday lovelessness, true.
But it is of that kind where two worthless halves
constitute an *abstract* whole.

And while art is realistic in its portrayal of what repeats,
it lacks a sincere basis as a thing.
If we had experiences, like they say,
we wouldn't need to produce them as above.

I wish to say that love as Love does not exist *right now*.
Made visible, inflamed,
even those capable of this love
must lie to one another to keep this flame burning.
But first we must produce a relationship
(with ourselves)
to even see to *that* yearning.

46. electromancer

I asked her how the paint party was.
"It was great…really fun."
I guess a paint party is when people do molly and dance to dubstep
while getting glow-in-the-dark paint thrown on them.
If only she knew my life was glow-in-the-dark
like a jack-o-lantern with a fire illuminating its lack of guts.
You can see right through its eyes
to the wick of its soullessness
eternally melting like the wax for Descartes
that mathematical refugee of the ephemeral's breadth.

Fun is distinct from joy.
Fun only occurs structurally in the promise of anticipated gains
in the weekend for the week
in the model for the series.
Fun has one prepared for it. It is operated on.
One wills it
plays it from beginning to end like a video
with not a contract but a Law.
The generation of models by models.
Fun. Anticipation. Planning. Wishing.
Being prepared is an effective way to kill Life.
Being shocked is an effective way to kill Life.
Fun is a safe way to *buy time*,
where the fate of energy is to burn itself
and burn its own ashes like the H-Bomb—
like the Sun as it burps and blows it in Mrs. Earth's face.

Fun is distinct from joy.
Joy is a shock but not of the unique,
a possession but not of the grasp,
a disturbance but not of destiny.

Spunctum

A meandering doomsday device of the nerves the mind hates,
it is a carpet bomb of ex-neuronal stragglers,
the disinherited of the CNS revolting and drinking wine,
a gorilla escaped from the zoo raping women
and getting away with it because he isn't black—
an immolation of the routine
where fun is routine.
Even some persons' shit turns out to be more beautiful
because it is joyful.
Others who like to have fun don't understand their joy.

The fun moralists are killjoys with armbands.

They need paint.
They need to paint themselves black.
They need to paint themselves neon.
They need to paint their nostrils white
their patriotism red white and blue
their politics blue or red
their vitals green
their Truth clear.
They have it soaking in nail polish remover
and get heady off the fumes.

The madness of their fun is apparent
in their willingness to work so hard for it.

47. *the models before the runway show (The Problematic of Liberation)*

"Do we seriously have to *walk* out there?!
UGH! This is so fucking ridiculous…like *who the FUCK* walks?!

Critical Leisure, Book I, Volume I

This is disgusting."

The models look so angry
as they meekly skulk across the runway like Diana dying in the tunnel,
the only place where the cameras were not around.
Only for the girls the cameras flash like time,
thoughts,
the sudden appearance of the masses in the late 20th
after the rabble of the 19th
or a fox—
a foxy coincidence taken as a sign by chieftains
of many religions.

The models look so angrily into space,
the only place they can look,
hounded by the many and objects with no objective.
They are models
and being-a-model has them by something,
just not their selves since they are not very seductive.

They are models, but they still have jobs.
Rather than the princess and the pauper
the latter becomes the pop-star
because the modern pauper, the homeless,
cannot convey the medium and even princesses 'have jobs'.

They are pissed off
like slaughterhouse workers taking their angst out on the animals

like technicians at the desktops with one more teaspoon to go
before they end up with 13 tiaras and no alibi

like children with morning wood

Spunctum

taking the SATs at 6:17 AM on a Saturday

like primitives working the diamond mine
selling a cinematographic humanism
or posing naturally fatally for the documentary.

They are as unsatisfied and unsatisfying

as Kramer with his indifference or hatred
getting shunned by the New World Order,
seduced by the heckling "nigger"

as the vegan who adds meaning to her diet and to the world

or the punk rock girl with moral principles

as Jews in Rome

as history on film or in the history books

as technique and technology

as the medium or the message

as communication or para-communication or instant-
communication—
three forms of ecstasy.

They are either sluggish at the lack of a scale
or anorexic from its omnipresence.

That is why I suspend judgment.
That is why I don't date models.
How can you date something

that because it isn't made of carbon doesn't bio-degrade?

Only do we *fuck* each other in *both* senses occasionally.

48. dating=restaurants=jobs

Remember when we planned how you would get impregnated
by one of your brother-in-law-the-lawyer's cohorts in Washington, D.C.
and how you'd divorce him, and we'd raise the child together,
unemployed and taken care of by a hefty alimony settlement.

It could have worked,
but we got to the abortion clinic before it opened at 5:30 AM
and while you went behind closed doors,
I read The Flowers of Evil.
You came out. You didn't cry.
I watched you give the receptionist your credit card
and we left.
I don't know what happened in there.
You shed the remnants from our union for the next few days.
I yelled at you on the way home
because the aborting process took 4 hours
and I was going to miss a French midterm at 9:30.
We were both aborted that day.
And I am sorry/glad about that.

…

You were still working at the country club.
You were about to graduate and have to pay back your loans.
I am glad you paid off your credit card debt.

Spunctum

We both lost our insurance in January.
The reason you didn't have any money saved
was that you always bought us wine
and insisted on taking me out to dinner.
You got your wish for us,
but it no longer involves either of us.

When the women sit across from me at the tables of the restaurants,
they don't know of you.
They'd call you a whore if I mentioned our story.

But the table is between them and I
and the dining room is loud.
Even if my elbows extend beyond my share of the table,
I cannot hear them.
If anyone, it is me who leaves my position
to go over and sit on their side.
But the table folds and shifts and stays between us.
They know nothing of us.
They ask what I do for a living.
They assume I will work for them.
They think I will earn their attention
They even expect me to pay
for the capital necessary to produce such a relationship.

I know you and I have tried to produce our happiness.
And we made things worse,
but we were crazy for one another
not with or because of one another.
And we both chose the restaurant over the meal
and the meal over one another.

We will continue to haunt one another for the rest of our lives...

probably not.

We are that much closer to each other in *that*
than those feeding people, dating people or working for people
are to one another.

49. new delays

...worked at Walmart for 21 years
until the Drug and Alcohol Administration
sent a sleeper cell secret shopper to erase her
...was fired because she didn't card the 47 y/o man
for a case of Bud
...the small town has no jobs.
Just fast food and Walmart jobs
and cash for metal and cans—
resell value of your energy being pennies to the dollar.
(The local dentist operates a side business).
And a local employee is fired b/c she didn't adhere
to a code that abolishes judgment and recognition
...21 years is erased in a flash like races who vanished in the trade,
scattered and categorized with strangers
because familiarity is dangerous to a Totality.
(That is why comedians magnify gesture.)
Victims like these show the luxuriousness of the freeze-frame
of the former residents of Pompeii.
Their ashes will outlast our bytes.
You can print out your Instagrams on marshmallows
so you can really eat yourself and your 'art',
where an art has its conceptual foundation
in common with reality television ghost-hunters.
You can't use judgment in a place of business

because everyone is a potential double agent.

Terrorists don't wear uniforms either,
so we all become foreigners.

50. porn industry

Gaia takes smokestacks as dildos
and squirts on the horizon
but doesn't do creampies.
The excavator cups the world and says cough.
The wrecking ball invents Miley Cyrus.
The pipeline bukkakes' the sky
the loosest goose of them all—

but even the loosest goosey is a limit.

The artist-philosopher makes headway at the forefront,
the meta-forefront.
S/he says fashionably

"EVERYTHING MUST BE RE-VERSED!"

51. closed captioning provided by Christmás. Live más.

She had a disgusting sense of moral worth.
She would have died had she lost the opportunity to give advice,
even though her moral code often came from Hallmark Inc.
She really believed in the movies.

She commended American politics for cleaning up after
Watergate.
She felt like an adult after traversing Disneyland.

Like they say of many housewives,
she held things together—
a glue trap hanging from the ceiling to catch flies.
Don't all housewives model themselves on the first lady,
the woman behind the man?
She was more like the surge-protector beneath the fake Christmas
tree
choking on the plugs
that stick to it like dead ladybugs under the lampshade.

Like the hub with its convenient switch
that lights the fast-casual aura of a holiday so distant from itself
that to form an opinion on it would arouse suspicion,
she powers the oxidized haze of a filial torch
that laments its yearly experiential gatherings
too meaningless to disagree to.

If Joyce Myer PhD said "Christ wills it,"
she would prematurely age herself
in the gas station bathroom interiors of hospices
consoling the deteriorated minds of people
as dead as keychain electronics—
too dead to acknowledge her efforts or their own emotions.

Emotions dangle
like the earlobes of the elderly in the plastic deformation of old
age.
The cause of aging may have nothing to do with loss
but with stretching
like spit that can't be sucked back into the mouth

Spunctum

after straying too far from it.

This death occurs midlife
midsentence
perhaps in the mind of the woman who, for lack of her own devices,
would stay up all night consoling a sick dog.
And maybe she is right, maybe that's all there is.

God harps on the existence of the Devil.
The Devil denies the existence of God.
The modest and the talkative, in denying one another,
rely on each other to have the status they claim.
They bounce their identities *off* one another.

They are like the master whose autonomy
is staked on recognition by the other,
whose autonomy is insufficient to underwrite its humanity.

52. Daytime TV psychology

The needles left little tissue
in her face that was without the lush exuberance of an aerated lawn
that grows back fuller in its destruction,
slide-showing the PowerPoint memories of a full life
in its upkeep.
She refuses to live to make a power point,
a technique of graffiti artists who sign their existence anonymously,
requiring only that a window-shopping consciousness
recognize it while driving by.

Critical Leisure, Book I, Volume I

The upkeep
erases memories and the continuity necessary to remain a person.
The needles disengage the psyche
and the skin (vanity) reacts to a series of social tests
like the backs of children being tested for allergies.
Only nothing is unconcealed.
What is unconcealed is the facelessness behind a body
that was nothing but a sign to begin with.
The new face is a Las Vegas
in the cultural desert of the American West.
The toxins, escaping the needles like children exiting the hyperreal
as their bottoms spark and hiss down dry plastic slides,
cut off the circulation of the face
like the Hoover dam ties the tubes of the Colorado.
It shows the body relates to itself spatially
like the suburbs relate to the metropolis, forming the 'metro-area'.

There are no monkey wrench gangs fighting for the humanity
of the damned-to-waiting-rooms in cosmetic surgeons' offices
and this accounts for most of us.
They fight for the liberty of dust
pigment
and rocks,
for fish and country,
while education like ecology forgets about the human
as if the human were the fat thrown out after lipo.

Anthropocentrism is necessary
and whatever intellectuals ignore, hipsters criticize.
That which they criticize—the unusable—
'must' be taken up and made useful by artists,
so we don't die as a species or whatever—
which entails also the death of the individual.

Spunctum

Artists are salesmen, mostly.
Well yes, we are
and some of us have become aware of that.

53. the dresser

It isn't a dresser. It isn't even an image.
Photography gives the meaning even of meaninglessness
frivolity
and irony,
adding the narrative of insignificance
to something otherwise less than ___.
The hopelessness of an ironic smile on the ignorantly, vulgarly
aware.
It isn't even a thing.
Yes, apparently mere material isn't as base as it can get.

"What is it then?" we ponder instead of dialing the suicide hotlines
where we are stupefied into *surviving*
by talkers who've never lived a day in their life.
Those who've lived for a second know what it's like to see it all
perish
and to want to alongside it.
As Honor does.
Except, like a forgetful dog
we, the Onerous, wait for our vanished master
in the middle of the street.

Its peculiarities aren't even peculiarities.
They are not even the playing out of a flawed design
or a tension.
They are calculated, planned errors,

pluses or minuses of a capsizing curvature.
The drawer not flush with the body, jutting out without standing out.

A million versions
in a million American housing units
for a million ___s to contemplate
as they live through another night,
too unambitious to commit suicide.
Or else they wait to fall asleep giddily
as the Rect(al-)angular, anti-geometric Light—
the ectoplasm of the screen—
produces evaporites in their brains like slugs on hot pavement.
Their hot, mucousy brains digest the barriers of reality
like caterpillars
and they melt into a higher order World of Dreams,
a world with no future.

54. vociferous hallucinations

The entire body of the fly dances across the computer screen
with greater fluidity, gravity and purchase
than these eyes that seem not to even look any more,
not like the eyes of our grandparents used to do (did they?).
And even they accumulate skin dust on Naugahyde lazy-boys
with eyes that never even make it successfully
to the edges of the screen.
Per myth, you could see things then.
Even if they were useless, you got a good look at them.
But does one *look* at reality
any more than I *watch* reality TV,
or is it background ambience while I'm working?

Spunctum

My cognitive mapping skills
seem to almost fair better in open world, sandbox video games
than in my life.

These eyes scan.
The body grips the neck like a 15-year-old
sweatily aiming the scanner gun at the checkout counter.
The head juts out of the neck, forming the elongate gun-shape.
At the end a clear piece of plastic— the face—
houses a red laser that diffuses the objects it gives the up and down
without ever going through them.

The way we look at each other is not the same
as *when bodies mattered* (materialism).
We can no longer even objectify one another.
But what is left behind?
The image?
But no.
Having abolished bodies, we have abolished the image.

55. stop revolving

Like skeptics sitting Indian-style with arms crossed
tilt their head to one side or the other as dogs ought
and as mystics blow ash from filthy cracking hands
to breathe new life, *prima materia*, into ore and sand—
while it's the poor, the wretched who *believe in* the Bible
that only aristocrats can pump Christ's blood is liable.

It is love that we know as anarchical
and lust as the *highest* stage of any love

that will soon be theoretically responsible
for the slaying of symbols, of turtle doves.

Joy the slayer of rationale will make the new terrorist
without schooling knows no words "determinism, heritage."
The wit of the juvenile delinquent that has no desire to rectify
will avoid without knowing it "fun" or joy objectified.

Free spirits will paint concrete images with bombs in stock.
His refusal may be inactive without a past. A *no show*.
No matter! Having never watched the news she'll know
where others are dead in life death is longer be a shock.

Her 'party' without leaders, strategy or organization
will neither search for, find, nor *know* one another.
Without vocabulary for fellowship, comrade or brother
her intuition speaks: "personality begets self-objectification."
Not the wishing kind yet fountain-like splashes s/he arouses
knowing transcendence is sold in concert and theater houses.

No enemy to be *won over* will be his,
for s/he knows no watchmaker has decided this.
Never will s/he 'shoot birds' this semiotic tease.
It's a *system of objects* s/he'll smell as deceased.

56. the demand for poetry, poetry's deferral

See the people stuck to a courtyard
like boogers traded by children to the underside of end-tables.

Some walk upstairs like zombies.
They bleed corn syrup.

Spunctum

They lack a founding principle to underwrite their hurry or
stagnation.
And perhaps my concern for efficiency, or momentum otherwise,
is the drive behind my complaint against them,
an effusive silicon desire implanted in me.
But they stand on escalators and even Sisyphus shows contempt.
Some even stand on moving sidewalks.
They block the sidewalks in perpendicular groups,
homeless chromosomes pushed around by the gel of surroundings.
They are gunk making the social
flow *more tightly* at the margins.

There are cities I've heard have phased them out,
but they became upbeat *local* hipsters.
Slow traffic stays right usually,
but in general, the people here wear concrete shoes,
think concretely,
vacantly but perfectly illumined by the sign.

The bird is symbolic of freedom—
the bird that pecks puke out of its mother's mouth
and shits sterile white
regal purple
envious green
or gloomy black periodically.
Thought is a periodic ally
because it adds periods to an otherwise unreadable complex
sentence
that fancifully skips its heavy truths with little Lilliputian
explosions
that tickle as frivolous micro-narratives—
micro meaning *invisible* or of no concern.
Useless signification magnified by mirrors
that eliminate and birth differences with each zoom.

Poetry does something different with this because it has a differ-end:
to dis-pense, dis the pensive.
Truth leaks,
hardens
and fossilizes the words careless enough to penetrate its syrup
that leaves out details with an inventive self-cruelty,
barbarizing itself for the challenge of its readers
who aren't mere readers
and can't win without barbarizing themselves in return.

57. *Carpe diem poem for the brain-dead*

When the tubes are tied
and the wind lubricious and penetrating
and the family members selfish,
stay distant on the path to glory—
like the skin of your sex now covering a hole in your head—
so that neighbors can come and visit and take pictures with you
and keep up your Facebook profile,
answering all the accumulating mail in your person.

Before death runs out,
seduce from beyond the grave
you silent cactus lushly removing all traces of itself from the desert
that fills our water-headed thought like a family of ferns.

"YOU ARE BOUND; SEDUCE, THAT IS, SIMULATE!"

Spunctum

58. Mistaken Success Ethics

YouTube gurus for DIY crafting
would look at me and start laughing,
say "We crafted happiness," blink
& personalize everything, and the sink!

"What kind of coffee, would you like?"
"Just coffee would be really nice…"
w/o preference you show weakness
or are an Indian painted *with Greek-ness*.

Is Heaven less a product of White-ness
than brand loyalty or 'I like this.
I think I'll take it home with me
& Airdrop it into my identity?'

You don't need to exercise to be on 'roids
when the question "how" is what style avoids.
You are no less threatening in captivity.
Meme animality in your photogenicity.

A thing out of its context stings
sensing that that's what capital brings.
A monkey in a little red tunic climbs
or a person paid to dance holds a sign.

A cat held by its neck like a little yo-yo.
Tourists photographing Whiskey a Go-Go.
See the animals like junk on QVC
like a news-bit on World News BBC.

Give the masses a task like informing us
who per Star Sign know about each Cusp

and the headlines will have been puff pieces
more vacuous than what astrology preaches.

In classrooms across the world there are
contingencies of less & more, near & far
that prevent some and expedite others
b/c "Where schooling fails Life has it covered."

Life is not a commercial for pharmaceuticals
but we're offended about nicked cuticles.
And still we keep relapsing on Christ
like we re-made the film Poltergeist?!

Like Sisyphus not only might we backslide
but might go on Back to the Future: The Ride.
If we remembered the Bang where it all began,
we'd catch our childish selves dick-in-hand.

To celebrate we fire Patriot missiles into the air.
On the moon forensics wouldn't find specks of hair
just moon rocks as empty as hotel rooms
because Mexicans had to sterilize the boom boom.

Domination. Rebellion. Repression. Domination.
Someone wears a smock to study moral patients.
And if we are headed towards the Absolute
scientists dig in the world's anus w/ ice cream scoops.

But freedom has always been put in powerful terms
and it can be fishy to adapt and completely relearn.
How my mother who'd collected commemorative plates
would rather store them in boxes than throw them away.

My poems. As soon as they find their rhythm

they tend to end but that is not always a given.
I'd call it a technique, but it probably isn't.
It's more a dumb mistake they'll make a cool gimmick.

59. "Follow the light with your eyes," said the policeman

Life can produce you like an assembly line
but you must learn to stand up straight
if you want your body to be aligned
with the mechanical segments of Fate.

To put on a shirt you raise your arms
as when you pray to Allah Buddha Jim.
Like Babysitters' Club bracelet charms
if time doesn't skip it at least skims.

If faith can make dying women Care
with much greater Efficiency
there's no need to officiate Book Fairs.
Their children consume proficiently.

Education is no different than Disney.
It makes little Hopeful hearts flutter
that once would've worked the chimneys
and hands pretend at work squeezing utters.

If Jesus became a hologram we'd be aware
of His reality more like that of Mickey.
Out of water and color he'd make chairs
for those that were shocked but not picky.

If I learned more about Life feeling her up

Critical Leisure, Book I, Volume I

then were she prudish I'd grow dumb.
How are you supposed to drink the Cup
when you're always biting your thumb?

I wrote in the Form so I wasn't forever a Kid,
but I know it wasn't any better
when my ego forcibly strapped down my Id
and then asked it "Please bite the leather."

The newspaper includes a list of sales
and the comics section must be hardly over
because we still look for the Holy Grail,
only now with the Mars Exploration Rover.

And our mission will then be complete
if we find another galaxy in which to live
and on Earth II leave indentions of our feet
us prisoners desperately constructing a shiv.

When you can helicopter in a famous utopia
and drop it in an uninhabitable desert
where highways are the copula…
did Los Angeles or Baghdad come first?

Apparently, we came from a fertile crescent
but my Croissant was not made in France.
My clock will not give the time at its present
because it is always moving like confused ants

that can't remember where the trail leads.
They must always be going both ways
so that their population feeds
their Will so that They aren't lead astray.

Spunctum

So it takes a communitarian effort
to accomplish the simplest of things,
and it takes a lifetime to build a fort
that protects against the lightest dings.

But we will launch off Earth before
we have solved any of its problems.
And we will have plans for what's in store
even if we're stuck here. Its nose goblins.

It also takes a hammer to pry out a nail
and teacher you dug into this scholar
by showing me that Big Names can fail
up against an Unknown from the holler.

Even if I think my own writing sucks
and that poetry is nearly dead—overdone—
I am not a saintly figure on a crux
and I think that Sartre is really no fun.

I still like to read less than write.
And that can seem so un-democratic.
I don't even see what I'm doing as a fight
and I am less happy than ecstatic.

Less do I want to be hip, happening or funny.
I have gone 26 years in isolation
but I'd still probably not fuck a Playboy bunny
any more than participate in Wall Street Occupation.

Critical Leisure, Book I, Volume I

60. Door to door thief asking to borrow butter

The best salesman is psychology
and my soul is best wasted on my shows.
I should hope that stars' apologies
divert my affections from the ghettos.

If culture's the seduction of sexuality—
the fallout of its particles ex-terminus—
I've never been a virgin *actually*
that invention for religious permanence.

At Heaven how could we look away?
At any level there is so much movement
and if you didn't ignore all the play
how could you make any improvements?

We progress because of our stupidity
and never would wonderment suffice.
It would be impossible to achieve lucidity
if you got hung up on all the Life.

And there wouldn't even be surfaces.
Without surfaces we wouldn't labor.
How could we commit to purposes
were we *always* curious about behavior?

Imagine old dock workers in their machines
performing their miraculous destructions
if the microbes and galaxies were seen
at the level of reality not of production.

What if the majesty is reserved for a few
who cannot even speak about it

Spunctum

since it has a dialect obscured by The New
the language advertising has crowd-funded.

See nature thrown back from a screen
and you will see it feel it safely
from the perspective of dirty corporate deeds
that involve one's orally fixating.

Oh, they finally added shows to the ads!
And if I was the CEO of Party City
I'd search Google Trends to see the fads
and sell USA costumes for consumptive unity.

I have followed trends never blogs
but have never cared as much as liberals.
Actually, I think politics is for the dogs
because I guess I have different goals

like fucking, getting high and sleeping.
I don't even want neighborly love
if I have to hear the Garbage truck beeping.
I always know where I am when I'm bugged.

There is a screeching in my head I bemoan.
It could be the silence of the electronics.
It's more like feedback from a microphone.
And how I'm kept in check when catatonic!

Is Porn my Life? Could it really be?
I know it's not real, but my body differs.
Simulation is no *imaginary phantasy*
but an infinite vacuum of attachments like the Swiffer.

The Word program recognizes brands

before technical or art terms.
The pleasure is all a part of the scam
but asceticism is like smoking Sherm—

it puts gaps in your brain y'know?
Keeping up takes a lot of energy too.
Some get high on the past, some 'grow',
some get stuck and sniff the glue.

61. I am not the Kafka of the iPhone generation, but whatever

I am in panic about every poem I might lose
& indifference isn't for lovers but for cold prudes.
Some beautiful women will sleep with anyone
and poems are about the same—always undone.

Why commit yourself to seeing past where you end
or to highlighting what most people only skim
unless you have some sort of bent to
liquefy (by vomiting on) what you're into?

Forgive me for having no Kafka on my shelf
and for not writing a lot about the Self.
I'm more interested in junk that exceeds
the existential things to which the senses lead.

"A long, prolonged derangement of the senses"
is a phrase that Oliver Stone clearly invented...
or was it Jim? How can you even tell?
Forgive me Rimbaud if I wasn't born to sell

Spunctum

like the real life Catch Me If You Can.
I am illegitimate, but you must understand
that I am so with dignity not with purity.
I'm not tight enough to want security.

To need security you have to have something.
With nothing you're much more into humping
but even then, you need a prophylactic
because even sluts have plans & tactics.

Poetry on the other hand may have no plans.
Nervous sweat positively correlated w/ use of fans
is nothing new but something Old and Dirty
when death and life were a little *too* flirty.

But always on the move, poetry lets go.
You will hurt more resisting the to and fro
like riding a jet ski against the yachts' wakes—
and who relaxes who doesn't wake and bake?

You might have thought poetry Big & Tall
or like journaling worth nothing at all,
just another confrontation on the way along
or a score kept during drunken ping pong.

The former is hyperbolic the latter only half-wrong
like a person shaken by the gong.
Poetry is important and not when considering
that it's only good when it isn't glittering.

Sure, technology can certainly help
with the dissolution Cormac McCarthy felt.
But poems will never be made into movies
except ones that on the book are improving.

What is a poem but a constant remake?
Who reads out of respect? Who for escape?
And here I panic if I'm ever to lose
a single keystroke if I didn't choose.

62. Only my life have I written on an iPhone, never a
    poem

Maybe I learned how to speak
without understanding what I say
and put God's WikiLeaks
thru the shredder by mistake.

Satan was Lucifer after getting fired
when he became so unemployable
that destruction was all that inspired
him seeing as it is enjoyable.

I was asked to relay a message
but I developed China syndrome.
Television alleviates Redness
and the *panning* of Bentham.

It is hard to notice typos
when it's Being and Time you're reading
because it looks like old winos
made up words in keeping

with a story given to police.
My mentor was not Husserl.
She was a little more petite

Spunctum

& under more pressure—a pearl.

Anton Newcombe was still producing
at 47 living in Germany and tweeting.
I bet at 47 publishers will be refusing
my work still because it's fleeting.

When your topic is traditionally Being
including the entities that there are
you end up always writing what you're seeing
and *obviously*, you always lower the bar.

"I know I'm not lying b/c I have things to say"
is what George Washington told dad
so no wonder to pipe the American Way
McDonald's provides monopoly gamepads.

Capitalism has been global so far
and extinction is more imaginable than its end.
The future is unpinned from the taskbar
and combatant is indistinguishable from citizen.

I guess poetry is like any other way to see
but needn't disappear for all that.
It can stir up shit like a dirty martini.
Getting shit 4 free makes it a democrat.

No! Poetry is not political! It functions
to eclipse the politico-moral with grace…
or without the slightest compunction
and with a shit eating grin on its face.

While it is a riot it is so comically.
And while it might provoke a crisis

it doesn't do so histrionically.
Who's *seen through* the screen of Isis?

The violence done is but that of a tease.
And would you say "Poetry was asking for it"
when it went the route of the honeybees
and collapsed from an unrealistic chore list?

I guess poets liked to do like children
and spit and suck it back into their mouths.
To see them tick we have to kill them.
They won't yield the pleasure of an ouch.

63. Exegesis exceeds Jesus

There was always something quite excessive
when what came out of the image was authentic.
Giving thoughts as they came was impressive
when for lack of Others computing was autistic.

Failures in communication can occur in person
and unifying enclosure can occur over a distance.
After the abolition of distance *thingness* worsens
and the relativity is entangled in the instance.

Love is like a photo. Having scaled the contrast
and the saturation we overwrite the original.
Seduce the object of focus to a context-less past
and fill in the meaning through a pigeonhole

when you can organize a population of words
into an effect that to find words is a struggling.

Spunctum

It is like shooting ducks in a barrel when afterward
the Ferris wheel is *vertiginous* from the nuzzling.

When mere speech can produce an experience
the Mary problem is more than a thought experiment
but here experiences are only seized at variance
and similarities are lived. Isn't that a predicament?

We think that we pass into adulthood
free to write our future as we choose
and that we avoid evil by doing good
as if by winning it is impossible to lose.

But we are never free of our only childhood
that through disappearing can resurface.
By each trauma we come a little closer
to thinking of our loyal negation as worthless.

We carry a previous germ always with us
a purse from a former million-dollar engagement.
Without our microbes that antibiotics bust
we become allergic to our ancestors' amazements.

We go on as living traces of a former time
that wasn't measured, organized or even spent
who because we left reality for the sublime
out of infancy had reality to invent.

Dinosaurs and lizards insects plasma cells & sperm
and once we buried our shit we discovered gold
and eventually heated straight hair into perms
and turned fossils—already signs—into casted molds.

We have a taste for the beautiful, but always go wanting

and get a passing taste before we swallow with gumption.
We don't even believe ourselves when we go flaunting
and our aesthetic enjoyment always turns to consumption.

64. National Poiesis Party

Poems are but simulations of emo
and a donning of appreciation.
Poems about Nature are just nature shows
and that's important for the station.

So poems are like little advertisements
that secretly say "Pay me for not working."
Poets invented PR with their enticements.
Homer as useful as Miley twerking.

The Babe might as well be a soft-shelled crab
and the way she looks at Mom is kind of creepy.
Eyeballs never grow but grow darker by a dab
of death until they become an illegibly beady.

Poets are against finality but so are capitalists.
But the former's task is to give the latter a face?
Presented with Final Solutions they get the gist
while the latter turn Nancy Drew to Nancy Grace.

Look at someone today with googly eyes
after Googling the term "Femme Fatale."
Check Readers Also Bought for another prize
after reading reviews that make or break sales.

Poets aren't so very different than tailgaters.

Spunctum

The drunken kind & the kind who ride your ass.
I have never caught one saying "Fuck the Haters."
Passengers turn windows into TVs as signs pass.

A one-line poem on a bathroom stall: "pray and spray."
Anarchists are right "The world is trashy."
I guess poets *must* be statists to say
"I know it's made of petrol, but I can live off taffy!"

A sweetening of the Word causes blood-sugar spikes
as the audience now tainted must re-inject
those juicy fruits gathered by labor-less psyches
if they don't want their bodies to reject

the insulation and insolence offered as a Shield.
Audacious has a double meaning when citing
your professor, mentor, or expert in a Field.
They won't like it if they didn't put it in writing.

Poets slander people afraid of transmission
especially when their intentions are candid.
But I have never been one to ask permission
& for movers have homes' painted walls sanded.

Poets are not philosophers. That I have experienced.
For though you might have thought otherwise
the latter choke on their bureaucratic sentiments
when they see their fineries as 'more radicalized'.

About some of their brightest they ask "What have I done?"
when a hiccup turns into a whole detour of ethical wrongs.
Poetry Tat has never committed itself to being won
measures its marathons like its weed in 1/8ths, or furlongs.

65. Ripcord of daily rip-off calendars

We waste our lives like a calendar
made of white printer paper.
Every day we tear off and surrender
a piece so the landfill's vented vapor

can breathe more easily.
And on every sheet, there's a fun fact
about Today in History.
Even stupid set-abouts say how to act

and that means use objects
according to their uses
all the times you can discard and reject
that won't count as abuses.

I have never been depressed
but I have injured myself to grow.
Not New Age. I'm not Snake obsessed
but like everyone else I hate the Po Po

until they save me from another.
I have always thought people wholly good
until I watched human history putter
ignoring the No Cruising signs in the hood.

I once watched Fight Club when high
and took a razor to my leg spiritually.
But you can't even organize just the guys
because they represent strength perilously.

If we were to listen to Montaigne
who said every man knows what's bad for him

Spunctum

we would still be Kurt Cobain
and kill ourselves for our death-mask's grin.

How does the dishwasher fill
itself basically every single day?
Because it wasn't designed until
after consumption had become a faith?

And how many dishes do you need?
It seems like one would be enough
unless the technology is another mouth to feed
that cries like children do for more stuff.

It will take my whole life to erase
the way of Nature each of my parents had
always written all over their face
and even then, my children won't say "Dad.

We're glad that you came a little closer
to achieving fulfillment than those before."
Still will my mountain turn to a boulder
all the way down the effects chain to a spatial pore.

66. I am better than you because I am better than me also

Truth is just the moral of the metaphor
and metaphor is infinitely more important.
The former is a sign put outside the store
and its message is imported.

We ask "Does Truth really matter?"
It's either relative, subjective or real.

It has its source in "What's the matter?"
You'd think only there is it a big deal.

Even the self-evident is spoken
and we believe in the definition.
To be actual you must be a token
that discredits other renditions.

All my life I am a fraud
and I have read most of Freud *or*
I am still fucked by God
and fabric someone had to embroider.

Time never passes from semblance to truth
and we have reworked what we will edit.
We'd never stop if we didn't die as brutes.
If we've made it in our image: auto-fetid.

67. CA Hon. ES

"In language there is the rule" they say.
And you crank the AC when it's cold outside.
The Law is something you must obey.
The rule is what you can't help but abide.

Like how with one's Sign one enters alignment
like background checks & auto-complete searches
the Law leads inevitably to confinement
and playback afoul of illusory purchase.

In language there is the rule but no Law
& speech cranks up the AC when it's cold outside

so it can pull a down comforter up to its jaw.
See how wasteful! Just to make a place inside!

Kids go on play-dates to raise money for others
and the poetry must have really big Balls
to write about frivolity while again undercover
there are about 40-50 third worlds involved.

If you write get to know writing not just yourself
because language can never quite be yours.
And writing is not always a *remedy* for bad health
so neither can it prescribe Againsts or Fors.

Authors shouldn't go on shows talking politics
because that is what taxes pay some people to do.
Some writers freely offer what makes them tick.
Did you know Einstein had political opinions too?

It's hard to separate the art from the agenda.
Not to mention the original from the copy.
But do we really need to see the pudenda
if its past its prime old flaccid and floppy?

68. Broadway for Christ-bone

I'm like "really?" That is my only mode: flabbergasted.
Gassed (vapid) and flabby (loose) in a single sneer.

Most often, I think there had to be some sort of mix up—
my world is a little snow globe that hasn't been shaken in years,
yet still works.
Do they still sell?

Critical Leisure, Book I, Volume I

Is there a way to individualize (authenticate) a profile (a sketch)?
It seems like people are trying?
Most often, they come off as vulnerable or cold.
They are either too open or too closed.
In my life,
I am either sacrificing lil' immediate goals for a long-term goal
or a long-term goal for all these little mini- and/or micro-goals,
but they almost never contribute either directly or indirectly
to the long term.
I am not a very good Hegelian, but I try
(Hegel also failed at Hegelianism).
Then, I feel like I fucked an ugly person (the old me)
and want to gnaw my arm off.
I end up losing a hand and whatever I possess or grasp with it.
The only two ways to overthrow the system
are either total boycott on purchasing
and "shut-down" or total waste and expedience.
I am a flip-flopper like John Kerry or the Dude
and I think concerned people notice.
It makes both extremes seriously question my authenticity
and that's flattering.

Someone went to Cambridge and graduated magna cum laude
but started a shitty pop group and got 68,000,000 hits on YouTube.
I will never go to Cambridge.
They do not <u>except</u> rednecks.
When I graduated from a state school,
they did not put an asterisk beside my name in the lil' recognition
email.
I both blew it and made it
and that's fuller than just making it.
I was going to burn my diploma,
but I wouldn't have made a video of it to share,

Spunctum

so what would have been the point?

The masses increase, the few increase.
In their increase, the few become the many.
And someone finds that disgusting
and gives everything up to maintain their dignity.
Venereal horror makes neat Cronenberg films, but infection still sucks.
People think I am sad when they discover my withdrawal.
I must be threatening
or must want to be, according to a Theory.
I've never burned any cash, but I've made it
and that's just as good.
I have an ID.

What constant increase produces
is a fewer few and a few-many,
where the few adds up to millions
because the population is measured in billions.
A few, a many and a few-many,
but the few-many never thinks it's a many
and because of its denial, ever increases.
The few is few precisely when it becomes
a bad sample of the population.
Someone posts pictures of themselves
putting a Baudrillard text in their mouth,
asking "Am I doing this right?"
It is a tasteless metaphor for consumption
that *catches* my attention for the moment
(emotions are *given* photographically).

That doesn't mean anything
but *counts* for something.

The face of the crowd is always lifted,
but it never looks any younger—just tightened and alienated.
The few shrivels up like testes
in the cold air outside the hot tub of style.
The many is on a regimen of pills that increase the size of its members.
The few-many makes fun of both, calls itself stable
and blinks like a liar.
Like a bunch of colored party balloons,
the few-many elevates itself uncontrollably
until it pops one by one from the crispness of new air.
It is captured on a video
and included on a clip-show called "UFO Sightings."
Then the few follow suit
as disgusted viewers.

69. Thorazine Fanzine

The ants try to find their cars
and die on the parking lot vinyl floor of my apartment,
me, sucking a spider's asshole through its eye sockets
with the vacuum cleaner
leaving a few behind to catch other bugs
checking lovecompatibility.com once I learn the birthdate and name
of every new woman.
If I was a good liar I would have a career—
because I lied about having one
not because lying is an entrepreneurial skill.
And I'd probably get tons of pussy, and I am very horny
(BECAUSE SOMEONE SAID SO).
For now, I can cook,

Spunctum

I can hold an interesting conversation
if you like negativity
and I can make you look good next to me.
Other than that, I am a piece of shit so far.
That's only per standards that are not my own.
But that is mostly it.
That is me from without.

You told me that you used your engagement ring
to buy new breasts.
So basically, you consumed the breakup.
And on top of that, you desecrated yourself
(without desacralizing yourself)
by ingesting the gooey extract they use to make computers.
You became a fusion and refusal
and the refuse of the domains of Authenticity and Artifice—
a Simulacrum like me,
disinclined to analyze but inclined to speak in terms of value
and prostrate with the language of advertising:
the wit of seduction *that goes without saying*
or wants by denying.
Shit, someone mined your titties,
out of some stupid shithole of a rock
in an even uglier place
out of your average no-man's-land.
So, predictable.
They probably died or got cancer.
Maybe they even got sick
and their whole family starved to death.
And someone probably got you on video waking up from the surgery
with some more idiotic, quirky shit to spew.
Your tits are factories manufacturing in-home security systems
powered by the raw materials of despair

that was so bad it made you wonder
if it really happened in the first place.
I know you were shocked
but now you carry the weight around on your chest
rather than inside your nerves
waiting for the circuit to change.
Someone was brutalized by the prospect of everything
when they had nothing.
Another had everything but the one thing they wanted
so all the other things were consumed by the one failure
and demeaned.

I asked you what they felt like.
An utterly ambiguous question the more I think about it.
"Like boobs...." you clarified.
I wondered if the boobs felt like the fake boobs
or if the fake boobs felt like boobs.
But if one, then the other.

In any case, we met through Communication,
and that is so much different than community.

70. KT, Try Standing

She was not a cancer
yet to others she was another excuse to get high.
She was a growth,
an intensity swelling in multiple areas of my soma.
Cancers precariously attack the body,
but she resided in my psyche
and while she expanded there
she did so like a memory foam pillow

Spunctum

a giant Hindu pillow that could rest an elephant
where the elephants are
Out of Their Habitats Endlessly Rocking
out of discomfort
alienation
and confusion…
just to stay sane…
and above all to "live" secondarily.
Perhaps they are driven by a faint memory trace
but a pebble retains the memory of a boulder
and a boulder that of a mountain.
That is why simulation is such a worry.
It almost detaches Being from Temporality
and thus, the memory trace from the thing.
And the trace is our only Hope
(if we are *merely just*).

I guess she was a hard pill to swallow, but she got me quite high.
And she was a Cancer.
I don't believe in astrology
but I asked her when her birthday was, so I guess I do
or want to somewhere, somehow.
Wishes are more effective when you put them into signs or objects,
hence why the genie lives in a bottle.
I guess that is why I write.
I do not always like it, but it is my soul
and I am suicidal otherwise.
Can you be suicidal without ever acting on it?
Can you be a thinker and not think about it at some point?
No one has never been *faced* with the nullity of existence
and I shudder to think about what completion would do to
lovemaking.
I am not a doctor, so I do not know the answer to those questions.
But I'm not sure if doctors know either

because they seem to have their shit together,
make lots of money on kickbacks/salary
and be happy.
Plus, they get off on helping people like me.
I think zookeepers get the same pleasure when they nurse baby animals
from a technological tit, *their tit*.
I do not have health insurance
and must pay a penalty to keep living without it,
so I don't know why I'm talking about this.

Her father had cancer, was a real cunt
and once called me to tell me to stay away from his daughter.
I didn't understand at the time and told him he had the wrong guy.
But I think he was right.
Plus, he had cancer, so I went along with it.
It was 6 years before I spoke to her again.

Nevertheless,
when she was *fresh* out of rehab, she came over out of the blue—
daughter of Proteus—
and got high with me.
I really had no idea she was in rehab.
I didn't have a Facebook mainly because shit like that is dangerous
for people like me with psychological problems.
It's like having free license to further ruin your rep.
I guess that is justice.
It is one of our many freedoms and that matters.

After she got high and after I got high off her attention,
she left to go do something at her house.
I was a little naïve
but that's an argument *for* my love or *for* life.
I guess I fell for something…

Spunctum

Two things, including her.
She never came back like she said she was going to.
Luckily our encounter was so brief
that I hadn't enough time to process it
or to start drawing up plans/indulging former wishes.
But I was *pretty sure* (not sure) that I had killed her
because she didn't answer my phone calls.
She must've been exhausted from her experiences and the weed.

Maybe I did know she had just gotten out of the institution.
Thinking back, now *I think I must have*
but have been telling people otherwise.
It has been a lie, sure, but no one really cares about the story
anyway
so it causes little harm
and harm is what matters to people.
We go about weighing these conflicts
by largely arbitrary moments of choice that occur so quickly
we don't know how we ended up with one or the other.

Apparently, addicts are not supposed to get high at all,
not even a little gravity bong.
But she got this love addict high off her presence
and no one called her to tell her to stay away from me.
But maybe she stayed away by way of her own subjunctivization
and ultimately, by her distance, did me a kindness.
The come down sucked
so I took care of that with other expedients
like memory.

I was her best friend in high school, maybe even throughout it.
Well, I was one of them.
I once waited after school with her for her boyfriend to pick her
up.

Critical Leisure, Book I, Volume I

He was late.
I'm *pretty sure* (not sure) that was after I went to her soccer game
like she asked.
He shook my hand and had giant hands and a bad temper.
But he thanked me for warming her up for him.
I guess I was the valet who he tipped by not giving me an ass-
beating.
That is worth something, even if it's only a deterrence.
I guess I felt like a stupid piece of shit
but also, *pretty cool* (not cool enough).
It was worth it I think, both for her sake and his.

I am not high right now I don't think
although here she is again
and it might be fucking my creativity.
Her and I are talking over the internet.
I figure she could use it, use me
and I am not worth much, so it costs her next to nothing.
I am like primitive tool
that hasn't been replaced after 2,500 years of invention.
I guess I am not a piece of shit either.
Neither am I a square.
I am interesting.
I am slightly depressed, that's why.
I am not depressed *because* I am interesting, of course.
It's vice versa.
We are both fucked up in the head
because we lived our lives Unshielded and Open
and although that led us to fuck up our lives on multiple occasions
it strengthened our character, facilitated our honesty
and muted our prejudices.
At least it did for me. He he, I do not even believe that.
I'm glad space meddled.
As a division, it Opened us.

Spunctum

Otherwise, we wouldn't be here talking...
listening or projecting ourselves onto one another, both desperate.

Being strange and recognizing one's estrangement,
when co-opted, can be a deterrent against others of a dissimilar
type
as a farcical aura of advisement,
a Shield that both protects against externalities
and protests Closure as a soft barrier like the crown of babies.
It is a selection and *a mode of selectivity*.
Thorns and roses.
Brett Michaels already said that but without this qualification.
I must be a hack, not a poet—but the scythe is an agrarian
apparatus.
Heidegger is agrarian, I'm like him.

We needed egos to Shield us from the Trauma of the suburbs—
its vacuity whose desert of the real opens a space for poetry,
mine—
but we were too young to have fully or at all developed them.
We needed them because we both come from a shitty place
where there is 0% crime
neon green grass
lots of free air conditioning
decent food
gas money
where you can shave with the shower running
and flush your cum down the toilet
along with the toilet paper you dried your dick off with.
You must flush it down
because seeing your cum in the toilet is not only embarrassing
but kind of sad and offensive.
And Life doesn't dissolve for a pretty long time, considering.

I guess it isn't water insoluble even if it is susceptible to water-
logging.
I guess that's why Lil' Kim got her stomach pumped.
Too much consumption in life can back you up and bankrupt you
with the help of specialists.
I guess even discharge can accumulate.

Everyone has gotten married at 26 according to social media.
Many have gotten hyphenated names.
Apparently, that's less sexist.
They are doing their part to progress and transcend social norms
but still retain their free comfort.
I think that having a degree
a job
and a wife/husband
will look good on them at the reunion.
Some people do drugs.
Others have kids and get married with careers.
How can you say one is more illusory or delusional?
My ex went from Prozac to pre-natal.

I will not *Attend* the reunion
so I don't know why I Care.
I'm at the reunion now.
It's called remembering the past.
I can even remember feelings I had.
That's my re-sentiment—that's unlike resentment.
But I will just look at the photos on Facebook
and complain some more—
maybe write a poem about that.
But here I have beat myself to the point.
I will have ruined my career
with simultaneous inventions I share with myself
at other times in other possible worlds.

Spunctum

I'm not exactly sure if someone hasn't already written
all the poems I *have* written (by a sweatshop of lashed id-ioms).
I wonder if there was never a Bukowski
would someone have still written what he wrote.
I'd like to think that without him
those poems just wouldn't have existed.
But I am not 100% sure and that is not enough.

I am constantly deleting/creating profiles
because I am curious but a little disinterested.
Well, I guess when you are brutalized and a little nauseated,
that's a sort of interest.
But maybe it's just curiosity. It could be worse.
I could be a dog waiting on the hardwood floor
by the door to the garage.
I guess as a person who believes in love, in anything,
that's what I am sometimes.

Some people stay up all night Facebooking,
but it is just nighttime here and daytime where they are…
I usually stay awake
because my guts feel like they are being ripped out slowly by crank.
Or maybe God is holding my internal organs
like I grab a handful of goldfish crackers.

People that have careers
get on at 7:30 AM, 12-1 PM, and/or 6:30 PM-12 AM.
I try not to get online at other times than those
so it looks like I have one too.
They probably don't think about that, but I do, so who cares.
I have learned not to say too much on there
so as not to give my identity away.
And somehow, I don't know how, curiosity kills suspicion.

Critical Leisure, Book I, Volume I

It's a kitsch thing.

She and I were kind of buddies. Why give that up?
I didn't break the rule of pussy
and put her on a pedestal.
That rule is for pussies.
I just treated her like a creaturely being.

In earlier life, I watched her go for shmuck after shmuck
for about 3 years.
She probably thought that I loved her.
I would have not been the only one.
One time she called me
while I was at my girlfriend's mother's apartment
because she had taken a lot of pills.
I didn't call 911, but I did try to talk her down.
I watched KT lose her grip or her footing softly,
in a cool manner, from afar, in passing.
I never knew if anyone else ever noticed, even her best friends.
I never asked anyone.
Maybe she was one of those people like myself
who fall through the cracks
half-despairingly and half willingly,
a Manchurian candidate armed with suicide pills and a backstory.
Maybe it was just me. A total projection.

Her friends had no crazy in them, even if they were 'crazy partiers'
(crazy in their affiliation to the Party).
They probably weren't clever enough to see what was going on
(of course, *I was*).
If I made a movie out of it, I'd be Woody Allen—
in my own past, talking to myself directly to the audience.

It takes character to notice something like that.

Spunctum

Many of the people we've known are not characters
but mainly are series of reactions.
For some reason, she carried a little more force to me
and my lies were antennae feeling my way around.
I'm not sure if I was honest with her or not
but I looked at her a little differently, I think.
She was so cool.
The weights on shoulders can make some more powerful
like Vonnegut's Harrison Bergeron.
The strong can increase in size and intensity and cravings
when contained.
Joy contained (by metaphor) accretes aggression.
Cycle: rebellion, repression, increased domination.
Cycle: morality → loss → nihilism → reevaluation → skepticism
→ aesthetics.

Some of us function through dissimulation
and the involute aggression leads to implosion.

She told me she spent a year in prison.
She could have been fucking with me.
She was attending her sister's wedding on Monday
then she was *headed straight*
for Christian fundamentalist boot-camp/rehab.
She made a joke about snakes.
I wondered if they were going to perform an exorcism
on her drug/behavioral demons
and then pray for success.
Once the demons are all gone, will *she* be left in there?

I'm going to watch the Exorcist.

71. STARBUCKS, variety, and freedom

{poetry generating technology}:

Simulators/Sychophants/Symbiotes/Symbols
Tout/Tickle/Tease
As/Angelic/Anal
Religioso/Ready-made/Rheumatic
Baudrillardians/Bukowskians/Beatniks/Buyers
Upcharge/Upsell/Uphold/Universalize
Choppy/Catastrophic/Chaotic/Chance/Christ-like/Crocodilian
Kitsch/Killer/Kinetic
Stupefaction/Security/Sex/Sterility/Satellites

How much time could you spend here?

There is a secret technology in the slash
linking it to *the feeling of Starbucks coffee* ^{TM}.

Expedients/repeaters/time-shavers/space-savers
is not a sentence
but it isn't merely a word either, obviously.

72. The red, the white, and the blue

As the first piss of the morning slaps me in the knees
because its stream is multi-directional
surely the scientists have confirmed
there is no essential difference between laughing and crying.
The same mnemonic contraction and hypertension
of the muscular exactitude.

Those who live with the rigor of corpses understand not to do either
and do not age in their 'wish-less' lap pool of teleology.

My offer stands:
I want to break into houses with you
and defile empty children's bedrooms
and family rooms
or fuck you atop a pile of bodies we've just beaten to impotency
or something like that…

blood, cum and the tears of others
are the red the white and the blue.

73. Things Bukowski taught and did not merely teach me

When you write (moral) poetry
the lines *should* look COOL meme-ories.
When you shit it out onto that fucking machine
but not merely that machine

it must look cool,
        have COOL FORM
like the Holocaust
so that when the cameras shoot stark panoramic shots via drones
from cool, impossible angles—
music image text sucked up our proboscises all at once—
we 'are' inside it.
You just show up to the poetry,
the pan-opticon of poetry,
the punctum of poetry—
all from the *resting place* of COOL FORM.

Critical Leisure, Book I, Volume I

You're unsure where you end.

Flash it across   the   screen
in COOL FONTS
presenting it as:
being simu-typed
being simu-handwritten
       including simu-editing
simu-erasing
simu-crossing out…
being simu-meta-pata-holo-micro-conjured,
raising itself like the fakir's rope or like sponges.

Drawing a blank here. Are you getting it?

………Informational (or worse, *informative*) saprobes?
………………Magic? Fatality? Illusion? What?
This is shit. This is all shit. Fuck.

The FORM must be COOL meme-ories.

If there is going to be a documentary
the FORM must be COOL meme-ories.

If there is going to be a portrait on the back cover
the FORM must be COOL meme-ories.

But what if I write (derogatorily) quasi-dadaesque pastiche poems?
I write representation of poems, never poems themselves.
Isn't that it? Isn't the The Form? Nonsense commercial art?
FORMAL NONSENSE ART!

Spunctum

74. the webcam girl next door

I have seen many things:
a man stick his entire bald head into a girl's Virginia slim
a girl put her mouth up to a hole in a bathroom stall
and become a hole herself
and a girl finger gangbanging herself, all holes finger-filled.
I have seen emetic BJs
poop play
and pussy boxing—flurried like the speed-bag.
But when one of them asked you to put your fist in your pussy
you said "No, I will not put my fist in my pussy!"
I knew that you had boundaries
and class
and glass anal-
double- and triple-anal dildos.
I had to have you.
Good Golly Miss HollyCumslightly!

Baudelaire had his whores
and would have asked if he could stab you
and shove his hickey dickey in the hole, knife still in,
used as a wedge.

Van Gogh would have emailed you a jpeg of his missing ear
after you told him you liked him, because he listened to you.

Bukowski would not have sent you any gifs
saying "That's a nice cunt you have on your hands.
Nice. Not spectacular.
I've seen better and worse, but nice."

"We should stop seeing each other by turning off our laptops.

If I could get the poems you shoved up there upon request
that would be great…"

That's all that *I* could say.

75. A scene from Family Guy but sadder (read by the House
    from Amityville)

They sit several rows ahead of me with suggestive travel bags
probably to see family, the only time they
Get. Out.

Not speaking to one another, he looks down at his crotch
like queers dragged by a '72 Ford pickup down dirt drag-strips
and she looks out the window,
probably dreaming of when her cunt was still warm and sensitive,
now as draft-less as air-pocketed cement and underwater caves,
her body abandoned and consumed by some little shit kid
from the little shit genetics of a little shit man—
Nietzsche's little shits—
and the football stars or nerd millionaires she could have fucked
and the will to power she could have committed to
and the lotion-skinned bartender she could have fucked in the
bathroom
but she's here on this half-ass train
with this half-ass silence and simulation
from a half-ass guy and his half-ass love
fucked, nothing BUT fucked
like the rest of us.

76. zero emissions worse than thought experiments?

One day, we will only get a certain amount of shits per week
and even then, there will still be shit.

One day, we will take pills to make our shit smell like cascading roses
and even then, there will still be shit.

One day, we will have an economical diet
and will do inventory of our diet
and calculate the expenditure of our own shit
and even then, there will still be shit.

One day, we will *receive* (that sexual innuendo)
pamphlets passed out at mandatory visits
as a model for "Keeping Shit to A Minimum"
and even then, the shit will flow.
Baby will it EVER flow
like the fountain of the Alpha and Omega
given freely to him that is athirst,

but there is no free lunch
because even then the man athirst
will piss in the river.

77. 'You better redneckonize' (title of an NYC skin graft found after the seas rise)

We will improvise in our raspy-voiced vice
like the obese on opioids
or a 200+ pound whore fucking without moving an inch.

We will improvise and impoverish
like Wagnerian Tyler Perry
and in our cool reticence, we will require little participation.
In our piquancy, none.

We will discover less in truth
and *find* even less in Happiness
than we will find in the neck cheese
of former Mrs. America or Mrs. Universe—two identical things.
Such is the secret destiny of America, like all discourses:
to be a winner on its own show.

78. pre-emptive text poetry [poetic transference that is more A.I. than A.I. and thus wins (by losing itself)]

There is a new automatic writing and emotive power
and twofold a new relation to the world
that's shamanic in origin and technical in destination.

I surrender my poetry to Google
and in doing so, I surrender myself to the world
the only sacrificial justice for my coming into being.

Google:

"___-___."

As soon as I attempt to take this leap of faith
and finally allow the computer to express itself through me,
its mediatic Medium:

Spunctum

"Google Instant is unavailable…"

There may be a fate and there may be a sign,
but both are ambiguous
and the instant is typically unavailable to us on the spot
in the brute auto-correction of its obvious stupidity.

79. Katy Parity – an empirical study of Katy to be
 rejected by the current paradigm of Katy

Felinity and fur below the knees,
probably on the V for Vendetta, respectively.

A delightfully chokeable neck.
Nape like magnetic tape.
Harpies nesting in her hair ceteris parabus flowing down her faces
like the shirt-ends of insecure fatties constantly pulled down,
discarded babies off Spartan cliffs
or dim-sum flowing from a loosening hymen—
sudden return, compresence of symmetry broken.

Jaw-line like the fins of sharks served in Japanese soup for
$250/cup.

Eyes beam unto my soft-served guts/brains/spirit like the
NASDAQ,
like light that will never reach the circumference
of an expanding universe,
the skyscraper sunlight that disseminated the collapse of The
Towers
and raised morale in the hands of rheumatoid arthritis
bejeweled in semen

pork
and Purell.
Her eyes are blue.

The freckles are barely visible
like the stars from the immanent parking lots of the hypermarket.

There is a fine line between coquette and riotGRRRL

but today, only revolutionary women are beautiful
(to the point of banality).

80. Katy Parity II – what doesn't let you die makes you weaker

She once told me "You're not as clever as you think you are…

you're not cool like you think and your poetry isn't that good either.
You're not shit…" (that double negative that still forcibly 'negates')

"You're not good. You're a pseudo-intellectual."

…as she pressed her backpack up against her breasts
in a climax of volatile repulsion
and ascending, abruptly plateauing Life.

"It's not OK to take my things, to read my things.
Ask before you look at anything that's mine."

[She still believes in private property and a private economy

Spunctum

as an anarchist.]

"Is it ok if I look at your tits?"
...I thought it was kind of clever.

The first time we met, she said "Everything is politics..."
"Fuck politics," I interjected, *"it's not for everyone..."*

"Look around. Everything is getting worse.
It's getting *uglier.*"
She's so attached.

"You're very attractive," I exclaimed,
and I was dead
and spaded by her exacerbated Beauty
like the end of her immaturely Satanic tail.

81. Katy Parity III – The Anarchist Anarchs

She wears black eyeliner and black nail polish
black t-shirts
and black jeans with white chalky stains on the ass, I've noticed,
from sit-ins on concrete sidewalks.
She smokes cigarette butts she finds on the pavement.

Black on black on black.
Sometimes no bra.
I notice by the orientation of her breasts.
Hair 'naturally' black and artificially, that is, naturally anarchic.

The eyeliner is a cultural artifact of the West,
but it works by removing the eyes from the rest of her

so I am watched by her entire body
faced like the cereal aisle with banal freedom
banal choice
banal strategies
and finally defaced in a contest of doing/undoing.
Such is the re-enactment of strife.

The nail polish appears fresh
and is kept up in a tele-agonal adversity of dominating/freeing
the opposite of the Christian doctrine "Teach a man to fish."

The anarchist girl, because her Absolute is not THE Absolute, enthralls

but because I'm no fonder of anarchists than of the Law,
I "dutifully" (she accuses) accept the sexual tension she implants
in my scission.

Wear all the black you want my anarchistic systematizer,
but your white light imploding—dis-emanating—
from the single point *that's your Nothing and my mind's eye*
sucks away my shadow like the ocean edge before a tsunami
before the white heat that follows
disallows any participation on *my part*,
forcing me to consume you
like the atom bomb forces human cells to inflict cancer on themselves
in ecstatic radiance.

Between Screen and the Real, woman is tamping aureole—
interstice.

Spunctum

82. Iron(man)ic strategies

What would irony be in a culture of simulation
copy/paste
and useless functions
yet nostalgic perfection and reproduction,
where the fake is more exciting
loving
giving
virtuous
and more efficient.

Irony is a political alter-native.
Irony is a polemical alter-ration.
Irony is a pesky simulation—a fatal seduction—
in a time where nothing happens
because everything has happened
beyond the iron curtain altitudes of extermination.

What if *things* reversed? What would irony look like?
It is a reversal? What is a reversal of a reversal?
(The significance of the death of Socrates.)

Radical sexism? Radical racism?
Pomo sexism, pomo racism?
Hatred and indifference is the norm.
We must be more indifferent than indifferent: blithe.
More spiteful than spiteful: simulators.
10 truths and ten scorns a day—
the outcome of liberation that is the final solution
to the problem of freedom.

83. Holography

Some tattoo on their eyebrows
some their lipstick
their eyeliner
eye shadow
blush
and interest.

Some tattoo on their soul
with a jackhammer of their own surveillance.

Some inject their faces
until they are crisper than a potato chip bag
and every time they talk
all you hear is the crinkling of the bag
and you would prefer the bag to their face.

Some inject their armpits
that tense up like a cat struck by lightning
as the arc of their fame
descends like the arched back of the ecto-static kitty.

Nothing is more of an implant or injection
than your moot-point Humanity
and there's nothing terser on this earth.

84. The In-Betweeners

We were not sure any longer about categories
and everything seemed broken down into pulp
and even seemed fictive,

which made creativity impossible, as it become secondhand
reflection.
But *that* those words no longer had the zing they once had
in a more modern life
and *that* the mode of poetry no longer delivered punches
attributable to boxing matches…
it was more like city lights and traffic
played on fast forward for several hours
to a music file recycled short of every minute
like the touch of something unfamiliar and wet in the dark woods
but with an unconscionable Self.
Something out of fashion
and embarrassing like melanoma
or sun-tanned skin like potato skin,
poetry was supposed to produce a buzz.
Bzzzzzzzzzzzzzzzz!!
Like the sound of a washing machine
or just the high frequency buzz of silence today.

We were unsure about traditional ways of life
like true and false
good and bad
or nothingness.
We were a culture of the eye
and micro-monitored everything to a squiggly on a monitor
like a crease in between two legs.
Computers were already disappearing.
TVs were disappearing.
The robot no longer fascinated like it once did in the '50s.
All the technologies tended towards screens.
If you were lucky, you'd meet a girl willing to fuck on camera
and you could fuck her in the streets
in an abandoned home
or in the wild.

She would be *more willing* than most
(where the will now means "responsive to pressure).
Because we were so penetrated by visions because we absorbed them
we were unsure amid all the doomsday predictions
what the end of the world might *look* like
but we were sure that if it happened we would know it
because it would give us signs of its occurrence.
But we began to wonder if it had already ended.
Maybe the end of the world was nothing like
what the models showed it to be.
Maybe it just looked like the virtual reality
that seems to enwrap
augment
segment
and enrapture everyday life.
Our memories were penetrated
by pseudo-experiences and special effects
and the way we consumed media
turned towards how we viewed ourselves
and now we are unsure
if anyone can do a commentary on a state of affairs called 'today'.
The peep holes just show other people looking through other peep holes
and the monitors point us to other monitors.
And because we are so used to dealing with dinosaur machines,
totally unspectacular and unfulfilling given the models of the future,
we interact with others in everyday life
as in a chat room
or a virtual space of avatars and *mere possibilia*.
But there are none
in the disparity and intractability of the in-between times.
And it may even be utopian to think *that* way.

Spunctum

85. Perspectival ___

If you are not first, you are last.
That is a truism down the ages.

Don't mind that it was used in an asinine movie.
That just dissuades the intensity of the phrase
like the recycling center
masks the facts that the times are a giant landfill
and that the recycling center also produces waste.

1% and 99%.

We are all fucked by it.
Whether it is utopia
or capitalism
or poverty
or saturation
or Life
or freedom
or a woman a man or a tranny or a queer
or others
or sobriety
or madness
we are fucked by it.

Put yourself first and you are fucked.
Put others before yourself and you are fucked.
Put one foot in front of the other and you may be alright.
Maybe not.
Put beer before liquor and you may be alright.
Maybe not.
Say yes to the last and you may be alright at first
but if it lasts you may be fucked.

86. The Mouth Also Eats

We like to
talk
talk
talk.

We even write poems about the ecstasy of communication.

We like to communicate so much that we eat it.

We like to communicate so much and so redundantly
that we communicate Communication
and then we eat it.

We leave a copy of Hemingway on the dresser in case someone enters.

We put guitars on stands.
We put journals on nightstands.
We put drugs on mirrors on the coffee table.
We clean under certain circumstances and are pigs under others
and the information line is crystal clear.

There are phones that mimic our selective attention
and ability to reduce noise.

We enter meta-
communicate meta-
and that's ok because we will eat it and it will be gnawed
and if we are lucky
decayed
dead
done.

Spunctum

Let us only hope it trickles down to parasites
the ranks among parasites
the whole Order of them
phyla of them
rich and poor alike.
They will have their parasites.

With mucous (the *stopped up*)
THE SITUATION HASTENS!

87. No Former-Marine-Lovers!

You held the gun like a remote control
and the war flashed before your very eyes, your life in fact,
like images on a screen.
Events unfolded in the war like the schedule of television
programs.
It was a 'safer' and 'cleaner' war.
War was treated like death,
like a series of causes,
and all its negative effects—so we wished and assumed—
could be eliminated by us
but that attitude expedited a series of miscalculations
for which it was impossible to calculate who was responsible.
Each day seemed like progress
but we had been in the desert
with each day unfolding *verisimilarly*
mirroring civilian life in a pre-programmed, neutral way,
so we didn't know what was going on.
Everything was so micro-managed and pre-packaged
like stamps on MDMA that appeal to children

we lost track of everything that was happening.
And nothing seemed to happen, most of all.

Combat seemed to be button pressing.
You didn't come back a man like our grandfathers did in WWII.
If anything, that war was above all Human—aka Bourgeois—
the reverse of the Holocaust.
You and your old lady fucked back then like it meant something.
There was still a future, a project,
since things were unsure and mysterious.
And people were angry, the productive kind of anger.
Now, you basically fuck your "partner" like a sandbag
and he/she has been keeping in constant contact
with a series of ex-boyfriends.
Having forgotten your position in the household
It was hard to really remember what your place ever was *in any case.*
Things just plain didn't make sense.
Things didn't seem to be in their right places.

They find fish fossils in deserts
and warm climate fossils atop Mt. Everest, probably.
If there is a norm at all anymore
(no longer Protean) it is seismic and all-around collapse.
If the Twin Towers could collapse like that
as if there was nothing to them at all,
anything can.
You are unsure whether that is a good thing.
You can't even hold a steady position anymore.
Goods are bad and vice versa depending on how you look at them.

Your rifle did the killing for you and the pills thought for you
and the steroids exercised for you.
Thrown back into the world, you hesitated at simple things.

Spunctum

Unsure of where you stood on things and with people
you were skeptical of something as miniscule as everyday life:
a worse relation to it than general thoughtlessness
and taking-for-granted.

The gun gave you the illusion you could just change the channel
like the magazine or the scope
by joining the war and killing.
The woman gave you the illusion you could just change the channel
by being with someone and fucking

but EVERYBODY KNOWS THAT'S NOT TRUE.

Still they seem to tune in anyways.
Or they have the illusion that they can change the channel
and just be alone, immune and immutable,
like the TV gives you the false dichotomy between the world and itself
since it can be turned off
like a woman who says she is turned off
as a part of her erotic rape scenario.

The difference generated by mapping and demarcating
(the channels were their difference)
gave you the illusion that there was a channel
specially broadcasted and suited to you
and the image feedback generated made you friends
(that's just what friendship was:
piggybacking off the current polis).
Marines were jar heads because we embodied something
(Nothing?).
That is what made us fascinating like the ill or the mad in times past—

like the hermaphrodite.

It wasn't the fact of having *seen* atrocities.
We have all seen these things regularly on TV, and they are dull, not shocking,
a part of the day to day, moment to moment buzz
like the rattling fences of Nascar as the cars circle at 250 mph.

It had nothing to do with heroism.
That wouldn't have made sense to people outside of the current era.
They would have looked baffled
as they were raffled off to whoever drew first.

88. still young and like me

I see through its posterior windshield into the truck in front of me at the stoplight
as a young guy gives his girl the middle finger playfully
and as they begin hand-fighting
she gestures to jerk off his middle finger.

I've experienced it but feel luckier to witness it.

They are going to fuck each other when they reach their destination.
At least someone is getting it.

Life is beautiful from certain positions
usually from behind
and romantics are necrophiles.

Spunctum

89. the former granite capital of the world

The countryside will give you the best solitude you've ever had.
It's only *Beautiful* as an extension of city life
otherwise it is a terror.
It will be brutal as you become decolonized in its brilliance
that will vaporize the most talkative people,
those vampires who don't see misery built into the land
using anonymous tags.

You turn your radio off
and wipe the ectoplasm off the steering wheel
driving *through it in it*
and you can see it.
It's as simple as a sensual centrality.
You can see it like dried blood on scabbards
in the clay-stained foundations of the houses
looking deader and more sensitive to it than the people.
You can see it as the 15-year-old gets off the garbage truck
as the prettiest girl he's ever seen gets cash for cans
while porn-tycoons get cash for chunkers like her.

Don't turn your radio off EVER.
Don't stop going to the club the game the bar the concert the theater
the café the demonstration the job EVER.
Don't remove yourself from your crowd
or take off your stylish clothing
or stop reading historical literature
or getting it from the cinema
or debating politics EVER
because the future will confront you *from behind*.
And if you're not ready for it with your morale
since the fancy people won't prepare you for it

it will face-fuck you
until there is a strand of thick spit connecting you two.

It's the rurality of the present.

90. the primacy of melancholy

It's all will to power, baby.
Happiness will give it up though if she's drunk.
it's all about the works
the smiles.
But you don't want her because of the pigs she's laid with.

What we call Happiness is not enjoyment.

91. kill fast boredom

People can sense my arrogance.
Even when my intentions are good in concealing it, they get it.
They can hear it in my quietude,
in my laughter (even aimed at myself),
in the generic and the interpersonal.

All I want is a little arrogance to match my own.
I thought I had it with her.
But she hates herself by putting me first.

I think women will sometimes give into the coven.
In the commune,

Spunctum

everyone is given a task that will speedily (not boringly) kill
boredom.

She can have that.
I'm better on my own—bored, still arrogant or confident,
but I hide it well.
That's what you must do *inter pares*. *wink*

She *tried* her *best*.
She bested her goal by trying. I'll give her that.
She's *got fight*.
She possesses the verb to bring me down to earth—
the *particular*.

I can't go where the masses have a primitive epilepsy
over a shrunken-head social
because all the signs trying to recapture it flash on
flash off—*reflectors* at Night—
in a montage factory where the people respond
like they did to Pharaohs: with their lives.

Don't ever try to pull a gal from the coven.
They'll collapse like leavened bread
if you peek inside too early.
They're bitter and seemingly "jealous of the cock"
so the story goes that maybe they didn't invent
but keep in circulation with their subversiveness.
I think it's getting to be the other way around
and maybe men identify with the female in the porn
with her endless cumming.

You need a good one, good *on their own terms in isolation*
(from even yourself)
that's their goodness—their relation—

but not *total* isolation, since you could territorialize that,
which would make them disgusting.
Alone, they no longer count as Woman though.

92. the folding of events and info like time and space will take you back

The montage factory is to me unveiled sitting on the porch
of a person-I-know-called-a-friend's house
unemployed
couch surfing it
and watching the unquantifiable cars pass
as they take work home with them—a synonym for death—
every few seconds.
But I don't watch like you think.
They are *just there*—close-quarters, objective and indifferent.

Speech is at its highest point in the montage factory.
You can passively be yourself.
You can detox, as indifferent but not objective, since with gifts.

You *give* it Nothing
a simulacrum of a gift
a present with nothing in it
and thus a non-representation of a present.
It cannot respond.
I could *give* as much of a shit about it as about those cars
and as about the trees.
If they weren't there, you'd make it.
You'd be alright. You're only accustomed to them anyway.
They are nice now, sure, I agree,
but I couldn't care less about those *things*.

I'm just dependent on them,
and when they are gone, the future won't care either.

93. dawning on Eve

The little lovelies will hate the rich and the politician
but they will not beware of parties
and they will always vote for and promote
themselves.
They will exhaust all that they can offer
in merely designating Themselves in a style addressed to
Everyone.

The social network will allow as much freedom of good health
as the nature preserve does natural freedom.
The preservatives *do* lengthen life.
However, life lasts insofar as it's *on sale*.

"You cannot disturb the social since you are already a part of it"
simultaneously means "You must disturb the social at all costs"
like a fire that is constantly dying.
Life needs to be stoked (like surfers).
Scientists can install excitement about life.
Sociality is both sacred and anathema, typical of death—
and preserved and buried, typical of the dead
since they must remain happy in death.
It is ceremonial*ized*, i.e., not ceremonial,
relived and reenacted like Christ
but without symbolism.
Church at its best is pure reactivity
the way the brain secretes its own productions as it reacts to drugs.

"Has it ever been any different?"
One now wonders this, *but not for the first time*.

94. we gush redundancies

Our communication is stupid.
It is a weakness.
It is more contagious than a pre-school and functions the same way.
You won't change it, but it will dissolve you
traumatized
saturated
symbiotic
planktonic
and suspended near the surface,
worse off than waders who still have a bottom.

It is precipitated by a loss.

You will be nothing but information,
subject-less *yet easily identifiable*.
You will live as a thesis for an argument for a total program.
Glorifying your new intellectual-spiritual cerebrospinal software
you will be scanned
updated
upgraded
and you will have so many **things** to talk about
to so many people like you (you as one of the people).

The message will pass through into your blood (your depth?)
like a high-altitude blood transfusion
like liquid feed cooled to gelatin

Spunctum

and it will evolve with the prosthetic ambience of DNA.
It will absorb you—like among like—via information.
And every part of you will crumble off during the meal you are like hard-shelled tacos.
Each meme will contain residue of everything that isn't yours.
How do you know if you are even You?

You will be propagated,
your individuality violated in situ by a prosthesis of the prejudice,
intellectual mitochondria beneath your radar needing your information
without needing you.
You will be active in this process.

Through communication, you will participate in a system
constantly putting itself under a microscope
the magnification indefinite because the system redefines its totality
from each sample it takes from itself through your consumption-labor
and it will set the pace of your life as it laps itself.

You will participate in a system
constantly glorifying itself into the hole
renouncing itself
constantly updating itself on itself
just like little you do
and glorifying itself through renunciation, through a hole,
because a saturation point has been reached in you via everyone else.
You will become as lame as the 'New Left'
and turn to DMT—the God-porn—
and you will follow DMT and God on social media.
The nostalgia will kill you.

You will become pious and you will be the favored child of God
like little Lucifer doing His work, doing *all* His goddamned work
and stealing from the cash register minutely and quietly.

We're as poor as hell absorbed by heaven.
It's a matter of pooled time-points.

People are not equivalent to themselves.
And if they are, AVOID THEM AT ALL COSTS!

I'll leave the communication to lovers
whose feelings are transmitted in mucous
fear gazes contradiction tension and gestures.
And for whom communication is obsolete.

Happenings—die twice.

95. carrion

She would tug at my cock like the lever of a slot machine in El Dorado
when I didn't even kiss her.
I would just lie there squeezing her plump red ass
pulling at it like it would come right off
and become an extension *of my body*.

Those were good mornings when the sun showed through the blinds.
My parents surely heard us upstairs.
It had to have been better than the Today Show.
Good nights when the neighbors would leave on
"those fucking driveway spotlights."

Spunctum

She hated them. I kind of enjoyed them.
She'd go down on me and I'd watch her plump ass
red from all the groping
thrown up in the air like a cat that objectifies your fingertips.
I'd tug and pull at that thing that deterred me from her totality,
where fetishes add up to no one.

She gave me so much
and I'd yank at her mid-section and hoist her rear-end up to my end
until her vulva,
watering like Pavlov over his contribution to the community of theories,
or like death or any other sort of immortality,
draped right over my face—
that shroud of Jesus with the spiritual mark of a face.
"It's prickly down there."
"I don't care."
I'd light up like Christmas children in response to the lights
but she couldn't see that.
I'd have to wring that thing out every now and then like a dishrag
performing Chinese water torture on myself.

I'd spread her cheeks apart
and her tight little asshole would hover above my gaping mouth—
the fan-duct rupturing the bathroom ceiling and sucking out the death.
I'd scan the area
and would find ingrown hairs or pimples (I'm not sure)
scattered about but I didn't mind.
I was in dog eat dog heaven.
The dimples on her ass would disappear as I'd stretch the cheeks apart
tugging and pulling as far as they would move.

She had an ass that, dumpy on its own,
really shined when squeezed and stretched by another—
an interactive body.
She was the most beautiful girl I've ever been with
(and she wasn't pretty).
Something about her imperfections being pluperfect schemata
that initiated me.
Something like that drove me mad.
I almost thought she'd stay, too.
I didn't pay enough attention to her to give her reason to stay
or to think she might leave me.

96. I wrote this for a girl to seduce her and read it to mine when it got bad. Neither got it.

She had the fair skin of a greatly cold-hearted, calculating
and overall evil Scandinavian legislator-princess.

The aristocratic eyes that demand softly.

She was Delphi incarnate
(she spoke vaguely and tricked people into fucking themselves).

Within her, non-local and unified in the Indo-Dionysian,
were innocence and tyranny.
More Nordic
coarse
disciplined
skeptical
than the Venus in her *North Face* fleece.
How I wanted to breed with her
with the most Viking and barbaric purpose!

Spunctum

I wanted her blood in vitro.
In wine, I would take her communion
in the most Pagan and unintelligible sense (I'm vague too).
She made me "unique."
She was a liar.
My love was endocrinal and psychotropic—*simulacradelic*.

Why is it that I feel as if I've fallen in love with an ivory statue?

The pornos just don't do it anymore—*they're too realistic.*
I stopped believing in good sex.

Boy I'll bet she has a warm, ripe little cunt, too.
Other option:
more porno as I masturbate myself in her cozy hobbit hole.
Could life get any more perplexing?

97. CRACK

We thought if we made goals we'd be less anxious.
We thought if we were more informed
we'd be at peace out and about.
We thought that causes and effects would allow us
to prevent the worst.
We thought that instant communication would make us more
sociable
and less isolated
but it didn't even make us *feel* more sociable and less isolated,
just freer.
And freedom, we've learned, isn't everything either.
We thought that if we realized all possibilities
things would unfold stably

all we'd have to do is consult previous data.
Monica Joey Chandler Ross Phoebe Rachel
supposed to inculcate an outpouring sociability and sentimentality
and transience.
Beyoncé supposed to make us dance, stand up for ourselves, vote
and debate—
and per the latest model, THINK DEEP THOUGHTS.
MJ supposed to make us feel superior and sane.
Homelessness supposed to give us something to overcome and
avoid.
Obama Hussein Bin Laden supposed to moralize us
and give us someone to hate
blame
play ball with
or believe in.

WHATEVER.
Just
LET FREEDOM RING YOUR BELL
like a steel baseball bat knocking the stitching out of the only ball
so that the game ends.

As the entrails of the world unwind, *the crowd goes wild*
while I stay immeasurably sane.

98. Reductio ad Worrisome

People always looked up to me *but never at me*
and wanted to keep me around for their own
and thus all the right reasons
but still liked to keep their distance
as from cutie pandas capable of pulling your arm from its socket

Spunctum

like a carrot from ingratiated, pugilist earth or virginity taken twice,
though still kewt and cuddly
and with a hidden, imputed desire for connection.

I was a photograph of mad
 exterminated
excoriated Nietzsche
cross-eyed, drooling and gurgling my ABC's
in between grunts of anguish
or at least perceived anguish from a perspective
and fed baby food by my basest advocate
and most untrustworthy believer, my sister,
without the hope of death
life
or even the death *qua* life that the philosophers have been advertising
as a legitimate alternative:
a wallet-sized graduation glamour headshot kept by Nazis
for to brag with a shared sense of accomplishment
as Hitler defecated on women's faces to get hard.

They didn't know me
and because they didn't, they still had a task
and wanted to be around me, always waiting for an explosion
fruition eruption disruption dissolution and other -ions
or an act of terrorism.
It was the constant threat of terrorism that made people socially curious
 since they collectively forgot about the nukes (same difference).
They were unsure, unlike they were with the social,
what inputs would get what outputs.

They knew they had a little piece of me inside them

and that what little they had remains
like the conniving sperm that slips away or in too early
with the odds of a competitor of doping Lance Armstrong,
like the memory of an abortion
or the slag that fills the cellophane mountains like CO_2 in a 2 liter
or bile placating ulcers.

They thought interacting with me
would somehow make them understand themselves more
in their own psychosis.
They have been fed the old proverb KNOWLEDGE IS POWER
their whole lives.
(What good would the constant stream of info be otherwise?)
I do not blame them.
But they are no freer of their madness
than are Nazis of the Jew fostered and harbored in the cavern-cunt
in the back of their minds.

That is probably why they end up hating me.
Pessimism is an easy enough diagnosis.
But I think what they really hate is the deep connection we have
probably about ready to skip town
pull a knife on their boss
mainline a razor blade like blotter paper
delete all their profiles and phone numbers
(two tried and true forms of suicide)
and drive laps around town in a smoky car
guzzling 2 Buck Chuck like the Joker through Gotham
like a gas-station thief joyriding in a stolen cop car
blocking 17 lanes of traffic
as the commuters get closer than ever to one another
and the gap between the copter and the criminal
and the news story and the crime
grows greater and greater.

Spunctum

There is something sinister in my composition (calm position)
(the inner life that has resisted realization thus far)
that can seduce even the clearest of mothball minds.
My brain is dirty but still as washed as theirs.
Still, if all goes well they will be faced with a magnanimous "Or"
as they ride their paddle boat rigged to explode
into the levies of their psyches before a hurricane—
their hurried cane.

99. Unintentional Competition

It's windy today.
"Fuck windy," I think to God.

I look up and say to myself
"Fuck you God. You can try but it won't work today.
You couldn't annoy me if You wanted.
I'm not up for it today.
Too sleepy!
You made me this way!
Your wind is weak and Your work has been dull lately
even if you have always been blunt with my fate.
Creatures can barely function anymore because they are *too
functional.*
And they basically all look the same talk the same
and annoy with minutiae
like the wind that messes up my hair and my look
simultaneously
although I admit they aren't as stupid as anything produced by
humanity
that are also produced by You by extension."

In the end, reverse psychology doesn't work.
God power withdraws when provoked
leaving me with objectivity that spells death.
But it's a bonus knowing somewhere something (*not someone?*)
is fucking with me, doubling my offer for a limited time,
like the distance necessary to cross the road for squirrels
unaware of oncoming traffic.
Something that says "Come on Eve. Eternity...let's wrap it up."
Something that seduces and makes your action *voluntary* (reward-
less)
like Socrates talking the jury into killing him.

The splendor of revenge comes in reversals.

If you are naïve
when things go well, you'll take responsibility
but if you're a real sucker, you'll pay dividends when they don't.

100. the gymNazium

Mirrors on the walls
the ceiling
the floor
and even more reflective ones on the spandex behinds
of thirsty, starved women beaten by the Man
by feminisms of infinite varieties
by themselves and fat-free buttery spread.

Their mirrors are concave.
Do not look at their behinds
or you'll see an ugly, unrecognizable, but creepily welcoming face

Spunctum

looking back at you guiltily, perhaps of nothing/everything.
Only moralists can lack guilt.
As those asses bend like taco shells
and twist ties that keep old opened things fresh
you are unsure where to place responsibility or blame.
Is it oneself or few or many?
Or everyone or God or Devil?
Or laws rules necessities chance?
Norms
deviations
individuals
Reality
geniuses
viruses?
Or God or Devil Man Woman or women?

The water fountain is all the way
at the other side of the irradiated structure, opposite the weights.
If you get thirsty, the rules are that you appear in stride,
show yourself during your trip in exchange for the capacity to
drink.

The Greeks went to the gym to 'connect' compete 'talk' live and
fuck,
right?
What's our excuse?
All masculine desires have been enumerated
and each pretty much counts now as a Natty Right
(*for women, the equivalent*).

I prefer Natty Light.
It is honestly shitty.
At least you can engage *it* with a collusive, shared hostility
and miniature reciprocity like a Dare.

Critical Leisure, Book I, Volume I

101. The Renaissance man who does everything half-ass

When you are in bed nowadays
the time runs out of the clock like constipated shit
and you think you are never going to get out of there.
Your imagination runs rabid like dry-rot coyotes
or el Chupacabra
herds of ants
un-balanced ceiling fans
photographers on the courthouse steps like logos *qua* fire
and you've been half-dead for a while
half-alive for even longer
dead silent from the get go
and good at blending in with the locals
if anything.

The cosmos sprinkles all kinds of radioactive decay
over this body I've come to despise like everybody else
who either don't care on purpose
or care spitefully and bitterly
as I play back old memories like voice-recorded shopping lists
like aftershocks from the movie Tremors
or particle- and/or wave-motions.

Sometimes I feel like someone else is pulling the strings
to the extent that when I try to move the strings tangle,
challenging the puppeteer's artfulness.

It could be worse. I could be someone else, anyone else.
Fuuuuuuck *that*.

Bring it on God, my sprained cheerleader,
You imaginary son of a bitch that created me
whom I recreate to battle with

Spunctum

like the computer against which I play chess
and preserve by negating
in a post-cognitive, meta-conscious simulacrum of value.

102. le chat noir, le trou noir, la boîte noire, le trou du cul noir

I'm kind of fond of my brain.
I take care *of* it, not *from* it,
nourish it on what it wants:

facts, fakes and Nothing.
I run forensics on my life, on *Life not bright enough for the black light*.
Still, cum glows *everywhere*.
I'm a bad generalizer as is *human, not-enough-human*.

I feed it like an old bum gives communion to birds
big, fat, stupid birds—
rats with wings fat off boneless skinless Christ
the kind that make you think
"What if steak had the skin on it like chicken?"

The brain, *this* brain, eats birds.
And reproduces like spiders in the back alley and underneath houses.
And no one ever sees it again.

"Probably fell asleep behind a back tire
before they pulled out of the driveway to go to work."
It moves on.
It always does.

But it surpasses you, only passing on its indifference
and that is special.

Poets put out food hoping for its return
but they unfortunately believe in inter-species friendship
and economics.

103. a metaphysical reality

Perhaps it is a metaphysical reality
that a girl with a nice plump ass will never let you see it *head on*.

You reach down to pull up her skirt and she flings herself around,
no matter how unsuspecting she is, to face you.
"What are you doing?" She giggles like a pervert.

The only time you get to see that thing
is when you've mounted her as she lies on her stomach
and the perspective is never right.
Sometimes it looks weird, almost square, during those moments
that hint at the body horror of those of us off-screen.
It's not a good feeling but not bad either.

This all probably applies (like make-up)
to Truth in general.

104. a seductive ugliness

Only 4 miles from my exit.
Haven't moved in 30 minutes-1 hour.

Spunctum

No signs of movement ahead.
Nowhere to go.
Just here on the straight metro highway.
I watch the inmates stake at the garbage.
One lucky son of a bitch finds a discarded box full of porno DVDs.

It's like TV with lost remote, this life.
A DVR that selects your line-up:
the limits of the field of your perspective.

"Someone better be fucking dead to have caused this."

105. new-age old age

It used to be that the near-dead would sit by the phone
the door
the mailbox
waiting
but today it's the youth.
They wait *actively* by the monitor.
They clutch their portable phones like they're dicks that might fall
off.
They're always looking for something to do
while they're doing something else
for people to do things with when they're with others.
They hate being alone but carry their lack everywhere they go
and interpret it in all those around them
who don't save them by simple proximity.
They can't stand to be alone because they are quadrupeds.
They have midlife crises in their teens
twenties
or pre-teens.

Or one week to week in a meaningfulness that gives them credibility
that they think defies space and geology,
one that scientists or philosophers must not have experienced.
We have liberated the untapped Jetstream of childhood
and exported all our stress.
This because they are constrained to *this* Freedom among many others
and thus, never bound to *it alone.*

106. Mudlarking in my living room

When I came out from showering she was reading Sexus
sprawled on my couch.
I plopped down next to her,
cunt pressed up against my leg
like a steamroller to the hot, wet asphalt.
"It's pretty warm down there."
She ignored me. Pressed her face deeper into Miller
than her cunt into me
like an armoire of Narnia
or a Japanese peep show where the nose is pressed into the vulva
for micro-magnification and micro-logical surveillance.
She looked sober *in some ways more than others*
but drunk off something like us all.
Eyebrows tensed like 9 irons on her fair-skinned face
like a tee shot during a business venture
or any interaction with others.
Something we can no longer grasp without a hold on it
unprepared but *prepped* (like thawed frozen foods) for it.
I put my hand where a cunt might be, were it not for the tights,
and I said things to her like one is supposed to.

Spunctum

She didn't budge.

Every now and then she would laugh
and rub her bottom against my thigh
and curl her heels and toes,
stroking them against my calf tangled in hers.
I ignored her.

I was wondering if it was me or Miller that had her
so I sprawled out.

I one-up Miller every time but only in certain areas of the body
like the present is a permanent one-upping or annulment
of the already dead, segmented portions of the past.

107. New Year's is a man-god leisuring atop a mound
     burning all his possessions, no different than grunts
     peeling potatoes

Nietzsche said "Let everything with a shaky foundation be pushed
over"
or something like that
and you quivered as I yelled "I'D FUCK THE SHIT OUT OF
YOU"
into your ear over the bar noises
that kill everyone as primly as dog-show silences
and golf commentary whispers
in the back of that bar in Charleston on new year's.

You told me you'd only had sex with the guy you were with
and I thought he looked like a nose with a body
like on the old nasal spray commercials

and he memed fiscal cliff, so my friend stole his cigar.
I listened to your story until I interjected "I think you're fucking crazy."

I couldn't help it.
It was your fault you told me that dumb ass story.

And then there was your stare like a tractor beam or a harpoon line
or wench
or a laser disintegrating last year's man.
A terminator sent back in time but confined to the present
to consume my past in good faith.
Really, it was just a fetish.

The past. A night on new year's or not.
It is where you will create (never find) a will to chance
or free amphetamine given in solicitude and solidarity
that you accept without recognizing the giver
or the kindness of a stranger more than those who know you
precisely because they know you
or a sum average of what people might do
because it is important to read them off in the future if possible.

Sometimes, every new year's is appropriate. But maybe not.
You must also let your mind explode.
As if you *could* consent to that.
Just drink the beer,
the champagne the Jewish girl stole from V.I.P. and handed to you
before even looking at anyone else
when she didn't even know you,
drink the shots paid in full by whomever, the vodka and soda,
smoke the pot and take the amphetamine
but sober up later.

Spunctum

How many double-blind yeses can be given in a night
whose results you can pretend to have intended later?
How many fake deaths undergone?
They are important for unacknowledged Nays.
Synapses firing at higher speeds
in a more void-like and unavoidable space
but not as fast as the years pass
nor as fast as the hate crimes or the dissipation of love
like scattering roaches
that hide under the Place that Keeps my frigid nourishments
from spoiling in my soul kitchen.
I shock everyone with my partying skills
and my ability to die (lose the ability to decide) repetitively.
It is power slipping through my hands like cum I extracted myself,
and your friend invited me back—
just to be polite though.

I never invited you to the bathroom.
Blown opportunity freeing me
from burdensome VIP status!

108. The Screen-Effect of the Object

As the Feds raid the Filipino boy's room for downloaded
material…
as the eyeballs scan Consumer Reports for assault rifle reviews…
as the Prime-Time judges hit green buttons titled YES
and red buttons titled NO
as if the color-signals were insufficient for viewer comfort…
as people kill themselves just as gruesomely from too much
confidence
as do Self-Loathers,

sufferers of boredom and an intractable profit
that comes with an upping of the stakes
as the rest of us meander through the lucid, black-lit crime scene
incapable of cogency...
as the escape of the generalized exchange of sentimentality
and motivating affects becomes more and more unavoidable...
as a Rags to Riches tale is screamed into a mic \for sissified youth
whose first sexual encounters will be watched or participated in
via screens or tubes...

as there are chicken wing shortages before the Super bowl...
as psychic vampires up the stakes...
as your intestinal waste becomes the property of McDonald's
Inc...
as the actors' faces are so tight they cannot express emotion
yet express a sort of falling short, signified by tightness...
as each point in a Pissarro is counted in case you just HAD to
know...
as the 'clean-up' campaign is more 'evil' and 'offensive'
than the 'smear' campaign...
as you are only capable of yeses and no's...

as we drown sooner from car pools than quicksand
and it costs $2,000,000,000 to mine 2 grams of material on an
asteroid...
as life and death occur under the same sign
and as the money floats but the testicles never drop...
as the closed-captioning occurs in advance of speech...
as people fuck body parts unattached to bodies.

The metaphysics of the Code
and the relation between the operator/screen/object
that has disappeared from the monitor
is like this:

Spunctum

if you throw something in its place with too much force
it goes into its place and bounces back out.
Nerves produce this effect.
Our everyday experience of objects is one of a secret collusion.
We hold them responsible for things and hit them
or get frustrated with them and throw them into their place
and when they go in
like they are supposed to on a linear trajectory
and by Fate seem to jump right out from a hidden connivance
we laugh *on the inside* at ourselves.
This is what is meant when the other is penalized
by one's 'throwing freely'.
No doubt the scientists have begun to feel the same way.

The only way the things stay in that place
is if they are devoured by a Form.
But who is *stylish* enough for that>>>>>

VOLUME II
FLAVORING

*The contents of this
section are mimed
and any semblances to truths are
pure Luck. TV has a philosophy.
As they are the poems do not.
May the readers consume
them out of taste and
never nutrition and
even prefer them
in a way that
fattens (is
bad for)
them.
Ok?*

Flavoring

109. the Lovers

Enamored with her immediately
he forgets who he was yesterday
and only by slow recovery does he recall his criticisms
unless the gaps can shut themselves up
and accomplish a momentum change.

One lover accepts defeat
in response to the thoughtless mojo of the other
encroaching with stride into their enemy's territory.

How difficultly we stack ourselves and lose them overnight
like a bank-roll.
How easily are we hypocrites with anything that seems a relief.

There is a worthless part of ourselves, our pretty young cheerleader,
yet even if we kill it in us we go accepting it in others.

They hangout once and share the whole week
and suddenly he is a sad dog wearing a cone around his big head,
secure from the rupture of his stitches on which he may gnaw
though he looks pitiful and stupid.

110. The Scene

They are stuck together
like the sticky, comfy white rice in the cooked California rolls
pinched between their chopsticks
and the MSG spice immaturely fills them
but quickly wears away.

111. Instant Stardom

The people are real people.
The food is real food.
The history is for-the-first-time-ever.
The time is real time.
The communication occurs faster than death ever could
and there is even a lag between the cumshot
and the orgasm
between the brain and the mind, maybe.

There is no longer any privacy.
There is no privacy as a baby
no privacy as a toddler
as a child an adolescent a young adult an adult,
and when you are dying, they hide you.

ALL THE WASTEFUL MAGIC OF EXISTENCE
WILL BE PUT TO GOOD USE *TAKEN OUT OF YOUR HANDS.*

As data, your birth
your circumcision
your first kiss
the loss of your virginity
your wedding
your wife's pregnancy
your funeral
will be shared at the discretion of your moral standing.
And the urn containing your ashes
will become an efficient profile picture
because a picture in cyberspace is worth *exactly* 1000 words
but does not fade like an inscription on a tombstone.
They will replace tombstones with screens
that play slide shows of the life that you shared

Flavoring

and never kept for yourself
and the dead will require power to stay dead
because to even remain dead will be to *show signs of your death.*
Otherwise, you'll disappear into non-existence
and having never existed.

Everyone has learned the 11th commandment
"Be Happy and Show All the Signs of Happiness"
in conjunction with the maxims "You reap what you sew/
get what you give/
karma is a bitch"
(that sickly, transactional view of the gift)
so they pay attention to each other
to get a little bit of it in return
even though who gets it and who does not is a crapshoot
of the algorithm.
And even if they recognized it as such
they would feel Special as lottery winners.
They go around giving compliments and they get complements
and live on cloud nine or the 9th hole
and even read their stupid joy into Kierkegaard.
They poke one another with their Likes
like children repeating "Dad" 30+ consecutive times.
They drink from the fountain of youth
of their own and each other's buttholes.

The recognition of all by all IS ABSOLUTE SPEARMINT.

112. origami thought

All these little phrases from elsewhere
these ideas picked up discreetly

like prostitutes by politicians in the secret of the limousine.

The words we adults pick up like children repeating the curses—
they are forgotten but do not leave,
demoted triumphantly to the background.

Detached from their original context, they come out of us anonymously.
And we think ourselves original—
free like God uttering the Word first.

113. Meth Ode

People are always trying
to trick you into believing that things are harder than they 'really' are
to make of themselves something greater than *what* they 'really' are.

They think Method—the one that they use—is the best, untransgressable.
All their work is suddenly voided
by one with a genius they invent and attribute to who they fear.

But let's perhaps abolish the worth of genius
because even they know not what they do.
It does not necessarily follow 'all are special.'
The truth will become perhaps
it's as if all who are free persons can do anything.
It is happening
not as progress from genius
but as a lo-fi effect of the proliferation of a genetic, digital genius.

Flavoring

Anyone can make music poetry art architecture
and only a fool thinks they are special
in the so-called excellence of a discipline.
That excellence is only a function of the constraint of being oneself,
a waste of energy.
But there is no method, no beforehand, just performance—
that meth ode,
an ode on crazed productivity—
and those rigid 'folks' (where the folk is the laid back)
look down on you
as on a fool's wishing for and trying on the clothes of the emperor
because they're nothing beyond the blockade of a neat system.
They treat the value of all their knowledge
as if it gets them to infinity and a place beyond infinity.
They look down upon us from within range,
swinging like orangutans from their bubble-wrap chandeliers.

Persons even file (like taxes) the non-ethics of the Therapeutic
as if it will give some foothold or style
to flatten the ass they have filed down to a triangle for all existence
so that they can finally sit down
instead of constantly standing up for themselves.

114. Try ills and tribe elations

A dog plops her head on your lap and keeps you company at a party—
a furry end-table—
when all the human beings pass you like columns on a bridge.
A little girl waves in the neighborhood
where the adults stop with their children,

grab them by the back of their neck-like shirts as you pass
because you are a potential pedophile
murderer
or Helter Swelter with sex appeal.
A single copy of a book doesn't wait for you but rests opportunistically
in a place it doesn't belong
like vague lovers somewhere you don't believe in.
The span of a life reduces to a time-lapse photo
on a phone set stationary on the coffee table.

How we become so dead to life and yet so obliged to it.

How about something I cannot feel, see or experience
I can still speak.

How we can liberate only what is already dead to who discovered it.

Why I'd rather close the curtains and turn on the lamp
instead of read or write with the profane daylight personalizing me.

I have a friend with whom I relate on the basis
of thinking everyone is ridiculous
but the truth is we are all ridiculous.

Try as hard as you may to not be so ridiculous
and you will be doubly ridiculous in your trials, Whitey.

115. Excellence, Human

You cannot fall back on a large penis

Flavoring

or a big truck (second-order penis)
or a girl with ass & titties
or a sports car
care
indifference
the ability to fuck great
Love
the potential to do anything you want
(all third-order penises).

You cannot fall back on Desire (a pocket pussy)
or neighborhoods
or a good family
or an enormous income
a good past
a bright future
electricity
(all pocket pussies).

You cannot fall back on a talent
or a great photograph
or job security
or a trip to Asia
India
or Europe.

You cannot fall back on faith
a big clit
manicured balls
or atheism
skepticism
nihilism.

You cannot fall back on cynicism

no gag reflex
or beauty
knowing/feeling/having what you want
or ignorance is bliss.

You cannot fall back on promiscuity
"doing what you want when you want"
or laughter
a second childhood
or something
or nothing.

You cannot fall back on someone
or no one
or many
or yourself.

You cannot fall back on the Revolution
Dialectics
Work
or Technology
Nature God Science.

You cannot fall back on wine
or pills
sobriety
determination/routine/sleep.

You cannot fall back on children
or maturity
or retirement
or leisure.

You cannot fall back on friends

Flavoring

fetishes
family
Monuments
artifacts.

You cannot fall back on writing
or doing
or proof
play
reality.

You cannot fall back on criticism
or consent/dissent
thought
forgetting.

You cannot fall back on video
or medicine
or poetry
or introversion.

Life is not a Trust exercise.
But it Dares you to treat it like one
like a woman dares you to hit her.

116. the value of the intellect

Bukowski was 'real'
because he didn't *want* to write but had to do *something*.
L.A. forced his hand.
You want to so, you imitate him
share your love for him on your social media account

or tattoo his face on your torso
or "When the form appears the spirit wanes"
on the ventral side of your wrist.

James Franco with a PhD and a book of poems and/or short stories
Directing, acting and teaching acting classes.
Me, 26 years old, stealing drugs from my dog
and wine and power from my parents,
not getting an M.A. in philosophy
having seen the slavishness of candidates,
unready and unwilling to get a paper published
as an undergraduate, grad student or nobody.
These active/passive obedient fools—
each with a virgin's confidence—
want to sip wine at university cocktail parties
or follow their boyfriend across state lines
into a doctorate program.
They are the servomechanisms of corporations
Instagramfacebooksnapchattumblr
or Nothing.
They will be trusted with Knowledge and The Future
as they sit in a classroom in front of a laptop
looking up features of the lecture on Wikipedia.
And I'm glad I guess because I'm not gonna do all that.
These fools afraid of neurosis, not over it,
unwilling to let go—suckling morality—
who go to costume parties
read graphic novels intended for adults
and host potluck dinners
will get tenure and preach reform as *the* anti-capitalists.
They are fooled by their happy,
grazing in the greener pasture of the Id's baby-colored excrement.
These fools with their Great Answers
and Great Questions

Flavoring

who please teacher with a little glint in their eye—
unsuspecting of group psychology
and the belief of soldiers that insurmountable odds are nothing
compared to their 5 Hours of Energy,
that the person next to them will dissolve
while they will continue forward forever—
who all raise their hands to criticize one little lamb
after having nothing to say for a whole hour.
They all jerk themselves on their Progress
and work themselves poor at being the life of the party
when they aren't touring to conferences as undergrads
to get ahead of their pitiable peers,
taking selfies at them
and checking into them on their social media accounts in advance.
You don't taste the cum
when you're deepthroating the cock like a good little girl.

I have NO need
to travel to Philadelphia China Paris Olympia Niagara or Tokyo.
I have no need for experience.
It is absurd to imagine it possible.
Foolish
weak
and progressive.

As if growth came *naturally* from it anymore.

117. tech support

We have abolished the personal illusion of transcendence
and the allied, peculiar prospect of infinite fantasy
depressed as it were

but comforted by the secure theorem of the end of History,
focusing our efforts materially on the immediate, immanent present,
a point at which Freud's liberation of Death has made death oblivion
and nothingness
so passé and unmentionable that when it isn't on the news
in the joke
behind the irony
or on the front cover of Entertainment magazine,
it is in the cartoon
bloodless but obnoxious enough to notice.
We with abstinent irony and sapiophiles' ideas of beauty
at every 'moment' cower
and will nourish the Fantastic as if it [Death]
were more than the passing rushes of our lives and culture.
Irony, cynicism and Godlessness.
Gallows humor
gaming
and indifference.
Nihilism and free association.
Free education in audiobook form
the annihilation of sound in sampling
the verbal love of transience
The Moment
ephemerality
anonymity
all have gotten us no farther than the fire ant from the ant.
There is no magic in our fire.

The haters of tradition and those of change
the haters of free verse and those of The Form
the ape from the ape-man
the ape-man from the primitive

Flavoring

the primitive from the cultured
the cultured from the cosmopolitan
the genius from the neuronal man
or the citizen of the world from the space-man.
These are all ordinary forms of madness—
a projection of an original lie
and a Sign referring to another Sign *ad infinitum*.

Poets
and scientists and philosophers
having to market themselves
and generate a need by endlessly deferring problems
or by inspiring and exaggerating possibilities
complaining
embarrassed of themselves and society
hating their genius
peddling to the many as out-of-context rock stars in shirtless
ensembles
alone on a stage with machines playing for dust mites
that are un-vaporized, still filling out clothes with bodies,
skipping down a yellow brick road
of rocks spray-painted to look like crystals
until they sink in the middle of the bog—
their Wishes—
calling their ripples Art and Meaning.

But there only corpses are preserved
by the humic acid that tans their shriveled bodies.

118. the 69 position

As our childish adulthood goes,

we are those football players
whose education is pastime and whose passing is guaranteed,
who would celebrate and taunt
for but fitting into the mold of their assigned position.

To ourselves we give halftime reports, both expert and viewer,
dumbly and mostly unnecessarily,
for but the sake of *attention at ease*.

119. pinch me, piñata

We are shuffled out into the world
by old folks playing with us on a Cruise
after they put our foreheads to the bat
and spin us around with their game-knowledge.
What was simulation is felt as real
and the rotations of a good childhood send us stumbling with drive
towards the undercoated chewed-newspaper we whack repeatedly
whilst blinded
until candy spills out like crazy
and the elders applaud and join with renewed shamelessness.

120. fear of the dark

The television lights up the black room
like pretty women were once said to do.
It populates the room like all-nighters
and watches over you as you're sleeping.

The television is a computer

Flavoring

and the computer—it is a TV.
And the game system is both moreover
but still it refers to other TVs.

The television has applications
like the application of bright makeup
sold you by the ugly cosmetician
at Macy's in a full Galleria.

I've met people who cannot fall asleep
without television their souls to keep
their form sustained childishly in the light
as it presents their dreams with being-in-sight

a plated, inedible and tasteless garnish
of representations of signs themselves.
"Was once God and women served this function."
Now they provide *that* assumption.

121. backup drive

The jealous bug nibbles my ear like a beautiful sucker.
Daft yet aware of her own limits,
she lets all the brutes ogle her and label her a stupid bitch.

Her best friend Flattery
goes down on me in tiny increments—
soft, slight pecks that leave wet prints.
I track her through my hairy jungle cleared by spinning metal razors.

Ugly but highly literate, she punishes with self-esteem

while her tall, thin and delicious friend acknowledges her folly
by laying with her abusers, trying not to disturb their sleep

partly deadened and dignified—
with an obliviousness to fate…or highly sensitive to all.

122. the one and the many

Most Personalities are hairs fallen off the head of Humanity
clogging the shower drain,
so you must wade in the pool of your own murky soapy debris.

I will die in the ambulance
because a Singularity did not pull over, on purpose—
while the police use their sirens to speed through red lights
daily.

123. Met Ru Paul; I tan

Damned by the gods to his grin
of cops eating for free in the Waffle House
of church-goers packing consumer goods
into little pastel-colored backpacks
to send to Appalachian kids who live under a leaky tarp
for their bestest Christmas ever
while he must climb the stair-master
as he watches daytime talk shows on seventeen different TVs.

Watched by the TVs in sports bars that *look down on him* like
heaven

Flavoring

or watched by coffee-darkened eyes
that eye him like brief yellow lights.

Nihilism is no longer an abstract belief
but a concrete condition of our world that peaks up at dawn or at dusk
like sprinklers quenching the golf course.

124. Now

I have no access to wealth
but I have access to Hollywood
and I can freely advertise my whole being
ash to ash
on the medias
like a puffball mushroom
dis-integrating as its microscopic spores get carried away
by the network wind.

I want to be responsible for nothing
and I should go to jail.

Freedom is always a phone call away
and that means it is never on my side of the line—
that of a gentleman caller.

125. Textbook Rioting

For my mother
vacuuming was a spiritual activity.

Sometimes she did it first thing in the morning
before she did workbooks about the Bible
as church was the new or original profit school
and sometimes she did it in the evening.
She was "stupid" and "weak" but she knew it.
She told me so
and was self-conscious about it.
She was one of the sweetest, most spiteful women I had ever met.
I wasted the intelligence she so desired
and that could have freed her financially—
even though it put me in the hole financially—
or prevented her from staying with my father
until it was too late.

I will never get any Likes
while the former love of my life will get 150 Likes
for her 8th baby photo of the day
and she will snag several Likes when she shares an article
titled "10 Amazing Things That Will Happen
When You Learn to Enjoy Being Alone"
although if you were truly comfortable being alone
you wouldn't need to read
let alone share an article that legitimizes and encourages your aloneness.
She never enjoyed hers
until she became a housewife on the military base
trapped in her own private existence,
increasingly dependent on her husband
her child
and favorable articles.
To be fair, I could have the same relation, I suppose, to my neuroses
to philosophy
and to writing.

Flavoring

If I had been put through the ringer by some person
politician
or corporation
I could sue them and win for millions of dollars
but you're not allowed to sue Life, yourself or God
so I am still broke.
I am not damned by a central authority
but from all around
by each person in their own unique way
and the Law bars one from taking on many.

For some it is religion
for others, it is technology and the extensions of man
the social
mankind itself
or a more direct form of inebriation with drugs
or alcohol
or sex.
But no one ever said you couldn't be engaged in more than one
at the same time.
There are days on which I consume more alcohol than food
even though they say to take your medicine on a full stomach.
Homeless people use alcohol to defer hunger.
I guess I could be doing the same.

Some people become whole through their sacrifices
where caring for another, these people say,
gives them a reason to become stronger
to persist or to strive.

I am bottoming out like a jeep rental jumping dunes
plummeting like the no-longer-necessary parts of the spaceship
after it has reached space,

disintegrating into ozone.
I am a gel capsule stuck in the esophagus
dissolving but still conspicuous.
I am a centipede in a cave
feeling its way around
feeling each contour and concept
with each of and all its 1000 legs.
I am the Mexicans tacking on the roof in the rain in Pleasantville
or washing the windows of Goldman Sachs from the scaffolding
as the sun reflects off the mirrored edge
like the sun through the magnifying glass
focused onto the ants by a weak and barely curious child.
I am the 64-year-old chosen off the street
to get a makeover on the Today Show
and in tears over it.
I am the celebrity look-alike in the porno.
I am the rape-victim who's expecting
and you cannot abort the memory
of aborting consumer capitalism.

I am a consumer of philosophy music food emotions friends film
my body my appearance and my pleasure or dislikes.
I have become dependent on either focusing on the positive
or focusing on the negative
each making the other worse and more thoughtless.
I get even more uppity and full of shit
when I claim to have found a balance between the two.

You name it, it has its expert:
parenting
puppies
the nude photographs of Walt Whitman
containers
hygiene

Flavoring

cooking
sex
cellphone applications
the chemistry of silly string
first century mysticism
cave-dwelling insects
the revolution
or using the bathroom.

Solace and suffering sandwiched between bipolar technologies
making it nervously through baggage claim—
I either drink like a man or an interring coward.

126. the feeling of being lied to

Here I collapse as someone whose legs fell asleep
while they were taking a longer than average shit.

127. vacancies for vacationers

Concerned less with Death than dying, it is true.
If I said I didn't care about losing my hair
as much as losing (to) you, I'd be lying.

Life's form is a riddle unaffected by arguments.
If you heard I didn't stare into the peep show *for a fair*
before the door was shut and sealed, you misunderstood.

128. (Total) Field (Vision) Trips

Care has almost always been
an indecisive accidental lie.
Like jerky we're sliced quite thin
and hung in strips to dry.

Our culture is processed meat
composed to resemble filets.
You cannot tell prime from cheap
except by what about you it'll say.

Our streams are bottled water
Coca Cola without the syrup.
Air conditioning makes the world hotter
like a cowboy without the stirrups.

Our land is filled like a Twinkie
by key-chains from a guided tour.
The one thing that is truly kinky
is the ethic that we work for.

The rural kids go on a field trip
through the local processing plant.
To the military we are little blips.
In our private opinions, we're Gus Van Sant.

129. D, none of the above; E, all the above

Creature of Eros creature of Death
will you go Right will you go Left?
Leftly you lack force to subdue a love.

Flavoring

Rightly you only push and shove.

Creature of Night creature of Day
will you screen or will you display?
Behind the screen of night you conceal.
In solar heat you fester or heal.

Creature of Lust creature of Self
will you pursue or will you engulf?
Lustfully you overestimate another.
Selfishly you become the Father.

Creature of Sight creature of Mind
is it inconspicuous or rather a sign?
Looking you see only figures.
Thinking you always say "It figures."

Creature of Thought creature of Speech
will you know or will you teach?
In knowing lack the potency of sloth.
When teaching you are the froth.

Creature of Writing creature of Film
will you waste words in details or skim?
Wasting you are a monstrous excavator.
Skimming you telescope the escalator.

Creature of Television creature of Gaming
will you go spectacular or go simulating?
Spectacular you surf your many channels.
Simulating you're the wax produced by the candle.

130. Lindsey Low Hand

Attention is a cash cow of the day
fattened by indigestible corn feed.
Caked in shit and touching they
are sent enflamed to nourish me.

The light shines focuses and spots
like the sidereal optics of the squid.
When you stop moving it does not.
When you died what your brain did.

The attention is given and withdrawn
and the starlets who cannot keep pace
show up more the more they are gone
stagnant in their variegated haste.

We are first aggressive in our attention
like infantile monarchs before jesters.
Then with our pity we execute retention
without recalling that we were pestered.

Originally it was the persons flayed alive
that united a people as they consumed.
Bees may work together as a hive
but hornets attack without energy exhumed.

We re-lay our flowery messages fast
so that Death is buried underground
so that we can embroider the epitaph
before the dead can make a sound.

So let us have our starlets eat them too
like the smart desire the stupid to criticize.

Flavoring

But a half-eaten large pizza we'd refuse
while we'd order one anew half its size.

Every civilization thinks it's the First
to have achieved wealth, liberty, happiness.
Every society thinks it's the Last at worst
and has its vanguards wearing strappy vests.

Every youthful assumption of novelty
every disappointed yearning for Nature
has the nativist heads forever bobbling
looking up at the presentation feature.

131. Mapping the Unconscious

If only I could take an inner picture
that wasn't merely breath on a mirror
I'd make a safe travel destination
and relate to myself as to my nation.

Into this electric world we are crammed
like textbook data before the exam
like a tiny car full of Hispanic clowns
that view the Template like a wedding gown.

The Unconscious is a prior invention
of ethnology and colonial expansion,
so that when everything's been discovered
we have the pleasure of being Covered.

For when our ego bleeds into the world
with thick cartoonish and certain outlines

that are less apparent on a Pearl
it's that we hunt from the concealment of a blind.

And would we enumerate our powers
that in one stroke could really collapse
we'd find our top-shelf whiskey sours
in the gap between the synapse.

And so even there is a distance
from neuronal hotline to hotline
that can alleviate our insistence
on sterilizing the Cut with betadine.

All our potency in a safe-keeping
that refuses the way of the travel-log
or the bucket list of thrill-seeking
and slows the frame-rate to pixelated blocks.

The drive to remain unplumbable
encoded into the drives themselves.
In their depth they are preferable
to memory-cores superficially delved.

The problem of the question of Being
Finally Solved in the profile page
when diversions are considered freeing
to the new ascetic or the Electric Sage.

How it is or how it is used
those are questions by definition
that mask themselves in the term "abuse"
understood by the electrician.

Far beyond discovery as innovators bar

Flavoring

the Unconscious is a narcotic safety
for you can't tell me who you are
without attempting to bait me.

But the well-travelled have long thought
themselves privately opposed to boredom
so that they avoid the problem more than not
by escaping the reversals before them.

And so it is these young persons Go
and think that with 'an experience' they grow
like the twenty-something with child
who's suddenly wise and no longer wild:

the safety of the dictionary-thesaurus
and the intervention of the chorus
like the safety of a coming insurrection
when a fantasy too can cause erections.

"If you build it they will come"
has more depth than your interpretation
for what's produced by the humdrum
is your misapprehension of saturation.

Even in a corn field a crowd can show
and make the country into city-glow
where to apprehend is to know and stop
while apprehension is an inner block.

The free, liberated and the transcendent
have an Unconscious they think unaffected
like a corner-man with whom they reckon
as their rocks they can win last-minute.

And so their freedom is a little drone
extending out of their stomachs invisibly
a useless umbilical for these clones
a bendy-straw of amphiboly.

Their Unconscious is like the bars
with their representation of freedom
that discloses itself in the gaps large
enough to extend an arm's reach in.

Yet, the world gives us its reach around
and jerks us beneath the tablecloth
while we try to mitigate the sounds
of furious pleasure before our boss.

132. Dr. Jekyll skinning my hide

My rationality is like a housewife
whose job is to spend all my money
running errands all day
and calling that productivity.

My living space is always under construction
or is being redecorated
so the marriage between Heaven and Hell
doesn't become dull with the children no longer at home.
And the material holding the floors together is always drying,
so I can't walk on them.

Flavoring

133. Primitive Pop Culture

After I'd shot my cum in a ghastly mosaic stuck to her stomach
I felt more like myself than usual.
I felt over-it—the Over-Id.
Part of our dilemma is the lonesomeness of the Id
that hasn't its rival-become-friend or competitive lover
like the Ego has in its superior.
I had already forgotten what'd *just* happened leading up to that
like neurons repellent to internet content.
It wasn't your typical case of ADD.
But I felt like any other disaster capitalist from the suburbs
where the childhoods
sparkle like buzz-saws in unfinished houses.
She said that I felt good.
She was a moral realist
just returned from New York simulating the U.N.
a model itself become realized in the micro-model for academia.
"Putting your clothes on so soon?"
I've never been the type to linger.
I shit and vacate the bathroom/
get what I need from the store and leave
before the crowd leaves/
never go to the mall that cuddles you like cancer,
like she did me.
It wasn't that the fuck was bad—I came.
Though the means don't justify the end.
It wasn't that the conversation was any duller or more predictable
than any other.
If two people can disagree
they can pass the free nights and weekends—
the whole of adulthood.
It wasn't that
I had other girls to fuck.

This was the first orgasm in months I hadn't given myself.
"I dunno."
"You could just take them back off and stay in here with me."
I started taking my clothes back off
now already caked in cat hair.
I wasn't really the type to cum twice
but I thought I'd go ahead
and fuck her until she uttered a password of satisfaction
so she'd shut up.
When she said "I'm gonna cum all over this dick"
I knew the rickety carnival ride
could come to a comfortable halt shortly.
These days, sex is like the possession of cocaine
you are guilt-tripped into its expenditure once you possess it.
You end up snorting it begrudgingly
too proud and transgressive—perfectly moral— to flush it.
It is like a cigarette that tastes like shit when you light it
that you smoke to the filter without regret
but without consent, either.
It is like a day
at the amusement park when the rides are such a bust
that you await your vacation from it in reality back home
away from the shit-park
where you can feel the motor memory
of the tubular acceleration of the rides
in the promise of your own bed.
It is like a vacation that doesn't fulfill the postcard
that only gains its appeal in a revisiting of its photographs.
"Don't you know that the future society— society as it is now—
has no use for writers?
The new society, computerized and illiterate, will not support you.
You're out-moded by the superfluity of narrative
in an ADD culture of simulation."
"All the better. And neither will it *you*

Flavoring

ascetic, rapacious *woman*—
that concept of your mother and mother's mother."
I am afraid of fucking this one more.
She seems to like me, this one.
Fucking and liking are combustible
as contents in a bottled disinterest.
She doesn't even know me.
I've been the asshole the whole time
trying to avoid this very situation.
If she wants to see more of me,
let's face it,
it's because I put my clothes on right after I fuck her silly.
There are criteria of judgment
that prefer 'real', in-the-flesh shit like this
or else politics wouldn't function.
But sometimes it is just decent (no longer *descent*)
to not be nostalgic for it.

134. There are other ways to win, but just playing is one
 of them

There are poets
who are like stay-at-home fathers to their works
who don't have the femi-nazi in a feminine leg lock
or at least in a superficial abyss between two bodies
cordlessly identifying against each other
those who think they can move up the ladder
without also moving away from something equally enticing
who engage in their art like a Skinner box
and believe in a hard day's work of art.
They ultimately forget the spectacle is no longer needed
that simulation is enough

and just feels more decent as disaffection
offering opportunities for the entire central nervous system
to feel all the affects at once
numbing each other—
each commutable with the other—
or to feel an embodied montage of affects
so quick that it gives you the feelings
that good, pinpointable, moral things will not
for their involvement of action
and time.

God is dead because he is *out of fashion* (He has no clothes!)
and no longer has the same effect.
God's boring because He's everywhere
built into the foundations
to the extent that to speak of Him is to say too little.
If poets have not forgotten
it is only by force of their flexible, candy-coated, pastel absurdity
and their giddy, supple, mix-n-match superfluousness.
They intensify as surfaces
and their depth is no longer a criterion of their worth.

Seduction is 100% cash back with 0% down
the hyper-inflation of wages detached from labor power.
You even seek truth (impossibly) in death.
Mystery is your petite death.
You cream in your panties
as each hard truth starts to ooze.
And after each truth reaches a harangued summit in the duplicate
you get chills—an immediate effect of ecstasy.
You smoke each crystal of spiritual *fatum*.

You trick yourself into a happiness so tensely hot
like a trick of the eye

Flavoring

produced by a water glass of the contents beyond the glass
a happiness bleeding together a series of passing signs
until you are capable of nothing *but* ignoring them
in a path—any path—
arbitrarily, sartorially, forgivingly close-minded
a happiness like a test of an emergency broadcast system
pistol-whipping your amygdala
as you do the twist to a soulfulness that cajoles
like a tenor dial-up modem of dopamine
that blots your synapses like ink squirted from an octopus.
You can vacate,
but you are tethered on a circulatory flotation.
To those who are impatient about knowing who they are:
try very hard to escape yourself
and you will gain a significant lead.
Spectacle is dead.
You cannot *show* people anything anymore
certainly not yourself.
They have to feel it.
But they are as desensitized to the violence of the system
as they are to its death.
They are all apophatic capitalists
little supermen who fall just short of transference.

Have poets ever misunderstood this?
Definitely. Me too.

135. No complainandum. No explanandum.

There are those who complain
and those who complain when others complain.
There are those who decry explanations

and then explain why there is such a demand for truth
in our contingency
through genealogy
though genealogy has also perished via genealogy.

Absurd Complaint:
A man attacked by a dog by chance
ends up with the jowls of a dog.

Hyperreal Complaint:
Freshly prepared from pre-packaged ingredients.

Situationist Complaint:
Graffiti-less cities, ooo wee.

Instead,
let *us* break *our* bread in a bakery with no ovens
that sells its products fresh off the truck
fresh off the assembly line
fresh out of the factories
fresh from the lab.
Let *our* omophagy
be a devouring of mannequins:

ourselves.

136. Hope floats, but so do dead bodies

The prayers are impersonal
and the self cannot be regulated
any more than Christ is interfaced by God.
This time the presuppositions are humbly cynical simulations.

Flavoring

The lies were realizable desires
but the simulators are already realized, not subject to desire.
Sinless hoaxes that have outlasted guilt—
an analysis that would not impress
new youths electrified by the consequence-less marathon
of post-History.

The suicide kid becomes the most popular kid in school.
Having been decoded,
little fragments of him codify a reproducible whole.
Each monad of his bodiless meaning
magnifies his spirit indefinitely.
The bodiless art has so little effect
like education
like seduction
that it saturates high schools where youths laugh it away
and press *previous channel* during commercial breaks.
You can see its picture-in-picture
in the close-up panty scene of the cartwheeling cheerleaders.

You can disrobe
but you cannot de-code.
That would require a ritual cruelty
and indeed, you only have open-invite events at hand.
But you do have enough disasters recorded on film
to stage the end of the world.

137. Authentically a machine

The ugly are the most alt.
They make their awkwardness more obvious than it is.

They reduplicate their ugliness
and project it outward onto you.
They punish outwardly
and dig (are 'into') themselves inwardly
involuntarily or magnificently
with the most stringent anaerobic pleasure.
They attempt to find themselves.
Thus, the *one* thing they lack: singularity.
They analyze.
They *Get By* (Pass Up) with Effort that expresses what they are
in the end:
clumsy, inchoate infinitude.
They clean us with an abrasive appearance.
They cannot disappear behind jarring garments,
and their *style* is hermeneutical and post-critically restorative.
Their mollycoddle is easy-going
in a world of enthusiastic young professionals
and stoics who shy from what is common.
Their simulacral second existence
will suffice on underpinning (by suffusing) *the enigma*,

that unused trap-door under the welcome mat.

138. Don't personify the magic away to avoid a void

Only the past tense is conscientious now, so:
it was like jet takeoff—
one's skin concave against one's reclining bones
brain against the back of the skull like fracked cemeteries
or sand on a giant bass speaker,
a balloon gorilla tied to a car dealership flapping like vaginal folds
in the deco wind.

Flavoring

One's inertia was used against him
or else he co-opted it and went Trump-bankrupt from it
increasing his fortune in the long-run.
People are so different (repetitive)
and there are just so many of them
that you must have indexes of power-ball personalities
to draw from (trace) to just say "Hey there."
There are singularities against whom there is no flight,
with and for whom sets of personalities are nullified.

It was like a smell that dispersed so uniformly so quickly
that one could not pinpoint its origins.
It was like Fate
where *Fate is only the type of fate Fate would offer* as a sketch.
When you thought about your life rationally
nothing made sense.
When you were capable in the negative
everything did
(because 'sense' lost its specificity).
Such a position will die from exposure
like previous Fruits fallen off the tree,
holes dug by worms turned into squats for whole populations of bugs.
Movement seemed the only mode of immortality,
even pathologically.
The kind folks offered dismemberment—
a good enough reason to live,
though life needs no reason to continue.
If you explained the luck away, for instance, that you made your luck,
you killed it
because it was always the object that *changed the course* of the future
never you or I who *altered* it.

Critical Leisure, Book I, Volume II

You were asked and made to ask yourself
"How do you cum?"
You hear that?
You can even take the complications out of sex.
Sex was limited to relevant (default) facts.
Having always been a culture,
once all the rules were codified, everyone cheated
and thought they could win.
They were like old women
fermenting/dying at slot machines with 2 penny jars to go
as caked joy powders off their sinkhole faces
like powder ejects when the Doctor snaps on the latex glove.
To the old ladies' advantage, they were seducible.
They knew the rules and kept silent about them.

You inserted your flesh cartridge like a credit card
into a tight, cavernous magnetic strip.
You never saw what they typed in as the amount charged.
This was what the phallic economy looked like.
Feminists couldn't help but rubberneck
at their own constant castration performance piece.
The phallus was coerced to adopt,
having grown impotent.
It adopted women—its best patrons.
The secret closet
within which women thought they'd encounter the secret
and unleash it for good
was just filled with junk truth that crashed down onto them.
They were buried beneath the wreckage
within a structure that was itself constructed by men.
It was a Feminine victory.

You never did anything good

Flavoring

because you never did anything evil.
No one wanted to play with you
because you never kept score.
That only reminded them
that they couldn't beat you.

139. Transience. Pass it on.

The idiots are going to be idiots.
Don't accept them as your own
but don't imagine that you're any less bound to a floor
to an asshole
to up and down
to chance
or at the very least consumption
or publicity.
You are no less subject to rule
to law
and its lover, transgression—
but also, you're an object and rule over law as an object.
The status of humanity has its scene in a boil-in-bag brain
talking. i.e., not saying anything on a cell phone
about a basketball game
as if it is the *final form of play*,
but it is only a final solution—a guaranteed sociality.
It's as if they are 7'4" heroes themselves
giving meaning to a mark on a ruler
like a child attributes noises to ghosts.
There is no known difference between a pair of sneakers
and Olympic gold.
They are right about that.

Don't insult them
because it will insulate your bondage to their scene
and will have come morally, fearfully,
since you are a creature unlike the creature they are
even though your insularity is its own apophatic doxa.
Don't insult them.
They are too out of their minds to internalize it
and too in their heads to comprehend themselves as such
or to comprehend themselves in/without a common world.
Hegel understood capitalism as a self-fulfilling prophecy
and could bet without gambling
that the rabble would never not be produced
though he underestimated its scope.

Why don't they jump onto the train tracks?
They would if they dropped their cellphone down there.
Why don't they kill themselves?
They would kill You over a mistaken $15
if conditions led to it.
What is that force inside them you?
That pulsive force?
It is probably dumber than they
yet more genius than you.

Intelligence is dead
and floats to the surface
and bobs without capsizing.
A smarter, less knowledgeable way of being
experiences going under unlike a baptism.
More like a playful otter
tricking humans into calling it "cleanly,"
demeaning it yet making it what it *is*.

Flavoring

140. Mayan doomsday/book of Manu

It was the last day.
The day the/a calendar ended...
but the calendars end every year
like gizmos
except that gizmos don't die—
they disappear and reappear willy-nilly,
i.e., at the whims of whoever profits.

They can be called upon or into question at any time
like the pheromones of death
emanating from a woman with hyperhidrosis
smelling of hellish sweet rolls
as I peel back the graffitied walls of her personality
like a tear-producing onion
as my fingertips graze across her plush, ragged, tender red skin
upon command, jerkily,
like the metal claw from those cheap machines
that used to occupy a space near the exit of Walmart
except they give prizes
as all the water from her body ejaculates droplets exploding
through air
like hollow point bullets
like the interstate cutting through the city without touching it.

I live each day like it's my first.

The conspiracy theory
was equally productive of day-2-day interactions and conversation.
Mayan or swimsuit calendar?

Those guys and I blew down in that recording studio
that lacked guitar picks and commodified women.

I complained about dick shrinkage
but what was more troubling to me
was the shrinkage of *any* future
also the planned erection of any other
in the form of a pill
being a pill
being stiff and nearly caught *horizontally* in the throat.

I had no choice but to make a pact—
to snuff out Life like a Dust Devil
but never look directly at her,
throwing her away, locked in an opaque bag, indeed *in the bag*.

The world *truly* ended

but not any more than it illusorily does from one moment to the next
as I write poems
that constantly change the subject.

141. Blown

I stare at my phone
opening and closing apps without any pattern,
aptly wasteful and vapid
like the white clot perfuming the rim of my nostrils.
Fingers pattering against the touch-Spleen
like obese kids with fat Mickey Mouse hands tapping on shark tanks
or chicken feet expanding on a conveyor belt like blown glass
by the mechanical inferno,
only they are more aware

Flavoring

and want life more.

I realize I haven't blinked in the past 7 minutes,
eyeballs dryer than the balls of pornstars.

The rhetoric is that I haven't opened them for 7 years.

You can only lay low for so long.
After a while, it's time to blow it all
(in the *normal* case, for the insurance money).

It was you that blocked my reuptake.
And you wore black like a magic 8 ball.
Every time I rattled you
you got hung up on the same answer
in embryonic fluid too dense for flow.

It said NO.

142. iDeals: new update available

He grabs Fate by the back of the neck
shoves her face into the headboard
and shoves it in dry right in her ass.
She lets him.

This is only for dramatic effect—
the rape porn of codified suffering—
as that stuttering sonofabitch Time gets it all on camera,
but there's no *battery* in it.

The hyperbole and precise accentuation—

the exaggeration of her wails—
were automatically successful.
Such is the message of the Code (not desire).

143. Plug-in scent

He stops me at the kiosk he's arranged for his club
and asks "Hey man um are you like a writer?"
"No. I'm Ariel motherfucking Samuel Ackrum."
"Have you been published?"
"Yes," I lie.
"Well here's a copy of um our literary journal.
You should contribute.
The submission deadline is Octooober 7th—"
"Does it pay?"
"Well um no, but it's publication."
"He he, forget it man," I reply with decency.
And I move on with two extra things to throw away:
a memory
and a thing shoved into my bag like insertion without foreplay
as if immediacy *naturally produced* intensity.

144. The one down on the end

The big stall, that's what you're Thankful for.
The one down at the end, the big-ass one
bigger than Delphi's cave
than some live-in pool houses
where you can shit in peace—a dead man—
shit until

Flavoring

you're on your tiptoes.

And there's even a mirror
so you can keep an eye on yourself
so everything goes according to plan
and the act commences with the delicate, precise machinations
of whipped ballerinas.

Truth requires even shitting like a dancer
apparently.

There could be improvements
don't get me wrong.
The TP is too soft and only smears the shit
like the security industry does violence
like programmatic information does irruptive though.
And since you're not one of those types
to spread the TP over the rim
you lazily risk Hep. A B C D E or F minor
but against the paranoiac's hygiene, always win.
And sometimes you find yourself
wiping shit off your ass cheeks,
not knowing how it got there—

but those are exploits to tell lovers.

You are as Thankful for the big stall
as you are for the petite table at the end of the large room
where you can sit down facing everyone,
all the people you will shit on
because when you look up between stanzas
there is still the Theater of Cruelty
to make it real.

[...]

In the Big Stall, you can shit thoughts—as unopposed as the random—
with moral fiber:

"I'm not sure if it was a chimera diverting me from what-she-is
(if that statement has any meaning at all)
or if she was the licentious daughter of Proteus
changing Forms
only when I confronted her about her is-ness."

145. Stiffs get to the bottom of things

The asshole sniffers behind me
talk about social capital
and eliminating private behavior
and correlation coefficients
and have Life in a stranglehold
with ropes cutting off circulation to her tits.
It's captivating
or unfree to watch—a pleasure of disgust,
a sweaty pleasure that excretes
like the uncomfortable come up on a psychedelic
or maybe I'm wrong.
And you see their square faces like Department of Philosophy Chairmen
like a Political Index.
And you yell with disgust and a mouthful of Asian taco:
"HeyguysI'mtryingtofuckingeatoverhere!"
And you're the only one around in an eatery—
full of men who are either lying or deadened—

Flavoring

playing with the idea of eating Asian pussy,
whether or not it's OK to even *think* those thoughts
in the privacy of your own head.
A homeless guy taps on the glass for change.
You meet him at the door
and the owner of the joint approaches.
"Sorry," you say preemptively, smiling a few moves ahead.
"Don't give him any more. He botha my customa.
I. Don't. Want. Him. Herrre."

"I'm a customer and I just paid you for your overpriced Asian fusion
and that is just another name—a metonym—
for 'do whatever I want'
and you didn't even give your daughter up to cunnilingus.
Where's your sense of reciprocity?"
Across the way, there is one of those "scary-black-men"
approaching everyone that passes,
gumming his jaw, grinding his teeth
or eating his own crusty face like pork rinds—
it's uncertain—
saying "Fuck you motherfucker" times infinity to them all.

That's about the way I feel about it too
(perhaps more prettily
but not necessarily in a *totally* other sense).

146. the writer I am

Sometimes the tears will make you laugh
and sometimes you want to drink while you drive
and not just before or after,

and fate is a bitch that mocks you with the softcore
and the past is a couple
that sees you looking at them through your rearview
and so proceed to make out
and Nature is a high school tease that only lets you stick the tip in
and Reality cuckolds you and insults you as you watch.

It feels so fucking horny (redundantly good/bad) to be alive,
anachronistically.

147. Anabolic Kleenex

There is no money for the racetracks.
There is no money for the whores
no money for the crab dinners
or *for money*
or the amount of alcohol needed for alcoholism
and socialization.
The social capital has been plumbed.
The info-capital has become a rat race
a gentleman's bet of its own accord
and still there is no money for racetracks whores lobster booze
because there have been no hours put in
no innovation invested
no putting to beneficial use.
It's $3.37 for a cup of watered down coffee beans
digested and passed through a small Nicaraguan rodent's intestinal tract
for added or subtracted flavor.
The toll costs [$market value$]
depending on the amount of traffic
to drive into the city

Flavoring

on $4.32 a gallon that is 17% corn waste pre-digested
and thus indigestible by pigs, cows and chickens
at an extra 42% added cost
and 33% of that is water that evaporates before you can even fill it
up
as early as March.
The birth rate increases more quickly than the inflation rate
but the birth rate of the few still cannot be measured
forestalled
hastened
prevented
produced or streamlined
to the disappointment of the grandiose.

You can increase your happiness for up to 3 months
with just 5 charitable deeds
studies show
but how many men will saturate their bald heads in ultrasound gel
and jimmy them into shaven Asian pussy for profit—
costly and non-profit on the part of the puss—
we currently cannot calculate or forestall.

As we cultivate our garden,
the amount of poisonous plants relies on the amount of good plants
and vice versa
but that reliance is too uncertain to be uprooted.

So, let us not do any digging and just let shit crop up.
What will the cost really be?

148. The basement of the Vietnamese restaurant and of my resolve

Sitting in the library facing the rest of the suckers strategically
like an object.
Every now and then
the Asian with dimples underneath her eyelids
eyes me up with futuristic speed and cubed form,
automatically, like the vector of Progress.

The recluses are people-watchers
like the individual personalities are for others to see.

I can't help but think of the image you left me with
in the basement of "Vietnamese Noodle Soup"
right out of the pages of Marat's biography or a book of coupons
with the sewers peeking in
like children frozen at their parents fucking violently.

I think of it even in the face of the Asian girls
strutting across the carpet without lifting their feet off the ground
with the shocked, instant grace
of a whore waking up in a bathtub
with a note stuck to her stomach using questionable binder.
They inch forward like wind-up toy robots
too functional to be useful.

As I scratched the crown of your head,
you jerked it uncomfortably.

"You don't like your head being touched, do you?"
"No...
it just reminds me of when a guy pushes your head down
when you're sucking his dick."

Flavoring

The head, though, has the most and shortest nerves.
I don't know this for a fact.

The image burned in my brain is more strategic,
Innocently,
than my facing the tables of Asian study groups,
licking my lips as they put on a show for me and God
who jerks off tantrically
without cumming until the Apocalypse.

It was always like we were on camera
and I liked that.
The best I could do to engage in such a potlatch
of information exchange on the hierarchized intellectual free
market
was to go for Oscar gold,
the highest, easiest honor
besides the one hyperreality confers when it teaches
disengagement.

As if my award could be made,
realized coercively,
any more phallic than it already is.

That is debatable
if not tradable, though.

149. The bleached asshole of capitalism

She handed me the Anarchist Newsletter
like the hombres of the Vegas strip passing out hooker trading
cards

where all you can hear is the clap-clap of the cards
smacking against the wet wrists of la Familia de los Penoches
like the muffin-tops of the men of the boardroom
or a room of their own
one's own,
anyone's own
slapping against the bleached rectum of the girls
down on sedatives/cocks/their luck.

I took a gamble and read the newsletter.

There were marches.
There were errors, presupposing a paradigm of truth.
There was a new many,
still a rabble like a newspaper
or *langue*
or a kicked can
or TV static
or Atlanta sounds
on WABE ATL, YOUR HOME
FOR THE CLASSICS
AND NPR ('Non-pretentious Rabble')
a rubbernecking crowd of oracle-ites
gaggling around a depth that disappears into itself,
impossible to verify.

150. the good life mmmmmm mmmmm good

Making life ethereal makes the good life a gas.
They know that it works.
They work.
They like things that work.

Flavoring

When things work, work succeeds, they succeed.
It beautifies them who are transparent—
unreflective,
transferring all the heat without getting hot.

The good ethereal life comes from cows caked in their own shit
with holes in their gut
so the farmer can reach in there, if need be, to tighten some bolts—
cows that fart all day long in giant compounds
utters dripping with puss
tumors in their balls
and cataracts in both eyes
literally good for nothing but dinner, manure and heat.
The good need irritable eruptions
and traversals
and the company of sniffers.
They love this ethereal scorcher,
trapped and smug in their own gassy bliss.

The cosmos?
WHAT THE FUCK?
ARE YOU KIDDING ME?!

Pppppppppppppplllllllllllllllllllllllllllll!!!

151. Suet stains in the Highlands

I turned away
from the 47 x 35" television screen hovering in the corner of the room
like the horizon beyond a disappearing-edge swimming pool
land-sliding into the Atlantic—

the ocean itself only an annex of the deco wading pool—
screened behind the captive shutter-shade mansion.
They were doing a WHERE ARE THEY NOW piece
on an orphan polar bear on the nightly news.
The microwave beeped
but I hesitated to gather the food from it
because of a laziness without intentionality
that shielded me from pessimism
coupled with a bargain anxiety of missing something.
My phone vibrated
but only from having completed its charge
in its pubescence.
I was as alone as ever.
I excelled in it and against all successes this one was in the bag.
I was like a shop-girl smothered by Saks 5th bags
as in a circle-jerk finish.
The first time I saw her,
it was like an emergency broadcast
that interrupted programming on every channel.
I quickly became annoyed,
mainlining my resentment like vectors of small talk,
feeling that I had missed some invaluable bit that has now
passed—
some irredeemable span of programing that I can never get back.
For people dependent on the everyday mode of existence
there are no moments of transcendence, *only interruptions*.
For some youths, blacking out is part of their plan.
I could have never anticipated
or, nevertheless, *precipitated*
the irony she would release in me like a wet fart,
one that would seep into my movements
for another chafing day.
She hit me like butt-plugged ecstasy
like the nervous pleasure felt by the guilty.

Flavoring

She was a Czech bikini model.
Age: 23. Eyes: blue/green. DDD breast size.
I met her on matebate.com.
Her profile pic gave the dizziness of flickering guide rails
keeping a healthy distance between a speeding Lamborghini
and its tempting disintegrative arc by way of the ravine.
at which the more you look, the more you think about hitting it
as you speed along—a would-be contact in a parallel fatal
universe.

History *is* a gif (right now…*historically*) that you can't respond to.
It repeats after it plays through its imagistic motions
without a point being received.
It is a DVD menu on repeat
that you wake up to in the middle of the night
too lazy to shut it off,
enduring it outright—neither angrily nor happily
but with a healthy, sleepy indifference.

152. TXT#hostage

I message her:

"This time I'm going to do it.
this time I'm going to do it FOR REAL"

She responds:
"you're too chickenshit
that's silly
you're not going to kill yourself over me"

I wish she said that.

She didn't respond at all.

She's right though.
I'd only do it if she actually cared
But it's worthless
I'm worthless
her worth is ambiguous but more probable than mine.

I message her:

"I don't think anyone will ever love me like you did
[you spoiled me you fuckin' bitch is what you did]."

I was right.
No one would ever be good enough again (for that version of me).
I didn't even think she was good enough.

Thus far, as my guts GUSH out on the floor everywhere I go
so I'm always tripping over them
and carrying like tangled corded phones,
unraveling like M.J. in his Disneyland mansion

her pussy gushes fragrant mists
that block someone's smell receptors
somewhere
somehow.

Commodity exchange doesn't understand symbolic acts of terrorism…

Flavoring

153. Life, questionable *thot* that she is

Indifference is more seductive than being seduced.
If life were a slut, the challenge—*ours*—
would be to resist her,
thereby resisting *ourselves*:
that part of us that is merely her ruse.

But since she too is quite stupid and indifferent,
we simply *must* have her—
that when she becomes too concerned with us
it becomes our taste to turn away from her,
which is only *her way* of being rid of us.

Do you not think God is sick of your prayers?
For I pray only that he stay the fuck out of my business
and get '*a life*' (which would kill Him), bypassing *all life*.
If the gods were irrational they'd have *good reason* to be.

Of course, I've heard there is an impossibility
of seeing without being seen.
I have not verified this with photographers.

Isn't it God's duty to be indifferent?
Forgetting is His job.
Luckily, He has a short attention span.

Do not become a para-suicide
because life, *thot* that she is, is unconcerned.

But if you think you are too good for her
you still acknowledge yourself.
But maybe if you just stop thinking about it altogether
mustn't '*your*' indifference also be seductive?

154. Jesus moonwalking on water *for viewers like you*

The instant of climax like molting cicadas crawling out
of ashy elbow earth
that tears like dried tobacco leaves during the blunt roll.
The blood of Christ:
a gag gift.
Christ on the Cross
the perverse the absurd the useless.
Midgets wearing pumpkin costumes, sodomized by donkeys.
Laughter at the dumb
the unfortunate
the injured.
Toilet humor. Flush, flush, bang, bang.
Blood Sacrifice of conquistador gods by their unfortunate
worshippers.
Devouring of and by The Other.
Vomiting speaking bleeding cumming.
Communion and daily prayers
in the instant of any-instant-whatsoever
a million tiny deaths Hallelujahs and cruel acts
laughter at tragi-comic death, canned.
Warhol prints of canned laughter:
pure evil
an intelligence of evil
slapping Jesus on the bottom like a fellow player.
Sex and death and religion and happiness and tragedy and cruelty

...talents.

Thought is merely an afterthought of speech.

Flavoring

155. Fast-Casual Tie Events

I've never liked the histrionically unfeeling
Mickey Mouse fast-casual joints
that you must enter as into a utopia
just so that your shit doesn't stay inside for another few days
but my dad knew a guy
and there was going to be free food
free wine
and free pussy
given that the fast-casual swank swanks
are typically owned/operated by upper middle-class franchisers
with prize wives.

And I don't know what it is about the Mickey Mouse club
and the middle class
but they produce great puss
with health insurance policies that include puss insurance.

I ordered the same thing my dad got
(because too much freedom is not *worth* it
and because they have 8 pasta styles
10 meats
22 toppings
6 sauces
and because menu items have names like "twist"
"twist and shout"
"mac-daddy"
to humiliate me censored speed *that I produce as I repeat it*).
I sat down at a booth with a relaxing view of two roast-beef danglers.
Don't let the tight faces fool you about the shape of the V.

They looked frozen in time.

The junk probably seeps through the skin
and has the same effect on the brain
the heart
the gonads
but probably not the gonads.

They were lucky that the Botox wasn't fresh
or the pasta
or the conversation. What conversation?

One of them reminded me of a girl that I once loved
who was a stand-in for a character on MTV's The Hills.
She was one of those fancy yet dumb girls,
wealthy and luxurious but with no culture
no taste
no experience
experiencing the world like a dog watching TV.
Not even any dreams, passions or desires.
She doesn't even fuck well.
You might as well fuck a sandbag
and she's tougher than a sandbag or a tank
and she'll squash your eyeballs
and your spleen and your nervous system
with as much of you in mind
as your image in the mirror has about you
as you stare into her soul, darker and less man-made
than a roofed box
where the cats shit in secrecy.

I once loved that girl, perhaps *the mode*.

She will one day marry a man
who wears purple silk shirts without the top 2 buttons fastened
and who rolls the sleeves up only once

Flavoring

and perfects them with cuff links he ordered from a catalogue
on a plane to Sao Paolo.
She will not be unhappy.
She will have a good looking-kid with the best hair money can buy
and the best clothes money can buy
and the best and whitest skin color money can buy
and a purple silk shirt to match daddy
when they have the glamour shots made.
She will consider them one of the greatest gifts she's ever received
when she's long forgotten and only para-forgiven
the beautiful dick that popped her cherry
after getting a hand job from one of her best friends
who's somehow related to the Kardashians
on the walk back up the long, grandiose, Hollywood-knockoff
driveway
to a gate where she was picking me up.
That was me—
sketch creepy forgettable unforgivable.

I hope that she has grown up
away from the Cancun hotel-parties
and the lake
and the roaches that always come back
and crawl back under the baseboards of Facebook messenger…

and sunglass shops
and Nordstrom Sacs Fifth D & G
and handsome guys with nice trucks
two dicks
and no dreams,
who majored in physical therapy or marketing
and pretty girls that nibble away at her time and life
like someone eating dry ramen noodles on the 4th floor, alone,
overlooking a retention pond.

235

I once loved that girl, perhaps the mean.

The other lady came over to our booth.
"Would you like some wine," talking to my father.
"I'd love some," I responded.
She looked at me and didn't say anything for a little too long.
"How old are you?"
"Me eh? I'm 29 my dear…"
I handed her my wallet and received a bourbon glass filled halfway with wine.

She came again with the same awkward pause
and this time I gazed into her eyes
and saw right through them into her skull
where there was an obnoxious pinball machine
with bumpers that didn't work
so her brain just kept recycling through the machine.
She asked me more often than the others, though,
if I was good on wine.
But I never was.

Like life-in-despair, I let it ride.

The strip-mall had a reflux
and more people, more suburban simulators, more secret shoppers came in.
More spiked hair
more baked potato skin
more goatees
like frames pinning a mouthpiece to a blank-wall face
more steroids and male enhancement pills and One-a-day Men's ™
more jeans and oxford shirts

Flavoring

more Christ and more Women and more right answers and more
success
and more superiority.
There was a man that walked in very obnoxiously and over-
dramatically
with a tan, spiked hair
a goatee
big muscles
but not very much height
a Christ-on-Cross necklace
wearing jeans and a white silk oxford shirt
and a woman on his shoulder
right answers success and superiority like Death didn't exist.
He went up to my wine lady.
They hugged
and I leaned over to my dad.
"That guy goes ass to mouth spasmodically."
We both laughed

at him
at us
at life and death and world.

It was the highlight of the evening. Negativity always is.

156. The sex of Rhianna, the sex of Martha Stewart

"Feel so alive...
                      ...alive...
alive...

alive...   alive

...alive..."
Rhianna is a sex symbol.
Why? I don't know.
Could be the fashion
the attitude
or whatever
I've never seen an expression on her face that isn't abstract
minimal
or *intentionally* blank.
Her appearance streamlines her appearance tautologically
descriptive but without explanation.
I've never even heard her speech/discourse.

And because she sings

"I feel   so alive"
in the trompe l'oeil non- or micro-tone of Martha Stewart,
simulating non-joy and non-life and non-illusion
and a Hobby-Lobby aimlessness or functionality
of micro-managed art.

I question whether she does or does not feel the ecstasy
of a life that is too quick to stick.

Like that, I question whether it is music
or text message
or extinction
or the farting noise made by a juicy-fruit vagina in jack-hammer
porn
(in the sense that the jeep wrangler
or wooden roller coaster
or free fall is sexual)
or the sound of an eyeball moving
like the supermarket self-checkout swipe.

Flavoring

THAT IS LIFE.
I'm not sure.

157. your days of plenty are numbered

Death will park his horse in the hall
and it will shit all over your wetvac'd carpet
and he will come into your bedroom, into your bed
and pull the covers over your head, hemming you in from all sides
and let out a flaccid wet fart
after eating gas station taquitos for seven straight weeks.
And as you microwave in the thawing gases
your skin turning yellow from the sulfur like some Egyptian child-king
he and his horse will lay with your woman
and she will scream bloody murder
about how much she is cumming
and her orgasms will be plotted, like the land He seeps into,
on a Microsoft Excel spreadsheet
but you, like the masses, are uncertain about physics
and *physis*.

158. Title does not suffice it titillates

He pulls out his identification card.
Every time, they look at the card
and look at him and say "This you, right?"
as if he's not real,
trying to pull one over on them and make them lose their job

and their License to Serve.
And he once was
still is
will become that kid, probably.

It's not their fault.
No one trusts anyone anymore.
There is a puritanical paranoia so deep
that The Credentials no longer even suffice as suffibulum.

I cannot even be a mere object that simply is what it is
apart from the decoder.
After presenting my identification card
they look at the person on the card with logic and dogmatism
and they look at me with suspicion
that has become detached from skepticism.
"So you've gotten a haircut since then have you?"

"Yes. I have changed from the person in that picture too.
I have always changed.
I've shed 2 pounds of skin and microorganisms since I entered
this joint..."
(the segmentation of a greater body that allows it to run
and to carry itself through shifts in environment).

159. 'the destiny of a theory'

As with everything that flows
what matters most is that you pinch it off at the right time.

And as with everything that is pinched off
there is a residue that remains inside

Flavoring

and behind.

You must pinch it off at the right time
if you don't want a wet mess.
'Poets' (or just me) and skeptics and scientists know this
and ONLY the wipers of asses after them
(everyone).

This is to say that liquidity is dangerous to all Forms,
Properties are dangerous to Substances
in this economy.

So avoid the corny filler of technique
you little shit.
The Kernel of Truth is only visible in shit
whether it holds itself together (becomes a system) or not.

160. "Evian is naïve spelled backwards," said Janeane
 Garofalo

I don't remember what is said at lunch because "I smoke pot 24/7"
but her eyes look the same
still flat-chested
everything is the same.
Hair still dyed
pussy still shaved with skin irritation
no hairs on her knuckles because she bites them off.
Still, this time her feet look worse than they usually do.
"I have bleach foot."
Her feet look like a leper's
or a zombie's
or the man's on Ponce playing a shoe string

strung through an empty box of tissues.
Her flesh has been eaten away like a raisin
mangled like el chupacabra.
"Let me kiss them."
"No…….no."

We get beer.
We come back to "813 Cuntcliff" and watch bootlegged movies.
Kiss.
"Can't we just have sex," she asks in a struggle.
"Take your panties off."
"I think I'm done with my period he he…"
"You know what I say: 'if the river runs red, take the dirt red.'"
"I'm not doing *that*."
We proceed until I look down where it looks like a murder scene:
thick brown blood staining my couch.

There it is. The scene. It is still there. I think.
"There is still a history," I try to *repeat* to myself
but it has little (that is, still *some*) force
because I doubt there *is* a history
because we've dis-covered everything in our re-covery
to the point of saturation, another form of concealment.
I could be wrong. I usually am and have been thus far.
"Past behavior is the best predictor of future behavior,"
says Dr. Phil.

I get her something with which to wipe herself off
but there is a stain on the couch.
It will be pleasurable to anger my roommate.
"How do you want it?" I ask
but only in the form of pre-emptive blackmail
in the form of an intelligence that keeps its enemies closer—
all the better to experience their weaknesses."

Flavoring

What happens next is pure simulation and the end of the scene:

she utters things like "harder I love the way *your* dick feels inside of me
I want you to cum in my mouth"
and occasionally "I love you."
Lies? No. *Not exactly.*
She believes them.
It's the integrity that makes me suspicious
and it is difficult to cum with all her technological perfection
so we take a break
after I simulate (as counter gift to her simulation) having to piss
and having nearly pissed inside her vagina.
So I drink beer and she drinks wine and champagne.

She tells me that she watches lesbian porn
and that she hooked up with her friend
and that they even tried to scissor (a sex meme).
"Oh yea?"
The simulation of interest that is reciprocity takes up most of my energy
needed as a counter-gift to my own indifference.
Lesbians are great.
Whores are great.
But she is no pure simulation
since she believes in the company that she represents to herself
and sells to those she wants to represent, too.
And instead of treating her like a whore—you know a professional—
I treat her like SOMETHING
because she seems to be missing.
She's no screen.
She wants to be a retreat from SOMETHING

but I only know nothing
and you cannot run from nothing.
Whores who would never use the words
truth
authenticity
nature
or any of that dreamy shit.
They're here to fuck and that's all.
A failed screen become a female bodybuilder,
hard-surfaced, trying too hard to impress
and only know how to via *pressing matters*.
I like the fat flesh, the ugly fat flesh of warmth,
squeezable like cherry tomatoes by inbred, ailing kings.
The luxurious illusoriness of the feel-good flesh
that appears monstrous to the eye.
I have not mentioned the fluidity of her personality
that she will freeze after he asks her to marry him.

Am I to jerk myself with a button-mashing victory
with her flat screen pussy?

That is all she wants.
But I can get that cheaper and more effective on the Internet.

161. Pisces is a riot

They want to fuck your brain—neurosexual—

but when they realize that it is plastic/
accidental/
improvisational
your love is swimming with the fishes,

Flavoring

one of which is you.

162. the playboy character of the world

It is always the front that says "This ends here,"
the liar who says "I swear on x."

The truth has too much to say

that by its proliferation and reduplication
it becomes unbearably obvious in its simulation.

It is the lie,
the discursivity of the lie,
that imagines some truth
but the *hidden* is merely the excessiveness of truth—
a bastion of truth and the only place
where there still is one.
But as surely as the love triangle will end
in the loss of both the seduced parties
and the death of the seducer
so shall the truth and its double disappear by this tripartite
narcosis.

The liar gives herself
unto the illusion of some truth, some Order of Ought, via
subjectivity,
but it is subjectivity that hides the fact that there is none.
Objectivity is true—but useless.

When people talk about themselves,
it is precisely then that we find them unbearable.

Not because of their ego
but simply because there is a discourse
where there are no words.

The critical attitude presupposes some end
wherefore the skeptical attitude does nothing except laugh
deridingly
at answers
and advice.

It is when in the wrong place there is something,
where there would have been nothing otherwise,
that there is disorder—
but disorder presupposes some order.

That is what I've heard.
So let me remain silent on the matter.

163. No Thanks – *a poem for a frenemy*

Thank you and no thank you
for the silent dinner
where, because there is no television in the room,
there are no consensual, mutual
or worthwhile topics of conversation
and no scale of conversion—
no version for lack of verse.
No meta-language,
nothing
because the only things that can be shared are simulacra.

Thank you or no thank you for the silent dinner

Flavoring

where the only thing we have to tune into
is the constant farting of an old woman 27 yrs. past her expiration date
at the other end of the table
as she shits her panties with the garrulous self-affirmation of a child
calling for her mother's rescue
in spatters of shit-bubbles
and spit-bubbles.

Thank you, but no thanks to the furtive triumph of shitting your britches
when the only freedoms you have left are the blowout of your intestines
and the hope that someone comes to change the pants.

Thanks, but no thanks to the extra few years
when the catheter is jammed up your pisser
that functions like a spaghetti noodle
that doesn't seem to want to conform to the rotation of the fork.

Thank you but no thank you
for "No Thanks"
or sober, orderly, solidaritous anti-Thanksgiving—
anarchist-vegan potluck.

164. Castigate me cavities/Identitus

People wanted a succession of other people
like a succession of images.
Children grew up needing activity
stimulus

movement
Progress
and other synonymous myths all the time.
Growth experiences are gross.
They are the consumption of the placenta
life incestuously consuming life.
The only thing 'in' life that is grossed is the GDP,
but that is *above* life, so basically nothing.
A succession of life moments
like a succession of screens in different restaurants, bars or homes
all of which are escapes from each other.
This was an extreme form of Hell Is Other People
and the most personable persons were the Corporations.
Women came with their own backstories
like American girl dolls,
their own brochures they'd hand to you,
gripping them curled like your cock
like a manual gearshift and as they really shifted gears
and shape-shifted like reptilian aliens but with more tongue.
You changed, things changed.
They imploded and were reassembled
in ways identical but not.

Relationship became just a word: Identitus.
    Love became just a word: Identitus.
        Words became mere signs: Identitus.
Relationships were set up like shop windows.
Indented, they flashed across the screen of life like stock prices.
But those *just made more sense*.
Relationships were speculative and that is unacceptable for Most.
Because they could not be calculated and had no truth,
they were abandoned.
(For what? Nothing?
But they *are* nothing! in a good way...)

Flavoring

      They were susceptible to a disease: Identitus.
Symptoms of "just being sick"
they manifested themselves only upon diagnosis—
symptomatic *of* diagnosis.
They even caused diagonal madness
and most of us were control freaks
with heads like aircraft control towers
even though the flight patterns were said to tend towards
equilibrium
like compost.

Any one seemed as good as another.
Choice gnawed at one's gut, one's freedom—
"one's gut instinct" experts say—
like Hell hounds who barked like DMX
after blowing a small fortune on crack and dogfights.
One beat choice to the punch.
Because frivolity was out the window
one could push shopping carts
into the streets and into one's conversations and love making
like the homeless and the content-less
like the destitute tactfully remaining barely intact.
Even they interacted with you more
than 'your own' desire.

There were no more dustbins of history.
People places events things ideas accumulated
together on the same level
all as signs
in an extreme form of the Western identity: Identitus.

One collected partners like future-vintage collectibles
or aware of their inevitable replacement by an upgraded model,

held out for the best one and found no one.
Objects were more functional
but people *attracted* nonetheless
(as intractable).

They had differences.
They were merely their differences—a homogenous system.
This was about the same fate
as if they were somehow essentialized.

They were fascinating with distinction
and that's about it.
One consumed their consumption of them
like producers consume work itself
and philanthropists consume their capacity to give.
It was their popularity that was popular
like it was the Ideal
that lovers often loved 'in' (or *above*) one another.

165. the Superman isn't real, he's Protean

Seinfeld was our brief Ubermensch
whose 'self-mastery' was a psychopathology of daily life
that implied an uncanny dialectic of inner subversion
unraveling the everyday metaphysically
like the Heraclitan '*Thought is a condom*'
and the dogs of war bark *at society*
like a subway rodeo clown spitting up blood
on the secondhand Dr. Martens he shines.

Things just happen

Flavoring

(irreferential of cause or effect).

In *chains of events*, fate segments itself
and gives you a metaphorical, euphoric striptease.

Penetration is a HUGE unconscious assumption…
reciprocal coitus (with the world) seems a flat lie, right now.

166. Sub-division Sandwiches

One day I'll have it,
my own little Hyperborean plot on a square acre.

The arcana of the modern world
will slither up through my pinched butthole
and I'll see the wisps of classical Americana spiraling up.
"The Earth is Hollow!" I'll cry.

…and in my own personal Aghartha
I will make entertainment systems from their sopping hair
I puke up to receive 'The Masters' on standby from the giant
screen.
I'll get lost in the profusion of details
that constantly escapes experience and speech.

I'll tattoo R on my forehead
and circle it with magic marker every morning
as part of my daily ritual that circularly encloses Reality.
I'll fashion gauche paintings of an old half-eaten bowl of cereal
left out next to an 'I Heart New York' coffee mug,
a folded paper-towelette below it,
and upside-down tortoise-rimmed glasses

all sitting atop a faux-alligator leather—
or real I don't know—
foot rest.

Neither privacy nor peace-of-mind:
complete with those little-shit kids next-door
who in climbing the fence to retrieve that fucking ball
they've been pounding into the side-brick of my house
for twelve years now
interrupt my concentration on increasingly-difficult masturbation.
They'll grow up to be little league coaches
who tip lackadaisically during 'endless' mimosas.

In my warped lounge-chair, I am at the beach:
I gaze at sweltering piles of dog shit
and plants I don't know the names of
except via the little name tags that come w/ purchase at Home Depot
that my wife stakes into the soil next to them.
I plug the headphones' cable into my ear.
"I don't think that's how it goes, sweetie"
says my helpful hospice nurse wife.
I've almost grown fond of the sound of The Highway
directly beyond that furry wood fence
beyond that bleeding tapestry of fungal-infected evergreen trees
I planted around each side of the acre.
I waited thirty years for them to grow tall
so that I'd never see again another goddamned good neighbor.
Even now I hear passing freighters as the whooshing of the tides.
Others might hear basketball nets.

One of these days I'm going to spread fertilizer
to liven up that 3 by 5 patch of yellow stain.
I'll have to buy a special machine that spreads it

Flavoring

and even that will require fuel maintenance, etc.

Graceland
Monticello
the home of Mark Twain
the cheap extended-stay hotel room of Jim Morrison…
when I'm dead some poor saplings—
my tail end as long as that of Ursa Minor—
will drop their poppy-colored luggage trunks
right atop my dead corpse
and rip up that vinyl 'wood-flooring' I so adored
to put down *real* wood…
deracinate those pseudo-anarchical trees I scattered at 'random'
throughout that perfectly flat square
to construct an inert swimming-hole.

In the Hypermarket, no space goes *unused.*
That is immorally wasteful.

On that day, the neighbors will welcome them
to mow their lawn on the same day they all do.

And never speak to them again.

167. twat-latch feasts and the NEW GIFT EXCHANGE

We moved on from a competition
of playful desire—seduction—
to one of the lowest point of desire:
aversion, prophylaxis.
It is indifferent and hatefully passive.

Now strategies of desire and of non-desire:
"Why look at me? I don't exist, you cannot meet me!
If you notice me, I'll notice but I won't notice you.
I certainly will not recognize you recognizing me, privately."
Ellipsis of the body.
Disinformation and disinterest resulting from *too much* desire,
too much talk about desire…
neediness and fascination with that *new need* yet aversion.
Because of the Children of Proteus society will dissolve into bits—
inert, kneady clay—
and I hope if you are reading this
you're not one of those anarcho-Romantic figurines.

When there is investment there is interest.
Desire as rhetoric and rhetorical questioning passing into
asexuality
as a blowback of integral role-play and transsexuality.

Remember the playback: good eyes up evil
beauty eyes up ugliness.
Yet instead of eyeing up, it's "Avert your eyes! Too much face!"
That is the same as "Look at me *with eyes only* at all costs!"
due to a saturation point of desire.

This changing room of insignificance/
fitting room of *integral trespassing*:
"Do not ascribe ANY meaning to me! I *stand* for nothing!
You *hear* me? I will not stand for your seduction! I'll *get laid*
instead!"
(*Free* speech?)
It is the opposite of infantilism.
It is a high fidelity of wannabe-indifferent compassion—
reciprocal spectrality.

Flavoring

Today, the compliment *offends*.
"Don't judge me favorably.
See, you can't I mock up myself already!"
Well, I won't appease your ingratitude.
I will actively kill you in my mind
without thinking twice about the 'nothingness' you hope to signify.

168. Occupy Nature—ONE LAST EFFORT LIBERALS IF YOU WOULD BECOME COSMOPOLITANS!

Humanity occupies 1% of the world's total population.
TF, I declare that we return to animal living.
From the fact that 99% of animals are ghost writers and pyramid bases,
it follows that *we moralists* must destroy humanity.
In fact, if we found out
that fish *accounted* for 99% of the world's population
(but they are carpenters?)
it would be wrong to have legs
and quadriplegia would be a necessary LAW.

Citizens of THE WORLD: *consider yourselves ungrateful*
(that is, unable to return gift).

169. Real world: Mongol edition

For you my dear, I will be the holder of shout-out signs (at events).
For you my little lovely,
I will be the follower of astrology
and collector of historic newspaper cut-outs.

For you my sautéed sex-fiend,
I will be the prize-bag of severed organs
found inside ready-to-boil chickens.
For you my gape of Venus,
I will be Merriam Webster.
For you nape of my death,
I will be the lab monkey with filial attraction to the stuffed toy-monkey.
For you subterfuge of my ASS Worship,
I will be the apophenic pilgrim professing faith in crud.
For you my stalked oblivion, I will speak in future perfect
and stick my head in between the rails
and put parental controls on my internet browser
and perform vivisection on puppies.

…the depersonalized—the innocent—won you over
and you moved out
and I would have had it no other way
because it's better *for me* to quit cold turkey than to wean.
But the offers stand eternally
like God the defector
in the moment, alienated from the whole.

170. pacifier laced with LSD

I was told once: that I was handsome (by the women in my family)
that I was beautiful (in a rejection notice)
that I was gifted (by dingbats).

All my treasures have hitherto been merely complimentary
accommodated for an event I didn't even pay for or go to.

Flavoring

…And when all the bets are off
the cocktail waitresses no longer come by.

When unnoticed I once felt considerable pride
like the prettiest girl not asked to the prom
but I think now that I'd fooled myself
with a runny caramelized (*concentratively* sweet) soul
murkier than Mr. Gloppy from Candy Land
but not as *generous*
generalizable
generic
or generative
as slime molds.

I am the most jealous cunt alive.

I still have the desire
of the Kid I project on the memory of my commercial childhood.
Still I want:
a Ferrari bungalow jetliner
actress/model/singer
love
French mistresses on each side
dropping bowling balls on the temperpedic mattress
and the wine not spilling…

a good God that favors me,
gives a damn
and favors me as the incarnation of justice
a Good woman who will be the man of the family
Baudelaire's Lesbians
Julia Roberts from Pretty Woman
leisure time
paid vacations during periods of unemployment

pleasure paid in full
...in other words

all possible forms of *mentholatum*.

171. the politics of the remainder will make you laugh

There are too many memes to recognize in a courtyard
some are lost to space
to cyclic time and to linearity
and I become confused
and hyperreality turns you off to the real *as much as* to the fake.
It is the third term whose affinities dissolve the binary
maybe.

One day the fashions of the Mormons
or maybe even the Muslims
will be 'In'
and it will be fashionable to dress Amish/Babylonian/Marxist/
NASA-esque/Victorian/primitive/etc.
and nothing will *oppose*
but the binary code will fool you into believing
that you can revitalize dead oppositions
when precisely opposition itself is dead
apparently even when we *oppose* its death.

Or maybe we're there now
while with this poem I'm behind—
dead, slingshoting myself towards it in the draft of 'my peers'
in a campus courtyard,
who I peer at bivouacking like Coptic friezes of black-tar
pavement.

Flavoring

I don't know.
How can you tell?

We are all hoarders of desperate meaning
because one day we will die hard or *hardly die.*
Death ≠ dead bodies according to this anti-tragedy.
So, we leave our space trashy-as-hell—
destitute, a substitute for destiny—
so that all the broken-down shit we've accumulated *over* the years
can be seen from the bypass.
nibbled on by Georgia red clay
like the little man from Twin Peaks eating creamed corn
while talking backwards.

In all this, in everyday life, there is allusion, resemblance, to the code—
to the mark—
and *there,* allusion no longer resembles itself
and illusion is dead to consciousness.

There is an air of rites of passage
in a campus courtyard as congested as the streets of Asia
(according to video)
that are probably faster/sleeker than New York

and Wagnerian melancholy is no longer an option or decision

and young Werther no longer must do it
because there is no longer a dialectic of life and death
and neither Romeo nor Juliet can die for anything
making the union unconsummated.

and I recall 'Bataille's inclusion' of an image of Chinese torture
as a man's breasts are removed along with his genitals

Critical Leisure, Book I, Volume II

in 100 pieces or 100 flowers
like a J. G. Ballard novel
in a courtyard just like this one
where we collide without buffer zones and yet never touch
for the same lack of personal space.

We each subduct others as we all converge.

BOOK II

VOLUME III
SPEED READING

*The following poems
are to remain unread.
They are to be glanced
over and passed by, but
the CliffsNotes are un-
released because they
are so new. So, may
they disappear in the
warp speed of our
lives Forever? Not
without some luck.
Gracelessly, accidentally, they
reach the Oceanic like newly
hatched creatures, in a
mob-panicked dream,
most of them eaten
by vultures.*

Speed Reading

172. Faux-Pretentious Intelligentsia vs. Poetry That *Really 'Kills It'*

She emailed me all she had written in March:
longer short stories I didn't read
but skimmed like I would homework assignments
or court papers
terms of agreement
blogs.
They had the fact that they didn't need to be *read or read well by me* going for them.
Still, one could not connect/disconnect with them
as with the web or the aphorism—
the firewire of the written.
One-part poet of looser verse, one-part reality TV celebrity,
she was an unknown writer—
the difference being I couldn't search Google for her
a much more efficient way to steal her likeness
and exhaust her resources.
The prose was not necessarily dense
but it didn't have the quality of poems
that are abridged like television commercials
that require only that you mainline them
in interregnums between puritanism and hedonism.
Poetry often made more sense by *what it didn't say*
to paranoid readers who the poets produced
by seducing dissatisfaction with the uttered.
That's old news by now.
Fuck Mallarmé for being born first.
Even poetry as such must be obliterated
as it begins to resemble Hollywood—
perhaps by the fabled 'heat lightning'
that drives the subterfuge of our Non-Event.
This poet is a lesser god banging on his drum,

asking for nothing but getting belief.
This poem is some 'heat lightning'.

Hers were not made for those who lack attention spans
like you and I.
In that sense, they were un-American.
Do not think you can fuck with the world
with a condomed *thinking-cap*—
the *fractional* cap of the ice *in toto*—
getting away without an exchange
and without impregnation or disease.
If Bukowski wrote machine-gun poetry
that swept streets and put peep-holes into windowless walls
then here is offered poetry that *vaporizes everything*,
uniting it all in almost-powdery weightlessness—
the lye for our zeitgeist—
making it all an even more mobile utopia
(less homely and more dispensable than it is in-itself).
You can snort it.
The poems will be *locked*
like technologically superior death-machines
to those who *have* fingerprints
they will be locked out if they insert password correctly
and the poems' data will be erased.
They fire only accidentally
with no safety or trigger
at the *focused whim* of the codeless.
The finger may not be on the pulse—
how could one differentiate between thumps and the buzz of the world
that no longer retains the upward-downward movement
of a steam engine?
Better, the cord is plugged in—albeit memory-less at its 'core'.

Speed Reading

173. A POV poem about an eye turned in no particular direction

Seeing a woman shoving a gigantic dildo into her petite cunt
from the perspective of the dildo,
to *out-measure* (measure more than mere measurement)
but not *out-perform* (perform more than mere performance)—
since performance no longer makes sense
in a valueless space of dispersal
that's curvy, soft and excessive
like breasts on the impregnable—
without any need for your humanity
to satisfy her supple, dovetailed life—
is like seeing *a world without any humans in it*—
a so-called Real World.
"It's going to be a good year," take 2013.
The info-action crashes networks,
as it pancakes out like her titties
when she lies on her back,
into a grid like the debris cloud
that waltzed in the general hurry of a N.Y. streetwalker
from Ground Zero,
calcifying the panicked mob
as they reaffirmed their lack of a terminus
more quickly in their terror than in their daily commute to
nowhere.
One would think the determinate to be *the case.*

174. the hotels are communities at last

What do you want to do with your life?
You will be coerced move to do it, even if it makes you shake,

like the Africans uprooted
and without a language to build solidarity with the foreigners
who bought them.
Luckily the suites are now like little gated neighborhoods.
The cum-stained walls are now fully furnished live-in spaces
and they are no longer in the bad side of town
they are generally close to hypermarkets in self-surpassing
business- or tech- parks—
where the world is a cosmopolitan live, work and play hotel.
The business men *live on the run*
as the hypermarket, vacation-style restaurants
for those who are just passing through—
which is the same as living—
gives them the runs, stocked by cattle farms
like junkyards where involute, crushed metal
spears the atmospheric sounds of a submarine turned inside out
or of people sucked out of the gape of an airplane cabin.
They travel nostalgically
since the internet has seamlessly killed movement with speed
and metadata,
reducing the everyday to the notification.
The times offer /experiences in a vacuum.
It is a preparation for space for Mars.
Machines monitoring and regulating bodies
that suspend agelessly,
reaching the extreme lower limit of the pulse during travel.
"Are we there yet?" is not asked from the tank
programmed to take you off standby when the destination is
reached
but not freeing you from it
because as soon as you come too, the instructions begin.
Malfunction and the instructions to repair the bubble
is the new *functionalized Destiny*
that resembles Destin, FL more than destiny.

Speed Reading

175. defecate the sugar-water of consciousness

If you want to know
when the sweet milk of a causally efficacious consciousness
gets chunky—
adding an unnecessary reduplication of chaos
rather than its generalized (pre-?) ordering
of the chaos beyond its network—
think, Narcissus,
of when you were considering the mirror of the toilet bowl
with your guts reproducing your image
as the propositional content of your thought
highlighted the Jim Bean eating out your guts
like Sonic rolling through the pipe, losing all his coins.
It is a near Pavlovian hypnotization
as of Alex choking on the Primal Scene.
It is likely that wisdom bars bodies from their telos
and cripples most.
Perhaps we are the strongest creatures for having to endure
such a superfluous torturer.
Wouldn't *that* be nice?
Most of us give in and provide the torturer with ourselves
and provide both with false information
to make it stop.

Information can only liberate us from so much thought…
we are hangover cases communicating through an equal link
between think tanks
and drunk tanks.

176. disaster socialism

Luxury made affordable at Ethan Allen.
DIY now more functional (and unnecessary) than ever
with a utility belt of gadgets—
batmen of the leisure class (who sleep *on top of one another*)
psychic vampires who will tell you
that *sucking blood beats sucking dick*
when shop class is soul-craft.
What is wrong with buying a higher caliber soul?

Do not shit on your plumber sporting a chin-strap beard
and dying nightly from sleep apnea.
Not everyone was prepared like food
for the cameras to enter daily life,
who did not 'sign-up for this.'
There is no signing-up to the consumption of signs.
But poetry signs-up by *one-upping* the sign.

You can read Ubu Roi while listening to Taylor Swift
with the freedom of blameless hypocrites,
a freedom that is not less than that of grocery store shoppers.

We will be freed of parenthood
and babies will be checked out from Rent-A-Center
for couples missing something from their lives
and needing to find their center—
"*MISSING SOMETHING? GET A BABY!*" the ads will say.
They will be public property for once—
to the communists' surprise—
like women were once imagined *insofar as they were privatized*
and thus, returned, will generate prestige.
"GIVE YOUR BABY TO CHARITY!"

Speed Reading

We will watch politics unfold on free-live-cams
as politicians respond to their fan-base's demands
getting themselves off as their viewers' benefit
from compulsive behavior and the escape from *the touching*.
Has it even been any different
since Socrates offered *his* little cock
to the god of panacea?

177. nights of the living dread

It's impossible for them to avoid it.
They all eventuate looking desperate by looking desperately.
You put a camera in the mix
and they'll eyeball it, give *it* the up and down,
like they're already famously enticing the audience—
before there is one—
with they're disappearance.
The fantasy of their sprightliness
is that *they cannot be captured in the present tense*.
We only see what is already gone.
Our idol is their two seconds ago…
soooo 2 seconds ago.

But in their effort, they are vulnerable.
Don't you ever look at them when they are inundated
because if you've got a good mental picture—a concept—of that face,
they'll know it.
They'll be threatened.
They will start to mistrust you.

Mostly, all of them shriek like banshees in you-better-believe-it
forms
or sirens
baboons
the exorcist.
At the point of climax, one sees their pixie trail
like a slug trail of becoming,
the ectoplasm or loot
of an indifferent, Holocaustic Alzheimer's death.

Where it was once a severance without compensation,
it is a connection to oneself—the orgasm—
like psychedelics are a connection to the surrounding order,
a technology of the brain ported in by its miniature.
There is no longer any *reason* to involve an Other at all…
plug & play from the little-system from which you accrete.
You stucco angel. Twice.

178. rim jobs

Death is *about* the most average thing on this fatidic Earth.
That is why we forget it
and forget tragedy (and forget courage).
It is the unavoidable common,
the blasé of *fashion become detached from the scene.*
Crisis happens often (to be managed
and stimulate growth and a technological regime change)
and life taken seriously is only a special case of it—
the surface of an Infinite Regress of spirited losses,
an epidermal courteousness removing gore from view
but goring itself with anti-bacterial warfare.

Speed Reading

If anything has been liberated, it's death.
If anything has gone viral, it's death neutralized
or the sum neutrality of anti-death.
The entrapments of everyday life
have made it easier to sever ties with others/world/self—
in short, to incriminate oneself.
The 'new' sociality is plastic—
connections can always be redirected
because they are all indirect.
And so friendships are as superficial
as the interaction between eater and waiter.
New pleasures are discovered out of new failures.
Spirituality is easily simulated like other appetites
via the supervenience of a meta-simulation of appetite itself.

Romance is a Q and A model.
On a date, you are applying to work at Target
at a little kiosk in the store—
with a 250-question psych. evaluation.
A supermarket convenience,
a familiar nature of Love
that takes into consideration your desires according to your lists.

How many times can we play the same game?
Loves are victories without gain—
become little fates passing through itineraries and security
checkpoints.
We are drifting to the center from x.
Loves like arcade games
that circulate back to the menu-screen once each game is 'won'.
New forms of control too
are tested on willing experimental subjects through digital media.
Governance-through-force polled low.

Romance *operates* under the same sign.

179. the anesthetics of banality

The 'bourgeoisie'
or the general leveling of *all into all and through all*
(unwilling to admit it yet not not unaware of it
like a man in a gorilla suit in the background—
we do not look as hard at our own lives
as we do optical illusions
I Spy
or Where's Waldo...
but we eye up the ones we find below us twice as hard
and decipher the terrorists from non-combatants
with an unrequited diligence.
Not knowing what we want, we are sure of what to avoid.
Our goals are Aways.)
clicks on links
until the 360 degrees of separation
has taken him into an *infinite retrogression*
of videos of people popping cysts and people getting pedicures.

The Optical Illusion does not enable one to determine meaning
(terminate illusion).
The observer effect is nearly eliminated in this Leibnizian
perfection
as the viewer is as irresponsible for his grasp of the image
as he is for red being red.
Of course, college graduates will introduce themselves as nihilists
with a penchant for insight into the way of the world
and undermine your values with a left-wing diplomacy—
parabolic cock favoring the left

Speed Reading

(or the 'western quadrilateral of a spherical world
that knows no cardinal)—
from regular (and *regulatory*) masturbation.

They talk about subjectivism and value-creation
as if they are truly free
to choose to be the relativists that they have become.
They are like those of us who *want to see*
the image hidden in the optical illusion
as if it were a sign of our mastery—
like a television viewer who identifies with the hero
and shares in the feeling of responsibility for heroic deeds,
inspired into mania…
Kafka-esque dreamers who'd rather be nihilists than simulators,
overlooking the supersession of the former over the latter,
but won't give up "intelligent conversations."

Of course, *talking* emerged *as a pastime*
only in palaces
remaining a means only in a continuous elsewhere.

180. post-modern chicks in a 'metamodern' world

She texted me the next morning
"another day another tragedy.
I'm assuming you follow current events"

"an early taste of death isn't necessarily a bad thing," I reply.
An early Bukowski quote isn't necessarily a bad thing,
prompting me to respond
is neither good nor bad
but annoying and unfree.

"lol right
and it's only gonna get worse
hang on 2 ur fuckin hats"

"I mean joggers are ridiculous and all—
but bombing takes a lot of effort and deliberation and planning.
It can only be carried out by *alternative capitalists* with a work ethic.
It's banal attacking banal.
Banal terrorism is as capitalistic and calculated
yet stupid
vapid
disingenuous
ingenious—
as petty crime.
Idiot feasting on idiot.
Rock sparking against rock."

"lmao at that having petty crime status.
Idk man the guy got away he can't be too much of an idiot.
anything less than genius is banal as fuck"

"I already wrote a poem about it.
Fuck genius. It doesn't exist."

"saaaaame. lol fuck YOU does."

"What a clap trap"

"email me your poem and ill send you mine. I'm a terrorist"

"No you're not. Why?
It's a self-less, other-directed act.

Speed Reading

You'd be damned to be a mirror image. Get a self"

"jk. I'm into shock value is what I mean"

"Nothing is shocking in simulation."

"yeah There's still shock value tho. it's definitely still a thing.
Everybody loves tragedy. Boston Massacre part 2."

There is absolutely no shock value—
the electrocution of everything
and the valuation of everything
occurs before the things themselves
like light itself, a medium with no message.

Commenters banal
as Texters banal
as Terrorists banal
as Joggers banal
as Kantianism banal
as Care.

As Satan discovered only too late and only confusedly,
God colonizes souls
the same way capitalism colonizes identities—
by giving.
I personally would rather be no one than have a cooptable identity.
But *no one* is only a temporary state—a convalescence.
Having created myself out of nothing,
now I cypher—
I follow the humor of the 'Amerindians'—
a silence that mocks the abject speech-conditions of everyday life,
whose fields of vision all curve towards the Impossible.

181. Baroque suppleness

It's no longer so much the stupidity of *other people* that drives us mad
but the stupidity of our technologies
(that make *us* stupid by extension
because we made them in our image)—
the oven that burns the sodden pizza
the computer that 'freezes' in the era after the cold war
the car that breaks down between two equidistant gas-station-clusters
the satellite signal interrupted by the storm
the vacuum cleaner with no suction that moves the dirt to the corners
the flashlight that flickers in the cave without a breeze
the lawnmower that doesn't cut the grass but throws dust in the face
the Kitchenaid that requires more steps and makes more of a mess.

It's not artificial intelligence
but artificial stupidity that will send us to the mad house again.
At least that is what the producers sell us
as we throw the remote across the room
because we must point it inconveniently directly at the receiver,
which requires us to move more than what is comfortable.
But our tech is not getting smarter
and neither are we
(we both 'solve' what are problems according to us that we 'created').
…
The persons and the personalized technology
are not mutually exclusive
and it's unsure as ever who is the giver and who is the receiver.

Speed Reading

We converge like security lasers interlaced as deterrents to movement,
and as triggers of an alarm
without ever stepping on our own toes.
Who will be conscripted?
Who exonerated?
Won't it be hard to tell what is a spandrel
and what a useful function?

182. the monogram of The Look

I've seen girls as useless as a hole
mediating communication through the dividers between bathroom stalls,
pussies as useless as assholes on opiate users.
I've seen girls as useless as speech,
almost wishing I could un-see them—
but not really or I don't know what.
Either way, it doesn't matter.

…some are as useless as Jell-O
teeth on a corpse
a wallet on a corpse
a legacy of a dead man
as History in the historical period after the humanity has left it
as a mouth on an imbecile
a tombstone for an Atheist
as Atheism and people who talk about Atheism,
who keep God alive by taking Him away—
what has always motivated the religious.

.

I bet they could pleasure me like a large mouthed bass
patch of soft earth
water
(can you penetrate water?
maybe water opens *as* you 'enter' it)
or a rhythm, gesture or hand-signal.
Sure, pleasure has become a sign-language
(replacing enjoyment, which was a sin-language).

They (the women) cannot be simulated *live* in their presence
as what develops only socially in their inheritance.
They can be dissimulated, though,
like I dissimulate my utter fascination and joy
at what they may become.

Now, I always see them running around
like insects mechanized by incomprehensibility.

Once they all are scientifically reducible—
integrated—
they too will be *totally* fucked
(and typically, fucking ends)
and the power they *historically* strove for will be voided where accepted
and they will be forced into repetition
by not just men but the Man (having become Him),
or worse, by people-people like my apparently backwards self
still anachronistically interested in them
their company
their homeliness
their character-armor
their reproductive capabilities,
everything old…
in short, little men who still have 'interests'

and are therefore unacceptable,
pretentious or whatever.

"You, Asian male.
How can you do your homework right now?
You never look up and yet it comes so close to you that…
Well, how do you not notice *all dat azz*?
I've read about 4 Nietzschean aphorisms in the past 90 minutes.
I can't read when there's all this ineluctable sex
being relayed through me!"

Physics will be something like alphabet soup one day.
Speech will be like the rustling of tree branches.
Artifice will not exist as a concept
and absence—including rest—will be the first to go wholesale
via a buy-in-bulk warehousing superstore called Encyclopedia.

Women's liberation is now sold to and heralded by juggalettes.

183. suicide warnings through text message

She says to me
"You know, I wish there were more good-looking people in the world."
"I know," I say.

The neoclassical body of a pixie,
smile like a Japanese cartoon pornstar fucked by octopi.
Her eyes are drunken X's and her pineal eye makes for a triple X—
Holy Trinity of mental DP.

I'd never seen such enthusiasm.
It's like everything I said 'blew her fucking mind'.
Right away, I didn't trust her, a Valkyrie rider with whiskey throttle

She sits closer to me than to her boyfriend.
The first time I met him he greeted me with an English accent…
I thought of the character Andy Warhol in the movie The Doors.
Neat.
I'll kill him.

She messages me:
I want to die. fuck everything. I hate philosophy.
everyone is full of SHIT.

"It's better that way," I set her straight about overcoming.

There is another a waitress from the Mountain people.
Tells me she's bisexual.
Quit meth about a year ago.
Quotes Nietzsche without knowing it.
Over-annunciates her words like Chomsky.
Uses wrong ones like "equivalate."
For giving her a ride home, buys me three beers and a pack of smokes
on her minimum wage income.
"They were all out of American Spirits, so I got you Camel Lights,"
she tells me in confidence.
Her breast jiggled like her nose when she smiled,
how could I complain?
Tells me about how she used to sell time-shares
and how she views other women as only sex objects.

Speed Reading

...the homeliness I can get over.
In fact, it's the homeliness we find exotic these days.
She shows me the liquor shot she'd created for the establishment.
"See the signature right there in the Bartender's Bible?"

"You don't need them," I tell myself.
Fuckable—maybe, only physically.
But the women of the internet, Ariel, that's where the (re-en)action is.

I try and think of another way.
They tell you that homeostasis
is one of the most BASIC functions of the body,
but I know neurosis better.
For fucks sake, I've only ever balanced on the plank?
There is always a fatter version of you
that bottoms out the scale and throws off its accuracy.

I think about and sometimes around her,
never past her,
old what's-her-name (yeah right)—
the one that disappeared like honor but not religion
like the Will but not the willing-and-able
like the West is going to
(perhaps Global Warming and globalization are ruses of the East...
death by universalization)
like Jack O' Lanterns after Halloween
and evergreens after Christmas
(I take her out of storage. There are paler preparatory rituals.)
I think about how I always wanted to be one of those *guys*
that walk on *their* women and keep them around
like a taken home pair of nylons socks you use to try on shoes

...that's love.

I see it everywhere like a nagging God,
but I'm too unfortunately kind for *that*.

184. Pandering, or the Inconstant Constancy

I spent much of my youth hiding among
(or becoming)
the average, the superficial, the cheerful
and the crowds thereof—
the sort of circle jerk where in-group conversations
seem like denatured hogs trampling one another to reach the trough.
Not hiding from the dreadful
from tragedy
the nothing
unknown
nausea
or any of those roses—
but from 'myself'
whoever I think that is now as opposed to whoever I thought it was then…
Maybe that me was the cancer.
Maybe this me is the cancer.
They distract us too much to answer.
I now think I was frightful of my coldness
my indifference
my total oblivion—
my youthfulness *par excellence*.
You only think of *youthful transitions* when you are grown
and *no longer inert*.
Still, I became many personalities
for I *had not* one

Speed Reading

and among group-think that entrenches itself *in* individuality,
that is terrible.
I successfully concealed myself at the right time
(*logic is backwards*).
I am/was necessarily flexible—reintegratable.
One would think employability would follow.
Perhaps an inner Child remains,
dunking my head underwater
in a pool in which I can clearly see the bottom but can't stand up.
I dive into a reservoir of the past and lose my shorts
when in the present I am forced to eat them.

In the summers of my youth,
the mosquitos would beat their heads against the window panes
at the mere sight of my being indoors alone.
I mistook it as a compliment,
where flattery is a petty noose.
They were gentler towards me than folks who tell stories.
Perhaps I used others as bait.
Never friends—prisms through which I refracted the impossible.
I inconsistently networked,
passed through personal relationships
like a bomb disabling robot unaware of risk
with an intelligence that has advanced beyond knowledge,
an evil intelligence without periphery that could be reasoned with.
A draconian sarcasm that knew how to crouch—a paper tiger—
and laugh
and keep thoughts to itself.

Good luck to the nostalgic suckers who see shame in their
sociopathy
or their even more absurd fellows:
those who simulate their shame to appear common—
the ones that are usually murderers.

185. Theirselfies (from the English *Themselves*)

She is sitting in an XXXL Elvis tee,
its graphics making it feel like it's been soaked in cum.
"What if Jews broke cum rags instead of bread," I wonder.
She is half-Jewish
and her father is a former basketball player turned millionaire
C.E.O.
She is following in his footsteps
and votes republican.

As we are sitting, her ex-boyfriend starts beating on the front door
of the condo her parents bought her.
"I told yoo I woulda married yoo
and yoo fucked that nigger bitch.
He's gonna cum inside yoo then leave yoo.
He should. Yoo should…"
He looks right at me through the glass above the door
like a person looking at the camera for a selfie then at 'themselves'
(i.e., theirselfies).
"I'll beat yur ass dood."
He turns to her.
"I know yoo think I'm stoopid
but
I know yoo think I'm stoopid
but
I'm smarter than yoo think."

I am scraping her pipe for resin
and she is the resin I am scraping from Life
as he stands there drunk off himself and losing
yet angry at death—equivalent to a hatred for Life
with its bottomless mug.
I smile at him and nod at everything he says.

Speed Reading

"God what the fuck?!
Oh my god, this is so embarrassing.
I'm sorry you have to be here for this…people are fucking crazy
dude,"
she says as she trembles like her toy fox terrier, Loogie,
that is more rat-like than others
because it doesn't grow hair on its legs.
And she is in the process of lasering off her pubic and armpit hair.

She's a trust fund baby.
Never worked a day in her life.
She's 22 he's 32…
I wonder how daddy feels about the scumbags she nurses
….including me.
She must be getting revenge since she cannot have daddy.
Maybe.

When we met, she told me that she has had multiple stalkers,
that men have moved half-way across the world to get over her,
that the TV show "Girls" is the Truth
because it captures the phenomenology of woman-ness
(like an electro-magnetic field generator intended to trap ghosts).
(You expect as much
in the muggy summer after budding History).

She told me she could write a book about men
from all of her experiences
that there are 7 or so fundamental types and I'm "a Tyler."
I encourage her to do so because I'm sure manliness is dull
and repeatable as a system of transgendered cross-references.

She seemed so sure of herself.
I followed.

She was beautiful,
shined like the gold dust of Elvis's suit printed on her morning-
after tee.
I hoped that her interest in me wasn't printed
but the hyperskepticism of hyperreality
is something Descartes never anticipated.
I had a "great dick"
and was "good example of the human form—
a mixture of all of the types" she's "ever been attracted to,"
but those are things new people often tell new people.
The only other thing she talked about
was how bad relationships are
and *how much* she didn't want a monogamist relationship
and how her ex said, "she is going to be sooo kewl when she's *his*
age"
because she will be more mature
and less likely to cheat on him,
opposed to her now supple young body
and her charming unconscious grace
(a tautological, self-reversing grace)
and the innocent diabolism of her choice.

I happen to like it, although you 'are' further from death
in the company of whores
than in the cinder cone of *her* freedom.

186. 13 years after the millennium 'failed' to *take place*

There were 'women' there ranging from 15 years old to 22ish.
They were wearing jean bikini bottoms
and the lower latitudes of their ass cheeks

Speed Reading

hung out like light bulbs partially screwed into their circular fittings
in the ceiling
but their souls were non-porous due to a sealant, candy-painted,
that their aerosol brains spray
after being shaken with the trauma of being.
Their messages are as salient as Salisbury Steak.

As they hump/dance stagnantly
to signify a dialectic without *aufheben*,
their heads chime like spray paint canisters.
They contribute to the global warming of culture—
one of convergence like disappearing fault boundaries,
a highly viscous magmatic culture that can't be dug up
unfortunately for the Foucaldians.
I am hopeful that at least 1/20 of them will go totally insane,
waltzing with the specter of their humanity
as death brushes their hair
and blows a shotgun of the smoky entrails of previous ghosts
into a phase change of formlessness between the ears—
psychical butter knife that spreads substance but can't cut it! —
their *only* hope of cutting the shit.

They all claimed to *be* bisexuals, but that was due to their naivety.
Sexuality is a belief system.
They thought that they were a synthesis
of two antithetical belief systems—
like 'alternative' and 'popular' culture.
I let them continue to bank on such hope
like parolees banking on reincarceration.
"Do I dare disturb hyperreality, me?" said Proof-rock
with his lateral logic.
They felt more whole like a solid-colored pie chart
when really there was a breach in their enclosure

such that nothing really took *shape*—
remaining lines.
They were at once uncertain about masculinity and femininity.
They were transsexuals.
The orgy had a festive, discontinuous (and renewing) purpose.
But the fuckfest's was more a screen of operatic, calculated pleasure
and transactional, flexible (and thus continuous) social relations.

Naïve and banking on History,
they still referred to their acts as free.
It was like the difference (which isn't one)
between a punk show in the '70s and a punk festival in 2013.
Polyamory is a term that cannot make sense now
even if the anarchists somehow win—

there is no more Love *involved*.
The many are incapable of loving
and must be liberated from such a deficiency
through the *techniques* of 'sexuality' and other-directness.
The body is related to as a thing that the mind operates.
If operated efficiently, at maximum capacity and speed,
the production of cum increases—
but only for the consumption of it.
Lewis Carol made the absurd a logical theorem of *devout ecstasy*—
because for him *the mirror ceased to be a surface*.
That was when anthropology and logic
still had a basis in superconductive entanglement.

These wannabe 'free spirits' operated
on the spooky entanglement the quantum theorists speak of—
thereby were they *relevant*.
And they were going to be running the economy in a few years

as efficiently as they tweet, fuck and dress.
Christ had probably won,
but only because everybody got a trophy without knowing why.
The trans- (from what to what?),
like the cis- before them,
lack seductiveness
since they lack seducibility.

187. vigilante castration

You can give a yes or no to your own death
within the countdown of your end times
that you are convinced each moment of your life is a hoax
(your life continues *as retro fashion*).

You can talk to others
who defeat you in their silence-filled words
like zombies gumming you to death
or like a retired boxer jabbing the heavy bag: you,
as you settle on yourself
like the sand of the generally unused bag.

You can create an identity after only a few clicks and drags
OR you can destroy an entire life's history
of anyone from any time
in a single click
as if God preferred to watch the same thing
undergo multiple, fashionable deaths…
in addition to those dealt each moment by time,
each moment passing being a recycling of the Big Bang—
static fuzz and buzz.

You can feel strong feelings other than the Universal
in which you are like the shell casings of buckshot after the gun
blast—
gutted but still in one piece—
although I won't advise it to You, socialite.

188. Pan's Optic-Con (like Comic-Con)

Tears alone in car
(and cracked steering wheel—wonder how that happened?)
and no response last night,
and the crack pipe whistles like rye in the immature wind
like a Combine
mowing down Holden's or R.P.M.'s neuronal connections
making them disaffiliated, unrecognizable and radicalized;
like burnt bridges that never fully collapse
or that once collapsed, damn the way up river
like phones on silent
and axes stuck into stumps
and knives on keychains
and the hind teeth clinching.

The hooker gets up and scurries away, out of the Holographic
Museum,
like a centipede.
She moves fast but in a curvy strut
that looks too meticulous to be effective.
Her ass pops like cockroaches on fire as she snaps her panties.

Did grown men cry in the wild?
In Rome in spiked pits?
…

Speed Reading

We're just not equipped anymore.
We're our own worst enemy.
We're full of shit, society and saline.
History fucked psychology
and generation after generation of Christ
made a world-historical malt out of our blood.
We foam at the mouth non-threateningly
on sugar pills,
reaching the end of the pipedream but not jumping,
even though we're fugitives.
Our God, Atlas, is blown shotguns by fellow Titans
and forgets where he put the world.

"Huh' name Life," the pimp says.
Big fellow, Godlike.
I traverse the moonscape of his neck rolls with micro-machinic
eyes.
"She the best you got?" I ask to appear like an informed customer.

"Hahaha yeeeuuuhhh…she a GAGGER!"

Pull the needle out
the spectroscope out
the words and not the words
and a gateway is left that the auto-immune doesn't patch back up
because the body is Patch Adams joking itself into painless death.
Soap is a gateway drug for liberation theory.

Wives leave and don't look back
like I don't look right in front of me
and while I blame myself,
they don't even have a second thought
or a first.

Critical Leisure, Book II, Volume III

Lovers, you are one 'probable cause' away.
Because there is no material love
and you should have enough respect for someone
not to love them with unchecked affection and object-anomie.
It is somehow lovely
and attractive when you do.
And *your* true love may begin there.

Once you're stacked on top of one another like cafeteria trays,
what 'matters' is that you take your helpings of mashed shit
with a pious grin
and a sharpening-stone will to file down your claws.

Don't ever let those *fuckers* get you *worked* up
while your unemployed.
They'll suck the life out from the cunt or the cock
and then try to kiss you afterwards.

The hookers—at least they have a little respect.
Probably because *they know how close is too close.*

People are going to give you Real Talk
Real Sex
Real Technique
never realpolitik (yea right)
and ask too many questions
or give too many answers
and tell you how ordinary your ambitions are—
but you must give them the shamanic mug
of Black Panthers without a goal.

And "there must be a point.

   There must be a point.

Speed Reading

There must be a point," said Dorothy in technicolor.

Why can't I just be one of those guys
Satisfied by talking about sports
…about anything?!

You beat on the door to a hi-fi cell that you believe in
as the guards play checkers, not chess
and go home complaining to a miserable, dumb wife
before passing out in a recliner.
They totally ignore you
and fuck with you like sad, bored, miserable gods
before they watch Rush Limbaugh.

"They ain't neva' gon' answ'r," cell mates are going to tell you
in Pan's Opticon.
But *who fucking* cares.
I'm gonna make noise but not too much noise—
something R & B…

but I'm not too attached to that idea
and that's key.

189. a more fat *I* – the happy revenge of the One (Or
     Philosophical Sociopathy)

Let me tell you about drunken megalomania
or the happy science of the One,
a nappy pleasure with more function than body,
a born(e) surplus
but One in which the observer effect is diminished

to a negligible recount that doesn't change who loses: a-more fat-I.

Let the mad be mad,
maddened like senile John Madden persevering via preserving Twinkies
like a drunk getting his stomach pumped live.

Let the tornado tornado.

Let surgeons perform surgery
in a carnival or exhibit or network television.
I mean…there is C-Span.
Presidents make incisions increasingly via guest appearances.

Let the studious study the *physis* of mites

Let the virtual consumers of virtual music virtually enjoy music—
be electrified by it, unable to elect without suggestions.
They, like others, revive something that *nostalgically ought* die
since it has already ended through its realization
and when it did/when it was we're not sure.
Of course, artists have no concern for originality or semblance—
let alone the artifice of the passions.

Let these romanticizers of art use art like a narcotic.

On the other hand, let the preachers of sobriety
seek their narcotic in preaching.

Let the child-murderer bite the head off the child like an ice-cream cone
and accept his punishment like any other luck of the draw
because "in civilization," psycho-sociologists say,
"we all draw straws for crazy."

Speed Reading

Let the biographer study the lives of as many others as possible
before he dies
or if he so wishes, the life of only one other—
never, EVER 'his own'.
For who would read the autobiography
of a biographer?
(Probably many.)

Let brand loyalty reign
like Tribes mocking each other with spending.
Let dams ruin ecosystems
like giant guillotines above genitalia or Gaia.
Let the titties grow further and further apart
like ice sheets on frigid women
with skin like discarded brail office signs after foreclosure.
Let the nerds take revenge.
Let women take revenge.
Let the majority take revenge in their silence or their commutation.
Let the Nazis Nazi
and they will always fulfill the eternal sunshine of a spotless
Nazism,
buried in some future vault when there are no more humans
to fuck shit up,
when the A.I. inevitably were the destiny of the conscious species
that poisons itself with ideals to live up to
and we are animals finally liberated from human thought.

Let us elect the first blind-deaf-mute-dumb president
for that is what *equality* permits!
On the other hand, let equity acquit the charged.

Let virtual agents make art for its sake
a revolution for spectacle's sake

speech for belief's sake.

Let artists simulate themselves as artists.
Let the depressed simulate themselves as depressed.
Let those who are definable define themselves before asked
and never or only ask them
as a form of amusement.
That wouldn't be unordinary.

Let confessors confess and aggressors aggress.
Let victims arouse the pity of the many.
Let persecutors persecute.
Let victims *be persecutors*
and snarl and grow fatter than Buddha the nihilist on denial.

Let a more fat I grow *here*.
Let it expand until you can't even recognize it
because it's edges are out of view
like the blob
yeast
single celled organisms
grey goo material dissolved from flesh and plant
by nano-robots gone haywire —
marketed on growth, not understanding.

From the primordial soup,
a return to a post-human soup
a trans-human soup
a cosmopolitan soup—integral reality.
Let a more fat I grow *here*
like sponges or moss or fungi or cancer or rot.
Let it perform metallurgic rust like Coca Cola.
Egypt's silent revenge from the frosted beer mug:

Speed Reading

THE BLOB OF FATE DAMMIT!

190. cookie jar TV

The people bomb left a crater 10:1 the size of the populous.

Death
the Devil
CEOs
and worms embrace the population explosion more than we
(or implosion, new beings being the fallout of others—
fissiparously emergent—
they feast on their own instability
and their waste produces their energy.
It is speculatively unexplainable.)

Pat Robertson
Joan Rivers
and others follow the lead of Tutankhamen
and outlast their own deaths by 50 yrs. and counting.
Bukowski only threw *his* clock out the window
because it sounded repetitive
as he wrote 10s of 1000s of poems about 7 things:
himself, fucking, work, women, fighting, drinking
and human stupidity.
They will charge money without equivalent in gold
for the energy the sun dispenses.
If they could, they would sterilize the sun and do away with
shadows—
that through a grievous metonymy, symbolize the Sun
(another stand-in for Death's creative luminance).
Perhaps they wish for their shadows to extend in all directions

by a light that does not occur from a perspective—
for such a condition would be True.

Once, people felt free to Oversee or personalize their own deaths—
one could choose b/w cremation or burial
open or closed casket
tombstone or mausoleum
wood or carbonite
granite or marble.
With the population implosion
we will run out of room for the burial of our dead,
unless we build upward—
perhaps there will be skyscrapers full of the rich dead.
They will be sterilized
and each facility will employ 2,134 persons
and 95% of them will be digital media specialist
(or some title hitherto un-invented).
It will stimulate the economy.
The poor will be buried in mounds that are ramps for Monster Trucks.
Cremation will be too costly
and likely utilitarians will have righted a huge oversight of humanism
and dead bodies will be *functionalized*
(that means liberated).

Bill Nye types sell existentialism to children,
when it is no longer a humanism but a product,
who unconsciously assent to the destruction
of one of the terms of absurdity—
that is, postmodernity now defined after its death.

The interest in this overpopulated
liberated

Speed Reading

ascertained life
is conceptually indifferent to the use of advertising on children—
perpetual movement, epileptic light, saturated color
capture the attention of the *en-listed* eye
(listable, serializable, indexable)
as post-hoc enthusiasm flurries the eardrum.
The brain is set on fire by *EXISTENCE!!!!!!!!!!!!!!!!!!!!!!!!!!!!*
at the expense of human exemplars
(that means Life—livelihood).

191. founded on a loss

The cops are as bored as anti-bodies in the Clean Room
and harass the innocent to fill the sense-ratio of the medium,
forget the station quota.
The celebrities are anybodies
and while they have everything *in potential*,
the luxuriant thrust of their intentions hits a wall of satisfaction,
where they successfully incarcerate themselves
(from *carcinogen - to cause to forget death*)
in a saw-dust bean-bag
of indifference and proliferation...
the cops shoot criminal suicides with non-lethal bean-bags
and charge them with attempted murder.

Don't fuck yourself with a blanket of positivity
on the beaches of an ocean rising from the melt
of ice still trapped from the Cold War,
the victory of which is a battle won for Global Warming.
You are likely to fill your crotch with sand.

Things have gotten so bad that we find Hope in the absurd,

whereas hitherto it has been the absurd man who is hopeless
and thus, transcendent through simply living.
What will we find out about this new 'character'
who is a blowback of the absurd figure?
Should she be something Invisible
only out of a selective *inattention*?

192. To the quirky characters they play: I love (am
annoyed by) you all…

Get buzzed off the Hunger
staggering like a delirious buzzard
less dangerous
than delirious consumers compulsively checking their phones
that pause when their operators look away from the screen.

You wear the Hunger like a lead apron during high-tech x-Rays
and it makes you a 'natural' Stoic
in a sleepiness that only comes again after you've eaten much lard.
The body has the "meat sweats" from its self-consumption.

Fad issues are raised feet-first
like pigs by forklifts before they're slaughtered
and to combat them, fad philosophical terms
become a part of productive vocabularies
and the world doesn't even care
that fads operate without negations or awareness
since the World itself has only ever been a fad—
and what could unhappiness even mean for the many anyway.
They contradict the proverb "none shall win"
and accessorize You into their verdict of contradictoriness.

Speed Reading

There are re-involutionists seeking to entangle things again,
to bend them like a Superman bends steel
into ellipses that, like the Earth on its axis, wobble
to slow them down a bit as they speed up stationarily.

Too much power wipes out power
as is witnessed in electrical outlets—
like at outlet malls,
one wastes a great deal of energy traversing the grounds
and leaves emptier.

193. burn fat by cutting out depth

There will be paleontologists digging up Juggalo fossils.
There will be REIs inside every state park.
Otherwise, there will be a proliferation of lawyers
nurses
and upstart recording studios—
the most in-demand professions.
There will be a genre for every band
and 1 out of 3 people will be in a band.
Reality show stars will only count as $3/5^{ths}$ a person
(*and in that they will flourish*—like a bored-out race bike (*goes faster*)).

The shitty won't be able to decide
whether they want to be solid or liquid.

194. All that is left is human

The only freedom left to us is beastliness—
Moreau's beasts are more human than we
in their revolt.

The Humanity is silence,
secretiveness
(and like Nietzsche says, 'endurance that is not merely
endurance')—
the gregarious ability to keep the tears to oneself in total darkness
like a beast limping into the inaudible woods to die,
where if there is no one around to hear it
the sonorous pride of solitude does not make a sound.
May the sound of the air conditioner muster
over your hopelessness.

When she tells you she is getting married in December
out of survival only,
you will say "congratulations"
continuing to mime the values of Western civilization
in total condescension
like everyone else has been doing under the low-pressure system
of hegemony.
She marries like a child pulling knobs and doodads
in the play-spatial vacuum of Epcot Center,
that is, like a good sport
who adequates the means to the end.
Those are private thoughts.

We are the woman aping her man in bed, laughing at him—
or worse, keeping still and silent—
as he gives it to her really hard.
Cry alone in TOTAL DARKNESS—enough at least to enjoy it—

Speed Reading

the final human dignity or opacity.

Plato—Au contraire mon frère!
There are dirtier, older,
more enlightened uncertainties.

195. most guidos

Mostguidos are hated as transmitters
and as parasites (fake places)—
they do not merely suck.
There is a transmission that could bind to your dendritic cells
and cause IBS.

Mostguidos are small and dumb—
they are dumb because they bug things that are bigger than them,
big enough to say:
"no, I will not kill you."

OR:
Mostguidos are capable of what we are not: a leap.
This leap is neither the trust fall of team-building exercises
the parachuted positive vibe of skydivers
nor the eternal return of bungee cords
to that bridge between ape and superman
—it is even without hope of YouTube.
This is the leap of a tightrope walker
who without faith *wouldn't* have fallen
at Zarathustra's chafing ramblings.

We smash most Guidos
and watch *our own* blood ooze out of them in profligacy.

196. "if I'm not comfortable then I'm not having fun," said Taylor Lautner

Baudrillard reporting on the war after watching CNN
and dying of his obsession: decline.
Foucault the sex fiend dying of AIDs.
Bukowski the last modern writer
written, directed and getting canned by Pomo-pornographer,
James Dean Franco.
Cobain's vigilante suicide announced on MTV,
solidifying his disclosure—
that for him was an act of acceptance,
giving the masses more than they could have Dreamed of
themselves.
The dress of Monica Lewinsky,
itself more alive and harder than politics,
potentially forensically revealing the semen of slick Willy—
may it retire in the Smithsonian!
Lou Reed collaborating with Metallica
and Microsoft Word spell-correcting Metallica
yet unable to recognize apophenia.
High stakes betting on the name of a royal baby,
after forensic teams have projected what the child will look like
in 20-60 years.
It will be given a cryogenic vault at the baby shower.
Anarchists exalt the characteristics through which are ennobled
spring breakers
without their wishing them.
To find TOTAL AFFIRMATION in the marathoning of trash
reality TV
in which the virtues are embellished like the orgasms of pornstars
is better—but impossible.

Speed Reading

Whether you renounce virtues or vices or the world or God or
yourself (what is the difference)—

if Life Is a Practice Test for Death,
May It Be Christmas-Treed...
then, exited like a classroom with the impatient giddiness of a
Child,
the child holding a Ruler
only to view the up-skirt perspective—
this world order's obscene exactitude that obstructs maturity.

197. obesity in nursing

It's a curious phenom' why the possessed refrains from murdering
priest
and from suicide.
The demons are so clever that they leave contradictions as traces
like good criminals or Las Vegas illusionists—
miracle workers notwithstanding—
where it is more favorable and eviler to give too much,
causing disbelief,
than to leave nothing to make it an open and shut case.
Only in that are they devilish
since they produce jobs
(unlike what men call "teases"—
who necessarily operate
on 'less is more')

...in exorcisms they make a lot of noise
but are too curable to be Evil.
Like mine, theirs is a soft violence
but unlike mine theirs is uncomfortable

and reaffirms faith once exorcized.

Compassion is typically crueler as a conscious lie.
That is many a discomfort.

198. secrets are anticipated

Her name came from Steel Magnolias.
And she was less experienced in bed than I,
asking me what I wanted her to do.
I couldn't even be responsible for myself.

She had a bunny named Bam Bam.
She slept with a teddy bear.
She told me she was molested by her neighbor for a year straight
as a child
and in middle school a group of boys stripped her of her clothes.
My own life lacked the oomph of childhood trauma
at the price of me being open
to the general trauma of life.
The flicker of her words,
trebled like breath against a microphone,
ringed in my brain like the cock of a handgun on a sound stage.
I died on contact.
I have asked nothing from women
but to be overcome as a fraud,
a writer who writes nothing but writing—
comfortable, spineless and to die for.
I bent poetry to the curvature of space
the language of advertising and the elasticity of the brain—
rap music
ambience

Speed Reading

or on the flip side, botulism toxin.
A murderous poet,
but not poetry through anti-poetry—
murderous only due to indifference, accidentally murderous
(passion).
Not a poet, not a writer—something older and dirtier
but less than 'new'.
Consciousness will not allow belief
in one's own authenticity or authority.

At that point, she committed involuntary manslaughter
permissible in rebellion.
She is fine while I consensually relinquish to her my departure—
like a rat that can't saunter back out of a stainless-steel water bowl
yet doesn't stop swimming out of *mere* exhaustion.

She had a potbelly
but her face resembled a Norwegian model
and an actress or 2 that I did Google image searches for.
She maintained the detachment of science
going to school for engineering.
Shortcomings and confidence
and a soft psychosis
that can be seen in someone without desire
who, beyond the boundaries and capabilities of our thought,
has a destiny—
these seduce more than sex is capable of.
I told her that because I didn't have a past
because I had no future.
When she asked what I meant
I told her that the TV—though it can't be turned off—
can make you disappear.
In a similar (heroin) vein,

because my identity lacks friezes in a way that makes it unmemorable
(which is to say unavoidable),
I don't exist.

We watched trash TV
and rolled around in its shit
and fucked in its mud-colored couch for several hours
until déjà vu wasn't suspicious—
the only commercials were for profit schools
attorneys
and psychological medication.
Not knowing what to do with the masses
(who are 'the residue of the few'),
it was agreed on by the U.N. that they be conscionable,
that proper funeral measures be taken so that their spirit may not haunt.
Trash reality TV is their nameless headstone
through which the living one-ups the dead and each other
in their simpatico pathos (ecstasy),
each *out of* a debt to the dead
and via a masquerade with one another.

We move mountains and bury trash
that of course must be vented to prevent an odorous explosion.

199. magazine attention

If it's a thing you want, you'll see nothing but it's properties.

If it's property you want, you'll see nothing but money.

Speed Reading

If it's time you want, you'll see nothing but events.

If it's money you want, you'll see nothing but time.

Wanting culture, you get nature.

OR wanting experience, you press record.

…

If it's events you care about, you'll see nothing but time passing.

If it's a stage you want, you'll see nothing but actors,
if it's actors nothing but a setting.

You're nothing but features. capable of attending to outlines an eye
that stops blinking when dead but blinks after a lie—
the movement through which rest deepens.

You'll dawn properties you don't possess
to impress people who would've been more interested in their lack.
You'll present things to people who prefer absence.
You'll make something out of nothing
and an ideal out of a moot point.
You'll rush and still be late
and you'll relax and be uncomfortably early
and if you learn anything,
you'll learn that learning often changes nothing,

that forgetting accomplishes itself more rapidly than death,
that people care less about you than you think
who you thought hated you,
that many problems are the work
of an imaginative ego that needs to overcome to feel power—

that pumps itself to no gain like promising sneakers—
these untruths and little-mourned miscarriages
are more important than the circumference of the Earth
or the amount of people you've slept with,
your twitter followers
or historical dates.

But you will more often forget this.

200. retard strength

The camera circles as the kiss waxes,
making the room feel like a 720° rotation,
and the joy shrivels like breath on a winter's window pane.
You're lucky if you can write something in it before it evaporates
but even the heart or dick you drew in milder terms
will disappear with the fog.
For once can't there be a dirty car
on which a finger doesn't engrave "wash me" or draw a dick—
two homologous signals.

You will not hear your own trial
until you have sampled 90 seconds of it,
the sample-rate being less than half actual quality
in a world of quantitative and qualitative parity.

You refuse to experience what cannot be researched,
but you research what you lack in experience—
if it cannot be miniaturized then it isn't real
yet if it's real it is already a reproduction *or that which can be simulated*
   …someone just internet searched "two-toned bowel movement"

Speed Reading

or "am I depressed/overweight/bipolar/pregnant?"

If it can't be made to speak its sorrow it isn't worth saving—
if it can't be magnified and repeated on a jumbotron it isn't love.
It is only love if you see that you are on screen
and can wave to yourself through the camera.

Truth, a dragon lady, waits for you in the lobby,
exonerating you from the indistinguishable smells
of Sherwin Williams
Discount Tire
and Hobby Lobby with a hint of the killing floor
as she swears you in.
She sports a kimono,
untassled but with skin-tape holding in her breasts
to visibly thwart/invite peaking...
Truth—that puritanical whore of America.
She will not look at you
like we do not look at those who are ashamed
because it would be too cruel.
Like many women and some men,
she must remove her heels to run away
and becomes short again.

Truth is, one is stronger drunk.
But because the blood is thinned, one shows more signs of injury.
What becomes important is that you laugh *with* the trickster god
that it may not always laugh *at* you.
Some suggest a sonic boom as a possible *causa sui*—
Nietzsche turned against this
but his first book still circulates.
Have we yet thought Life anything but the motion blur
of the thunderous laughter of Zeus?
Jesus was sacrificed, true,

but that's because that's the only possible solution
in such a hostage situation—
for God wouldn't have exchanged anything for Him.
Wouldn't the state of affairs, progressive time, have been much worse
had God paid the ransom?

Jesus was capable of walking on water
only because he had the tragic knowledge
that the oceans stem from the happy tear ducts of a God
who can't keep a straight face.
The trickster god walks on air because he doesn't look down—
and boy does he look goofy.
Nietzsche's tightrope-walker—
his audacious, manly philosopher leaping from temporary footing
to temporary footing during the seism,
drawing strength from wherever it will come—
couldn't sport such a cruelly *untouchable* humor
(in the sense of *being beyond caste*).

Grandmothers lift cars too…

201. The Revolution will not be tweeted about

The traffic moves like an accordion
and the acid kiss one of many left behind
erodes my esophagus
as chunks of memories ride it up and down like an elevator
with every button for every floor pressed…
I removed my 13th vertebrae for good luck.

The 23-year-old wins a lifetime achievement award

Speed Reading

in her planned obsolescence,
and if the terrorists attacked the musical awards show
the retaliation would be more expedient and enchanting
than that against 9/11.
A pop-singer's life is worth more
because it is so cheaply produced
but the only thing it seduces in its extravagance is terrorism.

Intent against the culture industry is more likely to cause WW3
than that against political economy.
Look at Manson,
the only difference is that Manson was put into play
and can be seen on YouTube
dying a natural, civilized death in jail
whereas WW3 or the revolution
will not be tweeted about.

(Terrorism is *different*
(it has no absolute meaning),
viral,
mass-mediated
and relatable to anything.)

The easterner revolutionaries
fight for Twitter as a fundamental human right—
as the Pope tweets
the President tweets
the Dali Lama tweets
the hobo tweets at the internet café,
as the wireless receiver *lets you bring your television outside*
because TV behind closed doors is totalitarian.
The war journalists will filter and mangle the giblet photos
with a preset.

The fate of all who undergo plastic surgery
is the face of Michael Jackson—
Universal Man—
The fate of those who have experience is to beat it.
The fate of the revolution is its proof in its consumption.
The fate of the imagination is still picture thinking,
but the images are the outdated, Cartesian ones of spectacle.
The fate of language in the acronym.
The fate of dreams
in premonitions that simulate themselves retroactively
in the virtuality of wakefulness.
The fate of actuality in the virtual.

While the laboratories slice life and the garbage cities block the sun
and the REIs exist only in cities
and the happy birthday song brings copyright infringement
and the cities banish backyard chickens
by which the autistic children break their silence,
do we spend our time in Rousseau's cabin in the woods
browsing WikiFeet? —
Even a brain in a vat would not free itself in its virtual reality—
an immortal would do nothing but read magazines
and waste itself forever.

202. The Give and take, or apophenia in practice.

Poetry does not work for a living
and might encourage others to do *the same* (by ceasing to be poetic)—
Rimbaud quit writing at 19 to become a man of conquest
and to work at finding treasure,

Speed Reading

which is a life for a life;
Buk quit the post office and wrote a groveling letter to get his job
back.
The strawberry blonde hippie
told me that my poetry makes it seem
like I work hard at having and reflecting on experiences
but I hardly do.
Here's one that I exaggerated in real time:

I was lying in bed with the lamp on
scrolling through my contacts to delete old numbers
(I'm not sure why people remain in contact
with the accumulation of people from their past,
yet once you delete them from your contacts
and realize that you truly are left to your own devices,
you feel like a piece of shit).
To those names-I-was-unsure-of-but-knew-people-with-them
I texted: "Who is this?"
"R"
"R who?"
"L"
"Holy shit. Weird."
"Sorry I…" I told her the story.
"Haha no, it's ok no worries."
"I really don't know where I got your number.
Are you still in Alabama?
Probably married right?
Actually that's rude of me to ask."
I was drunk on tramadol.
"Haha I'm 23 why would I be married?
And no I graduated in May and I'm in Atlanta now.
Actually staying at Mary's right now while she's out of town
haha."
"Dude I don't know

I feel like shit happens like that.
I graduate in December.
And that's so weird I was just thinking about her."
I'm not going to lie, I thought about fucking R—
for a moment, we all do.
She is a transient hyperreal dream—
a mere concept that doesn't fulfill its promise in practice.
I called her a few times,
even left her a message,
but she never answered or called back.
I would come to be thankful for this.
That's the thought I projected into the future
or embellished for readers,
so they'd get suspicious if they merely *sought* the poetic.
She texted me back when I texted her.
She said she'd be busy, like I'm busy now in the useless narration,
because the Alabama game was that weekend.
I was already on my way back to ATL,
getting on the train at 3:07 PM
when she gave me M's number upon a request
that I had to make.
"M?"
Of course it was, it was a shared contact…
I was certain it was her.
"Yes. Sorry new phone lost all my numbers."
"You wouldn't have my number anyway.
This is Ariel—I got your number from R.
You dt?"
"Hi Ariel! I am but in class."
"I'm about to get on Marta.
Meet up with me when you're finished."
"Def I'm out at 4 ☺"
"What building? Law? I'll meet you outside."
I waited for her on the steps by the entrance.

Speed Reading

She looked different.
Her face, like mine, had thinned.
But she looked the same.
We hugged and sat down on a concrete bench.
"Ok, don't get grossed out." She pulled out a pack of smokes.
There were two in her pack.
Pythagoras would have contemplated,
but it was just me doing that via hope informed by internet astrology
that differs from site to site.
We looked at one another after both looking at the cigarettes.
It was that moment of precision
that fell from some nowhere most confused minds spiritualize
when I first realized with my dogma
how big and brown her eyes were.
The triumph of my truth only won me 'descriptions' (repetitions)
of pure facts
that are neither ambiguous nor of any straightforward relevance.
In fact, we both have olive complexions
deep brown eyes and dark brown hair—
features that women in my life who are experts on themselves
typically find exotic, according to them.
Of course, they weren't to her because she had them.
It was relaxing.
"I thought you didn't smoke?" (I told her that.)
"No, I just don't smoke my own cigarettes."
…
She told me she ran into my old friends, B and E,
at a restaurant with her father.
She asked E to forward a message to me including her number,
suggesting I call her.
"That's so weird. I got your number from R."
"Wait, he didn't give it to you?
Wait, are you serious?"

She chuckled like a fat Amerindian holding a melting popsicle,
a figure of the trickster God—
"…wait I'm so confused."
The way she dragged out the word confused as she laughed annoyed me,
had me believing in God, like the Jews, as the sum of all fears.
"He [E—from evangelist, one who spreads the word] messaged me on Facebook asking me on a date.
Of course he didn't give it to you."
It had been over SIX years since we saw one another
and here we were sweating and conversing—
abolishing time and space with *superficiality and vapidness*.
There were layers, but all the layers looked the same
and when separated, couldn't be put together
coherently or incorrectly.
I admit I loved her back then,
still don't
but not in a romantic or sexual way.
It was in the worst kind of way.
A prohibition
an embarrassment
an enticement.
I prefer:
'it's like I loved her enough not to get involved at the time
but not out of self-deprecation
(from my singular perspective
but from neither the general nor the scientific)—
it was a seedy love that must be projected unconsciously into the future
that needn't bloom another season to remain fertile—
as a return of sick hope
a retrogressive logic
a hermeneutic of meaning
that starts with the moral and can only well up in abjection.

Speed Reading

I didn't even become self-conscious
until well into my twenties, after I wrote this.
And even then, it was as much a lie as ever—
though innocent for all that.

Some connections are incredulously instantaneous;
you come to know what is good
by being away from it for a time—
like despair—
by suddenly recognizing it.
But as suddenly as you became prone to its shock,
You later recognize the process as pathological:
"*That*'s what's meant by being *directed towards* the other,
not *bound by* it—
who the fuck knows what's meant by eternal recurrence.
Probably someone.
It says 'it's wrong to desire or the theory of desire is wrong.
Instead of going towards that which is outside your grasp
for the sake of power
welcome ones you cannot elude.
Desire is incapable of the narcissistic elation of lovers
who do not possess each other
but acknowledge each other as inescapable.
Deadly—risky but non-threatening
and pleasing like an addled snake at a secure distance,
like an inside joke.'"
I couldn't say *for sure* what it was—
maybe that her name meant "sea" according to Wikipedia.
It was something other than her,
something outside of her.
I could *desire* only what was strictly desirable,
that is, unattainable.
It was no quest—certainly not a determination.
A quest occurs begins for lack of a *destination*.

A quest is proven by the intangibility of its objective
and always mistakes survival for life,
repetition for perfection.
My self couldn't have been involved
because I didn't *want* her, not exactly—
there could have been a thousand things I wanted
as vaguely as animals want offspring
that she represented.
I perhaps knew I couldn't *have* her
in the sense of working towards having her.
Seduction has, luckily, not a successfully assimilated choice.
Here, the parts deconstruct the whole...
without destroying it of course—
it involves the accidentality of excessive gravitational forces.

Many women have beautiful bodies.
Many women have splendid minds.
Sure, she had them both
and we had history—maybe just a past.

She was the same but different—a vacuous phrase—we both were.
She was vacuous
and the superficiality sucked me into its bottomlessness.
Beyond a certain point—reached immediately—
I couldn't evacuate.
The momentousness of the whole non-eventfulness
locked me into a visual stasis.
It was a Candy Crush—something addictive,
expensive,
without end,
something flat yet imbued with space
but space that adds nothing to what emerges from its decadence.
These fresh-eyed glances
have discovered something new and unknown

Speed Reading

in what was just commonplace,
or else poetry has ruined the good sense that saw eyes as organs
—a sort of love that was already there to begin with—
Love re-remembered,
one that relied on every single event preceding it in the universe
to have existed.
Sure, so does everything else,
but maybe not necessarily anything all the way down to Nothing,
that thing that is preceded only by its reputation.
(Stinking of Plato!
These bed-rested wounds rotting, exposed to old, unchanged
wraps…)
(More pathology):
"Everything initial comes late.
When things happen twice, they are significant.
No need to increase the number of trials
like experimenters looking for irrefutable evidence.
Theories and proofs are too slow for Life,
as *rigor can smother joy*,
or worse, make it out to be *just another affect.*
They are worthless when the Luck is like a wishing well
that dries up with only one bum—you—around to collect.
Only lifeless fools play the lottery
when wealth is something lived
and something shared."
What she had not a lot of women had because not a lot of people
have it.
She was soulful—
she didn't need confidence like the 'liberated' women.
She wasn't timid
and she wasn't faithful to compensate.
She was thoughtless because she was *making* something of herself.
Her form made something of her

through which confidence flowed as naturally as the television
image.
A holistic self,
that isn't *total* for all that—
automatism of thought,
charm,
grace of a ratio—
an ego that trickles down to itself
for all its mimetic success.

When she was sweet, she meant it.
When she was a bitch, she meant it—
and it made her more Life-like.
I was the same way—but out of the way for her.
We had a similar ethos.
I was recovering from the poisonous effects of another—
seeking whatever medicine had dazzling effects:
the pseudo-art of an unbridled individual.
(What that really means to the naive
is that she had the health that I admired and wanted.)
Somewhere a guy is choking on his own vomit
because he forgot to roll over,
an apartment complex is burning down
because an old lady fell asleep
with a cigarette secured in her saline fingers,
a polar bear is stranded on an icicle 30 miles from shore,
and here M and I were thrown into each other,
a Crash (like a market crash or a caffeine crash).
I didn't ask.
(But am I still too dependent?)

Destiny is not contents, but a form.
And being formal, it does not content.
It is not a determination, but a cooperation—thus a concession.

It is a consensual relation of equality to a body that begs.
As an exchange, a Gift, it can be neither accepted nor rejected.
It is unavoidable.
Acceptance is a taking-in, a consumption—
you are what you eat…also with whom you eat.
Sure, avoid anorexia of Spirit
if you wish to Live like M does—
whether she knows it or not is irrelevant.

Just learn from my pathology.
She is boring now and her Life has become a System
(a symptom of the past).

203. Love is a hotline, make a B line

They come and then they go wherever they go.
They see the other as the new.
And, yet again, you're caught in their undertow,
and you drift as they are passing you.

They don't want art; they want artfulness that is bought.
They want a stable vacation.
And they never give a second because they never gave a first thought;
and they're not interested in your vocation.

They peek in with a playful but refined curiosity.
They want to present themselves to you forthright.
They listen with an unmatched non-porosity,
as *my* lightning reaches for keys by an awkward kite.

The vibes come, and they go,

and the memes pass with the vivacity of fusion.
The connections never quite stick, y'know?
The suspicious ones at once seem astral unions.

We, lusted after during the week and ignored on the weekends
by those that want virility muffled to a cat's purr...
It's hard enough to meet a real, in-the-flesh, friend.
In the end, the means she settles on repeat her, though past her.

204. ladies' night dubstep curry

I read Hegel's *Philosophy of Right* in the law building,
and the bros would pass by to the coke machine
for a little pick me up—
some would sit down in the chairs
(that were nicer than the ones where the philosophy classes are)
and put one earphone in
so that the sound from the other just dissolved into space
like the breath of a man screaming into your face
as the spit hits you like a cat piss-spraying its opponent.
We usher nothing but warnings and future plans—
but you said yesterday is dead
and that you were a different person then.
One bro sits down next to a girl
and another guy is stopped by him.
They are "holding down" this space
like they did their victims after the hunch punch.
He introduces her as "my girlfriend"
and doesn't give her name.

I wouldn't do that to you.
Hopefully you would object if I did.

Speed Reading

You wore a black high skirt
and a white sleeveless oxford with high top tennis shoes—
useless descriptors that will wear out the readers
or will give their minds a rest because they add nothing to the story.
When the Asian hostess asked,
you said they also come in blue
and that you got them from H(e) & M(e).
The restaurant was named Tuk Tuk
after the public transit of Thailand.
Countries individuate themselves
through the technology they produce—
if the Tuk Tuk is the symbol of Thailand
then it must be a real hip country.
In America, too, you are what you ride—women are men.

You said that when you get hungry you can't make your mind up about food,
that the music is either too fast or too slow,
that you are on "sober crack."
You were as all over the place as God,
who sleeps with every enemy
and convinces them of their necessary victory.

You didn't know what to think of the massive cultural convergent zone
called "the courtyard"
and thought you knew the ambiguity of your consciousness
but you were wrong about the extent of your confusion.

"Wait. I don't get it…can anyone do this?" you asked
chuckling in condescension as we walked with intention
past the stall selling hand-made jewelry.

"What? Too many memes and personal brands for you?" I asked.
"What's a meme?" you inquired.
As I explained you interrupted "wait am I a meme? Meme!"
in a cute voice.

It was ladies' night at the Ivy—
where the women, like the plant,
need a rigid structure to become elevated.
On your way to drop me off, you cut across four lanes of traffic
and each car honked at you—but I thought I was a good spotter.
When the pickup wouldn't let you over,
you said, "Gosh I h8 fat people and people who don't let me over."

You mentioned your presentation
during which you got embarrassed
because you used your lingo instead of formal language
after I highlighted that you said "bought'n."
You'd be writing law-books soon and defining oft-used terms.
For an 'appropriator' of language,
I sure am prejudice against incorrect grammar.
Or else I look for excuses to pick on the women I love.
The latter seems more justifiable.

You complained about the smell of my cigarettes
and when I mimed you—
"your cigarette smells and you haven't even lit it"—
you said that that doesn't even make sense.
"It makes sense or else you wouldn't have cognized it
to the extent that you could critique it."
"Well, it does not make sense."
I've never had the luxury of outright denial.

At the Thai place, you ordered one of your favs:
green curry.

Speed Reading

I had a tall whiskey on the rocks.
When we left I didn't hold the door open for a lady
and you gave me shit for it.
But I was either spaced out,
drunk
or thinking of you.
You informed me more countries are represented at a dubstep festival
than at the Olympics.
We argued over whether a dubstep show *counts as an experience*.
I think you won—
if winning means maintaining your position.
You made it seem like
because I have never been to a dubstep show, I have never lived.
I guess I am a bad person if I say No to Positive Vibes.
I started to wonder why I had been writing all this time
about people
the city
the feelings
and Ideas
the anguish, don't forget about the anguish,
when I should be writing
about ladies' night at the Ivy
dubstep
molly
and You.
I told you that drugs are the reinjection of experience
into a contemporary life that is unsure about experience—
a generation that never came to know Fate on a Walpurgis Night,
that knows better than anyone
that *the simulacrum is true.*

We passed the bowl around.
"Sorry, I'm hitting this twice, he he."

I felt the authentic remorse in your tone
and reasoned an authentic indifference to an objection.
Before you left you asked for a cigarette—
"two" I said.
"What does that mean?" you inquired.
"One for me, one for you," I insisted.
I walked you to your car to claim the black lighter you stole from me
but it wasn't there.
You claimed to have left the cigarette and asked for mine
but the cigarette wasn't waiting for me inside as you claimed.
You got away with my last smoke
my black lighter
and my disgusting heart.
'That means something,' meaning nothing.

In the future, dubstep will embarrass the children
whose parents were into it
and the dubsteppers will find the new genres obscene
and worry about the immorality of things,
ignoring the destructiveness of their own music.
But you told me that you don't twerk,
a word I wished I'd never written—
but You said it, so I did.
DJs will be ambassadors to exotic foreign lands
and do molly with dictators who travel through the cities in sky-buckets.

Geologists will find clasts of chewing gum and gravel.

Artists will release their art into space
and it will be objective art,
virgin
and unseen forever—

like me.
And…
temporary communities will still form
between people complaining about injustices they've suffered
as they wait in line at the cable company.
One old lady will say
"you [cable company] are no different than the hoodlum on the
street,"
which is funny because I also like to *watch them*.
But you wait in a line of previous identities you have become other
than
to watch Your Life flash before your eyes—
a 'free'-spirit who Wills to relive it on the screen of your passive
death.
Culpa levis in abstracto.

205. "Keep Rollin'," said Fred Durst

The off-ramp wouldn't let us in
and the parking lot wouldn't let us out.
The community wanes
when the economy drifts like a glacier over the land.
Community is the medial till leftover from the melt,
the popsicle stick after the popsicle
sticky with the residue of former sweetness,
sweetness that is better now because it is artificial
just like it was before.
The parking lots fortunately hide the desert beneath them
but they titillate wisdom as a wasteland of their own,
and the desert is no less imbued with non-meaning by the
Amerindians
(*for good reason*)

than the parking lots are for the culture we have ascended to.
The warehouse stores are built like Egyptian mausoleums—
they give the illusion of space
and the action within them obfuscates consciousness
but they express perfectly the permanence of death.
They are built into the peeling precipices of the green-screen multitudes
that in their proximity to one another signify the victory of something.
One-day Martians will treat the borderlines of the lots semantically.

How fortunate!
To already live as anthropologists merely by citizenship!

206. précis time

There are street performers on every corner
who don't do magic tricks,
play the sax
or bang on an empty container of spackle turned on its head
with a paint stirrer.
See the mime in their stroll?

The drivers even speed up as they get over to let you pass,
trying to get you in trouble
or because they can't break the law alone.

And it is no coincidence that Tim Leary made the transition
from LSD cults to cyber-punk.
We are all one via LSD.
We are all one via the Internet.

Speed Reading

We are hanging from the nous of culture—
and never has our blood been more concentrated
to the area above the neck.
De-oxidization will wipe out even the barrier reef that is our thought
…but we will cum harder.

It is of little significance that they call 'retarded'
those who have mental blocks.
What We call "retarded" is "what is unnecessarily rational
to the point of irrationality.
One who is retarded is double fucked—
once slowed by a personality
that has in mind only its freedom *above* everyday life.
Once again slowed by *custom that considers itself practice.*"
They are slowed-again, twice Late—
those who are out of flow, the Awkies,
those who get embarrassed and who regret.
Shame is intuitive for some.
For others, those spirits of flow, it is a double barricade.

And you complained about your outfit.
But You and others like you could do no wrong,
or if you did it would require so many extra steps
that you wouldn't waste the precious time
to fool with it.
I only work part-time on myself, so I'm often wrong—
perhaps wrong for working at all
because when I do
I am constantly frustrated.

(I'm still hopeful you'll waste
the time won by your provisional assumption,
your broken perfectionism,

on me.)

207. After Playland

He said that his LASIK surgery was wearing off.
"Sue for malpractice," she said.
"Well, think about it—law exams…
I use my eyes more than most people."
Lawyers, like us, use their eyeballs more than their brains.
Perception has probably evolved like soldiers or white cops
to shoot first and ask questions later.
The cult of the eye is made possible by the loss of ritual and festivity
and the neo-hippies like the other hippies
will revive the corpse safely
thanks to the omnipresence
omniscience
and omnibenevolence of the American military.
The loss of anything to see
corresponds to the maximal utility of the eye
and the complication of the understanding
to vision's technical perfection.
Absurdity, even when there is nothing to see,
creeps into the silent floor of the Law Library.
What?
Did they expect objectivity that can only be imbued in silence—
one of which even Mallarme was incapable.
(And who said breaks are what *generate* meaning?
Stability and spontaneity reciprocate each other in a greater structure:
poetry.

Speed Reading

But that's only one way, and becoming The Way, it ceases to be poetic.)
Blush and eyeliner on a woman does a better job at this—
the only beautiful objectivity that illumines and engenders seduction
as not a form of speech (but of silence the militaristic cannot accept).
Nay, it follows humans
like untied shoelaces from the feet of unaware adults,
like unplugged game controllers dragged upstairs by little peculiar boys.
The mystery schools were better than us but no different
in the savagery of their dictates.
We are uninitiated because we are too alive.
I say this as she hacks up a lung without complaint.
"Mew!"
He called her the creepy kid eating warm yogurt;
IF THERE IS ONE THING THAT HASN'T BEEN LIBERATED
B/C IT HASN'T BEEN FULLY UNDERSTOOD,
IT IS WIT.

For there is no entryway into the semiotic,
and if there is,
the gatekeeper has allowed us free passage to and from it
only by denying its existence as a place.
It is a utopia.
It is more like a hula hoop that can neither be maintained indefinitely
nor fully realized with the oscillation of the hips.

Hence why it—she—
is a plaything.

VOLUME IV
TR@NSFR@T

YOU CANNOT DRINK THE CUP!

Our culture is incapable of thinking poetically
—we are
archeologists of the Real, which disappears when
undug.
Our Fall was not from divine Heaven but from
Seduction
—quarantined, as we are, in Linguistics and the
Literal.
But without their third term, they too evaporate.
We were not born to be men and women, but
to Live in the future as soulful signs. If
there is 'Hope' for Us, let
us begin to consider
a comic solution:
may we instead
be devout
consumers.
May we rip
to shreds
and, like old
Maenads,
not merely kill God,
but devour the land and,
through the land, its King—Nature.
Only there does the Double inheritance begin,
because the 'Double' is inherent in the World.

Tr@nsf®@t

208. Autumn

In the country I can't work
but I go there to unwind and play
so I don't come back and jerk,
then hit the city by highway.

The pics move and make me less poor
like they do everyone else.
Of course, you can't know for sure
if you'll drown from the snowmelt.

The icy heat of the seatbelt—
the amputation of spermata
into the cool toilet felt
like nothing, like slicing ricotta.

Hyper-stimulation and extension
without a protective organ
is a blister cut to oozily ease tension.

The women in the courtyard,
the women in the films, ads, pop-ups
can be saved to a memory-card—
outside—to prevent nervous lock-ups.

Even a whole identity can be
amputated onto a network
but then the lack of privacy
makes every shock into a jerk.

When Satan fell, he lost sensation
and experienced Chaos retrospectively.
He had to *witness* the Creation—

and Light screened him out effectively.

Beetle Bug disappears in the Light
for the antennae are a hotspot.
Yet forever his battery life doesn't die,
being the extended profile of God.

Satan always did make God's skin crawl
as any extended organ would do—
a pinched nerve he got while sleeping
that Icy Hot attended to

but never relieved immediately
because comfort is an amputation.
Especially when it went conveniently,
Satan faced a shocking realization

that made him vibrate and swing:
he was the operator on the Cloud
and awoke when he fell suddenly.
In silence, after he witnessed sound

his appearance suddenly changed—
GodTV makes you disappear.
"The Majesty is for the poor," he explained,
"trust nothing demanding constant cheer."

Viewing from Heaven where community
is instant and total—mythic heat lightning
causes a surge of emotion, punitively.
Work is a form of relaxing.

By the time Satan first spoke to his men
he had grown a new organ of demand.

Tr@nsf®@t

His spirit had congealed into skin.
Facing only the content, he served the Plan.

All his speech was irreversibly translated
so that freedom became a term.
And the cool heavens were evacuated
too soon—that single mischievous sperm.

God outsourced all his labor
onto an alien territory out of sight.
When He begins to play the satyr
the bark is ruptured from the bite.

Satan became God's excuse—
an auto-amputation after he understood
Evil was a thing he knew not how to use.
And Satan fell off the edge of the Good.

209. You called me one of those literary theorist guys that I was shitting on, but said I just do it in the form of poetry

I have to do all this shit I don't want to
just to be left alone.
Everyone is always nagging—even the bums
the junkies
the communists
always bring up your failures.
It's like success
or wealth
or the end of history
is just a way of saying Fuck Off to naggers.

If no one can be my friend
without trying to trick me into becoming a better person…
thennnnnn… ( ).

It's not like I'm going to stop talking to these people
(against my best interests and my better judgment).
I'll entertain their fantasies about me
that are fantasies about themselves and their relation to the world.
They think I am them…it is a common mistake.
Our bodies look similar and we speak a language
and that suggests things.

I'm not as smart as they think or as perceptive as they think—
I'm not sure which one,
but not both and not neither.

I'm wholly seducible,
more sensitive than many
and thus easily diverted.
I *wear* my feelings on the outside like a shroud
and sometimes get tangled on others' flesh as I pass by.
Yet I am also more willing—
more willing to go along with another
and see what they are up to
to follow out a line of thought to its end beyond visibility.

I have an elastic will
always pulling me to a denser force or larger body—
unless I am tangled in the will of another,
knotted because I am not cordless.
Willingly, I am an outdated technology when the will goes
wireless
and can move without linearity,

that is, without a past or a future
(and for lacking them also without a present).
A wireless will runs the risk of a bad connection
and the loss of connection altogether.

This will watches me unwillingly but kindly
like a sober friend watching a drunk,
listens to my baby-talk like a therapist,
observes me like a primitive observes TV without speaking the language
like a scientist or curious child poking a dead man with a stick
or pulling the wings off a butterfly
saying "I'd like to know you *only a little better.*"

Like an understanding wife that cannot be hurt by your infidelities
because she is self-sufficient and so secretly knows your secrets
it always let me 'have my fun' and go on my trips
and without judgment took me back in
and nourished me back to good health
(since my desires were usually out of *this world*).

I was kept together by this thing
that seemed like it co-specialized in interior design and psychology.
It was my little world and thus also my worldliness
(my digitality).

I get teary when television commercials—
get sentimental and feel warm and fuzzy
when the contestants filled with hopes and dreams
make it to the next round on singing competition shows.

I am a dough-boy,
and my brain is a plastic sex organ furrier than a dirty tongue.

Meanwhile, the suicides outnumber the casualties of war,
pet-care is a $56,000,000,000 industry
(for just cats and dogs, the mainstream pets),
and the old men are dying from testosterone pills.

210. Trash-cam Lid

I can open my lenses open-endedly
when my eyes are behind a film.
The drops make them mucousy
like a lubed transgendered vagina.

The thumbs will no longer grasp things
The fingers will no longer point.
But the former will swipe a screen
and grow a new tissue or joint.

Without my lids for censorship,
the trash will get exposure.
My brain is cooler with holes in it
left by lack of enclosure.

211. 'What does Chuck Klosterman *not* write about?'

Suicide
real fear
cultural lies
characterological lies
suffering from happiness

pleasure in despairing
absurdity
anti-capitalism
the paper industry
compulsive masturbation
hardcore amateur porn and dildo robots
epistemic anarchism
Satan
commonplace genius
the stupidity *of* genius
the genius *of* stupidity
poverty (in the first person)
not being touched by a woman
suicide
the sort of boredom that inspires suicidal thought
manic or major depression
Thought
simulation
seduction
repressive de-sublimation
psychology
dread
resentment
alien-ness
or suicide

What do you expect when someone starts writing books when they have already written for ESPN other than that their readership is made up of the people who take the suggestions of Amazon or iBook or whatever over their own conscience—women wearing professional cocktail dresses on Tinder/OKCupid/LinkedIn/Tumblr/etc.?

Journalists write democratically for a 4th grade reading level

and win
(the opposite of playing).

Lena Dunham first played a writer on TV,
then wrote a best-selling book.

Baudrillard: "[cynicism]…writers
that write only the fact that they are writers…[cynicism]"

212. Poverty is a slimming diet, and I became a model because I had a pretty frown

The *kitchen*—the place where *food is prepared*—
is either a conspiracy or a scam.
I always have ingredients, but they never go together,
so, I am constantly eating out—
and the ingredients I have never get used so I have to throw them out.
But then I will buy them again at the supermarket—
the floor plan of which they say is designed to make you hungrier and more impulsive
so you shop more aggressively.
The kitchen, where they make what satisfies—
the one-man factory that comes built right into the apartment—
may be designed/could very easily be designed
with the same rationale.
And the living room is modern enough to make you hate being home
so you pay substantially for your own absence
and the mere possibility of a return.

I try to combine ingredients

and make 'really unique' and thus hip food.
(The difference between food pictures and ass pictures on social media
is up for debate.)
I have thought of myself as a chef.
I am my own personal chef and personal stylist/cameraman—
writing my fate like an easy A for following the assignment,
dreading how exhausting could be the tedium
of a constant, transparent, self-written obituary.
The division of labor was ugly, but shit—
without it our cheeks are spread even further apart
and our asshole opens and closes like a door on a space station
like automatic doors that signify the ease with which retail stores
bleed into the on-the-go crowd.

The food I make with random ingredients almost
always takes like shit.
I would be booed by celebrity chefs on a cooking show
and escorted off the premises by security personnel.
Everyone would forget about me by the end of the commercial
break.
I'm not sure if the shit I throw together in a pinch
counts as stoner food or not.
I do often smoke pot, mainly because I need to be hungry.
It can pacify cancer and impoverishment but cure nothing.
Maybe I will start a food truck…
I'm wondering why almost all hipsters are chefs or food
bloggers…
Maybe I could be a starvation blogger.

When I cook breakfast, the TV is playing the Today Show
and I want to believe it's live.
I think news anchors
are just viewers filmed reacting (corresponding) to the news

as they read it from the teleprompter *for the first time*.
I think what is more important for consumers than news
is people's reaction to it.
I like to be disgusted in the mornings to feel alive—
preparing for cancer, the beyond-death, with nausea
and getting cancer or losing death in the simulation.
Nothing says like TV
"you are in *this* world, *this world is real,*
no other world is like this world that is a crystallization of the others,
where the virtual is consumed as raw experience."
The kitchen is experienced as a restaurant—
this is great for business.
For a home is necessary to found that homey-vibe you find dining out.

I have been meditating by sitting outside in 90-degree heat.
I don't get high.
I have never really transcended anything, only condescended.
I sweat out most of the food
I have angrily purchased at some eatery I do not like but is convenient.
Then that pisses me off.
The food seizes my body with its solid magmatic runs.
I think food should be free,
but only the sun is—
and it is basically *giving* me cancer
the gift of the inhuman
whereby death thankfully still circulates
because I once internet searched
"suntan lotion conspiracy."

I really have nothing against it and am just lazy.

But I think sitting in the sun for too long
would be a terrific way to commit suicide.
It is sort of like the car-on-in-garage method.
If you kept putting on suntan lotion and didn't eat,
you'd never get burned.
You'd fall asleep in agonizing pain that lacks the value of a motivator.
I will kill off a character in a novella that way,
one on which I'll tell people at cocktail parties I am working.
One that I'll never finish—out of boredom.
There have been hunger-strikes—what about heat-exhaustion strikes.
Seems effective geopolitically.

So goes the speculative philosophy of our times
that still benefits wholeheartedly
from its misunderstanding of the very spaces it confines its action to.

213. The remnants of a poem I wrote about Iraq, having never been there

You can only dig through shit to find gold—
you can only reduce something to mere material
when you sift through it to find something else meaningful in it.
You dig through shit when you have a goal.
Everything you work on is shit...

Before, a soldier said "This is *my* rifle."
The two—one a person, one a thing—
had an intimate relationship
like a husband who knew his wife wasn't cheating on him.

He paid for her and she took care of him.
They loved each other in other words.

The situation is no longer a relation of compliance or patriarchy.
No Daring. No sacrifice for the end,
yet a constant fear of the consequences of commitments.

The gun jams—not because there is sand in the firing chamber
(that would still involve mechanism).
Today, the gun jams because of some belief the gun has about itself
or some expectation it has about the future.
It is integral and has total field awareness.
We humanized the gun at the expense of its functionality
and ours.
It will fire when ready, not you.

There was once marksmanship
and wars were won based on the ability of the marksman—
or by capital outright.
The former is no longer the case
while the latter persists because it has no contents—
but in a way beyond the utopia of critique, desire or use
(because operation is different than use).

The gun marks the targets for you
(the State labels the dead in advance)
and informs you of the appropriate time to fire.
You weren't needed for the war—
you just went to say "I did that" like a marathon runner.
You weren't needed, just your fingerprints, to activate the gun—
just your code.
And anyway, you never mattered as an individual,
not even as a labor power.

Tr@nsf®@t

You were information.
A single cell from your own body carried more weight
for you were a model
from which a series of individuals could be produced
more efficiently than if by sex.
Your judgment wasn't as efficient as an intelligence.
You were fatal if you had an intelligence of evil,
so you disappeared.

You were *an accessory* to the crime *of perfection*,
mucking it up thusly but sustaining the negativity of its
impossibility.
Not the utopia of an instrument
you were a nostalgic showpiece—
or someone to blame if the tech failed.
It was a video game.
Mountaineering.
Exercise.

And when you came home,
you showed up at the bar where the guys have tumors for biceps
as if they'd put a bar of soap down a sock.
Like they do in prison.

214. Pit of Balls/Parisian Occupation of Texas

If I had dicks for knuckles
I would punch you in the face,
daring you to chuckle
about my gentle pace.

If my Voice were fainter

355

I'd photograph my works and destroy
all the originals in a ploy
to become an *original* painter.

If I were more proactive
I'd slogan "Love to hate your city,"
capitalize on such ditties
and spin Evil on its Axis.

If I could let go of me
I'd be sure to Progress,
but the person in my place, you'd see
still got lucky on a guess.

If I wasn't so unfree
I'd pay for all your drinks and dinner,
but when I got up to pee
I wouldn't feel the winner.

If I was *in charge*
it was the rope around my balls
that made them large,
not the reading of John Rawls.

East and West play racket ball
in a courted monism—
in a gym where mirrored walls
play Tetris with edge-obsessed vision.

To do a cannonball
you assume the fetal position,
while I imagine the pitfalls
of the sun's nocturnal emissions.

Tr@nsf®@t

Bukowski ended up a guru
because everyone's a fiend,
but they *added* all *that* 'should-do'
to a man honestly being mean.

The same fools would ask Nietzsche
to provide a criterion—
something that while super freaky
could still *last* a whole eon.

No one knows despair
who always has an agenda.
They travel together and have affairs
with their satisfied pudenda.

Me? I'm lonelier than Bukowski—
who cannot himself be trusted.
The world carried on without me
just like it truly must've.

But then I go out into it
like a stethoscope to a wall.
And somehow into the stinking pit
I always drop the ball.

But every time I *am* listening
you rip the speakers from my ears,
knowing when I pick up on social cues
is the only time I give cheers.

215. *This is the life I chose*

Responsibility has a stranglehold around human life,
unappreciative of the weight or the seduction.

The judge gives us the option of either pain or stupidity
and we are usually coerced into a plea deal involving both.

"That's the life that she chose" is what they say about her
when she is strung out on the dope
that her dope-lover pricked her with like yesterday's love.
He says he will kill himself whenever she is about to leave
and excoriates her when she is home.
And she was once a straight A student—
her parents forced her, but she liked the credit.
And she was a pyromaniac as a child who butchered rabbits.
She thought the dope would pair with the art,
but the pathos just pulsated
instead of expressing itself in words.

Who would want to be there?
Who would *choose* to be there?
They sit up against the wall on a mattress on the floor
in the corner of the room beside a gun,
staring at a brand-new tablet pc and falling asleep mid-sentence.
Her consciousness goes off the rails
before she can't finish the proposition of leaving
because the tracks are on her emaciated arms.

I could break him when he speaks to her the way he does
but the drug-mind would call me a fascist.
He belittles the Mexican lady setting up his internet connection
over the phone.
He tells my friend she doesn't understand his sense of humor

when she tells him he's being an asshole.
He says something about tacos and something about Tijuana.

But "that is the life that she chose"
and I liberally refrain from intervening
because 'Nature is taking its course' and truly fucking *her*
rationality,
which feeds into the further development
of her penchant for a conglomerate nothingness,
a multi-rational incorporation of forces that—worse than
nihilism—
convinces her that she is free.
She says that she has "discovered" a way to exploit capitalism
in the greatest conceivable way.

She shows me the heels she wears to work:
7-inch mirrored-finished stilettos
so the perverts can get a good look at themselves
when she is on stage.
A little powder and glitter on her arms, ankles, feet and hands
and she looks sober and full of consent.
Make-up and make-believe
and she is a cover girl when the sheen of the pole certifies the
sequins
swinging like a grandfather clock in the digital age,
chiming the midnight of her free choice—
waking her but not making her rise.

People in award show audiences take a moment of silence
for whatever
and then give themselves a round of applause
for the depth of their feelings.
But a friend is in trouble
and because it is troubling, she is best left to her own devices,

her own 'truth'
and her 'choices'.
It is not my problem.
It is not my bad luck.
She is not my responsibility. 'She is responsible for herself.'

Because we are all burdens, us *irresponsible* ones
who learn the dimension of determinism and say no to achievement,
we become a drag
like a boot on the end of a $568 fishing pole.

A burden to the family
the government
the fellow man
to taxpayers and to God.
Those that are frozen like assets by careers
fear
and politics
morality
television judges—
those who are frozen like computer screens by insight and Eros.
They leave friends behind,
similar in behavior to the friends who go nowhere,
because "that's life."

216. Unjustly cared-for songwriter

If truth falls off the bone
we don't need to cut it up
'cause the privacy of home
determines when we cut a rug.

Tr@nsf®@t

One day I will be a "hotty"
when the sun's a supernova.
I'll massage your deserted body
like an unmanned space-rover.

Forever we go back and forth
and spin 'round like a bucket of water:
We let nothing spill as polymorphs.
Plus, Satan fucked Sin—his daughter!

Either afterlife or reincarnation
or decay that recycles nothingness,
our movements forward are frustrations
with no impression without a press.

Our distant entanglement constricts.
With lazy blood we moan "No!"
this organism from the sticks
who's imprecise without a Pro.

This Wissenschaft—of coat-hangers
unclogging hair-saturated drains—
is a burner phone for willful strangers
that leaves no causal remains:

our unraveled quilt become a rope
that suspends and raises us in reality.
Yet were it good, some wouldn't cope,
and life would be a real pity.

When our palms finally touch
the movie has already started.
And Here we *are*, if only *as such*,

alit by the matinee historically charted.

The spectacles always leave
an indention on the nose
when the way you perceive
generates a debt that you owe.

The tie off occurs on arms and boats
and the guilty tend to accuse
like the Silent withhold their votes
and the tenants pay more to renew.

Like the wax clasping the whiskey,
we have a tab *made to rip open*.
If only flourishing were a piano key,
we could pirate a compressed Chopin.

Like a drunkard working the stage
we go out in public mumbling,
but it isn't paramount to the age
that its performances are stumbling.

217. The One, Part II

Kerouac wore his flannel better,
but the grain on a film
can sell a knit sweater
better than the hem.

My presence is not a power-
to-purchase in disguise
driven to a killer

Tr@nsf®@t

to be recognized.

I don't want an impractical pet—
some pillow-talking elephant
that I won in a bet
that began with "bet you can't…"

We come from primitive mind
either desperate or maddened—
socially one of kind
when we come from the bad end.

I'll stay worthless
without money for Christians,
get the aggression off my chest—
byway of the wishin'.

Wish in one hand
shit in the other.
In the Clearing stand
attentively Uncovered.

Symbols are a shit show
and Nature Doesn't Care.
But I do! Soooo…
discriminate *That* from *There*!

The First Principle
is Break the Law
because God piddled
when he separated needle from straw.

If the Will was an illusion—
a post-hoc fable accompanied—

what madness could accuse one
of *acting on* thinking?

Hipsters squatting in timeshares
and churning out e-novels
think that Respect compares
to other-directed grovels.

Is it the Ride that's spiritual?
Or the falling off,
when you can't hear the bull
pass through the red clothe?

An elephant rocks in a cage.
The chains below her knees
weaken slowly with a discreet graze
so today she can Ground the trapeze.

Burn it all down won't you
to make keychains and stress balls
from the thickening goo
that seeps when the Wild 'calls'.

When the One began to sweat
the beads emerged as many
and eventually all those off-bets
made things *categorically uncanny*.

Now immersing it in *plenty flame*
the informed masses accrete
the distance-less Other lame,
rubbed raw by electricity.

218. Three O(D)'s

God looked at a few billion years
and Said "Let's *wrap it up.*"
It's like He too after several beers
removed the condom to test his luck.

Look at all our productions—they suck!
And if I'm to anthropomorphize,
I'd say God created us all in a rush—
a writer at the mercy of publishing deadlines.

He gets a rush paying last-minute rent.
Creating a Universe was resented as work.
Even if he was pleased, he's spent,
and Consciousness was an *unintentional* quirk.

Who cares? So God was a little lazy.
And what if the Good was *His boss*?
Maybe the World's Night was for Him hazy.
And maybe the creatures were for Him a loss.

It's agreeable to Lie when in a hurry—
to make a path one must clear it first.
That happens on one's toes as surely
as Asians dance through rain with dry shirts.

Some can write on a shifting train
if we bear down hard enough.
Our strokes are 'genius' only if we *misaim*—
instead of at the wrist, at the cuff.

The seas rise like a shaken beer,
and a space left to Nature is unrecognizable.

The sun is a glory hole through which God peers
frozen, fascinated, wholly incapable.

Some are duller than soap opera characters,
and that seems hard to pull off—
harder so than the rug beneath the barrier
to objective, in-itself thought.

219. Jarry-rigged

If men really are Pigs,
let them use their corkscrew dicks
to uncork a bottlenecked World,
hardly, as it were, uncurled.

Umbrella floats when you let go.
You stay gravely grounded though.
In the whimsy, at its whim you get
conventionally *more painfully* wet.

What is a talent but a ledger
that only exists *as it develops*,
something you can only measure
when you grind the reef to a polyp?

And why do I want to see
who loses the rose ceremony?
Is it that the human shows itself
in the illnesses disguised *in health*?

Reality TV is like the Holocaust
when what is shown is what is lost,
inventing what it's proven by.

Tr@nsf®@t

The experiment's the alibi.

The mutilated bodies of Iraq,
the bloated stomachs of Sudan,
the pigment-less skin of the salon
without slack—closed, smooth & tan—

when peasants quote philosophers
or brutes express their introversion,
DNA compares to synthetic polymers—
aesthetics of incursion.

I want to defile Goethe and Bukowski
by sewing them tackily together.
The cultural highpoint of Germany
can't withstand Jarry forever.

Put culture into a hyperbaric chamber,
get Klosterman and Sedaris.
But *all* the yellow words seem garish
when the lemonade left a canker.

220. incoming outrage against outrageous income (of artists)

Poem:

They sold little casts of my intestines
but I had to ingest the molding.
The models were raffled as funnel cakes
made of the impoverished smiles

of untapped fire hydrants in July on the North South East or West
end.
My stomach was always a public pool
stuffed with the offspring of the poor—
the lakes, cheaper, are too polluted
and the swimming holes of Before have been filled by the tire dust
dispersing from our wheels on the way to the pool.

The country?
Remember the country?
What happened to the country?
What happened to Kipling?
Bukowski tiptoeing through the woods and ruining a whole eco-
system.
It was like a giant tarp was laid over the country for fumigation,
if that tarp turned out to be a projection screen.
The locals looking up to God
saw only the haze of the city
like a chemical peel reversing the age of the Earth.

Thoughts:

"I'm glad moths don't fly into the whites of my eyes"
is a line Tao Lin would have written.

Poetry?
What happened to poetry
when it brought things together to tear things apart—
to rip open the language of its readers
and reveal the transfinity of *the relatable* with a sustained effort?
Goethe—he was a scientist and had love affairs with 19-year-olds
in his 70s with psoriatic arthritis
and a republic that knew him and found him dangerous
as he blessed the Nation.

Tr@nsf®@t

E. E. Cummings—who the fuck is E. E. Cummings?
Someone told me she had only read *him*.
She was getting a master's in philosophy
and planned on getting a doctorate in psychology
but had never read Freud.
Daniel Dennett is a name I would throw out.
Tao Lin—if I had an e-reader and enjoyed irony a little more,
maybe he'd impress me.
Maybe then I'd identify with my time.
Meta-modernists are a possible market I could exploit—
but I will not reach the extreme limit of functionality, irony.
Apparently, I am either pre- or post- millennial
and might be "the iPhone generation."
I have never tweeted,
but the person who wrote American Psycho, the book, said so.
Doesn't he hate women?
How could he understand *me* then?

The poets? Where are *my* poets? Could *a* poet be lacking in *his* poets?
Probably not.
I don't respect other poets.
I don't want to be tainted with their approval either.
I see them as backwards,
too caught up in either the infinite
(the pure circulation of words, nihilism without praxis)
or the finite (hyperrealism, pornography of the visual,
purely descriptive and ultimately acritical
or insufficiently critical insofar as, so their logic goes,
the real critiques itself).
They repeat what is and thus *say nothing*.
I could die without being published.
Without or with—no difference.
I am a poet—that is a limit.

If I spent more time grinding,
that behavior of the day of either spenders
or of strippers, pimps or prostitutes,
maybe I'd have love affairs
and fun
and an audience.

Reader concerns:

Ariel, what's your deal?
Don't you *want* to be read? Don't you want *to be* a poet?
What is an artist if not a narcissistic type
that deepens the false consciousness of his readers
who almost always think they are comparable to him—
and how pleasant *that* is!
If I was less afraid of the career suicide Ayn Rand comparisons grant,
I'd advise the talented artists to stop producing altogether…
they'd communicate their silence and the reality of the situation.

"Give us something to believe in!!"
(Even if such a belief is the belief
in the anesthetic irony that can allow the multitudes of the talentless
to enjoy the slow decline of humanity,
cynicism,
even Nietzsche can be read as making whatever shapely stupidity tolerable for whomever.)

Comments:

Even the disillusioning reinforces illusion.
Or else intelligence could be *finally* liberated with only its continued use

or its projection, condensation or installation
into the opaque object with 'artificial intelligence'
in which intelligence is merely the accumulation of discourse.
Intelligence become a fact
studied in a lab.

To the readers (practical concerns):

"I am not your comrade.
And if you have been confirmed or disconfirmed by me,
then you have misread me.

Reader response:

"But to get praise, one must give it?!"

My rebuttal:

"Be suspicious of those reading their poetry electively,
who are not getting paid for it.
They care more about community MORE than truth,
and so only get the latter as a deferral of the former…
They are either fulfilling their private need to express themselves
(not to deny anyone their narcotics)
or they are following public demand
to produce live on stage for an audience.
And who has ever trusted their friends or girlfriends
as their critics—
sweet old ladies aren't always good judges of character.
Many of them live with junkies
who slowly empty out their medicine cabinets.
Don't forget that payment was the only reason Buk read at all—
economic coercion.
He was honest. And his is the *only* legitimate reason!

Poeisis isn't poetic writing but life-writing."

To the critics (the judges or formants of public taste):

Poetry through anti-poetry isn't even new,
but poetry that doesn't break tradition is still shit to someone.
Anti-poetry's fan base is mainly 15-29-year-olds—
and when have they been credible when it comes to taste?
They are so inexperienced.
I write this at 26...*That* should alarm you.
New shit vs. old shit.
Black, hangover shit vs. green, leafy shit.
What kind of poetry am I writing?
Not the kind Heidegger examined.
Not in the American or French traditions.
Tzara would get knocked the fuck out.
The Greeks, at least *they* were manly and understood tragedy.
I am not the poet of the street or of nature.
I am not even a poet, *so I say*.
The poetry coming out of my ears, my nostrils, my eyes, my mouth
or my anus—
it is a poetry that gathers all the things produced hitherto;
it is just as Plato suspected, where high is low, and low is subterranean.
McLuhan or total field.
The hard-earned fame of Napoléon
and the instant fame of Paris Hilton,
and the transfinite Tube fame of amateur porn and Justin Bieber.
The effortful and the wasteful and the pluperfect.
The whole artifice of humanity—
poetry repeats it and says "de nada."
World production
world disclosure

world erasure
world fusion
world confusion…which is which?

How irresponsible of and costly for *real poets*…

221. life crisis or something

We sit *together* separated by a ground-level window,
as if not *in proximity*,
the birds and I—
they become visible in the perennially vacating trees
and puff themselves up to avoid the dissolution
of a temporary tundra,
snow-blind and without a backdrop.

We outlast it together,
the snow.
They by numbers and order and accumulated fat—energy.
Me indoors, depressed because I got no matches on the app
and in solidarity with creatures that should disgust me
but preferably wouldn't affect me at all
like I don't affect myself and thus lack difference and an image.

We are separated as if by a disfiguring accident—
something not partially unnatural,
too quick and straight for Nature's cycle.
The snow crystal displays a kind of lag in itself
and seems to fall only reluctantly
due to the quickness with which it formed.
This character transposes itself onto a slow accumulation,
the opacity of which appears spectral

as it thickens like stacks of bleached paper.

They strive in the snowstorm
as I strive against an illustrative mania,
an imagination that *puffs me up, topically,*
like the birds' physiology—
by way of being the topic of conversations between strangers
who are probably talking about birds over me.

They fight the cold while I fight the sad sads,
which I experience as if it never arrives or gradually grows
(presupposing a path with me as its destination)
but suddenly appears like Ms. Winter (single and harsh forever),
who always proves the weathermen to be ratings-increasers
and science to be a harried spectacle,
frustrated by the system of signs and by the *image's homage*
that its instruments hypertrophied and hypostasized in the virtual,
that changes the psychology of those
to whom it evidences its predictive superiority.
She appears *into Life* like the famous femme fatale *into the room*
(inhabiting the communication between the décor
in the space of their contiguity—the system of objects itself—
as sign among signs).
Nothing can be done to woo her.
The men sword fight over her with their erect cocks
that must function symbolically
exactly like the fossil or the image or the simulation:
to *extend death.*

Like ancient predators become miniature
and weather patterns become storm systems,
the slush of despair *bites*—
like a shark curious about a surfboard—
leaving a hardened, blackened organ that won't fall off on its own,

must be severed with the mediation of society
(but the roads are iced over)
and I sit indoors unshielded and equal to the birds
but less than them in my eyes
because I am worried about getting stiffed on a 9$ app plate
or getting a spontaneous BJ when I have toilet paper stuck to the tip
from prior masturbation.
This despair like an image
destroys and projects me as if my continued existence
were a constant resurrection
(which, of course, requires a crucifixion).
Rather, it carries me like a newborn by the back of my neck
as if by a cat who ate my undesirable brothers and sisters
like genes/secretions fix the birds
(while they only *move* us).

222. Tao Lin is a little bit weirder than I am

The screen reels. It realizes.
And what does it realize? Reality.
Like a deep cut.
It is damn near vaginal—
the abyss below the tripod that smelled, they say, like post-period pussy,
the stench of ovulation
that attracted those seeking wisdom to a death beyond the visual.

I ate pussy last night from behind
and easily transitioned to the asshole.
She was a dead fish—my technique was failing a misunderstood body.

I became embarrassed then forgot about it.

223. force-feeding optional

Living or income. Value or price. Humanity or humanitarianism.

We cut ourselves like some do:
with words or drugs/
through work or strike/
with sharp objects, sharp wit and intense orgasms.
To cut yourself you must be conscious—
for intensity, you must be tense.
Otherwise, you are knotted and all too acquainted with yourself.
Knights kneel, a position otherwise reserved for the beheaded.
Cutters are neither kings nor executioners.
They are too horny to work
but work *part time* to blunt their libido that's too strong for leisure—
that the libido,
become a kind of ultimate commodity,
denies work but denies rest in the process.
That the unemployed masturbate at higher rates
has not so much to do with excessive leisure time
as with excessive libido,
but not Freud's libido that was *a source of work,*
where work simultaneously produced the ego
and the object through which the ego superseded itself,
mitigating the influence of the inner authority.
This libido is more a floating, collective libido
that has the properties of information—
passing through everyone from without
and never quite leading to *actual oeuvre*

but to the production of signs that needn't lead to any action,
not even the poetic action words used to levy on language and life.
Being everywhere, this 'libido' may as well not be one at all,
since what is excessive is libidinization,
or constant arousal (attachment to and seduction by the object).

Always about to bust, cutters—
the accidental children of positive culture—
see the orgasm as an opening that is a physical loss
and an affective gain.

They know the sadistic freedom afforded to hourglasses
that function by being turned over, reversed.
They see their pleasure
as the scarecrow sees its stuffing carried by a wind,
that is, unable to see it!
Certainly, without the obliteration of the inhuman by discourse.

224. Kim KarDasein is a hot lil' Cummodity

Surrealism just won't die.
But the imaginary is dead.
The icon moves in the green glow of night vision on the porno
like a sleepy Komodo with the –Itus.

The words can mean anything, so they mean nothing
because nothing is easily reproducible.
Daily life of this jobless critic is nearly dissociative.
I'm running into the underpass from zombies wearing Go-Pro
cameras
in a zig-zag pattern to avoid and obscure their focus,
and yet the latest batteries started to go out in my Fleshlight.

The glimmer of vague hope flickers in my eyes
(and the hopelessness doesn't hurt as bad
due to its vagueness)—
I uncap my drive of its child protection
so that my inner light becomes a CRACK lighter.

The photographers lick me to death with aftermarket tongues,
long after the lube has lost it lubricity,
to make good on their claims
as affectionate cows whose rest secretes products.

In my dying climax, I make out with myself
during a private screening of the memories I hoarded in my life.
My life become an indie film,
low budget and rustic for how proletarian (*uneventful*) it is,
that feels unnaturally quirky and tries too hard to end ambiguously.
This private session of me watching myself jerk off.

Yet I fast forward to the good part *of the porno*.

225. what the hell kind of show is this?

The car is never going to stop
and turn around
and the driveway will hitherto
remain empty and spotless
pressure-washed (washed *of* pressure).

There will never be a knock on the door
with a soaking-wet beauty on the other side
who travelled by foot to see you in the rain.

Tr@nsf®@t

There will never be a double-take
or a call-back
or a suitcase dropped
by lone woman revealed behind a bus as it drives away.

There will be no perfect day
and no days at the zoo
or in a park
or in Paris—
not even Paris, Texas
where most people, says the movie, are only passing through.

The event is only aesthetic
when sequentially withdrawn from the whole of time,
that is, in its hyperreality.

226. we already live forever

The speed of infrared
of information
and the primitivism of the object
or the commodity
or the gold standard.
The chair-swing obeys gravity upon your exit.
Its swoon is the wave of your disappearance.
You can look at the ductile pendulum, tempting you into capturing it,
as a sign of your presence
your own history
and think to yourself in assurance that no one was on the swing
that in fact there never was a swing
and that there wasn't anything all the way down to 1's & 0's

(the conjunction being only provisional since the two are
ubiquitous)
and below them.

Moment approaching moment but never reaching the next,
never approaching zero along a decadent curvature,
slowed more and more by its own inertia
in contact with nothing but itself.

We are months apart calendrically
but light-years apart from one another,
so far that we see each other only after we die.
We never make astral connections with one another
because we are hung on our own and the properties of light,
our otherness iconized in and terminated by the computer,
like in a dream in which you are being chased,
running, falling, not going anywhere, but never touched by the tail.
(Perhaps dogs dream of being chased by their own tail—
in so doing they would be wiser than we.)

Even then there is a dark energy expanding the distance between
us
at a faster rate than previously expected by the Other,
while most of our inheritances are bloatware
that in their turn cannot be deleted.

We do *all* we *can* do:
consume our history
consume History as something that *can't itself be historical.*
(Maybe one day we will look back and remember
when people watched the History Channel week to week
after watching history 'as it happens' via the media—
they will be misunderstood and retain their strangeness.
With their heads shaved they would have looked their insanity.

Of course, there is also a grisliness to *our* upkeep).

We consume geologic history
in the form of liquid that in turn liquefies the human like a spider—
we leave an exoskeleton that is whitened
as a token of our truth,
that is itself an internalization without depth—
a digestion from which nothing is gained,
like junk food passing right through the body.
The gains, too, diminish, but at least *they* Return Eternally.

We are consumers and nothing but,
capable of nothing but (except poetry and gay science).
And we leave less signs of life than you think.

But that would not be right
because we ourselves turn into gases
that are much easier and less costly to extract.
Perhaps this is to our favor,
but no one any longer believes in *that*.

227. Akrasia

O little bore,
is my attraction to you a little more than a fatal strategy?

Is your beauty *really* organic, or is what I see
not a thing more than my fatal strategy?

O little whore,
how are you situated in the 'wherefore' of my fatal strategy?

O little whore,
will your fame transfer to me and reify my banal strategy?

Your intellect,
o talkative little bore,
I do expect is not a silly thing more than your ideology.

Your appearance,
o fashionable little bore,
is per chance not a visible thing more than your fatal strategy.

This *meeting*,
o friendly little whore,
is it more than an impossible fleeing?

228. The cornices of limits

Buried in the sands of Time is an IED of its own possibility.
You cannot see it
and by extension you are unconscious of its existence.
Your ears ring after the explosion
and afterwards you likely *hear differently*.
With explosive excitement there is an implosion of meaning.
It jars your brain and you become jar-headed—
that refraction of hard-headed.
Opened on the spot but not yet with anything to fill it.

When Time marks you *with your own disappearance*
sometimes you receive the change in difference
like a handshake of honorable defeat by a rival-become-friend,
but most often it is an agonizing severance of pay.

You embellish this new other
into an even more unrecognizable *personality*
(the supposed genera of the *person*).
You repeat the destruction with the baroque bombast of the wrestler
who really becomes an ahistorical hero
whose reverence approaches the subject of cannibalism—
beyond the mere sadomasochism of an actor.
You one-up Time with a simulation
that not only recognizes but accelerates the disappearance.
You give *expression* to the *impression* of a Fate.

229. Tattooed and pierced Christians

To postpone their big *finale*,
the workers like to dilly dally.
Their profiles say they love God.
They also love their iPod.

The *punks* all taking videos
and embellishing lil' idioms
that they searched hard for—
supporting the Marine Corps.

They don't just tell you the news
but what people are saying about it
and how it will affect *you*—
4th grader that defines 'legit'.

And these are the Active ones
energized by an inner God.
They move mountains for fun,

their presence more than a façade.

They like to keep their quiver full
but are choosey about perversion.
They must market Him as Cool—
sew the scalpel *in* as spacey surgeons.

While the rich jerk each other off,
the poor watch, criticize and scoff
and defer the eradication of idiocy
so they can lay claim to literacy.

All the work is oriented at a Beyond
and in death, you finally *get off*.
Not unlike the scum in the pond,
in trade—we're linked only at the cuff.

Americans have very large penises,
but the fur worn by Venus is
protested on social media
lightly and sweetly like the stevia.

The philosopher's stone
comes from the mac and cheese.
The psychologists postpone
patients' self-management as they please.

The red hair of the Devil
and the daily use of the Dirt-devil,
is for these puritans excused
…but group sex is still refused.

The Chinese exit the train
when a fellow man faints.

Tr@nsf®@t

If Christ cared about carpet stains
we'd not appreciate women's taints.

ALL IN THE GREATER GLORY!
But Christ emerged from a hole in the wall
and never left his number on the stall.
God had His number—*that's* the story.

230. Shel Silverstein Died in Key West, Florida

There was a guy in a creative writing class
that I took at a community college,
this gangly little white guy with glasses
and curly hair,
pale skin,
and a huge Adam's apple
who admitted he had sever stage fright *in front of the whole class*
and wrote a poem about having stage fright
when he was covering The Smashing Pumpkins
at his local church during a talent show,
chocked full of friends and family.

Fucking Christ…

He wrote another one about an asterisk
or a dwarf or dying star or something.
The last line may not have been "maybe even I was beautiful once,"
but it will do for our purposes here.

He complained to the teacher
when I insulted him via my assigned criticisms.

I bet he will be published, whatever that means.
If this gets published, it is publication of him.
Fuck.

But what do you expect from a species that could even pity photons?
Or write a poem about a nerd.
The same species that will give a hug to be sweet
and stretch their neck out hysterically but thinly,
as if touching their face to the other person
was the most grotesque thought or thing

Don't take this one-armed hug *those* poets offer you
due to the microphone held by the other.

Now back to you, Reader.

231. imposter syndrome

How things turn to their opposites
we scarcely see yet know.
As if I *hid* the artistic components
when I was a cool bro!

The drugs, the music, the internet
or the regular turn of age,
where youthful ties dissolve unmet
like school after spring break?

A profile deleted at its ignorance
was not a cunning vote

but wings that disappeared to a glance
like the flap in the fricative throat.

The relation of the story to the news
in the way it is spun?
The relation of events to speech
at the level of fun?

Like a chicken with gliding wings,
useful only at a throw,
I've endured like a rubber cock-ring
to last by ensuring flow.

My grammar only developed
when I became a mute,
when latency became a relic
the future could compute.

Met first with indignation,
whence they silence their alarms
every child who's *of the nation*
holds a copy in her arms.

Yet as from print to e-reader
what I first lost was space—
that with all leechers and no seeders
freezing *set* the pace.

232. Ego depletion

How exhausted we are at the choices,
almost herded through the grocery.

For we, *as if* hearing autodidactic voices,
revolve through—chicken on the rotisserie.

The decision is not necessarily the action.
Imagine if we deliberated on our steps!
We'd wander out away, but never back *in*—
and without energy to estrange or digress.

Like rabbits hooked up to cocaine feeders,
we are tired once we look at the menu.
We broke bonds and became cheaters
because we had to decide on the venue.

You ever opened the cabinet stunned?
Lost your appetite during the cooking?
To keep alert you'd have to be a nun,
but you'd get to do a lot of looking.

You almost wonder. It's like we *knew*,
and Bodies responded more than Thought.
But because it's irrelevant exactly who,
sleepily we *choose* to serially stop.

233. Give Nature privacy

Could you prefer anticipation to reminiscence,
a savory periscope for trampling pissants?
To get there, ask what is there to be done anew
when the Previous *essentially* obstructs the view.

What is a part to a whole? That's part of a question
that emerges like the gel from the pectin—

Tr@nsf®@t

and how is the Answer original from the Clue?

How many tokens from a type can be drawn—
likewise, how many novel tastes commercially farmed?
Distinguish how between atonement/attainment
when the fetish economy is a religious arrangement?

I remember my debts to Wallace Stevens
and acknowledge that the scenery across nations
are just randomized differences in elevation
daring the World—with the earth—*to get even.*

The processes, they say, are uniform—
and we are creatures whom 'mere facts' can harm.
But with dread or not, let's not exaggerate
the magic of what a hand creates.

Our artificial departures don't get far,
but it is better that we take the Bate
for without our illusions we lack a fate.

In our strife, I'll be damned if the covering fire
didn't give away our positions. Like narks wired,
we have had our soft sediments patted
by Nature, on whom we would have ratted.

What would it be to give Nature privacy
if our disruptions erupted from being too avid
and freedom wasn't action adlibbed?

234. Denouncing-nunnery

Somebody told me that my poems were "good,"
that I'm a good writer
but that they are not deconstructive enough
and might reinforce the mimed contents.
Poems are filled with nothing but feathers
and their contents burst out of them
when schoolgirls use them to pillow fight,
which is not a fight *exactly*.

The somebody who spoke thus
creeped into my head later and asked with victimized verve:
'Ariel, don't you care about global hunger
global economic disparity
global poverty
global misery
global war
global terrorism
global racism
global sexism
classism
nationalism?
Couldn't you write something about feminism
environmentalism
anti-capitalism?
Then your talents wouldn't go to waste.
You will never make it as a poet unless you *promote* issues."

I thought to myself about being the marketer
of the Revolution Reformation:
"You misunderstand me both as a human being and as a poet.
Above all you confuse poetry with journalism.
Second, you confuse journalism—that metastable positivism—

Tr@nsf®@t

with action.
Give me the tangent of at least a few remarks
on what I am doing—*my objective.*'

To begin, literature is *the* (only?) deconstructive art,
and were poetry ever reduced to literature
all writing fictive or scientific would disappear.
If I started writing on graph paper
not only would I be making *a statement*
(an assertion, or repetition of what exists)
I would get to explain *why* I did as such.
But here do not take my remarks *as explanations*.

I will not push the issues *because* to do that one must be
pathological.
Their logic must be pathos—
the pathetic whose pathos is both real and imagistic
insofar as it never goes beyond the thesis.'

'Doesn't anything matter to you?'
this other responds,
'are you an active or passive nihilist?
TO WHAT DO YOU BELONG!?
WHEREFORE ART THOU????
Don't you feel guilty when you are…like…informed
but *choose to do nothing* in response?'

To do that, one must be a voice.
A voice for the powerless
a voice for the disinherited
a voice and representative
for myself above all.
But you are the voice and I only *respond* to your absurd
questioning

that is, I calculatedly repress my intentions
in a court of appeal.

If I take at least one matter 'seriously'—
if you want to call it that—
it is my writing.
And if I represented one thing, one thing at all—
which I do not (redundantly) *'necessarily have' to do*—
it would be writing.
It won't act except on language
to make language collapse on its own weight,
to *terrorize* language
and make it show its Power
that will waste its own citizens to remain closed and thus significant.
If I chose to do nothing,
that would at least be something that I cared about.
Still, *you* are the one who *makes* me represent.
I express non-signification (not in itself but in *this world*).

I am sorry that my "care"—
an ethic that always ends up endorsing—
doesn't show through.
But you *do know* it is precisely Evil
that shows through the Good in its transparence?

And wouldn't the only deconstructive thing left for literature to 'do'
be to deconstruct deconstruction—
which is also the *most constructive* thing,
as writing "put to appropriate use" and thus 'credible' *as such*?

Only poetry could accomplish that—
because it doesn't understand what that even means,

Tr@nsf®@t

(a meaning above the everyday).

Here is one of many self-descriptions you will get
from this 'willingly' voice-less poet:

"I am like a black hole drawing the world towards me
but making it stop as an image just beyond my throat.
Having to always look away from it, I make it face me:
the juxtaposition of me the bystander against a world that—
though I can barely stand it—is made to stand up for itself.
I am a terrorist you might say—
but one that cannot be incriminated and is thus even *more*
annoying.
Nanny nanny boo boo poetry—
not anything like a rapist who forces his victim to *refuse consent*
and repress—at the limits of consciousness—their brutality.
This is a little non-consensual (for me) poetry.
It is not even a poem since it is a mere response.

I am not a solipsist because that is a theory.
But I am not opposed to drawing the world off stage with a hooked
cane
not so that it may pay me a little attention backstage
but to make it a little darker, less focused and the center of
attention.
The curtain is directed at an audience,
but I have backstage passages,
and like an untrue friend
I tell of the monstrosity the audience designedly misses.

If this were fast pitch, in which case poetry would be a fascinating
brute,
a fascinating woman sexed by a negation,
from which it isn't far off (because it's meaningless)—

the fast ball would not be frequently used.
Readers would get a little too comfortable
and accommodate their swing.

But poems are change-ups that give the illusion of a trajectory
such that by the time a perfect swing is already committed to
the trajectory changes
and the ball just scoots over the bat,
creating a barrier of air that repels the one from the other.
It is not far off from philosophy in that,
so long as a metaphilosophy still lingers,
even if its tattered maps really were deserted.

235. raspy poetry

I want to erase the poet's voice.
I am totally seduced
possibly dissolved
uncertainly inspired.

236. Animal Planet is strangely Human

I felt Lady Winter's fingernails
tug at and start to unfasten my belt
and creep caustically underneath my layers
as if pantheism heard my prayers.

I heard the drops from my nostril pound
as the cold gave me the reach around.
I grew frozen, hard, as if immediately sick—

Tr@nsf®@t

black as the desert seem from the Vegas Strip.

Nature, You are still superior to me;
you will always remain in my belly.
I can blame You when I'm in a rut—
or get drunk off You to numb my gut.

If You are a symptom I produce
when my personality becomes loose,
why do you come up my throat
from my gut like gators from the moat?

237. Bump in the Night/The bubbly girl on Train 9

The streets seizure
like a crony with his septum bashed into his brain.
The conversations on subways can be *felt*
like the buzz of the train
that works *with* your rigidity as it joshes you 45 degrees left
or 45 degrees right, until you're a perfectly rightly angled.

The people look down at the concrete as they walk
like they are children riding themselves on their own shoulders
but a little more like they are dead
(i.e., no longer dying, the hard part)—
as if they see their brain reflected in the *hardened* grey matter.

It looks like their brain on Alzheimer's.
A brain can turn to mush by one tap of the hammer
or it can take 5-80 years.
The sidewalk does the thinking/reflecting—
a warped shadow, never a false symmetry—

it walks for them
and they walk with it like the automaticity is offensive
to the legged finery of creatures.
It talks to them
as their thoughts bounce back at them from it
like hollow, inflated basketballs
that the inner-city kids bother the whites with at the amusement park
and overall the walk to the car is an empty form of entertainment
whose silence leads to paranoia in the echo of the deck.

The only silence you will ever have to yourself
is the silence of an audience just before the programming begins—
as descriptions about the world
are only supposedly those about a central nervous system
turned inside out.

"I know myself (because I 'think a lot of' *me*)."

I spot her out of the corner of my eye
(that is still Euclidean and Newtonian and yet round)
from approx. 30 ft. at the margins of the train
as it slows time for those looking in.
She had this look that said "get bent…" given to time itself.

At first, she wears glasses—the kind that swallow a woman's face
and serve as a centrifuge or diversion—either/or…

I can't tell if she is older younger attractive or whatever.
Even with all the details, I would still be significantly uncertain
whether she is good or bad for me.

As the train moves, the glasses come off.

Tr@nsf®@t

She looks like Amelia Earhart taking off her headgear in the movie.
She puts on sour apple lip gloss that makes her look trompe l'oiel.
Her face is oily, but it isn't a painting.
It is like graffiti—difficult to read on purpose
(but motivated by the rush).

And just for a moment, there is eye contact...
it lasts over 5 seconds.

I'm inspired to commit an act of insurrection:

I'll pour some ineffectual dish soap into a public fountain.

238. Inner Tube

You do not need the First,
and Presence is unnecessary
because it is sort of worse
than the copy, an emissary.

If you never met the person
that you hoped to marry
the love'd hasten, not worsen,
for profiles preserve their buried.

The passion is emaciated,
the distance visceral.
But the dirty stuff is mediated
like my lungs *on Albuterol*.

When the fucking streams frugally

you're not a mere spectator
but engage the lubricity
through an auto-regulator.

We will leave God the scorn
because it all happens in a flash
like the dicks going soft in the porn
until The Judgment is a blowout bash.

If anything's dead, it's men,
not merely Man, and technology
has gone soft. The masculine
stands insecure before the cunning.

Capitalism coopts the feminine
because the men are only *allowed*
and their supplies are limited,
but women can be endlessly plowed.

The feminine is a topical utopia;
the masculine is always getting spent.
The men are leaving the workforce,
and the ownership is all for rent.

When the gaps are filled, she can't think;
it's hard to move in the fluidity.
You can't tell the stink from the pink
when the Eye is separate from stupidity.

239. trick or treat, an inclusive disjunction

The trauma of a life

has before left me paralyzed
and *I* have had *far* less strife
than most other guys.

Previously spoiled rotten
and left stinking with shame,
though I've a spark I'm like cotton
without the butane.

The need to be a hero
and the need to be saved,
I'm as Roman as Nero
facing life by having coins made.

240. The fetish of love-making (or *love-production*)

I fetishize making love
and need you to look me in the eyes
when you're below and I above,
for wanting distinction from other guys.

If I am stuck with myself
I would like to stick my cum
on your belly just above your belt—
because together we are a sum.

The one you are with now
must thrust only blindly
because he is as dumb as a sow
if I'm to describe him kindly.

I never knew the beauty mark

marking the middle of your cheek.
Back then it was always dark
as we kept it tongue and cheek.

You'd sneak out & I'd pick you up
like an indebted hitchhiker after curfew.
To this day you kept your mouth shut,
and you never let me hurt you.

Your physical fitness worked but made
a triangulated and jagged back
exactly like a man's I'm afraid
with only a petite, boyish ass to smack.

And your clit would fold & dangle—
Like a cat, I'd nibble its angel-wings.
Unlike all the other women, your angled
thighs peremptorily lock onto me.

I a laborer and you less than a tool
that fits atop me like brass couplings—
we'd seal the pipedream unfueled
before you'd shop-vac my wet suffering.

Your flirtations, prematurely covert
and one at a time, were mine to perceive.
Not once did you think me an extrovert
with opportunity always up my sleeve.

Much time apart comes to a head
that can be agitated, picked and popped
when interiority that breaks out in bed
juts through continuous layers outcropped.

Tr@nsf®@t

241. We are all a psychologist's wet dream

I had nothing in my wallet,
but that's worth more than a credit card.
I ate some food that had been designed functionally—
anti-hunger—
and it killed my appetite without feeding me.

I was horny
so she got fake braces for her teeth because I thought youth was sexy
(but not as sexy as signs of youth
because they hide what was never there).
She said she liked to have her face fucked,
but it wasn't Facebook official.
Getting dentally drilled by an enormous cock is bad for your back,
but it gets lots of hits on porntube.com.

That is merely on the computer.

On the TV, people perform similarly hardcore acts on stage
in front of celebrity judge panels
for a million-dollar prize
in a game they weren't told existed until its live debut.
And don't we all perform like this for everyone (ourselves included)
from moment to moment—
in a constant failure
to live up to standards above and beyond the human
designed to wear us out spiritually
to make room for the religiosity of the Code?

Your life is a non-event
and the excitement is the electrocution of the medium,

charging and filling *the bar* of 'your libido'
(whence its containment and perpetual frustration/overload).

242. The elephants broke free

I'd be lying if I didn't want to see
all the captive elephants break free
and leave the global Miss America sash—
with their ribbon-cutting tusks—slashed.
Let them charge, trample and gore
like black people looting the shoe store
and cha-cha over downed circus tents
where silos accumulate endgame pretense.

243. Whiskey poetry or suicide

Somewhere, everyone was laid off
because they all stopped showing up.
They gave up the freedom to scoff
in bars where drinkers skip half-full cups.

"We don't do karaoke here," said the keep
and the syncopated melody in his voice
as forgiving as Jesus whipped the hill's steep
says "This weekend I finally get my boys."

There was a cowboy YouTubing Townes.
He'd scan the room with each sip of wine,
not looking at the beauty there behind
the bar in the cardboard Lost and Found.

Tr@nsf®@t

"Happiness is the greatest form of beauty,"
he said, but I knew I was an ugly lad
if I was a socially-constructed cutie
whose thought only touched the pad.

Sometimes people do themselves in
or their diseases provoke them to kill them,
little neural pathway plaque congestions
that haven't unlearned previous brilliance.

Psychic disorder, or rather brain disease,
is more than a mere good excuse—
if it were license to do as you please,
we'd have stayed unrepressed & in disuse.

I have lived quietly among a sleeper cell
who'd destroy me if triggers aroused.
With a nice, safe tan from a personal Hell,
I Keep my experience Housed.

The brain emerged as an expensive taste,
a customer service that exceeds its margins.
And if Ideas aren't already a kind of waste,
connections break as *matters* harden.

The neurons burn holes into themselves
become bile associated with increased salivation.
And if make-up were made of chalk…well,
let it add a calming closure-sensation.

In the mind, the singing acts are obsolete—
but they are little talentless fools with drive
that steal the thunder of origin when they succeed,

traveling faster than thought at the speed of light.

At our Best, we can always Go.
Luckier to be underwhelming
in a brief, brusque afterglow
than lost to information-telling.

Everything is a touching sob story
to antennae whose small frequencies
feel themselves up to a full-on worry
about the limits to our agency.

Of course, the word is not much to look at.
Like Eros & America it is a costlier detour—
at moments a nearly delightful one at that
that won't give a stiff drink a weak pour.

244. Harsh lighting

O cruel world,
you are my mirror on a day on which I look good
and don't deserve it because I bought nothing and put in no effort.

The womb is a body scanner at the mall
that articulates what style of blue jeans best fits the shape of your body.

In the future,
they will playback babies laughing throughout the office
and some people will be lulled into the docility of parenthood—
as parents that had children
because they could not handle their own freedom or individuality

Tr@nsf®@t

for lack of a project—
while others will feel post-partum depression about their labor
and through their behavior
seduce their bosses to fulfill a wish.

I feel like I am being face-fucked by Tyler Perry
Michelle Obama
and Rachael Rae—
but my No was ambivalent
and out of laziness rather than value or dialectic,
so the trial could've swung either way.
My body is just the string of vomit-spit dangling from my chin.
Or my body's like a McDonald's with a drive-through and no insides,
making it conveniently impossible to dine in.

I look out unto the world like a guest in the studio
smiling at the camera as it comes
but with a smile frozen on my face as if out of fear—
and yet I remain out of sight (or with sight that has run out)
because I am blinded by the totality of the lighting
that makes me look good and real,
a car rotating in the showroom
or a fat body rotating on a weight loss show as they give the statistics.

BOOK III

VOLUME V
FREE ADVERTISING

*The universe itself has always been poetic.
God's audience got impatient, so that God
spoke 7+ billion years into a week's worth
of events, and God's audience took their
tantric notes on that extemporization
and organized them into a small
puritan's Kama Sutra: here,
you are Roofied by
these copies
with no
origin.*

Free Advertising

245. an end to mourning, to mania, to melancholy, to another her/me

She showed herself again in July
when he left her because she would not love him
and he knew that but can't keep a secret.
And she would have stayed had he kept it to himself.
I welcomed her appearance.
She was more beautiful then
because she was reminded that we were made to die.
And her appearance had never so realistically reflected
the monstrous experiences she kept secret
so *she could stay*.
We agreed to be friends.
We both did so with hidden, seductive agendas.
But we both knew it impossible.
In the Historic District, she would grab onto my arm
like a high school girlfriend in a haunted house
where what is scarier is the hysteria of the mob
in the cramped corridors of the 'postmodern' social structure
that meanders with no end in sight like Snake ™ on old Nokia
phones.
A few tugs (lies) on my arm that day
and we were fucking on the couch.

We saw other people but loved each other.
We *fucked* each other,
diverting each other from all-too-linear trajectories,
killing each other softly with our words,
convoluting one another's meaning
by using our threatened meaning to entangle the other,
denuding but not denigrating each other so that both disappear
together.
My life would have been *total* shit

had she not made it *shitty*,
volatilized it
deracinated it
threatened it
like the curiosity we get about our own death
when standing on the edge of a rooftop
cliff
or bridge—
a high point
a dead end
or a way across
(smug in our freedom to hurl ourselves off
to whatever solid ground that is *beneath us*).
A life is useless
like poisons outliving their owners by 100 years under sinks
if it doesn't get you high.
A truly elliptical encounter is hard *to come by*
and has nothing *to go by*.
It is a by-gone nothing.

We fucked each other, and that's what's at issue—
because *getting fucked* is immaterial
in that it dematerializes whatever matter is at hand
and elevates overdetermination to indeterminacy.
Otherwise, we would have reached our destinies too quickly—
and become fatally complete.
Hers was the necessary injustice immoralists speak of
about which only the impatient complain.
But I am a mystical logician of prophetic presupposition
for which form destroys essence,
where both are bound *indifferently* and accidents are possible.

She had sex with my high school best friend
in November—

Free Advertising

drove 45 minutes from Savannah to the Marine Corps base in SC
just to have sex him (but they didn't *fuck*).
The plan B nuked the growing being lodged in her fallopian tube.

We saw other people but were jealous of them
and of one another.
She wanted to meet the anarchist with whom I was sleeping
to get a sense of her own superiority.
When that never happened, she spoke of Brandon.

She met Brandon at 37 and Main,
a bar where young men go to be preyed on by 'cougars'
in the lil' Jersey-shore-town of Buford, GA.
(Who would want to fast forward their life like that?
Why go for older women when the young are still in your reach?)
He was two years younger,
made dubstep music on his personal computer,
wore diamond studs in both ears,
dressed like a futuristic Asian
and bar-tended for a living in Kennesaw, GA.
He was a throw-away childlike she was.

She spoke often of his stupidity,
about how he didn't read books—
"That's unrealistic," I would quip.
The way she spoke of him I thought he was a big joke to her.
She was sharper than ever
but blunter than her approach to proving it.

She studied anthropology and spoke Chinese—
read Foucault and Hesse,
liked the dialectical struggle for recognition in Dylan
came from abject poverty
and divorce

and molestation
and Crank lines on gas station toilets in the middle of nowhere
with no civilization in sight.
She snorted ecstasy off a bathroom floor when she was 14,
was abandoned by her mother AND saved by her
so was always confused.
She was inconsistent,
both comforting and alienating,
peppering her love with entertaining hate.
She used to look at her ass in the mirror,
making it bounce by sandwiching it b/w her tiny anemic hands.

She had no tits, just nipples,
but showed them off like they were better than breasts per se—
she never wore a bra in the 5 years I knew her.
She listened to Vivaldi and the Misfits
quoted Zizek and Legends of the Fall
and spoke ill of women.
She morphed often.
The punk
the Nazi
the nerd
the proletariat
the woman of class
the drunk
the health-nut
the hater of blondes
the blonde
the Goth
the business woman
the Washingtonian
the Georgia peach—
an aspirational 90s Barbie.
She judged men on the size of their dicks

Free Advertising

and started fights between men
because she castrated with words and created debts.
She once gave me a hand-job below the surface of the table at
Ichiban
without me asking—
she had depth.
Nevertheless, she was 'The One'
of a kind
and changed my life—
she basically supported me for 3 years
even though she didn't make much at the country club
where married men dreamt of Face-sitting With Her.
She embezzled their money and brought it to me.
The first time I brought her around the people I knew from my past
she fell, drunk on wine,
and her legs spread
and gave some guys the chin curtain with her panty scene—
she would have shown her cunt
split in two by her thong underwear
to the world
and called those offended "sluts."
We once said "shake and bake" in unison
and pounded fists—
a typical cosmic union emerging from the banal,
the poo poo art of cultural runoff
(there have to be waste management practices for cultural myths
too).
Geeks like us receive the hand-me downs of culture,
getting our rations of mythos sparingly
with a sense of post-tragic duty.
We were the microbes
happy with the throwaway pulp of juiced culture
the nutrients of which are wasted in the process
for the first-class citizens of culture

who territorialize their mythic surf-spots
like bohemians do Wi-Fi hotpots.

She was the first to call my dick beautiful
and I got an erection right then—*see how the sign stands*—
it was humbling.

This woman who was more punk than the anarchist
who was a puritan in her political aesthetic
and more cultured than the first daughter
(as a product of a forgotten rural landscape,
a useless function and desert)
or *the woman behind the man*
with its ambiguity of leadership/servility.
This 'woman'
whose greatest fear and most intense hatred was complacent
mediocrity
was impregnated by Brandon.
He was small.
He failed the PFT for entrance into the Corps twice
and had to quit his job
to do weight training with other prospective barbarians.
They were to elope in December
over the break between boot camp and basic training for
deployment.
She had a miscarriage after their first attempt
and he consoled her w/ re-impregnation.
It was about pride at that point.
I heard she was diagnosed with endometriosis
and had a scare with diabetes.
She had to quit the Adderall
Prozac
Lexapro
wine

Free Advertising

and hair dye.
During the pregnancy, she lived in Marietta
and still commuted to Suwanee to the country club—
a 45-minute drive.
Her old Camaro with the duck-tape window and no AC finally died
and she had to drive Brian's Jeep while he was away.

The last time I heard from her, she texted me just to say hi.
When she wouldn't talk to me over the phone,
another degree removed,
I spoke my mind about the absurdity of her decision
to marry a jarhead and be a military wife—
because she hated all that once.

She lays waste her powers—
become an authority monitoring civilization to outlast it.

Of course, I rationalized something beyond my comprehension.
The person I knew went somewhere and never came back
like spouses and parents people have told me about.
I fucked her and felt potentially to blame
for her shipwrecked fate,
but remorse is not the end of seductions,
though it is seduced.

I was like a missionary perplexed by the rejection of Christ
via the *coup de ta* of the locals—
stunned illogically
to the point of absurd vulnerability.
You Complete Me became *You Totalize Me*
which can be read *You Make Me Vulnerable to Collapse.*
Could there be an evolutionary selection
for the hostility of seduction?

I wondered if she would ever resurface.
She couldn't see me again
because we threw one another off our orbits.
I kept drifting
while she hit another gravitational field.
I kept loving her trace—a stupid emotion—
because her spirit lived on in me
as if I was the sole recipient of a secret message
drifting in the trash circles of some ocean
inherited by a drifter on a DIY raft,
dehydrated and maddened by the God of the Mayas and
Heliogabalus.
The one that gives an unreturnable gift,
asking for death in abeyance,
a counter-gift that only serves 'the function' of *aporia*—
I was a terrorist
who got to the black box before the historians
after the vessel disintegrated
along with its essence
but not its memory.

246. The Dentist

They put 32" flat-screens in each tiny room
that functioned like a fissiparous cell.
The lady got into my mouth and started calling out Kafkaesque numbers
to the young girl shadowing her
but didn't tell me what she was doing,
and I didn't ask because she was inside my mouth
like the Indonesians in the sulfur mines.

Free Advertising

The television was tuned into "The Doctors,"
and it was an episode about medical malpractice.
It seemed crazy to me
I was experiencing the health industry in both of its forms—
'real' and 'simulation'—
all at once…
not twice since the two are basically the same.
I was billed for the TVs—
not merely the one in my little cell
but all of them in all the cells.
It's interesting that alien-abduction delusions always involve surgery
and Godlike whiteness on the operating table,
pulling your soul out by the teeth
then probing your anal cavity.

She nevertheless kept looking up at the programming
every minute or so
while she was in my mouth like a Nascar pit crew.
I look up at the fluorescent light,
doing my best not to look at her as she says "Now turn towards me."

I admit it was the FASTEST anyone'd ever cleaned my teeth before.
She clicked a little stopwatch that measured to the yoctosecond when she finished,
always trimming the time like the fat
that pulled at her bicep like hot candlewax, dripping down its solid base.
She was proud, and her boss was happy.
It was good for business.

She asked if I'd prefer grape or raspberry fluoride.

You even got your choice of color
when they gave you a free toothbrush with $180 purchase
if you had insurance.
I didn't and don't.
I preferred not to have a preference
like child that has trouble with eye contact…
it was like picking out a woman at the bar
and going home horny because you didn't get the one you wanted.

The doctor came in and asked if I'd been writing lately.
I said I had.
She asked if I was drinking energy drinks while I did all that,
assuming I do so late into the night with work ethic or
derangement.
I said no, that I prefer whiskey without soda.
"Is that OK?" I asked.
"Oh no, we encourage that," she said.

There was a poster that asked
"You probably don't have oral cancer…
BUT WOULDN'T YOU LIKE TO KNOW!?"

Cartesian doubt and capitalism go hand & hand
(not like Thelma & Louise…I wish).
If only I could DEMONSTRATE that I am human

…not a straight up demon.

247. Moving Target

The people all look dead
but without that lazy gleam that made Pooh ecstatic.

Free Advertising

Or half alive and that is worse.
All these demands
desires
and needs that haven't been fulfilled in so long—or ever—
that they are no longer attended to or are still obsessed over.
Forgotten on the exterior and forgotten on the interior.
I can hear walkie talkies that sound like space-Nazis
and cards that sing the classics like "I want candy"
when you open them with minimal effort.
The little microchips cost someone's livelihood 30,000 miles away
(What is the circumference of the earth?),
but for us they only cost our intelligence…
which is cheaper since it has never been developed—
the deterritorialization of the brain.

Someone asked if I had the right to be there…
that is, if I was a paying customer.
I didn't blame them for asking.
They worked at Target, but there was also a Michaels
GameStop
a Payless Shoes
and a plus-size boutique for women.

From the infra-privacy of my car
I cordially managed a scene and answered them:
"I suppose I don't,
seeing as I'm penniless and cannot afford to shop here,
but this is my home and you are disturbing me.
I will park somewhere else if it will make you *happy*
[your happiness bound, as it were, to the mandates of work,
That religion of snug coziness].
I am adding a little life to this place."
I am probably the only poet to ever to seek respite
in the shade of the trees that never grow but never die

in the grassy islands that keep the parking lot
from appearing a moonscape
but still appear to be mirages conjured by the heat blur
emanating from the car engines that never cool
during the efficient mindlessness of shopping.

I followed suit (or *called*, as the poker players say)
and parked in front of the Michaels
out of the old man's walking distance (the Target section of the lot).
And when the employee from that establishment—
that *supports art*, nevertheless,
that discipline that nowadays begins from an active consumerism
a lack of autonomy
and a stalemated economic blackmail—
came up to my window or my stoop
to solicit his company's policies
I went over to the Payless section
(although what demarcated each from each I didn't know.)

I stayed there until the same thing happened again.
Luckily, by the time I wore out my welcome at all the other places
all the "original" (nowadays only meaning prior)
Target employees had gotten off work—
sort of like how moralists get off on the misfortunes
of those who do not submit as they have totally to unforgiving rules—
so nobody would recognize my unkempt yet beloved Beemer.

I kept looking around for women who might take me home.
I almost made a sign that said
"Homeless but handsome. I can make you happy.
Will you take me home with you?"
Instead, I had forehead pimples.

Free Advertising

And that made me look like Lee Harvey Oswald
on the little grassy island between parking spots
upon which I shaded myself
and wrote poems that kill presidents without making the news.

Like the card singing "I want candy"
like Whitney after the Crack had caught up with her
I will go anywhere with anyone
because I'll take candy from strangers.
I'm as useful as the card—
a gift that will be glanced over,
read speedily
and thrown away after someone says "Hey, that's kind of neat"
with an anticipatory cadence
and performative gratitude to justify a wasteful purchase.
Miley Cyrus started a campaign to end homeless youth
but I am no longer youthful
so I am wholly to blame for '*my*' situation.

Maybe I will get robbed living in my car
of all my possessions
including all my poems trapped in a computer
like natty gas in shale.
When you're broke but not homeless
only the poor will help you
because the rich assume you are homeless and thus don't need help,
so if you're homeless but not broke the poor will probably rob you.
I will not scream for help to bystanders
because they carry fat pocketbooks,
avoiding the riff raff of Wally World—which is included in their bills.

They are all Germans that would turn me in—the Jew—

to save their asses.
And to think…civilly, I 'need' them to satisfy something.
That is a hostage situation.
Hell, in other countries they pass by dead bodies
like we roll past stop signs.
If you die in a parking lot they will cover you up…
because nobody wants to see that unless they are in the theater
where the air-conditioning keeps them sane.

We climb up mountains to reenergize our lives—
where it would have been a total waste to the nomads of yore
whose sovereignty was expenditure, retrospectively.
And we read Deleuze to say "Yo, *I get it* so hard right now"
but we can't explain it to someone who's never read it
and call that Politics.

You run away
after charging your phone for an hour
and the sound of the vacuum cleaner
buries the silence of you storming out.

I hope the next lover I meet is *really out there…*
because I don't like it here.

248. fetishes

She had the best mouth any of us had ever seen
and the rest of her did her mouth justice,
but I saw the way her jaw turned as she came,
how it distended ear to ear like a hammerhead
and how it looked like she had 60 teeth (the movie Coneheads).
She was a cabinet with a drawer pulled open,

Free Advertising

closed by the maid
to no longer show someone had been there
in a room with no one in it but the maid.

You ever catch a glimpse of her at a weird angle
or think that dealing with her
is like dealing with someone who, out of her mind on drugs,
can walk the line and say her ABC's backwards—
the embellishment and passivity of you rolling your eyes,
thinking "Yea, yea, let's roll this along?"
(The impossible exposes itself in sex
with perfection that still cannot shut off the mind.)

"God, the horror it's scary to imagine
you could look at Cindy Crawford just blinking
and think even she was just another woman,
that the same food becomes a Nazi if eaten too often over a life—
that one can despair from a hello, also."
Sublimation produces shit as a concept—
value produces lack (if you're a moralist).
But why?

All this data that I processed
multitasking (and so not paying close attention), nearly overheating—
it not only ruined the mouth, but the rest of her too.
Had she not seen right through me—
had I been a little less transparent—
she'd have realized how that face transgressed the rhythm of our dance.
Had she been a member of a tribe,
such a liberal exteriority would have been punitively unstable
for the rhythmic order.
I was a concerto spectator

who found her audiential movement at the music of life
unruly and distasteful.

The nearly unnoticeable letdowns of the prime specimens
carry a thousandfold greater weight
than do the hideous flaws of the Worst,
unless you likewise fixate on those—

but that would kill you, not merely *turn you off*—
maybe even kill your boner towards all of humanity.

Isn't that an *additional* little death?

"How could you let a mouth like that go, man?
Won't you miss the BJs? You may never find another
like that one again…"

"I don't know. It seemed honest…"

There is no straight path to forgetting,
and the best way to *build* a relationship is to lie;

to hold onto anything is to *withhold* much…
unless your values are your values.

249. when I shit in winter, I point the heater towards me

The artist that expels the ropiest solid shit
will have the most people climbing it.
And when they all slip & get Indian burns
they'll curse the rope for being unlearned.

Free Advertising

They fall to the Ground and lack a foundation.
Everyone produces *by consuming provocation.*

250. Light-writing in caves

Grow the organ out of your back
because the mice need to hit the sack.
And point out all the beauty you've seen
like the weather man before his magic screen.

If you post on a prayer page
do you address God in ALL CAPS?
HE is a JEALOUS god I think
when he sees big black women in penis-straps.

I forgot what He said when I was born.
I danced when no one was watching; I hid.
He responded "You won't fit, son, you're too big."
And the hole from which I surfaced had to be torn.

I lived when everything was DIY
but no device was, as claimed, user-friendly—
mimicking the cool disinterest of the guy
on the website modeling the Henley—

as if between subject and object
representations were the mediator,
a fruit medley for some manic insects
that only appear *above the floor.*

I am but an object out of use.
I need to be possessed and owned properly.

I will not admit of any abuse
even if made into a publicity.

However, you can't run out of tokens
when trespassing to solicit taboo.
I hand-balance atop and 'above' totems—
never freely but because I felt I had to.

Because future is inanimate and dark,
for the poet, flash is a must.
One remove from Lewis and Clark
he must wait for eyes to adjust.

251. her salience

You were going by a different name,
avoiding stalkers who you had a knack for collecting
like hoarders unwittingly accumulate the packaging
along with the product.
I thought maybe you were either trying to impress
or get revenge on your father
(or me, the easier, more present target).
Your parents were getting a divorce.
That's the first thing you said
when I asked you how your holidays were.
Then you said it wasn't a big deal and didn't want to talk about it
before I could ask you how you felt.
You said that you were practicing narcissism
and were a conservative because you thought being evil was more
fun.
Your hands were shaking when the bartender asked
what you wanted to drink.

Free Advertising

I watched your precious, trembling fingers
crawl across the laminated menu
like a politically powerful self-loather crawling in a sex dungeon
upon the commands of Mistress.
I suggested that you had formed what they call a "reaction formation"
in which you exaggerated social traits and appearances
because you were timid and detached in your depths.
Sociality is nothing but a tautological advertising of itself
in constant panic over its dissolution
and you felt the demand for the don.

You said that you try to dress like celebrities.
You were wearing a cable-knit sweater
leggings
and a windbreaker jacket tasseled around your waste,
those useless details called an outfit
that allow the body to escape by crowding it.
You had a dream about me
in which I was making out with my sister
though I don't have a sister.
You think I'm free,
and when you think of me, you're more apt to dream and break taboo,
even though I do neither.
You think I break norms and I do important work consciously.
But the truth is that I'm just a bad liar and so transcend nothing
by being left out.
I seduced you.
That is an important work.
That is *the* important work.
I destabilize personalities or attempt to—
the passive but not merely passive strategy of the object.

Like primitives for ethnologists,
the discovery of your object is the mark of its death
and already a sign of a victory you do not profit from,
but in fact lose the very thing *you were aiming for*.
Like reality TV, the discovery of your object
implodes the active and the passive
and leads to their reciprocal deaths
like mirror twins
on the screen for which the image is sound-generated—
the reversibility of the real and the medium,
where the real is the medium's alibi.
Poetry is a laser that explodes the plasticity of its subject.
The poet is the other that gives the gift of his death
in exchange for the death of the subject of the poem.

For you, I represented the ideal of transcendence—
I represented possibility
and the loss of possibility that comes staked in a life without
everything.
Like me, you thought the world was full of shit—
all narcissists do—
but you were subjected to the need to participate
inherited from a father who was loved by all those he stepped on
to get where he is.
So a distance grew out of that
until the simulation killed alienation
and you were this malleable form beyond a mirror form,
perfectly destroyed and thus easily built on alien foundations
like whatever the market deems *now*—
you could change essence,
change structure to give form to yourself,
though the metamorphic possibilities you had
were determined by finitude.

Free Advertising

You looked at me a lot that night and I felt more extant,
the feeling one gets just before they disappear—
the last look of the antagonist
before they lose their grip and fall to their death.
You looked at me like I wasn't blocking whatever was behind me.
Sometimes I forget that I exist.
I imagine I—like objects to infants—
really disappear when out of the immediate sight of others,
that I don't at all exist in their minds.
Nevertheless, I was no phantom.
I was a *simulation* like you—
that is, I was dying long before I realized I was dying,
a realization that would hasten the process,
and my image was like the object
frozen and stretched in its brilliance at the event horizon
long after it disappeared into the black hole.
I occupied the limits of the social
as the social is as meticulous
addictive
and pacifying as the technology—
and no one's sure which came first.
When you spoke as if I was a thought in your head—
that someone could be thinking of me
outside of my own presence and beyond my own presenting—
I was surprised (not a normal reaction).

For a night, I wasn't an alien—but I wasn't real either.
I orbited around you during your full rotation.
I disintegrated when returning to earth—
a bottom-up consciousness
that does tricks while it descends with a slope of 0.

252. befits the muse

We were murderers of reality.
For someone who was an agnostic about the referentiality of words,
I sure did *say* a lot—
too much, to the point of annoyance.

Ironically, the death of metaphysics made the universe a vast void,
leaving words to form clusters
so that the void could be navigated
by reducing the distance between each cluster of words
via a curvature of the space of meaning.
Instantaneous communication
has reduced the distance between words.
Metaphors string together *immediately*
like particles at the quantum level per string theory.

When I awoke, her cum was flaking off my dick
like the sidings of old houses about to be torn down
after the elderly who inhabited them has vanished.

She was a narcissist,
clinging to the solid
rigid
secured (wholly inward) ego
clinging to itself as an antique for which the value appreciates
in direct proportion to the age of its death…
like God.
Hyperinflation of a mono-ego
That, like an international ego, can travel anywhere at any time
and form no lasting connections.
I wondered if that was because she like I was *too caring*.
I am too caring to care.

Free Advertising

When one pretends to still have what one no longer has,
that is simulation.
We still practice things we stopped believing in
because we found them dead years ago—
our simulated feelings make us do it.

She was so behind the times, although I told her she was "with it."
It was not her fault: the times are always behind themselves
(backing themselves)
and democracy still functions
via social distinction transferred to 'the subject'
by objects the uses of which are visible
and have no relation to the experience of the user.

It's like time stopped in this Global country.
It didn't stop when I was with her.
Our time, on the contrary, was expedited—
like it occurred by not taking place, drunk.

She knew that I wrote and thought that I wrote well—
so she exaggerated the writer I am.
I, of course, could not *decide* (formerly, *determine*)
what was real and what was not
and am generally paranoid.
I couldn't be sure she wasn't *putting on an act for me*—
because she was so *honest* with me,
endorsing that what she said would *reflect itself*
in the poem she knew I would write.

Like photography, however, in poetry too
(since it is now an extension of photography—
where all speech is generated via electricity,
the benevolence of utility companies
and reverse-engineering philanthropists,

and all words are now screen-projections)
the performative mask almost always comes off
and the face is shown in its bluntness and absent virulence.
No one can be sure whether the bluntness and virulence
is an effect of *photographic reality.*
Poetry is always written from the destruction
or destructuration of beauty.
Poetry begins
when appearances and meaning speak their destruction
in uncertain terms
like the Holocaust victims who forgot their 'experiences'.

Neither one of us cared about New Years.
Neither one of us cared about much at all.
We liked to sleep and do nothing.
We liked to get drunk and occasionally snort drugs.
We liked being, but not performing—
yet we were both hyperaware of conventions
and performed with a perfect, smug exactitude.

Still, we were strange,
not estranged and recognized as such.
Things that normal, more flexible people completely ignored
were thought-traps for us,
catches in the zipper of time,
blemishes on the veneers
of an apparently rich, essentially decaying world—
behaving as if it had drunk coffee (oil)
to speed up its lethargy for events, postponing the crash for later.
We woke up every morning
as if we were on a strange planet collecting data,
looking at things as strange
curious
fascinating (but uninteresting).

Free Advertising

It was as if both of us had taken too big a bite out of the world
and spat it back out.

I asked her
"What's it like to have huge tits hanging from your body like
that?"
"Um, I dunno,"
she said in her usual condescendingly awkward and monotone
voice,
"it's pretty weird.
I find that I have to lift them up
to make sure I get the soap out from underneath them."
I wondered if she'd ever sucked on her own titties
like they do in porno.
I can't imagine why someone would do that.

Tits represent both the bounty and excessiveness of life,
its absurdity and the fear of that excessiveness,
where big titties become limits to the perfect function of the body
and whole persons become reduced to parts of the body,
servo-mechanisms of them.
The parts of the body become autonomous
and rationality is destroyed.
Poetry inhabits the former meaning and—
though poems are partializations of a massive whole
whose reality is beyond the limits of discourse—
poets interact with the minutiae of the body
and the fragments of the mind,
neither of which relate positively to a fear of the totality of each,
neither of which constitute its negation.

She was a Christian who believed in reincarnation and the soul.
She didn't believe in romantic love.
She was OCD and had a phobia of Styrofoam called Styrophobia.

She believed in predetermination
and could justify anything with ideology
but didn't need to because she could deter anything
and simulate all the rest.
She removed law jargon from her speech when we conversed.

I said I thought a lot about (meaning I didn't know)
what it means to have a body and what it is like to have *my* body.
My mind was constantly occupied by *it*.
It's like they wasted a perfectly good
useful
functional
employable body
on a dead-end consciousness, one that said No Doing
but had all the desirable, valuable social functions.
I was a lush, unused plot of land owned by an "old soul"
who wouldn't sell it
and who let weeds grow until the lush landscape became infertile
but still usable as mere land.
All the talent
brains
looks
sociability
personality
and will wasted,
not to become a junkie, but to become a poet—
that is, to "do nothing,"
which probably means "nothing that matters to anyone but me."

She hates me because I said her dog looked stupid,
and she picked up the tab for our drinks while I was in the bathroom.
She respects me and thinks I'm making a choice not many can make.

Free Advertising

Not many women have found unrewarded sacrifice amiable?
Or maybe she really does think I have a destiny—
I'll let her prophecy become self-fulfilling.
Maybe she is blackmailing me
or trying to inspire me,
possibly both at once—
any of which befit the muse.
And I'm *pretty sure* we are soul-mates,
but I don't believe in a soul or in hard determinism
and she thinks romantic love is a waste of time.
I have never been anything other than a waste of time anyway—
so we are perfect for one another
at the moment.

253. falling asleep second

It is hard to sleep
when you don't want to disturb the other sleeper.
The Obligation is the basal freedom
of which superheroes are best capable.
Following another is indefatigable
as an alternative to the voluntary *enlistment* of
(or *segmentation via the production of*) oneself.

I watched Gangs of New York to better understand Marx
and it worked (so I stopped trusting Marxism).

The members of the A/V club are typically deemed the smartest
and the existentialists embrace comic book fanfare.
In their downtime (their time of decadence),
anarchists read graphic novels and revile the apocalypse.
Tragedians talk of being 'painfully lucid'

in interviews with Entertainment magazine.

The Japanese at least are honest and see God in the machine,
little Spinosyns—hence 'post-modern'—
since they do not *compare* the object to God,
seeing the object itself as alive.
On the contrary, they compare God to the object,
hence the Eastern notion *wu wei*
(there is no such thing as Tao*ism* since a *Tao* that cannot but coexist
and thus interact with Confucianism and Buddhism,
that *Taoism* inherits the systematic nihilism of its enemies).
So I like the fake, Americanized version of the Tao
better than the original/
But precisely in God's objectivity does God win
(the dealer always wins, but only because he refuses to be a player).
Since God is *in* things, it is also an objective victory for you.

God is perfect. His death dies.
The machine is elastic. Its death lasts.
The brain is plastic. It dies constantly and thus constantly defers death.

And here I am uncomfortable
as you sleep beautifully, trivially and perfectly untouched.

In New York, sleep is considered laziness.

254. The diabolism of the mirror

"You are one handsome motherfucker…"

Free Advertising

I said to the Oedipal man in the mirror,
"but you are not Ariel Samuel Ackrum, not the REAL Samuel Ackrum,
because you are just light reflecting off (never *being on*) a surface…"

"You are one seductive motherfucker…"
I said to that Thing bouncing off the mirror
"but your symmetry is ravished, your face defaced,
trans-literal because you are merely light.
Yet in that way, you are quite faster than Ariel Samuel Ackrum…"

"You are one sly motherfucker…"
I said to that crystal behind the light in the mirror,
"but *your sheen is impertinent to your being*,
unlike my olive complexion that rivals the streets of Prufrock
Sao Paolo
Buenos Aires
or a car commercial filmed on the cliffs of PCH 1.
Yet you are more perfect than I am because of your obedience…"

"You are a subject," it said back to me.
And somehow because it had what I didn't—an image—
I think it got the better of me.
But the image in the mirror
only conceals the death of the logic of the mirror
by simulation,
so I win.

Ah ah (no) is ha ha backwards.

255. teen mom

As with the rest of the Liberation,
they edit the subtitles when the baby speaks so you can understand.
No more speech as destiny—
not just a shock but a ray of lightning gathered from the sky
by objects attractive for their comparative height
jumping from ground to ground,
always having already occurred yet not impossible—
never hitting upon the Same twice, even pluralistically.

Are you *receiving* this or *taking it in*????

…to decipher, *you must recite.*
And how servile that is.

256. Merry xxxmas

Newyearsvalentinesbirthdaymayda
yindependencedaythanksgivingchri
stmasNewyearsvalentinesbirthday
maydayindependencedaythanksgivi
ngchristmasNewyearsvalentinesbir
thdaymaydayindependencedaythank
sgivingchristmasNewyearsvalentine
sbirthdaymaydayindependencedayth
anksgivingchristmasNewyearsvalent
inesbirthdaymaydayindependenceda
ythanksgivingchristmasNewyears

Would you rather plumb the first few seconds of the Big Bang,
get inside the head of a madman

Free Advertising

or relive the true jingling of the Christmas bell
when the mucous membranes of St. Mary
underwent seismic shifts *ab nihilo*
as spermata caused mob panic?

As we floss this year's yuletide pomp with last year's butt hairs,
Disney mountaintop-mines Parnassus
(without a home, the Muses circle overhead like buzzards)
and what would Christmas be
without both the 72-hour marathon of a Christmas Story
and December as a month-long pre-game prolongation of
Christmas?

The only thing worse than the proliferation of media rooms,
the new mangers,
is the nostalgic referendum for 'real connection'
and 'real communication'—

there are more words than things
and more objects than organisms.

Legitimation is miraculous.

Christmas is an inside job.

But no more than human interaction *in general*.

257. 'if babies ruled the world, there would be peace on earth.'

Sometimes things appear darker than they are
and the days appear later

only because you've forgotten you're wearing comfy shades.

Sometimes it is indecent not to
and retinas are burned more efficiently due to the bright side of things
like the sour brilliance of food coloring
corresponding to represented flavor.

And in a conforming world,
systems of non-meaning and of meaning *equally descriptively cohere*.

The kids all look up to Rob Dyrdek and I don't blame them
because it—Life—seems more trivial under his banner,
when such an encounter with the absurd
is a pre-req' for Existenchillism.

…I just like to add difficulty to things where it is lacking,
that's all.
That means I'm what they call a 'neurotic'.
I don't even undo (because that takes work).

There are those who are never serious and those who are needy
and some people shit all over everybody abstractly
whom everybody finds praiseworthy.
While others flip through family photos and see death as eminent,
others see it as bodily immanence itself
and are cranky when you call them at 9:40 AM on a Monday.

258. the fat lady sings in auto-tune

The girl was so goddamned adorable

Free Advertising

I wanted to cannibalize her in dollops of thought.
She weighs probably 90 lbs.
and has no butt at all and sort of an under-bite
and obviously reinvented her alternative self
when she found her new audience of college students
and subway predators.
I once followed her an entire 4 blocks
because she was wearing a see-through white Mormonesque dress
and grandmother lingerie and white stockings—
I walked in front of her from time to time to make it less obvious
and put myself out there
and whether she picked up on it, I don't know.
Women who are awful socially, in groups,
can appear endearing when they leave the train alone
as if they're going to waste
or are truly nothing alone.

Most, these days, you'd rather creep on than know.

259. Now and then

Where the Giants once piled
the bodies of the meek and mild,
groping towards the heavens,
these bodies too small to climb even for the greatest Greats
who, grasping towards the Natural throne
and naturalizing their opposition to social constructions,
became naught but decorative plates
and downward slipped as if Sisyphus stones—
a peripatetic Cupid got bored of poor Gretchen
& accidentally shot his poison-tipped arrow into the backside of
Apollo.

Now, anonymous peons jump up & down on metaphorical game
shows,
touching
grazing
hugging the host,
winning his favor and *defaulted* kindness.

260. Spelunking

Our bodies become spackled together
as sexual skin makes the sound of farts.
And where Eve's fig leaf departs
your prickly genitals rub me like heather.

Heavy breathing takes the place of voices
and all communication becomes obsolete.
This freedom has nothing to do with choices!
I noticed before you cum you secrete!

I mash and mold your rear like dumplings.
I feel your overworked shins tight as pegs.
I want to craftily dash in through your legs
and like an escaping prisoner, go spelunking.

261. I never saw her outside Gainesville, GA

Her legs were lamp posts telling my form—
leading me astray in the sulphurous mists of an industrial park—
as firm as newly formed tissue

Free Advertising

and as smooth as freshly hardened asphalt,
wrapping around bones as sturdy as those that upheld the obese.

Her tame cheeks bulged like a malnourished belly,
though clumsily still restrained her begotten beams
that would shepherd in the sternest sea captains.

Brief grazes and nudges that removed like sternward swabs
followed me like a caste
…they left me with the bitterness of incapable custody—
a sainthood that robbed me of the title of Absurd Man.
I was a custodian…
arranging neatly all our streamlined exchanges
in poignant yet clear and concise retaining bins.

262. The main attractions of vacations are tourists

The taxidermized animals—scruff and voodoo-less—
machinically deter that the *public* are taxidermized themselves.
A Carnival—the *side-show* attraction is Nature herself.
World's largest squid specimen in preservatives.
Carnivalization of the objective world.
Consumption of all the Stuff accumulated in this objective use of space.
Consummation of a type of relation to the world.
Authentic re-imagining.
Mediocrification. The Abu-Ghraib of naturalism.
Divisions—bars, glass encasements—
heighten the illusion of the *non-object*. We call it a "public."

"Please do not approach object—stay on this side of glass!"

There's just something about the pure magnitude of the superstructure
that renders structure dysfunctional.
The vaulted ceilings, the floor plan,
the industrial lighting that does without shadows because it's so infinite,
the absence of reflections,
the 360-degree camera angles
and yet the utterly linear design of the labyrinth
that *prides itself* on eliminating personal responsibility.
Everyone is a germ marring the perfection of the structure.
Everyone wins—no dead-ends, no bottle-necks.
No *shortage* of swarms and buzzing—
only a collection of autonomously controlled beings
free from the need of security
could crowd themselves together here
in these oppressively open corridors
without touching or being touched
and without a crowd ever forming
because for a crowd to form it must disperse violently.
People pass through like in airport terminals.
They consume reality not anthropocentrically,
but in the name of God TV, a museum world without a curator.
Boo's and Ah's stay courteously silent.
Manifest, that is, Visible Destiny—
the itemization of a world already *totally* indifferent to items.
A world with no other value than that of its mystical
spectacular
iconographic
photogenic consumption—
a world whose *only* value is to not be valued.
Photographic flashes snap on and off—
momentous poses that break flow everywhere with micro-discoveries,

Free Advertising

models,
reproductions mixed and intermixed with *real things*.
They will 'enjoy' it, *no doubt*, after further review.
Later.
Screaming children are signs of the horror of this experience.

"Get your finger out of your mouth.
Now one more time."

Smiles are those of the future—
a pre-emptive happiness that deters the possibility of sadness.
They are unintentionally revealing.

263. Muham-club-med

Alas, after this fractured life of work
finally will we have eternal rest.
Doubtful. Even work-release at best.
For someone must heave heaven's corks.

Who will soak the favored feet
of hierarchical archangel battalions
and to ward off the vampiric heat
cultivate the garlic and the scallions?

As the masters frolic Eden's Garden,
we will without looking stroll hurried past.
Just as Upper Egypt's ancient caste:
to the Underworld as oxidized bodies harden!

Rain is sweat from angelic workers' pores.
For a thousand years Peter reads us vague rules.

And still before entering they assign us our tools.
Oh Hell, at least Muhammad promises whores!

264. arcade-goers are better off gamblers, prisoners are better off cheaters

I was told by her that it was game over and I was all out of quarters.
Having been sucked back into the Real
like a stringed puppet when the show is over—
and more alone than in a parking lot
(where the West is a parking lot safari)—
all I could do was beat
on that dinosaur game-machine
of the responsible organ severing itself from my brain,
for I mistook the message for the medium.

The nurse, obese and not looking at me—
the bartender, without acknowledging the space I occupy
after I've been standing there trying to get one for 10+ minutes…
they ask what they are required as teenage
middle-aged
elderly cashiers do—
as family
friends
lovers do, coaxed but not exactly coaxed into communication.
"I'm doing well, how are you doing?"
The manual doesn't go that far
and the cashier returns my card and looks around me at the next person
because now I'm just in the way,
making her job more difficult with my humanity.

Free Advertising

I understand and move aside.
Do not betray 'everything flows'.

The compression of Life into 30-minute intervals
that aren't commercial-free.
The compression of 1,000,000,000+ neurons into a yes or no.
The compression of continued artifice into automatic familiarity.
The compression of territory into 30 square feet.
The compression that poetry *maximizes or amasses*.

The people still watch the movies
the people still celebrate the holidays
and wear business suits and birthday suits
and see life as a finished work of alien cause and effect.
If the People meant more to you than the 3D-rendered pedestrian images
you run over giddily in the video game
and if your shit didn't always smell
just a little bit better than everyone else's,
you'd not have survived this long in the generalized exchange.

Of course, when you drink from the fountain of youth
you are bound to get Montezuma's Revenge.

265. ultrathin condoms

Some are better at hiding from it than others
so good that they don't come out when the game is over
after whoever is *it* stops looking.
Others focus on it so much they forget it's just a game.
Vampires and fairies, neither of which are human—
both being inferior.

These creatures are like the transhumanists
who, like the Nazis, made their mistakes by taking a metaphor
literally.
But what is eternal Existence (eternal platitude)
to a poet who *lives eternity* (in my case, infinite divisibility)
moment to moment—
each moment being perfect,
that is, being with a beginning and an end.

Go to any Neighborhood
(a hood that opens to no engine
but perhaps covers the reaction on the face of the beheaded
so as not to offend the executioner)
The Neighborhood is the white dove of a broadening middle class
and the crumbling gargoyle of a sky-scraping (pap-smear)
peacetime.
Go there and move door to door:
amid the trimmed lawns,
you will see cars with the windows duct-taped to the frame
on tires smooth as eggs.
Behind the brass knockers,
you will find refrigerators
in which 85% of the food is past the expiration date,
carpets that cut the bottom of the feet like Plexiglas.
Unkempt rabbit cages
seven dogs (all miniatures)
4 cats, fur matted,
and a parakeet that sounds like Liz Taylor hooked up to a
respirator.
There are 19 Busch beer cans in the living room
where the flat screen LCD HDTV helicopters above the fireplace
like FEMA over the floodwaters—
the nicest thing in the house,

nicer than the arcane food proving *post hoc* the cupboards aren't
bare.
The house still has tarps hanging from unfinished renovation
projects
and the smell of death
has been less deterred than integrated into aftermarket scents.
Third worlds are threats
examples
possibilities,
that make first worlds hostages of their security.
Death is present beneath the good.

Truly, we must watch our steps
upon these alters that make holy the trashiness of life.
Hoarding is the opposite of valuing,
i.e., it is value pushed to its limits.
Precisely in virtuality is everything saved
because it is weightless and means nothing.

266. They fatally groom you for it

I grew up thinking my dad's an asshole because he ignored me
wore a scowl all the time
and walked in the room without saying a word or looking at
anyone.
Nervous, I'd leave.

I used to wonder what the fuck his problem was.

They don't tell you about it.

When you're a kid

they tell you you're gifted (to raise their self-regard)
and you believe them.
You go on field trips to universities
and you think you are included
and are convinced that everyone is prosperous
and everything will be all right forever
because the going's good now—
your own operatic, miniature world as staple as a globe
but the basketball doesn't spin on the finger forever.

They don't tell you…

They don't tell you no one gives a shit.
They don't tell you that even the people who share your shit-pot
will hate you and think they're too good for you.
They don't tell you the public-school system is worthless
and that Harvard
Yale
and Stanford
won't hire you as a janitor or cook.
They don't tell you about the whores
or the aloneness so hard
you have to invent a 'personality' to get out of it
and worse, use it to seek out the others you have to "*work with*"
(or in your case, for),
which is everyone within the constant reach of mass
communication.
They don't tell you about the father-figures
who want to make cheese wiz out of the bottom end of your gut
to become your better half.
They don't tell you about being a stranger
to everything and everybody
to humanity
to you

Free Advertising

to God
to godlessness
to lovelessness
and sobriety (not morally considered).
They don't tell you about what the boredom will make you do
what space and time will make you do—
your parents battier than hell,
using sounds to survive in limited spaces.
They don't tell you
about no sleep and no fun and no one
and how much you're really going to shovel
(with a tool that costs a year's paycheck)
and how deep you're really going to dig yourself
(and how China will reject you).
It comes fast. Hard.
Sometimes it is an ability. Sometimes it is a terror.
Knowledge of Ability. Knowledge of Terror.
You can do nothing with either
that doesn't do back to you.
But somehow you always wondered
from the time they sent you to that school where those virulent kids
spread germs and snot and hate and stupidity
with the discipline and dedication
of those who make crop circles

…dear god

…my father's not an asshole at all

…the world is worse than he lets on
with his miserable everyday demeanor.

267. The Opioid Cure

I picture you.
I picture you and me.
Or just you and I am looking but you can't see me.
I picture you as being unjust to me.
I picture you at the expense of me
and you with me mutually, unnaturally.
I picture you and me in the film Billy Madison
and the slots throwing up the bank
while we hold our liquor that turns to heroin.
I picture me at 22
finishing the Flowers of Evil in 5 hours
in the waiting room of the abortion clinic
and what you'd have thought of me then.
I picture myself in your favorite movie "Fight Club"
kicking my boss's ass
and you swabbing my swollen face, getting wet.
I picture you telling me the reality of the situation.
I picture us taking pictures
of people photographing the artwork in the museum
and moving OTP to fill galleries with our punctuality.
I picture you and I walking through Austin, Texas,
passing up SXSW
while you are getting a master's degree with your doctorate
and gaining negative wealth—
you in a floppy hat looking like Edie on her pills.
I picture me leaving your office as you shake your finger at me.
I picture you stopping me in the courtyard
and telling me that I have an air of trouble about me.
I picture you blushing
getting embarrassed for me while reading my poetry
and forgiving me quickly afterward
(because my poetry never claimed to be good).

Free Advertising

I picture you on your knees beneath me
jerking me and looking up at me anxiously and hyper-consciously
asking with your body language "am I doing this right?"
as if you don't know…
and I know you know but you don't know it.
I picture you having a good laugh *with* my poetry
as I am thinking of you from 300 miles away,
thinking about you laughing at me and laughing with that you.
I picture you getting a smartphone
and thinking of my poetry 15 years from now
thinking "Ya know, I could've wrapped his skinny little ass
around my finger.
But he was right about a lot of things—and quite handsome.
I guess that's why I put up with the rest of him."
I picture us having a good laugh about capitalism—at it/with it—
drinking cocktails and snorting Xanax
as your husband mows the grass, all his allowance spent on me.
I picture myself writing about you from the perspective of a
masochist.
I picture myself writing about you from the perspective of a sadist.
I picture myself writing about you in good health,
and you shaking your head at my grammar
and me rolling my eyes.
I picture myself writing about you
from the perspective of a maniac or a depressed.
I picture myself thinking of you
and then thinking of what other people would think
and then getting embarrassed or feeling ashamed but forgiving
myself
shortly thereafter.
I picture myself thinking about you and thinking "Fuck everyone."
I picture myself thinking of you
and then thinking of what other people would think
and then feeling sovereign or seductive as a satyr.

Critical Leisure, Book III, Volume V

I picture you in a position of power.
I picture you innocent in your stern, lighthearted demeanor
lawyering me.
I picture you innocently and indulgently,
I murder shame
and take off with the idea of you
like a monkey in the city climbing the tower with the blonde
as the U.S. Army becomes a bucket of steamed mussels.
I picture you too on your own, living without a thought of me—
just another student passing through and ogling the goods—
another awkward man-boy with a limp dick and hard head.
I picture me leaving with your transference
and saying 'I'.
I picture the ego death I will experience
during the psychedelic experience I have of you.
I picture you dressed like Sailor Moon
chewing bubble gum and gnashing your teeth at passersby.
I picture you as a manner-less beggar
who gives charitable suckers an outlet.
I picture you thinking that everything is absurd.
I picture when you said sometimes you just "think everything's
absurd."
I picture us talking shit, shooting the shit,
shooting a bird at god from the perspective of human psychology,
shooting down theories with low-powered rifles:
thought to-go.
I picture you teaching me a thing or two about life
death
sex
my neuroses
and hermeneutics, sending me away better (but not richer).

I picture you.
I picture you before the picture was taken.

Free Advertising

I picture you loving me on the other side of the screen.
I picture you 'picture perfect': *out of the picture* subjectively.
I picture you loving me without a screen and without a clock.
I picture you without adventure,
bored
regressive
and reverting to me.
I picture you wrecking your Poncey bike
and breaking your arm at the elbow without whimpering
but looking to see how others will react like a child.
I picture you playing the accordion on the street
and nobody tipping you or looking you in the eye.
I picture you tiptoeing up behind me and covering my eyes.
I picture me getting angry at you
for surprising me with your good fortune.
I picture myself unappreciative of you but with expectations.
I picture you running up to me at the airport
when we have never met
and I have a sign that says your name.
I picture you googling things that I have said
and becoming experts on them.
I picture you entering my name and birthday
into a love compatibility calculator,
but that's just what I did.
I picture myself playing Internet tarot like slots
looking for a sign
when the bone thrown by God is the original murder weapon.
I picture you in a lab coat with nothing underneath it
labeling my organs.
I picture you coming to save my life
and thinking I wasn't what you expected, wishing I was dead.
I picture myself telling you this is unhealthy
and crawling back into a hole for another 30 years.
I picture us offline but not speaking to one another.

I picture who you *would be*
if you were not who you (*or I*) said you are.
I picture you lying to me because you wanted me
and I smile.
I picture you photoshopped onto another person.
I picture you photoshopped onto an animal and back onto yourself.
I picture you getting off too much and becoming boring.
I picture me whipping you
and you waiting for your turn but never getting it.
I picture me being with you because it's easy
and not because I love you.
I picture myself as your absent father
and you holding me accountable
but loving me harmfully to yourself.
I picture the single feature about your body
that distracts me while we are having sex.
I picture me finishing my business via side-entry the morning after
because I drank too much whiskey last night.
I picture you speaking the same words to someone else you have to me
and it makes me want to think something clever
like "I have a harder time saying hello
because I have a demanding time saying goodbye."
I picture you behind the Minotaur.
I picture you free with in-app purchases.
I think of you as free but not premium.
I picture you as a free trial with offer.
I picture you as bloatware and me as a new and unused OS.
I picture you as a photo backup.
I picture you liking my poetry only because you like me
and that making me disgusted with it.
I picture you with custard running down your chin
laughing out of your nose as we eat falafels.
I picture us both being uninterested in New York

Free Advertising

L.A.
or Austin
Portland
Seattle
Denver,
but then I realize it's probably just me.
I picture you sick of traveling with me
because I don't want to do anything.
I picture us clicking—
you as a girl in an ad that popped up on a porn site saying "click here."
I picture you as what I've secretly wanted.
I picture you as my wishes coming true.
I picture you as the realization that there is nothing in reality *for me*.
I picture you as a voice telling me to not kill myself
and that making me want to kill myself more.
I picture you getting wet over my mind
and our bodies never touching.
I picture you tickling the asshole of my poetry and beguiling me.
I picture me begging you not to go,
reliving the previous insanity of an original abandonment.
I picture me and you
and you in love with or sick of me.
I picture you being the reason I got over her
and then realize that was 6 years ago.
I picture you with many expectations and anticipations
and with a reality too.
I picture you mothering *me*
because I wouldn't have any kids with you *or with me*.
I picture myself creepily dropping my bags
and resting on your thought,
wearing out my welcome and leaving in the night while you're sleeping,

drunk but impatient.
I picture the picture you have of me and want to murder him.
I picture the… [n, n+1, n+2…]

268. we are all flat screens on which our lives play out for others

I wish I could TiVo all my poems, so I could write them all later
and binge write them all in a lazy day
and then not tell anyone
because the poems I DVR'd were from long ago
and by the time I have written them
they are an older version of consciousness.
And maybe I can criticize after I fetch
prepare
and eat my dinner
and receive sexual satisfaction
in this future-perfected world of my presence.
You! Tapioca!

VOLUME VI
LOVE_IS_AN_ANONYMOUS_CYBER BULLY

*Only prisoners can refuse
their last meal;*

*only genius can turn the intellect
against the 'intellectual'.*

Love_Is_An_Anonymous_Cyberbully

269. Singled Out – the underscore and space

We even represent space secondhand
and 'space' itself is already a representation (with no represented).
Attempting to *represent* space,
we put a sign in its place,
thereby creating a 'place' and destroying space,
which becomes an *additive*.

The underline highlights meaning.
The underscore highlights absence.
The former produces what it 'singles out',
the latter seduces what it *eliminates*.

Silence no longer speaks itself when one considers its meaning,
when one understands it relative (and subsidiary) to speech.

All space in this world is underscored,
for sale to developers—a potential business.
Is identity underlined or underscored?
Or worse, both?

270. I(E)dentity (IED entity)

It wasn't truly indifference
because the indifference was *held together* by a fascination for it.
The options *were* homogeneous—
annihilating the former glory(hole) of desire (lack) and
proclivity—
the *weight* of options.
It wasn't out of the question
that my indifference towards all possibilities—

an effect of a curious fascination and hypercriticism—
came after my discovery of poetry,
but it could have come before, making poetry just an alibi,
an early death or late birth.
It is 'probable' there was no before/no after—
that I had no childhood no past.
It would have been impossible to determine when exactly the change took place
even if one could 'best estimate' when it happened.
The recognition of simulation and of the sign
comprised the active/passive positions.
Life became a question, the response to which was obligatory—
not sovereign.
In a world in which even silence was made to speak,
in which absence was *made* 'to present itself',
I grew tired of being myself—
where *being oneself* was a desperate signification at all costs.
Behind all the signs I had accumulated,
there was nothing—an uncertain nothing
that was *less than* mere absence
disaffection
boredom
exhaustion
fear.
I hated speaking of myself.
I never wanted to be an authority.
All human interaction became an interview, a poll,
specialized *interns* as we are in *who* but never *what*.
Listlessness arose with the forced communication of my being
via lists of properties or sayings
or whatever is readily available in hashtags.
People still argued, still wanted to be convincing—
but I didn't care about others' conversion.
I didn't care about my own multiplication.

Love_Is_An_Anonymous_Cyberbully

I was labile *because* I didn't care
about my or other's beliefs about Right, about consistency.
I didn't try to produce a general happiness
because I knew there is no better or worse,
at least as far as the exchange,
just the 'different'—
that there is nothing not subject to the weight *of my options*.
I found it profane to have preferences *when they lead to arguments*,
to making believe, to recognition.
I had no attachment to the past
any more than I had to my own excrement
which was no longer *mine*
but something impersonal after it was flushed.
I had no attachment to '*my* future'—that careerist jargon—
just a relation to destiny: myself.
My aimlessness was understood as an illness,
so that skepticism suffered and the study of life became endorsement.
I was boring, unchallenging—
that is, challenging through an almost Native American silence—
uninspiring.
But I was indecisive—I made sacrifices to write,
to attune myself to what is only *an activity*,
never to embody what I write but to write what I embody.
There's no way to measure the success of either—
an important aspect of freedom.
It is also possible I write by default.
But is there a difference between sacrificing choice and defaulting—
ridding oneself of blameworthiness by being less than irresponsible?

271. Bulimia et cetera

My poetry is de-personalized.
It is non-creative fiction (fiction that is *received* from the world—
where the world *'is'* fictive,
i.e., written with too many details to be identified with).
The choice with which writers are presented are academic poetry
and poetry that bleeds out of an open wound ethos or pathos.
To the latter, what doesn't squirt out of you
like blood from the neck of the beheaded
like cum after celibacy
is profane.

My poetry is bulimic, the third option,
where the purge cannot disambiguate the natural and the academic
in a reversal.
It requires a minimal gag reflex.

My poetry is not customization, the new aesthetic.
And *aesthetics* no longer exists because it has become a *need*.

272. Famous Last Words

It took a 'trivial' everyday trauma—one delivered over text message—
that reduced love to an icon or an emoji,
both watered down and washed up,
a love that she could apply to me—
the career-less 'writer' living invisibly/
silently with his parents in Cumming, Georgia
with no job
no health insurance

Love_Is_An_Anonymous_Cyberbully

and no social media accounts—
from her headquarters in New Orleans, Louisiana
and to someone else, somewhere in France
who she described to me as "efficient, as close to a robotic model citizen
the government could produce."
The passion still filled me
like popcorn filling the microwavable bag
but I was torn open from the top,
emptied to a buttery film that lined my inside edges.

It took that irreparable featurelessness
of a love that could spread coldly
like information covered by multiple websites
like the news story that somehow no one reports on first
because the reporters from every outlet are all already there
as it happens—
a searchable love
a love of forums
that aerosol love that couldn't be sold to minors
and thus attracted them more.
It took that big finale of movies
that cut to the credits without ending
relieving the imagination of its former horror of possibilities.
It took that unconscious search
for trembling strong enough, insignificant enough
to trick the body out of indifference—
that one last hope
missed like an episode of your favorite show
that can be recorded and watched later
without the interruption of commercials
only the channel was only available
for a free trial weekend…

the tears destroying the tears
leaving you with the wide-eyed, wide-angle look
of those you cannot communicate with
whose pointless human appearance
you can only look at in fascination and speak to like a dog,
that is, to and for yourself—
because your own body
your own consciousness must keep you company
outside your own body and consciousness
so the beyond doesn't swallow you up
in its *thoughtless brutality*.

It took that repetition of history,
that distant familiarity unforeseen and thus willingly pursued
like the spatial disorientation of fighter pilots
who, upside down, follow their instincts by pulling up
and crash into the ground.
It took that ripeness of a new profile created in the database
and thus stalked with spam by fake profiles
or sent ice-breaker messages by 'gold' members—
when the prison is no longer the remainder of society
but society the remainder of the prisons.
It took that disconnection from every practical option
person
thing
where the only option left is to document your own disparate
demise
for people that are not yet born and may never be born.
It took my lover's last words to me being "Ok."
Finally,
it took that guilt of naivety
of one who wants neither to be fooled and crushed
nor to be anally cautious—that other morbid foolishness.

Love_Is_An_Anonymous_Cyberbully

I lack the functionality of a death *instinct*.
I will kill myself on my 27th birthday.
Then at least I will have the consolation of a project—
to produce myself later
be myself later by dying arrogantly.
Not because there is any special significance for that day.
27…why not 32
48
or 64?
Numbers have no significance in themselves,
like me,
they don't even have significance in relation to enumerated things
but only gain their 'meaning' (their functionality)
via their position in a series.
Not even out of some hope of an artistic apotheosis—
my poems will be inevitably read by creatures that I can't even hate
and contrive every day to speak with or to ignore,
whose possibilities for 'life' embarrass me.
The unknown writer—the writer of his or her own scene—
is a paradigm now and even the possibility of a silent death
of a tragic despair other than the melancholia that outlasts the mourning
of a former nostalgic pathos that's been expropriated.
At best I will make the entertainment news—
or a *quick and thus readable* post by NPR on Facebook's news feed
for individual profiles to scroll past.
A truly valueless existence, not even worthy of suicide,
where suicide too is a readymade nostalgia.
Certainly, it will not be to join a mysterious club of pathetic loners
(I am writing)
or to provoke copycat dawdlers.
I offer the collective festival of death

when even suicide is treated as accident.
I will kill myself on my 27th birthday
because that day has the insignificance of a Wikipedia page—
because it is a readymade
and frees me from the calculation of a whole life
(but banally, by calculating my own death)
the inescapable industriousness of company who share spunk like files
and love with the spasmodic alertness of cocaine-fed rats…
a body gone cold like the water of a bathtub
that can be heated with hot faucet water and drained simultaneously
while a newborn is birthed into flammable water
somewhere you and I will never go.

There is no way to die well anymore.
If you are imprecise with your suicide
you will be surrounded by police—the repetitive of life—
in a hostage situation with yourself, shot in the chest with a bean-bag—
how I already feel so they're late.

273. Famous Last Words Cont.

In a safe way,
suicide was as artificial as anything else.
Taking your own life was like burning your diploma,
which they gave out to everyone—
like God and conservatives did lives.
At best, you could video it and post it online,
making it a publicity stunt.
At worst, you cared how many views it received—

Love_Is_An_Anonymous_Cyberbully

though dead to begin with (like the university).

Madness was no longer a revolutionary form of revolt—
therapy took care of that by becoming a free app on smart phones
with licensed therapy bots standing by 24/7 to receive your messages
and message you back positivity—
therapy without a clinical setting and without meaning
and madness without a head and without any meaning.
This did not mean that madness spilled out into the streets
like the revolutionaries had always hoped either.
No, it too was contained in the virtual.
It too *was* virtual.

The joy was different:
neither nature nor artifice,
no longer interpersonal since the interpersonal
was only mutual reactions to media designed to simulate—
i.e., stimulate and signal—conversation.
Joy has always been artificial, but it was once *singular*—
even when shared.
The Other still came with all its horrors
but they were sarcastic horrors.
Whether with medication
applications
television shows
video games
drugs
or the anachronistic Hegelian idealism of behavioral therapies,
the joy came from somewhere other than the Other of the self.

[Suicide has become uninterpretable under such an order—
the Technicolor world of mass tech geekdom
and the continuous cosplay of decade-ism.

The suicide is a publicized mistake—like Watergate.
It must be paid for
in meaning removed of all its personal freedom and dignity.
Reality in its Lazarus reflex
or belated boner
(in its most literal sense) by psychological appropriation
must deny all possible objectivity,
treating it as all other events—that is, by isolating causes.
Suicide at best is taken as a pathetic cry for help
that negates itself by being accidentally final.
Of course, all finality must be punished in the world of capital,
where energy must be recycled to ensure future recycling.]

Suicide was *mine* (impossibly mined)—
Saddam burning the oil fields.
It was me.
It was *for me*
my story
my meaning
—it symbolized my own life, a slow, managed and profitable
suicide.
She told me she never wanted to hurt me,
that she'd "forsake anyone" for me,
and all I ever wanted was to be loved by someone I neither chose
nor pursued
that simple love that seems to take such a ridiculous amount of
energy
and cause such devastation to extract—
a fracked love whose spillage could mutilate unmade lives
in the process of coming into being.
I have never wanted to spoil someone
who would give me the only thing I wanted
but I have had cigarettes put out on my forehead by passive gods
for what feels like my whole life.

Love_Is_An_Anonymous_Cyberbully

She has shocked me back into feeling with her vague pain
that she has not given me yet,
a pure experience that destroyed my knowledge of what I want.
Because the future has disappeared,
I cannot leave her to these men she wants to love while she loves me—
wanting that capacity to love more than one person
recognized by herself *through my recognition of it*.
She challenges me to up the ante with only her
with her multiplicitous love.
My love wells up
and I give the only pail in the global village to her.
I do not believe the others will have thought of these things.
I do not believe that they will bleed for her
as I am at the mere paranoia about her disappearance
as she turns my guts into addled snakes
that pierce my belly with their jagged tongues
and rattle a cold chill up to the hairs on my head
from the bottom of my spine
like a strong man hitting his mallet
on the pressure plate of the carnival game.

274. Suicide

You cut something short that occurred insignificantly,
throwing you into a world of Hurt essentialized,
the Many essentialized,
a flaccid, private well-being and big titties.
Sure, you can throw it away like a hallmark card—
and like the card, you courteously wait to it throw away
because it is *from someone*.
Still,

a life is that stupid saying of unimaginative wishes
underneath the cover art the participant must open
with limited space to sign and write a little note.

A planned death is uglier than a planned pregnancy—
a planned Future.
To say you will die on a Tuesday is worse than Ruby Tuesday's.
Your life will be a buffet from which you got no seconds
but still paid the same price.
You beat yourself to Death—you murder a future you
in your drab, over-spoken sadness
that doesn't deserve the name Anguish because it is made an
Example,
a personalization.

A death that is a sure thing—
not formally but contentiously—
is a comfy exit that dings like the gas station door
that says "push" and eliminates all anxiety and Embarrassment.
A death worthy of Disney, the place of wishes
and color-coded parking lots so big they taxi you back to your
domain.

Only in the everyday near-death—
uncertain of your own wild, archaic impulses
a gambler with yourself with each day awoken—
only in the death unspoken in a minor Accident
are you beautiful.
You can die and live
without asking whether you are worthy of either
and when you ask too many questions
with a macabre slavish enthusiasm,
you become a drag to be around—
and death Screens your calls.

Love_Is_An_Anonymous_Cyberbully

You cannot call forth death and leave a message—
especially one without motive.
You mourn your Beloved with avarice
and your 'history' of torment denies Torment.
Your stories are paraphernalia that contain the come downs of life
in chiasmic bastinadoes—
your poisons are not poisons because they are figures of math
and mix easily in a philter.

Confine your death to a death bed or a note—
you will appear willful with softened insides thinner than pureed
fruits.

Can you, by chance, quit without becoming clean—
indulge without becoming addicted?
Life demands it.
It demands there be no Way out of your sorrows or your joys
that suddenly dissipate senselessly and lonely like merging clouds.
And who said bodies are any different?
We fall into our Talents as in a dream
and wake convulsively with a beating heart we ignored at bedtime.

You have traumatized me out of decline
with your 'resting bitch face' that targets insufficiently
and turns around to *nothing at all* and says
"You are behind my expressions, always."
Laughter bursts cruelly and admiringly
through that conniving disdain and returns to the sewers—
conventicle of Grace.
You kiss me unexpectedly like poppies pressed into salves
and settling as jelly at the bottom of the jug.
I blush like a toaster.

I can only hope—
that daft, diffident centralization of accumulating words—
that my death will appeal to the banausic glacis of the Adam's apple
that feels a repugnant splinter of the neck—
where puberty is a kinesthesia of death.
Let me be ripped more easily than the leather of the couch
that sticks to your shirtless back
by formerly friendly chimps—
have my body thrown at the family-oriented tourists
in the form of shit.
Put me on a gag reel next to someone
who hang-glides into electric transformers.

Life cannot be cut too short like hair on the self-conscious.

275. Campsite me

My fire is a divot in the ground walled in by rocks that are not flush,
burning crushed beer cans, empty cigarette packets
and plastic eating utensils/napkins—
pissed out the morning after.
My fire is the symbol of "leave it how you found it."

My fire is a warm patch of charred earth,
still noticeable,
still signifying that others were here,
but with no coals or embers,
discovered by people who came too late
with a quickly declining sun and only wet wood
and leaves that burn too quickly to get anything started.

Love_Is_An_Anonymous_Cyberbully

My fire is a fascinating spectacle for pyromaniacs
or the fire used by arsonists to burn others' possessions or property.

It is still *my* fire *they* use?

276. her candlelit viscera

She was compassionate and warm
like desert pavement
that makes the horizon twerk along the soundstage of solitude
in its skimpy cutoff text.
She was reflective,
her wit hot as the macabre windows of the Towers
as the mirror images of rich heroes
free fell to their lackluster deaths on television.
She brandished her living space, the handsy instant of her oblique life,
with modish men and women—
flexible, mobile and convenient—
as an adaptation
to the disturbance of personal space by functional liberality.

I imagined myself faint and choppy in an unbroken mutable process,
fading in and out from the black box of her Lack
in a future in which she was gone—
almost totally gone like the third plane—
where I could only make out the fragments of my desired past-self
in the classified scene of her disappearance.

I imagined myself in her desire—
as less than I am
as more than I am
as exactly who I want to be
as nothing.
Could we have fit into one another
like grommets hugging the horizontal pole above sunny windows
closing the curtains to an uninteresting but fascinating Fate?

Did she fear me as much as I feared her,
the fear you devour in mistrusting yourself
when standing near an unenclosed edge—
that *you* might *fling yourself* over?

I didn't know. How could I? It didn't matter.
As infuriating as I found her,
that abyss-less face behind a Mardi Gras mask,
and as underwhelmed as I thought she could have been by me
as by an email list
of faces she'd forgotten before she awoke next to them
upon noon's swipe,
I couldn't turn back without joining her along her lead
wherever that may have been to—
down the drain
up shit creek
or back to square one.
I *assumed* she'd accompany me to myself
beyond myself
neither closer to her or to a goal—
but somewhere.

Love_Is_An_Anonymous_Cyberbully

277. the soul escapes as an odor

What is this feeling of too much traffic
on the information highways of my nerves,
this feeling of having been caught on fire by the defibrillator
this feeling of fuzz
as if the snow is being churned by the spherical liquid
of my glass, global body,
this feeling of carbonation that makes my blood sparkling
and thus hard to chug,
this feeling of Life exiting my body too early—
only to make me wonder if I've rather *outlasted*
my own death, who moved on,
whose potency I avoided like a promising job interview
or like estranged labor altogether?

I spent my entire childhood
escaping the asexual tribalism of the miniature,
my whole adolescence expending the pubic force of ambiguity,
my brief young adulthood
researching the informative wisdom of the aged
with spoiler alerts forewarned but included,
and now I will spend the rest of my life wondering
where those 26 years disappeared to.
Now, they seem like an expansive open-world
whose freedom was mutilated by the narrativity of a linear game
that demands you forget all the details
other than the progression of the story.

I don't think I've ever been this afraid before.
I even don't know what triggered it,
but something jumped out at me that must have been waiting
programmed to drop into the corridors of my time
after I stepped on a pressure plate scaled to my exact weight

that itself was activated only via a motion sensor
that detected my movement towards the exit—
the horror houses
of Life essentialized and monopolizing itself in human
consciousness.

It's like I entered the atmosphere of a planet
whose gravitational pull ruined the uprightness of my body,
making me slouch to that hybrid primitive
trapped in the transition between ape and man
but dying out because it can't compete with either—
only I was moving in the other direction,
a body busted into slack by something invisible
that has been given a name.
All the blood was being pushed to a lower sphere of the brain,
an almost worse fate than being stood on your head
and having all the blood rush to it.
The latter is a Coldplay song or something,
so fuck me, right?

It was this boogeyman only grasped in its effects,
that is, never localized to a place that housed it—
the horror house of Life has no walls
but is contained by trompe l'oeil Blue
so that we are an unfolded, opened can of sardines
spoiling in a water that's taken on our flavor.

Love had my heart pumping like Dread—
where the anxiety will destroy whatever possibilities were left
with its schizoid anticipation.
You couldn't be an asshole, but you couldn't be sweet either.
You were either psychotic or adorable.
You always had to watch what you said
for fear you might say the wrong thing and be abandoned—

Love_Is_An_Anonymous_Cyberbully

Love modeled on the presence of the Father
and the terror of the collapse
of the basket that carries all the eggs.
This Nightmare Simulacrum
of a life as brief and as segmented as a dating show
where a screen divides you, the contestant,
from a 'love interest' you may potentially *win over*—
but win over only with your responses, not your seductiveness.

I was a hitchhiker and hers was the first car to stop for miles—
and I didn't even have to wave my hands like a desperate maniac.
She just pulled over out of the blue.
She wasn't headed anywhere near my destination
but insisted I'd be somewhat closer to it—
or at least would end up in a different place
that would require a different, perhaps more scenic route to it.
She may have dropped me off next to a road with more traffic,
so I might have better luck with the next ride.
At least her car had no other passengers in it.

She appeared as either a savior who would nurse me back to health,
someone who would sit with my exterior as I lay in a comma
and welcome me back into consciousness
with a sweet, unrecognizable voice,
or she appeared as a hospice nurse
helping me to die in comfort.
She could nevertheless have been the one
to administer the lethal injection I signed up for
when I became the charismatic leader of my own cult of personality
whose only member was me.

In *this* life, I am having a demanding time bending over

as if there is some giant inside me wearing my flesh as a body shaper,
constricting its internal organs and popping its blood vessels
while making it appear more beautiful.
Could she have been in love with me—
where I was this presence that left its body,
hovering and floating around that body,
filling the room like a terrible odor?
My guts were garland
whose individual tassels fell to the ground as fluff—
but made of Plexiglas that could've bled me internally
without me having felt it.

278. Subscription-based 'experience' economy

You threw up in your mouth a little
and it was the best conversation I had ever had.

I am the vomit in your nasal cavity,
crust at the sultry ends of your retching lips.

Time is circumcised, segmented like an earthworm
and splits into two acephalous worms.

The mucous descends from my dickhole
like FBI down from the chopper, breaking the windows.

Your head from but an opposing view is shaped like a shovel
with your chin in my abdomen.

Homogenous death is the barrette pinning your hair back
so the vomit cannot contact you.

Love_Is_An_Anonymous_Cyberbully

You love me in monthly installments,
and I provide straw-poll services that may 'turn you out'.

279. depth of field

Her nipples were like radial dials on a remote control
that I could use to pause and rewind my life—but larger—
the upright body being nothing but a dick-shaped remote control
with the mouth being a dick-hole,
ejecting an invisible laser of 'work' to a sensor.
It was a situation where something was blocking the receiver
so that for the remote to work, it had to lapse its function
making you get up off your ass to use it—
where its function was your motionlessness.

The breasts have already been exhausted
by fruit, jug and headlight metaphors.
Hers were like tails on a dog:
useless, except for communicating signs to creatures—
specifically the present humanity—
who could interpret them
only via recycling of readymade social connotations.
She didn't want to have kids.
I'm not even sure she likes to fuck
even though she fucked nearly everyone
who wanted to fuck her
which seemed to be a lot of people.
I think she really wanted symbolism
dearterialization.
She wanted rules
to be ruled

to be told what to do without being forced
a voluntarily servitude as a response to seduction.
Love, at its height, reaches a point of ambivalence
between rape and consent,
enjoyable begrudgingly and as mimesis—
one of the greatest human passions and pettiest forms of condescension.
She said love was a weakness
a disgust-trigger
a social construct.
But apparently for her, sexuality was not, the body is honest.

Consciousness is a neurobiological phenomenon
that runs throughout the body
like a Yucca plant that spreads as it is destroyed.
Still, consciousness exists in a tension with the brain.
The body exists in the world,
where the world is nothing but the history of signs—
and feelings that are the living vestiges of signs.
Neurobiologically I am hers—conscientiously I am mine
and vice versa.
Our love, deconstructable as it was, was 'real' *I think*—
beyond language, beyond the body…
a phenomenon the presence of which one cannot speak of
but can merely acknowledge the possibility of
even if the imagination can only violate it
with the future projection of a past.
I chose her—but I didn't choose my selectivity,
a truly affinitive selection.

She hated liberals—yet engaged in the 'free love'
based on the sexuality and carnality of the 17th century and the 1970's,

Love_Is_An_Anonymous_Cyberbully

that ideology that imagines it can affirm and say yes to many, to all—
without destroying affirmation proper.
She was too cynical for that—a sort of nihilist, like me.
Maybe sex wasn't an expression of love.
But if mere bodies were sufficient objectively for sex,
why not just fuck objects—
why engage in this nostalgia of 'human' bodies?
We nevertheless eminently subjectify the object
and objectify the subject—never having either in their purity.
We acculturate each other's nature
and naturalize each other's acculturation.
I liked that she could fuck other men like she could fuck a doorknob
with the door still closed and locked.
A narcissist, I bid her reduce every man to a commodity—
my little slut and lover.

But who cares about being desired
by creatures who's socially mediated lives
take the form of interactive reality television, interactive pornography?
The attention she receives,
master that she is,
is the attention the person with food receives from dogs,
the attention the person with cigarettes receives from bums.
It is not attention,
 but a sublime, measureless attention—
the attention produced by seating,
a waiting room attention, the attention of a faceless crowd
whose individual bodies become mere reflexes
rolling in the Circadian rapid eye movements of the crowd
with its hyperbolic, thanatophobic cheer.
Anonymous sexuality was not anonymous

because it was attention as reflexivity—
the irresponsible-responsive determinism of a structure.
Giving into the body *has become* giving into governance.
Ironically, she hated the police—
an anarcho-nihilist libertarian
who was a Republican for PR purposes.
The variety of men and women
is like the choice between Tide and Gain
Cheerios or Honey Bunches of Oats—
a freedom that destroys the ability to choose
via the overabundance of banal choices,
the incredulous stare produced
by the restaurant menu
that ends with a compulsive purchase
and the 'I guess' satisfaction of a day of shopping with your
spouse.

So what IS freedom?
Because it is always what exists on the other end of a screen,
I 'choose' not to pay attention to it—
like news, it doesn't affect my life
and if it does it's too late for me to do anything about it.
And so, she can *keep* her freedom since I cannot *give* it to her.
But she can keep it only because it truly isn't worth shit.

I would not crop the enormous photograph she is
to a portrait of only me.
But I hope I am in focus in it,
with all the others blurred.

Love_Is_An_Anonymous_Cyberbully

280. Immaterial Shit

I enter her (with the enter key)
like radiation entering a cancer patient,
making her ill by curing her
(neurotics always receive health as an alien, unwanted illness
because of its association with reality)
slowly decaying the masses inside her
with my unstable half-living
…only when I pull her hair, it doesn't fall out.

She enters my mind like critters in the attic
whose manic paces drive the homeowners insane
chewing through the wires
and moving the insulation around to suit them,
so that the heating bill goes way up, unnoticed.

Her head dots her body like a question mark
when she buries it in the pillow
while her back is arched
and her ass is the tallest part of her evolutionarily absurd form.
She is an ice luge
pouring a cocktail of Vodka and Xanax
into the delta-shaped mouth of God,
committal only to fratricide.

When she is bound
gagged
and blindfolded—
unable to anticipate the discontinuous timing
and random forcefulness of my strikes
and so, driven unnecessarily to an ecstatic break-boundary
and seismic shift beneath her skin
by her own imagination—

I am Fate. I am Nature
History come back from the dead
whose uncertain wrath has no concern
for the limits of consciousness.
It's homeopathic.
Pain is often an agreeable remedy
for suffering that recycles disillusionment.
And it is a sort of anniversary for us—
since we never expected one another
and were unsure of the pain we may cause one another.

S & M is our schooling in suspicion,
not faith in Nature or in Fate—
or faith *in* faith, which all faith requires.
What prevents such an infinite regress of faith
is that sex ends like our love did
in a two-hour span
from "I love you and miss you so much"
to "this relationship is too conventional for me"
over text—
but not via the systematic neuter of society…
what her French lover boy offered that I could not,
conventionally.

281. almost everything

She knew everything about Elvis
tort law
Kim Kardashian
buzzwords
and simulation.
Most of what she said, she meant the opposite of

Love_Is_An_Anonymous_Cyberbully

and knew from experience that most people have faith in words.
She felt guilty when her brother was charged
with attempt to distribute
because she taught him *how to deal*.
She was going to kill herself, but only told me—
knowing I'd mourn her more fiercely than an elephant
and preserve her memory in the Ideal because I'm naive.
She said 23 was a neutral time to do it,
but I didn't have the heart to tell her it doesn't get any better,
no time being better or worse
when the years resemble the work week,
when the lifespan—
with its infantile, vivacious Sunday and its two-day retirement—
resembles the work week.
Her ex-boyfriend murdered a 17-year-old who tried to rob him
forced her to have sex with him every day
and came from a father imprisoned for raping his sister.
Her father was a basketball star
and a chosen person
and a CEO of a federal bank and loans
and she was born with 5 bank accounts.
It's no wonder she was in search of the limit-experience
the infancy
the pre-linguistic—
because beyond everything, which she already had,
there is only nothing
(or me, good for nothing).
She was always right
loved by everyone
hated her name her body and being a woman.
She liked unrequited love
had bad sex
dated a boy with a dick that didn't work
another with a negativity that was negated in the repression.

Her heart was full
and she was full of shit
full of love
full of truth beauty hate confidence impatience
and unacknowledged fear.

She didn't wear heels
like the women with bent toes and moribund, blistered feet
that think you will give a shit about their sex appeal
their expectations
their favorites
or their subtweets.
She had little legs like chopsticks you must break to open
that most men either gave up for forks
because they are too stupid
or used with a sense of culture because they are too stupid.

She had resting bitch face, but she didn't Sleep—
unless it was until the afternoon—
and was just a bitch.
Men thought she wanted them when she was nice to them
because she was *normally* a cunty bitch.

She had everything
but loved me because I had nothing…except 'genius'
resolve that can't be bought trained or God-given, only learned.
I am 'free'
and *because I am free, I am worthless*
and because I am worthless, I will not *amount* to anything
and exactly in this world is freedom *considered failure*.
I have written more in 4 years
than Rilke Yeats or Rimbaud
haven't read a single poem
or been to a reading

Love_Is_An_Anonymous_Cyberbully

and don't give a shit about David Foster Wallace
DeLillo
or Vonnegut
—whatever baristas read.
I do not write about cybernetics or quantum physics
or the Revolution—and the demonstrations and festivals
to me, just mean more traffic in the same way as do the streets
that are closed for bicycle races or filming.
That people film the police
is only part of the television industrial complex.
And the paranoid counterculture
farming organically in the boonies
see Nature as a bountiful, miraculous Producer—
the weak aren't afraid of bullies
because God is bigger than thee
and the philosophy nerds mimic their professors and SEP
and believe their articulation is a mark of distinction—
hoping for the Wikipedia entry.

She had everything but me,
who couldn't be found in a thrift store or Saks 5th
or a dining hall
or volunteering in Africa
Southeast Asia
or Habitat for Humanity.
She had everything but me,
whose presence may or may not have been beautiful,
whose life didn't make a difference or a baby
or a Special Topics Seminar whose Truth was hoarded and buried
and lazy and fierce like an eel in the gulley,
whose desire was unspoken and unbroken
and unhinged and unwanted,
whose appearance was handsome
and useless

and prejudiced
stereotyped
and ignored.
She had everything but me, an 'outlaw' or 'outsider',
not just an outlier—
who wouldn't associate with her friends
because it was polite or right or good for her—
my God was just a private viewer
that paid by the minute
to watch me humiliate Him and break His balls,
whose followers just RT'd dumb, obvious shit He wrote
so they could get follow-backs and/or favorites.

282. flowery language

The waxy leaves of the houseplant,
its genitalia,
look like the covers of magazines
only they are not stamped with the *solicitous pose*—
the opposite of *enticing quality*—of naturalness
from an edited model whose lasered pubic area
is as swept and buffered
as a Target parking lot in which you get booted after 10 PM.
The whitish yellow flowers are runny eruptions
that look at me
like dapper, guiltless sociopaths sued for emotional damages.
The standby television does not reflect my bystander image
but engineers an ambience of my form
in its sleek, flatly hovering ebony.

Have you ever looked at objects
and thought that *basically anything can be a phallus*?

Love_Is_An_Anonymous_Cyberbully

My hands, what are they?
They are pegs or holes. They do not do any work.
I thumb her clit like a touch screen.
My fingers manipulate her brain states like digits on a form—
with the browser set to form-fill.
Naturalness is a myth, but it isn't artificial
since that wouldn't make sense either, *by extension.*

283. motion blur

I have to fuck her at the speed of society
at the speed of Buzzfeed Twitter, et al.,
or she gets bored.
The lack of effort such a *thrust* requires
connotes a pleasure that is *unrealistic.*
As I choke her, the veins in her neck bulge like microfibers,
giving me rapid updates of her hasty, grammarless pleasure
that gets concealed by countless subsequent posts
on the walls of her vagina.

She sits in my lap
as in the bucket seats of a brand-new red convertible,
gripping my arms like a steering wheel contoured to her fingers.
It takes minimal movements for her to mobilize herself through me—
taking her away from home,
away from habits and domesticity,
while offering another sort of intimacy and home.
I am easy…effortless. I am alien.
I can vivisect her,
have coitus with her brain with my three fingers,
implant a microchip of affection in her brain

and have her back in her bed by morning
with no evidence except an unbelievable testimony.

My pleasure is my cock's disappearance in
and return from her dwelling.
It is a playful transubstantiation of castration.
Seeing my entire cock disappear along with her ability to speak
into her mouth is even better.
I am a post-'feminist' poet
who understands that speech can offer nothing
other than #**meaninglessness**—
a performance intended redundantly
as a validation of *one's* own *zeroed in* beliefs.
The faster my thrusts become,
the less apparent are the disappearance and return of my cock.
The in/out loses its synthesis in the blur of a speedy repetition,
so fast that the repetitive imagery is itself blurred.
We are transcendent only by a death drive
unaware of its own circular movements
and projecting its own habits as facts.
We are two passive narcissists
specializing in each other.

In this world, no one can save you—
but you sure as shit can't save yourself,
contrary to what Bukowski thought (yet proved in his actions).
So you might as well do whatever you want—
though if feelings don't fuck you,
thought will…

and vice versa.

Love_Is_An_Anonymous_Cyberbully

284. "You're not going to like it when I get super tan pre-Paris," she said

I told her I wanted to fuck her into indifference—
which would mean extending her mourning,
emptied of its contents, indefinitely,
into disaffection—*traumatically*.
In doing so, I'd certainly be making her more relevant.
But I was too late for all that.

When I was done with my lashings,
I told her, her backside would be striped like a candy cane
and the elongate whelps would feel
like the dividers on the roadways under my car
as I drunkenly swerve over them.
Her tears would livestream down her face,
lagging and *ruining* my *jouissance*
by *producing* it—
beyond the scene's own use.
Forced to wait through her choppy displeasure
broken up by her own enjoyment of a future complaint—
to watch in between waiting
even though with the completion of the scene,
the fully buffered past,
the waiting will have been erased—
I folded her body like a PC/tablet hybrid
and carried her into the bedroom,
still plugged into her as she squeezed her sex muscle around mine
as if it were a stress ball filled with sand.
I put her tears on mute,
her face embedded in the pillow.
Upon discharge,
the timer on the advertisement reached 0,
saying "continue to site."

The face she made while cumming was cold—
like information—
her face a disappearing blue of hyperlinks,
delivering me to another place that resembled the previous one
with more and more links to separate us.
I found it comforting—she had my heart on ice
while I waited for it to be surgically implanted
in the chasm of my split body,
opened like her purse next to the bed.
My body accepted it as my own for once
while the purse accepts money
unconditionally.

285. the voice-over monologue at the end of the movie

I smashed my smartphone on the hardwood
and it was a symbolic act of sabbatical sabotage,
though not in any way carried out by a luddite—me.
To carry the double of the entire world
that expands daily and has no beginning
like the universe,
since it erases history with simulacra—
that is too much for a schizoid like me
for whom the world is already a vast, insignificant
(or unable to be represented)
mysterium tremendum.
There is not enough room for the world and its McDouble and me
all in one space at all times.

I am considered dead, repressed,
precisely because I exist only in one place at one time.

Love_Is_An_Anonymous_Cyberbully

There is not even enough room in a poet
for writing
the study of literature
poetry
and philosophy—
and I *chose* philosophy…out of fascination with its death,
but I *just did* poetry.

Like all relationships, ours was a cheap, material representation—
a souvenir—of a Great Beauty,
a lipstick smear that represented the kiss of Ms. Death
left as easily on the martini glass as on your cheek
(without a difference between the two).
What seemed like an eternal flame
was only the press of a Bic
whose button is neither more nor less convenient
than the old childproof flint gear.
Like our love, she couldn't bear her own soul's immensity—
reducing it to a collection of simulacra and slogans
she may or may not repeat
depending on how they poll
with a forever young, rapidly aging, ADHD audience.

We are singularities
that stake ourselves into a soft earth at an angle
to avoid rocks and roots,
to prevent the overpriced *3-man tent of society* from blowing away.

Still, she reduced me to a half-person…less than an object—
since her other, more well-adjusted lover,
whose traits I didn't want because I didn't have them
and didn't have because I didn't want them,
made up the other half—

so that I was pataphysically grafted onto him like a human centipede.
Of course, I was not the head or the heart
but the legs
the anus
and the sex organ.

She said she was selfish, that I am too conventional.
But she will not consider she regurgitates the fluid femininity
of late capitalism,
when the phallus is more inefficient and requires a break
whereas the clitoris-vagina can cum all day long.

That's why women can go shopping all day long,
gaining New York energy with each purchase.

286. Pathos? Sounds Mexican.

I have nothing to offer but my pathos
because I do not *enjoy* this life.
You can then read it as your own
but can only suffer truly structurally.
"Bukowski" or "Plath" or "my indifference"
can entertain or write *just for you*.

Here is my suffering for sale on the cheap—outsourced (invisible)
and the fruit of the labors of an inner child that lied about its age;
my love is common
and a movie.
Here I accommodate you with suffering,
so *you* experience something new.
Pathos, a simulation of knowledge

Love_Is_An_Anonymous_Cyberbully

that you can get from sit-coms or here.

Here is my loneliness communicated;
I do not care at all for 'fans',
those willing serfs who only undergo and never overcome.
I am not a loner.
Would that make you read me somewhat less?
Or could my emptiness fuel your projection—
that popular new, inexpensive 'installation' art?
Consume me as an idea
world-view
archetype.
Read me, professors, with your recycled, tenured spiel.

The sort of pressure spoof-news puts on the State,
let me volatilize and reduce to nothing, you,
victim-blamed 'reader' (viewer).
Only you consume your criticism
like you pay a boot-camp instructor
so you feel a little less guilty
for not expending all your energy.

287. leave the screen of wealth behind, blessed Capricorn

Sometimes the Beauty will hit you
like a pot of hot black coffee hits a robber in the face
by the *anyman* 'hero' (a dead concept)
defending Honor at *Hollywood Diner*.

Sometimes you must be a Cow with multiple stomachs
to process the blandness of the greenery.

Sometimes you must build up a pyramid and remove the top of it
to puzzle archeologists
and let the Dog Star gloom its catty indigo into your sleeping
quarters.

Sometimes you must transfuse your blood at the altitudes of a
private jet
so your stamina exceeds France.

Some halos are perspicuous
when they are made of thorns that prick with Kool-Aid.

Sometimes Red-40 will settle your stomach—
like St. Valentine in his thick, chalky, pink Abysmal Peptide.

Sometimes you must line the segmented sidewalks
with pastel chalks whose field of hop-scotch
trumps the white outlines of dead bodies in the ghettoes
and trumps scotch sipped by WASPs.

Sometimes you must hover around the dustbins of History
like ignominious, high-strung yellow jackets
that humans call "aggressive."

288. '50s America Today

I was born a habitual quitter
thrown out of heaven as litter.
While I'm in constant recovery
I try nothing on as the fitter.

Perhaps Jesus needed a sitter,

Love_Is_An_Anonymous_Cyberbully

so the barkeep added the bitters.
Then things turned from hunky dory
to History, a cricket's pitter.

God is a mixologist,
and we get drunken stomach cysts.
If we were all sapiophiles
we'd scarcely pursue truth's pecked kiss.

Vote Him off this rock, economist?
But History preserves what is His.
Don't let sober anarchists beguile;
we can only black out to forget.

Always already recovering.
But around my dreams, hovering,
I never realize anything
that I've repeatedly been uttering.

289. @n@rchy

The anarchists live in *proletarian estates*
that look like the guts of Urban Outfitters
but 'more authentic'…
they eat quinoa and read The Vegan Bible, a cookbook…
or maybe it is passé to read The Anarchist Cookbook
because explosions are so Michael Bay.
Having been born in the '90s,
they say 'it could have been different'
with a ludic affinity or consumptive affinity to May '68.
Occupy ATL was the 'best thing ever…'
yes, it was a thing

a happening
a be-in
an event
or a consumer experience.
They bang on drums outside the Prison
and call their racket 'solidarity'—racketeers of 'Subversion'.

The anarchists hold discussions
and host reading groups
and their favorite publishing companies are Verso and
Semiotext(e),
the expensive high-quality ones.
Fame, Wealth and Productivity are unfashionable to them.
Suffering is for their Schema, a form of clothing.
They like to 'up-cycle' abandoned spaces
abandoned ideologies
art-movements
musical genres
and people,
to renovate and beautify with unnecessary thrift.
They think video gaming is stupid,
so they make up their own more primitive, more 'real' games.
They do not even need a game-board
or a ball or other apparatuses,
"just each other."

The anarchists hate the liberals
but will get offended if you say "bitch" or "pussy" or "fag."
Likewise, they think Theory can change the world.

The anarchists project anarchy by wearing all black
LIKE TVs TURNED OFF.
But TVs set to Off are still TVs.

Love_Is_An_Anonymous_Cyberbully

290. Head-scratching contra head-shrinking

I laid my head in your lap.
"Ok, now I put my head *here*."
I grabbed your wrist like a policeman taking your fingerprints
and put your hand on my head,
the limit between your palm and your wrist at my widow's peak,
and your fingertips without finger nails
pointed beyond the horizon of my head,
down the column of my spine that upholds the Parthenon of my body,
down through the anus—Nature.
"Ok, now you put your hand here."

You stroke my head like an expensive garment,
textured.
I look up and there is the ceiling
your breasts,
the limit where the face extends itself out of view—
eye-level view—
and ambiguously drops into the neck
like the elevation of the shore into the deep,
and there are your eyelashes
your hair
and your forearm.

I am your Oedipal child, but I more resemble Narcissus.
I don't even know what I am—an animal or a camera.
And I am taller than you are.
When I lay on the couch,
an initiate on the altar waiting to die,
I am reduced to nothing, less than an infant, below you.
You could slit my throat easily if you wanted to.
You exhume my body, and it is a cold case.

Your fingers are gentler than fate.
They trick me.
You are going to cut my throat.

When you are a fully-formed-human, you meet the world at eye
level.
When you are a child, you look up at everything
but develop an intimacy with the ground,
the level at which most things are dead
ugly
brown
forgotten
interesting—
the level of *soft surfaces*.

I look up at you like at an adult, another species.
I am fascinated by regression and hope to undergo it,
but if it can be simulated, it must be real
and must be a dead idea.

I realize rubbing your snatch with three fingers
from outside your jeans
yoga pants
or cotton panties
is quite nice because the clothes get *damp* and *hot* like a bog,
whereas the skin is *wet* and *warm* like a bath,
and in a bog, you have no sense of direction.

How stupid—to have eyelids
and be incapable of shutting them upon waking hours!

Love_Is_An_Anonymous_Cyberbully

291. new management

Bosses are just programs at the end of the level
whose function is to deter you from realizing
that all the levels are the same,
that is, are not progressively harder.
Beating the game gives you nothing
but an instant replay
and credits only spendable in the game.

Progress is saved but unlocks nothing but memorabilia
of a game without replay value.

292. the cigarette

The feminine connotation of the cigar—
sleek
phallic
trans or hermaphroditic
and close.
It was a brief, useless oral fixation of death—like words.
It was a simulation of death, a loyal friend
a façade that drew in all the world to a little white cylinder—
test-tube of death
and the frozen sperm of an aging, incontinent male-order
finalized in the female.
The two of you had *chemistry* scientifically
with a faith-based naturalness.
You could go without smoking for 5
25
40 years
and taste its harsh slap

like a former love's who, undying, merely went aware to college—
the slap she gave you when you grabbed her and kissed her
because of her metastatic, cancerous ease.

It was the sweet evil of gossiping old ladies,
making their grown children guiltily care for them
and wave them into death
like a bikini model holding the checkered flag
at the finish line of a drag strip in the desert.
It *really did* reduce the world to a puff.

It said "life really is a drag…"

You smoked it to the filter
that turned to the savory, contented yellow of chicken broth—
that serial image Warhol had no need to 'originate'.

293. the singular plural

Be rudimentary, not rude.
Be petulant, not pessimistic.
Choose life,
unless death seems more reachable and realistic—
"I will die, therefore I am alive" the only 'certainty',
itself indemonstrable and fodder for ethics.
If death comes too close,
choose narcotics—
like a rose off the bush outlasting death by several days,
bodiless but not limbless,
in a vase of cool water laced with birth control hormones
toothpaste
and prescription pills.

Love_Is_An_Anonymous_Cyberbully

When life gets too easy, burden it with a heap of garbage
over which you play tag like a gang of orphans in India.
Skip over the wakeless casket lake
like a smooth, eroded stone
sinking but leaving brief, rhythmic ripples.
Love with the energy
of a red light beaming from an electric heater set to off
but still plugged in.
Let the tears spurt out like cum—
they say it's good for the complexion—
sometimes joyful and sometimes not,
yet as a never diminishing return.
Question whether your sorrows are a resource.
If you are feeling ugly, pick at all your pimples
as new ones form in the process
and go without a mirror, since, standing *before* it too long—
always assuming the image comes second—
you hallucinate anyway
until a confident insanity is reached.

Realize that life blows
like a Hispanic chef paid under the table
to blow hard boiled eggs through two holes in the shell,
one on the top and the other on the bottom.

294. "My struggle," a personal brand

Neither Christ nor Art
Culture
Wealth
Furnishings
the Country

the City
the Suburbs...

Neither Children
nor Childless Selfishness
Nature
Church
Philosophy
The Multiplication & Plurality of
Work
Policy
Friends
The Multiplication of Technologies
Lovers
Multiple Partners
Mistresses, Prostitutes or Tricks
Spouses
Cheating
Or Staying Single Forever...

Neither Yourself nor a Group, a Gift,
a Talent, a Science, a Planet, a
Universe, a Time...

Neither Hope
nor Pessimism
Realism,
Truisms
Proofs
Logic
the Absurd
The Multiplication of Perspectives
Ontology
Saying Everything

Love_Is_An_Anonymous_Cyberbully

Structure
Revolt…

Neither Good nor Bad
Hedonism
Morality
Body
Spirit
Mind
Seduction
Productivity…

Neither Hardness
nor Softness
Secrets
Transparency
Anonymity
Popularity
Coming
Going…

None of these matters can ground your being.
Only Being can 'do' that,
but it is too big for us and can only be represented infinitesimally,
abysmally specularly—like the moon qua cheese.
To interact with Being
would be like the water interacting with the glass—
but it is only that the glass is warmed or cooled by the water
or that the water is warmed or cooled
by the light or absence thereof beyond the glass.
Nevertheless,
the glass and the water equilibrate one another—
not so with us.

Critical Leisure, Book III, Volume VI

These cannot save you, but they can help you—
but only in the way Hospice Caretakers take care of the elderly,
bruising them in the bathtub and stealing their jewelry,
helping them die peacefully
forgetfully
sleepily…
when the Cradle *is* the Grave
so that you can't go from One *to* the Other.

The Wonder descends and recedes with Moods
and moods are more fleeting
and passing through is being conditioned to a backward everyday
life
—everything and nothing
health and sickness
solipsism and polymorphic absorption.

When we are in the Media Room or in the City
or waiting in line at the Bank,
we are snipers on a rooftop
Black-Ops personnel dropping carpet bombs on faceless thermal
images
contractors checking the live-feed of the Drone
Scientists looking at blobs and squiggles enhanced by mirrors and
light
…grace & prodigality—these only come.
But they can be more or less attracted,
or won *with some effort*, that is to say, wit, sprit.
They can be gained but *not only* lost—
buried alive in fertilizer but not dirt,
because fertilizer *intends* to grow things

Love_Is_An_Anonymous_Cyberbully

295. X Acto (ex-acted) knife

Her vulva protruded like the skin between fingers.
Her spread legs did not smell like a used book,
and I was illiterate in the crease of her body.
My mouth sounded out phonemes
with my face pressed into her
like into a massage table—
I couldn't make a /k/ sound.

At her feet like a dog at the foot of the bed,
watching
but changing the behavior of the watched,
I forgot the name of the Father.
I said she would make a sexy Goth,
that next time I see her she should dress up like Wednesday
Addams.
I'm not sure 'sexy' is the right word, since it implies an aura—
yet *technically* there is only a *configuration*.
I thought about Wednesday Addams being a child
and assured myself that that doesn't make me a pedophile,
even though I was in love with Christina Ricci
as that character
when I was a child
and retained that relation to that character in adulthood.
I wondered if a child watching child porn is illegal
or if it doesn't count as child porn
but merely as porn.
When the Infant is ripe,
everything is a pornographic projection of its body.

Once Life is loose enough for everyone to fit in
the tension necessary for production—ejaculation—
will no longer give enough friction to inspire synthesis,

of course, by then, technology will have *taken the load off.*
The era of tension was the era of heat—
Hegel's literacy was determined by the Gutenberg galaxy
from which History crashes glowingly with all its crises
like a meteor into earth, frozen but burning hot
(like a seatbelt buckle in winter)
and immediately starting to *cool.*

When the tension is cut with an X Acto knife,
the tumorous whole will exit
like the guts of a beached whale
shot out of its body like t-shirts from bazookas at sporting events,
made of fatty tissues that pretend at becoming an organ.

296. urgency and forbearance

The –ie, –i or –y added to every word
distilled the referent to a *mineral* spirit,
extractable and extricated.
The transparency of words required light
to be projected to other users.
Love was an emoji that in its cuteness, infantilized affection
to a subjective, narcissistic projection—a total lack of intimacy.
The babble of degree zero language
codified—coddled—the Eternal to an unclear will
to transcend archaic technical structures of edible redesign.
She played at speech,
intended to convince herself of newness,
by substituting former visitors for me.
When our relations intentionally went sour,
strategically dissolved by her—albeit unconsciously—
she gained a reinvigorated devoutness towards her former behavior

Love_Is_An_Anonymous_Cyberbully

like an apology intended to restore self-regard,
unintended for the other person.
Any rational person forgives with no concern of *post hoc* manners
and the stories that follow them.

The purification of speech,
not morally, via an artificial sweetening of abridgment—
not for the sake of efficiency or cost-effectiveness
but for entertainment…
because it was a thrill to watch people die onscreen
from the safe distance of being on the other side of it,
a self-inflicted violence
that followed the general numbness towards *violence become old fashion*.
A purification that reduced intimacy to a dead, flat screen
whose contrast and brightness could be set to warmth.
She adjusted the brightness
so that she could just make out the grey image of me
adjacent the matte black of culture—
because that's what the prompt said the viewer should do
for the best possible picture quality,
where quality meant the best possible quantities of black or white—
a sort of Aristotelian integral calculus.
A purification
that took the contradictoriness and instinctiveness out of intimacy,
and with-it passion
action
and power.
No more Power, just Artificial Intelligence and Terrorism to counter
because machines cannot die to symbolize the agony
of their colonization.

She followed her 'pleasures' like a dog
conditioned to remain on her side
of the invisible electric fence,
unaware that the signal producing the shock
would disappear once she got far enough away from home.
She herself said she liked her relationships
to be as far from her as possible,
that she hasn't had good sex in a long time,
that she had 'Nam flashbacks
about her boyfriend forcing her to fuck him every day—
she derealized sex, a strategy of prostitutes
and a consequence of a seduction-free sex.
I was a glass, a solid liquid,
that she could rim with her finger and generate a frequency…
a haunted house in which the chainsaw at the end had no blade.

Truly, I was a new possibility
overburdened by her unconscious
that halted her development beyond the current world order.

297. The tablet

"You asked for it, so we gave it to you,"
that Reason of advertisers and of rapists,
explains the menu change via the disappearance of the Author.

Perception is a cone,
an orange cone arranged in a series on the interstate
to express the demarcation of a work zone,
only there is no sign of any work being done—
and the work zone only functions to increase the traffic fine.

Love_Is_An_Anonymous_Cyberbully

With the tablet they are encouraged,
under the abstract and metaphysical assumption of power,
to produce themselves
to produce the social
to produce their desires before they consume them.
Like the system,
they produce nothing but signs presupposed by the medium,
signs intended to engender happiness conditionally
in subsequence.

The virtual is the ideal of capital—
that abstract material
that is the placenta of production
and thus represents the whole universe of production
as its narcissistic projection.

The virtual—formal ideal of the object (already a sign)—
is infinite, updated to the yocto-second.
Expansion of the virtual is the most effective form of consumption
that kills cozily like CO_2 in the garage.
It is consumption freed from space, a re-boot of the system,
representative of a structural change
and thus mask of a projection of a technical essence.

Love of the virtual persuasion requires no real investment,
no future and no work—
you never have to get over it because you never enter it.
Or else, you are hung up on past love,
inert,
insisting on the strength of a love that never dies
to the point of over-exhaustion
and hyper-cathectic withdrawal.
Too mobile or too rigid, needing a balance between the two.

The handheld makes hand-holding seem like a grotesque misnomer,
like touch in general—
especially the affective touch of the presence of another.
Are there still presences?

With the "touch-screen,"
we attempt to transfer the intimate, the embrace, to the virtual—
precisely that reality that cannot be *reached*—
as an extension of the brain…
and while the brain touches itself in its absence from itself,
it cannot see itself do so.

The virtual is untouchable…
and as such, it never leaves—
a sort of barbaric dragging of the fists
that interrupts the ability to raise them.

298. dónde está?

Life is Beautiful, sometimes.
Sometimes I see its beauty
in the teardrop tattoo on the 17-year-old criminal.
Sometimes I see its beauty
in the strange look a child gives an obese person.
Sometimes I see its beauty
in your long earlobes hanging from your dopey ears like moss,
like cum from your chin.
Sometimes I see its beauty
in your impatience that retreats as quickly as the groundhog
and never finishes the story to get to the moral.
Sometimes I see its beauty

Love_Is_An_Anonymous_Cyberbully

in the Bum asking if I want to hit the crack pipe
after I bum him my lighter.
Sometimes I see its beauty
in the pimple above your eyebrow or below the tip of your nose,
breaking the symmetry of your porcelain skin.
Sometimes I see its beauty in the glare on the television—
a hostile sun.
Sometimes I see its beauty when you swallow my cum
my strength
my awareness
my soul
and say "thank you, baby."
Sometimes I see its beauty
when you take a shit as I brush my teeth,
telling me not to look at you.
Sometimes I see its beauty in crosswalks unattached to sidewalks.
Sometimes I see its beauty
in cats only interested in you when they're on camera.
Sometimes I see its beauty
in the cigarette stuck to your dry, cracking lips
like a sewage pipe protruding from the Hoover Dam
a criminal is about to jump from,
like the ground engorged with Carrie's fist.
Sometimes I see its beauty
in lesser apes chain-smoking cigarettes.

Life is Ugly, sometimes.
Sometimes I see its ugliness in the Happiness of the Many,
the Clooneys
or the first family.
Sometimes I see its ugliness in little-league coaches.
Sometimes I see its ugliness in family photos
after the kids are gone and the grandparents are dead.
Sometimes I see its ugliness in shoe racks.

Sometimes I see its ugliness
in 'Nature trails' travelled by content cyclists
who look at you like a murderer if you stray from the path.
Sometimes I see its ugliness in stylish children.
Sometimes I see its ugliness in restored old houses.
Sometimes I see its ugliness
in the pillow-tits grazing my body
as the dental hygienist sucks all the moisture from my mouth
with a little white tube.
Sometimes I see its ugliness
in the published letters of literary giants.
Sometimes I see its ugliness in keynote speakers.
Sometimes I see its ugliness
in the music played at the restaurant that makes the idiots talk
louder.
Sometimes I see its ugliness in tanned skin
in whitened teeth
in shaved pussies
or unshaved legs.
Sometimes I see its ugliness in mandatory one-armed hugs.
Sometimes I see its ugliness in the promises of drunk talk.
Sometimes I see its ugliness in drink coasters.
Sometimes I see its ugliness
in non-stick cookware that isn't dishwasher-safe.
Sometimes I see its ugliness *in* beauty,
which always demands observance and expression.
Sometimes I see its ugliness in anti-bullying campaigns.
Sometimes I see its ugliness in standing ovations
that won't let me stop clapping without suspicious looks.
Sometimes I see its ugliness in Maya Angelou.

Mostly, I see its Ugliness or its Beauty in nothing in particular—
the two are within me without me wanting it.

Love_Is_An_Anonymous_Cyberbully

299. Ellipsis

The ellipses pop up on the screen of the messaging service
to signal what is about to be said
rather than what has been left out.

'Like' has given way to 'I mean',
and we have the absurd freedom of the elliptical machine
that is better for your joints
than the form of running the body produces.

300. Lubricate it with a smile

When you are fucked, lubricate it with a smile
because the friction of penetration
feels better than the warmth of solicitation.

When you are fucked, lubricate it with a smile—
lather on the Chapstick
like petroleum jelly around your puckered anus
and prepare yourself for the kisses of Death
that touch both cheeks
like the those of Queen Mary or Amal Clooney—
those models of femininity and reciprocity
warmth
and humanitarianism.

When you are fucked, lubricate it with a smile
while the fur is faux, and the feminism is faux—
when #ASKHERMORE is the slogan of the system
in which those who care *for* their body
(i.e., whose brains pity their body)

wear 1.2 million-dollar dresses
and have political opinions that apparently matter...
they too are representatives in their minds
that must lead or disappear.

When you are fucked, lubricate it with a smile
because the social relations are conjugal visits
during which you can perform a quickie
on your 'break'.

When you are fucked, lubricate it with a smile
because Oprah Winfrey is the model for social welfare
and was not around during slavery
or the civil rights movement...
precisely why Selma has become a 'deep affinity'
or consumer object.

When you are fucked, lubricate it with a smile
because the people are as diverse as the channels and apps.

When you are fucked, lubricate it with a smile
because non-profits dole out consumer goods
someone had to make as incentives for the commission
and there are as many band members
pornographic actors
and nurses
lawyers
early education professionals
as there are people in general.

When you are fucked, lubricate it with a smile
because humanitarianism signals the loss of the human
and homemakers
use 'more efficient' paper towel technologies.

Love_Is_An_Anonymous_Cyberbully

When you are fucked, lubricate it with a smile
because cars are still defined in terms of horsepower
and 'eclectic' radio is democratic and free—
as Wikipedia and IMDB
are mechanisms of Discovery, a.k.a., experience.

When you are fucked, lubricate it with a smile
because The Reverend Billy Talen, an 'anti-consumerist' guru,
is a character you might find on The Price Is Right.

When you are fucked, lubricate it with a smile
because you can have your dick-pics critiqued on Tumblr,
and Nietzsche
Malcolm X
and George Carlin
have Twitter pages sympathetic to Anonymous,
whose logo comes from a graphic novel
made into a movie by the writers/directors of the Matrix.

Lubricate it with a smile.
Lubricate it with a smile
That will double your order for free
and add in a free gift with shipping and handling.
Lubricate it with a smile that will get you $100 off your next bill
with each new member you recruit.
Lubricate it with a smile mandated by the glamor shot.
Lubricate it with a smile
that will take food right out of your hand during the safari.
Lubricate it with a smile that says "Oy Oy Oy."
Lubricate it with a smile
that is made in America and thus more expensive.
A smile that demands no belief, only observance.

Lubricate it with a smile
or don't and see what happens.
Probably nothing will.

301. melancholia

I am not made of memory foam,
but I creep to a form that obliterates all former impressions
while obliterating the memory of the creep to normal,
serially.

302. sequester me with your skirting fancies

Don't expect the Muslims to trade in their traditional wear
for nylon-blend business suits that erase Earthen ware,
or the Clown to trade in His rubber, reddish nose
for septum piercings and hippish hair that flows.
Let the Eagle sore without putting It on a Crest.
Let the whiskey put swarthy hair on your chest.

I, Agnostic Catholic who favors the tempo of Methodists
will not irritate the little pimple and swell it to a cyst.
Your Old Faithful will have its *hot* time cease
for tourists in Herringbone slacks with *permanent* crease.
The agrarians respected the Oxen that pulled the plow;
reduce your Project to the precession of singular Now.

You will have to take me, contract my contradiction and my worst.
You will have to let it mosey upward to a speck until it bursts
like a balloon filled by the haggard, 3rd shift woman in Kroger

Love_Is_An_Anonymous_Cyberbully

thickened in the "open 24 hours" universe of frozen Greek yogurt.
Peddle to the polis why from your honest crime you must die,
Socrates, who—Washington of Maraschino cherries—couldn't lie.

Suck the malted life of diners, drive-ins and dives
through a bendy straw of faith—role sevens and let ride
all your charming evil, not as a standardized test—
let the children fill with milk your fatty, veiny breasts.
Bid on me with higher note than others, bachelor for a night.
Let me simulate wretched acts, Key to ground the Kite.

I see in no living man a worthy exemplar.
Preserve me as a tantalizing myth, elastic Templar.
Accede to love me of the mortiferous 33rd degree—
secretly manipulate the chain of command I drag behind me
like a disrespected flag, a travel mug mimicking the Fleur de Lis.
Collect a box of belongings to burn that symbolizes me.

303. the togetherness of mixed media

My father once said to me
"I got credit for *something,* but I didn't do shit,"
the implication being he didn't even know *what* he accomplished.

"Isn't that what life's all about," I replied.
You're never responsible for a reply—
if you're pliable, you're liable.
So, who should I credit for my joy or my sorrow?
Viacom
Bill Gates
A Southern Company
my parents

Critical Leisure, Book III, Volume VI

a boss
God
Steve Zuckerberg
Parker Brothers
Sony
or Michelle Obama?
My father was playing a video game
when he said that beautiful, unconscious slippage of a truth.
He was talking to himself, thinking out loud—
I was a microphone set before a crowd of living furniture
holding up their camera phones like lighters,
when the person on stage has no choice
but to receive a candlelit vigil for his dead performance.
Every now and then,
he'd ask 'me' what he should do as a player of the game—
to make his comments
seem more like a conversation between two people.
What else is sociality
but this double monologue of commentary
about the open-world system of contemporary life.

My father's time was disfigured b/w work
drinking
video games
television
concerts
downloading music
drinking
eating cheese
and going on four-wheeling trips with his small group of man-friends.
He always had to be the DJ among his friends.
On top of these basic inebriants,
he often needed supplementary inebriants—

Love_Is_An_Anonymous_Cyberbully

that linked up systematically—
to supersede and bless them.

My mother used her two dogs
as an excuse to never accept invitations—
like she used me as an excuse to stay with my father.
She even once asked me if she should stay with my father.
I was nine. She listened.
She was the type of person who to an accusation
thought she could reply with "not x"
and have it be true—
as if speech was necessarily true just because it's free,
as if the function of speech was to restore faith and meaning.
Her time was divided—but mono—
b/w vacuuming
talking to her animals
watching television
doing bible-study workbooks
ironing my father's clothes
and answering calls every day from her elderly friends
as if she was a one-lady suicide hotline.
She had no choice but to be happy

Me, I wrote poetry—that practically wrote itself,
with me as but a button-mashing spectator—
while watching TV,
internalizing music with headphones
(which they now make for pregnant women
to stimulate the baby in the womb),
checking my phone neurotically for text messages—
occasionally drifting off
into never-ending search results for porn.

We circle ourselves in a spiral

like trees expanding but drifting further and further from ourselves
in the repetition of days.

304. our strabismic pauses

We spiraled around one another in bed
like show-biz, aquarium-raised whales
jetting towards
the curved surface of the water,
reciprocating one another's rotations
like pistons of a pneumatic language
that perishes
with her breathing my name.

Other women tried to match their own movements with my thrusts
and threw off the rhythm completely
like children whose swings have too much force of hope,
so that the higher and faster they go,
the more likely the tension of the ropes will be lost,
where the swing set loses its centripetality
and jerks them to an angular belatedness.
Their skin hit mine
like a net full of tuna smacking the deck of a boat,
handled by men with a better sense of direction than me.

We, on the other hand, had rhythm.
Although neither of us came because we were both drunk.

305. Contraria (formerly Utopia)

I am not a Man
or a Citizen
or a Writer
or an Intellectual
or a Lover.

I don't have an Origin
or an Objective
or a Soul
or a Saying.

I am not Who I Should Be
or Who I'm Destined to Be
or Who I Want to Be
or Who I Say I Am.

I don't Know
don't Care
don't Expect
don't Recall
and don't Need.

I lack Lack—
lack a contradiction
a word for Against
a Negative Language.

It has gotten to the point where I consume Negativity,
a ludic, harmless Negativity,
with its own brand of books and its own series.
Consumption through anti-consumption.
I collect 'revolutionary' literature—

because if I weren't available for consumption,
I'd be speechless.

306. A night on the town

The moon is an ass smashed against a passenger window at a stoplight,
funnel-webbed sky,
the under glow of cheaply accessorized certified pre-owned vehicles.
Its fullness won't make you more fertile
or increase your libido.

The sun is an emoticon, readymade sign that says
" [insert caption here],
there is only one Happening Place in the Universe...
we will bring the party to Mars."

The stars are stickers available to all
that can make a ceiling unique
but leave a paper trail if you try to tear them off,
the lazy lime green of ginger beer
whose useless calories develop taste
and dissuade the beautiful flavor
of liquor and death-come-early like Christmas.

307. black diamond cross-section of my expressionless face

The tears could slalom down the bridge of your nose,

zig-zagging like a fly open to your embarrassment.
They could jump off the tip
and do tricks
in puffy jackets of jarring
alacritous
epileptic colors.

It could be worse:
they could drip out monotonously,
quantized
as from a sterling, motion-sensing Kohler faucet
that droops
and represents the deeper sadness
that is the absence of sadness—
that shoe gaze of the Swan.

308. the rape of the lock(ed heart)

After a break from her, as from a piece of media
an object
a little monadic assemblage of technology,
I wondered: did she even have a personality?
Could this distinct person I came to know
really be something I imagined,
something I wanted to believe in because I needed it—
like she said?
I questioned whether this personage I had hitherto dealt with,
a sort of version of myself substituted for an absence,
had really covered over *her* personality?
It could have just as well filled in an emptiness
where I may have expected a person to be—
and because one cannot relate to the absence of a person,

I *had to* put something there to speak to her at all.
I have always been skeptical of 'persons'—
I have always found representations suspicious…
what automobiles 'say' about their owners,
they say of themselves.
I am not a political animal.

True, I was operating on that old myth
Essence-Appearance
Thing-Speech
Latent-Manifest
Progress-Metempsychosis.
But still, if Meaning had been destroyed,
so had Appearance along with it—
creating a sort of insecurity, a sort of inactive nihilism…
not unlike the rigid nihilism of my beloved.
Nihilism, says Nietzsche, is an absence
that masks a *deep*, reactive self-sabotaging pain
at the loss of a reality—
upon which a *morality* was constructed—
that never existed in the first place…
a revolt in historicity that ends in an exit
from the plastic order of Becoming,
and thus from Possibility altogether,
in a single, dead instant.
Likewise—another result of Nietzsche's astuteness—
it resembles that depersonalization
(what he called asceticism)
that results in a disgust at humanity itself
after the promises of the Human in its ideality
prove to be impossibly (or ambiguously) fulfilled.

She claimed to reject morality, its structural realism,
but only in favor of a hedonism

Love_Is_An_Anonymous_Cyberbully

(a moralistic interpretation of 'the free speech of the body')
that's only an impossible flight to that time *before language*—
the turn to experience that attempts to revive an affective precedence
as a sort of language of the Self in-itself,
a 'more authentic' discourse,
itself always-already a reaction against morality,
doomed to repetition
to failure
to a repetition of failure.
When passion dies, Pleasure presents itself as a rational revival thereof,
an uncritical, desperate (to feel) *persona*—
that fulfillment of the demands of personality.
The pleasure always only exists *neutralized*,
in a policed, controlled and overall external placebo—
never in an unsolicited (non-'personalized'),
interior experience.
The breakdown of the person,
a sort of rape by-product and terrorism,
always serves to seduce her to seek herself
in the system, current regime or model.
Always outside herself, she grows deader
colder
and more infertile.
Mardi Gras,
that 'event' during which the police give out beads to women
who only receive them with fascination.
Infants subject to the vagaries of desire
that consumption preserves and intensifies by never satisfying needs.
Women who are not even sure why they are there
but 'know' that they 'want' to be there,
yet end up only participating

because many others project *the look* of fascination.
The 'event' became for her a sort of flourishing,
albeit it cool, repetitive and brief.
Lacking Life
Pain
and the Symbolic,
it sells the *idea* of festivity, of human relationships.
After that orgy, you can only remain in a twilight state of consciousness,
attempting to recount the trauma
masked as joy in a failure of language—
a faithful limit experience.

It was that the spectacle of my own pathos—
the energetic, ever-exhausted battle with depression
with the intensity of Beauty
with the wonder and panic of creation
with the contradictoriness and constant tension
of a passionate hunger to live
to grow
to waste—
as something she didn't experience, only served to postpone
her own potential reentrance into the affective order,
the order of passion, of the human.

She was sexually assaulted
and sex has never been enjoyable since—
yet she couldn't stop having it
having but a 'fucked up' relationship to fucking,
an abreactive compulsion that resisted analysis
and *overcame itself redundantly for overcoming's sake*.
She refused to change to let me in—
killing spontaneity and possibility by having a resistance to dissolution,

Love_Is_An_Anonymous_Cyberbully

that necessity and constituent of growth.
It was almost as if her brain resisted apoptosis,
where alcoholism only offered a sort of simulation of it.
We already know neurotics view alternative perspectives—
analysis—
as a personal attack and suggestiveness,
an attempt to control and manipulate them.

Having damaged her brain with a self-induced epidural—
where numbed pain feeds back into a loss of nerve—
she felt no pain,
having lost a relation to her own pain,
losing the relation to the relation,
which does not mean she definitively lacked it.
She didn't want to have children,
a metonymous negation of birth—
where even the Self must explode into existence,
reborn,
born for the first time from a former nullity and disaffection
that imply a pain of birth,
so that your inability to relate to pain disables you…
from moving forward, of innovation (or enervation).

But she sent me alien messages, cyphered little attempts at a contact,
a breakthrough…
messages scrambled
incomplete
fading in and out,
a little black box she saved from the wreckage of a previous height,
a black box of a void,
a negrifying monolith that gave the apes consciousness—
consciousness through aping—

in its anomalous absurdity.
There were little hints at desire, pure desire,
desire for an active lack of project,
desire incompatible with consumption,
where neurosis is a form of consumption of one's own unwillingness,
one's own status quo of simulation—
where simulation is a preservation-function
of what is recognizably dead.

These messages hurt me, I felt the pain she could not feel—
I was the monitor on which she saw her brain.
I felt *for* her, never *with* her or *towards* her.
I preserved her pain
so if she ever came to I could reacquaint her with it as hers.
Whoever raped her raped me too.
Rape is a form of terrorism—
because it doesn't merely affect one person,
but the whole order of persons virally
or the very structure of the interpersonal,
replacing it with the extra-personal, the all-too-personal.
The world order is nothing but a systematic rape of this kind—
forcing us to take pleasure we didn't ask for—
suddenly,
indiscriminately.
Making us react indefinitely *on-the-spot*,
the melancholia of such a rape expropriates our beloveds
via an immediacy only resembled by death
that both the slowness of aging and the transitoriness of consumption
draw attention away from.

Love_Is_An_Anonymous_Cyberbully

309. the streetwalker

I walked through life,
looking at my image
in the reflective ground-floor shopping plazas of the skyscrapers
that direct me through the grid by disrupting it.

I walked, texting—running into people
and almost getting run over by automobiles.

And if I followed my bliss, I was jaywalking
and not being entertained—the latter: Sin.

310. She is a terror

We are these cameras that no longer take pictures
or capture images and thus steal auras,
but instead encode and store information.
We are these digital 'pictures'
who, because they are never final singular objects
but rather are pixelated combinations of effects,
can change our focus after already having been frozen to bits,
who can destroy our original code
with a screenshot of our edited copy.
And she saved a digital copy of a photocopy
of an autographed print of herself
to a personal flash drive.

We are deployed into a barrage of bullets
onto a garrisoned beach
as inputs to the artillery,
and we avoid gunfire

by diving into the water
to be drowned by the packs
designed to carry a little civilization along with us
in our descent
into the madness of war.

It was the sudden demise of the last love that was a terror,
and that love wasn't a love at all
but a cultural demand that developed
or became rational slowly over time.
But it was the sudden appearance of this love
that was more terrible,
and this was a love uncertain of its future—
a spooky love that might suddenly jump to another place.
A love without substance wasn't merely pulp-free
because it wasn't mere juice from previous fruits,
but neither was it a watery extrapolation of bitter concentrate.
The magnetism of this love
wasn't like those small, tactile magnetic slabs
with words printed on them
that could be arranged next to one another to form sentences
on a refrigerator in its hygienic whiteness—
a love without syntax because it had no periods,
that just kept going on and on until it said nothing
precisely because it said everything.

Out of my sight,
she terrified me like an enemy you cannot make out or blame
because it is located behind the eye
in the place behind *the scene*.
Consciousness is only the ground floor
beneath which each sub-basement has a boiler room
whose ductwork runs through the walls of each categorical space.
Her trials were parades

Love_Is_An_Anonymous_Cyberbully

trampling over this subterranean freedom she thirsted for,
yet the underbelly beneath the festive
was nowhere other than where the shit accumulated
in a giant, synthetic mass.
There, her shit no longer stunk—
and she was freed of the guilt of being herself—
but it only lost its scent
because only there did shit smell pure,
that is, no longer like individual diets
but objectively like shit did.

How did love become such an abstract,
ambient, component phenomenon?
Sure, bodies can only rub up against one another,
since only souls that can combine.
What is this open love?

Women become vessels for the void,
where to fill them with material
is simultaneously to remove the void contained therein.
And if it is not contained within them
it must be floating around somewhere else, dangerously.
To fill them with your love is to pressurize them,
to leave them empty is to leave them refillable and intact.
But as vessels of the void
they are but acute localizations of the void,
enclosing but a part of it, closing it off—
but making it visibly left inside.
With a woman, substances can be carried
from nothing to something
without spilling—
but the container loses its thing-ness
and becomes a reproducible, ordinary form.
Nobody wants that.

Critical Leisure, Book III, Volume VI

Lovers are the transparent glass
Keeping the waters and the sharks
from escaping into the observation chamber
where the spectators wander through
with the terror-less, univocal wonder of guided tours.
Whether you tap on the glass
has not even a negligible effect on the contained fluid
due to the thickness of the glass
that isn't smudge-proof.

She seemed to contain everything for me,
but pour it all over me too.
I represented transcendence for her.
I contained what she lacked, so that lack came too close.
But I didn't have what she lacked—
because as a container I also began from a point of emptiness.
And so we exchanged terrors.
Like can only be exchanged with like.
She presented herself, unknowingly, as something new,
something I didn't even know I wanted
until it was right there in front of me.
Knowing that desire is a learned behavior,
she constantly reminded me of how desired she was by so many—
according to which it was her desirability that I desired,
never her herself.
That way she could get through this closeness we were developing
without it *actually being* about her.
This clean campaign she was running must've been explainable
by the fact that she would one day be a politician—
and nobody knows they want to vote for a politician
until the politician says so.

The truth *was*

Love_Is_An_Anonymous_Cyberbully

I was part of the silent majorities.
None of that shit would work on me
not because I am excluded from the vulnerability of consumers,
but because she didn't have to do anything at all.

She was already a new lack where the new was lacking.
"Now I can lose even this," I thought obsessively.
Time lost itself to me—was seduced,
brackish,
allowed a break from itself so it didn't happen all at once.
That was a prayer
compared to the more accurate version of that thought:
"Now I will lack even this."
She emerged as a new need.
She was a new problem,
and she was the only solution to this new problem that was her.
And with this new taste that developed with her presence,
the entirety of my hunger expanded to a new appetite,
a new ratio and structure of an appetite.
She expanded my capacity for pain—
now a naked man whose shivers gave no warmth
but still used a lot of energy.
The world grew larger in relation to me
and smaller in relation to the cosmos
with her—
and my feelings seemed everywhere except contained in my own body,
the only thing capable of managing,
that is, rationalizing them.

And if I was to interrogate her,
she would only yield false information—my loyal terrorist.
Life like my desires was a gas.
It was tear gas but laughing gas—

the difference between which
amounts to a contextual value judgment.

311. etiology of panic

The battery of the laptop was dying
according to a message that it gave me (more clearly than a woman)
on its screen,
when the new form of The Window
is a block of information that obstructs whatever windows are behind it.
I was battered,
whisked away by a nervousness that was complete and utter—
milked by repetitive, inverse movements of the hands.
I had no phone because I destroyed it
for drawing things in too close,
a piece of virtual technology
that strove to put an end to the need
for all previous, tactile consumer goods
by creating a greater, more polymorphic compulsion.
Without a GPS that segments the world into its grid
its projections
its time and dimension of flatness that exceeds touch,
I was totally lost—
helpless
naked
alone
and reacquainted with that furtive memory
that all urban and suburban 'places' look the same,
cannot be differentiated and thus cannot be navigated—
a sort of ocean of gas stations,

Love_Is_An_Anonymous_Cyberbully

road-signs like already-dead stars
and various other consumer/domestic structures.
Flight came just in time
to destroy distance enough
to mask the lack of distance of mass culture and land.

I panicked like Abraham,
like Bukowski throwing mail into the cubbies at the post office,
like James Brown with his bell rung, chased by cops and the
Gospel—
I panicked like birds in a feeding frenzy
before a mere dusting of snow over the tennis court
netting the suburban landscape into a binomial.
I panicked and came in my pants—
like God splitting the continents with his uncontrollable jerks
or Jesus winning humanity
as if it were a kit for raising sea monkeys He won at the book fair
for selling His story,
even though He only won
because Father took the order form to work with Him.
That phenomenon of arousal-without-erection
at the experience of time-based anxiety
had not happened to me since Junior High,
trying to finish the biology exam
with seconds visibly disappearing.

I suppose I have to get off on anxiety
because I can never get off the clock,
unable to punch out without being the infantile barbarian
who lashes out at the terror of life
with mute, confused violence.

312. alcohol on psychiatrics

It pours out of you in dry sweat,
a sort of detergent,
a litter that clumps to the shit, transcending yet preserving the
smell—the morning after, drowning in a pit of colorful, plastic
balls
in a Seussical structure of play
modeled after a cosmonaut's small, providing metropolis.
You get trapped in a life-size birthday cake
you can't pop out of
for a birthday girl that slices the cake with you still in it.
It leaves you with a deep, somber resurrection,
a sort of depth perception you need to drive.
You comb through patchy, balding memories
like a chimpanzee picking lice off its mate's cranium.
Your teeth chatter like an antique bear trap
you struggle to open and set
for that rustic feel.

313. Today is just a show for now

The news team is a community.
Listerine produces floss that uses 'advanced technology',
and the 'iPad magician' affects 80 million viewers.
The journalist contributes to the investigation.

"Money can buy happiness—
so long as it's an experience, studies show," says NPR,
a State service.
The happy ending is always a hand job,
precisely when we no longer work with our hands—

Love_Is_An_Anonymous_Cyberbully

except to give massages and jerk one another.

I will not watch you carry your baby in the Baby Bjorn
like a GoPro cam suction-cupped to your torso, talking to it.
Unlike Siri, the babe is not programmed to respond to voice
commands.
I will not watch you make organic smoothies with Avocados
and bake vegetables into cookies
and talk about Darfur.
I will not watch your 14-year-old give Ted Talks.

Looking up your name on Urban Dictionary
can finally replace astrology and numerology and tarot,
and Vogue offers a Name
that will ensure your child's fame
prosperity
fashion
status.

"Crossroads has my heart"—an ad for a hospice.
Face fitness grows in popularity,
described as 'natural' Botox
and there are personal trainers for you face
who really teach you how to smile and scowl
without ruining that stoic, middle-class youth.
Human Rights lawyers make enough money to wear Prada.

The Lord giveth Chris(t) Harmsworth,
Death in Kathy Lee Gifford's neck,
homeless shelters,
the Civil Rights museum,
yogurt that tastes like key lime pie
and poems that are like advertisements/
the opening jokes of Jimmy Fallon—

representations of poems,
the signs of poems,
poems that are Dr. Phil interventions,
poems that are tracheotomies
allowing readers to read through their throats
instead of their noses,
sacrificing disgust for speechlessness.
The stanzas flash by
unrelated to one another like commercials—
and commercials are repeated like refrains.
Taken together, they form a break.

Like L'Oréal says, "we're worth it."

314. The way she and Saint Nick love me

When I was a child,
I would walk down on Christmas morn
with a blank sulk pickling my saturated face—
a look of sheer disdain,
bored at the fetid abundance before the unwrapping even began
that occurred as mechanically
as an electric whisk beating eggs
with the frozen smile
of ice skaters who may be killed for an 8.5 average.
I wasn't an agoraphobic child
whose relation to people could only extend to objects naturally,
but I always found people strange
facile
stupid
(though not stupid enough to be controlled by me).
I picked open the presents

Love_Is_An_Anonymous_Cyberbully

as I looked at my relatives enjoying watching me
and behaved accordingly,
having been validated.
I was asking them to myself "Am I doing this right?"

"Look what Santa brought you," they'd say,
so I'd look.
You listen to them like you listen to advertisers—
because they say "Don't think about it so much,
just let yourself enjoy it…Life."
After looking beneath the wrapping paper, beneath the packaging—
that phallic metaphor
(where *metaphor is phallic,* and *the phallus is a metaphor*)—
I'd end formally on the Objects,
but I'd want to look inside Them too.
I wondered "Is there a Function somewhere in there."
But you cannot look inside objects gynecologically,
you can only Use them on bad faith,
like women.
I once sat in between my aunt's legs,
turned around and yelled "Hello in there"
as if into a cave.
That is not an allegory.
But masturbation (pornography) makes blind more quickly
than exiting the cave.

I looked upon these objects
and looked around, expecting to be tricked—
like a scared little boy looks behind him
while he pisses at night.
I never heard reindeer or saw Santa—
who I only ever consumed as a cultural object like Big Bird or Jesus—

but experienced them *in their effects*...
like the Unconscious over which objects now have full control.
You are never sure why you like them,
you just do
(like Nike says, *"Nike ergo sum,"*
that messenger who expends no energy
because her shoes do all the work) ...
and probably *why you like them*
is because the reason why you like them is non-existent—
like when you love someone.
You marry with the same *passive collusion*
you opened presents with as a small child,
saying "OKAY, I guess I'm doing this now."

Santa with his red suit like a Corvette
welcomes you like the old lady into Walmart,
like Mammon into Hell
when he says this costs $250 without insurance,
then says to sign in and have a seat
after making a photocopy of your Id.
Santa, that fat, old fuck with a disgusting work ethic
and efficiency only matched by FedEx Int.,
that representative of a society
that cares for you and gives you security if you are obedient,
surveilling you and stockpiling your data
for your benefit.

I've never trusted anyone since Santa,
who says "Everything can be yours *if only you Believe."*
You bro down or you go down.
In this world,
in which you are either a zero or The One,
I will be the 3rd term—
the one we will never have a word for

Love_Is_An_Anonymous_Cyberbully

because it is beyond good and evil.

315. phishing for compliments

New York is so 20th century.
Patti Smith got by writing poetry a blogger could have written today
(only because he copies and perpetuates her—
mummifying and necro-).

What the hell am I supposed to *do*
but *perform* this wiener-dog poetry
that breaks its back if it doesn't get so fat
that its belly gives its insufficient legs a break?

316. Morning breath

Bataille's writings and dangling mufflers
suck the venom out of me, gargle it like cum
and open wide to show me it's gone
before kissing me sloppily afterwards
with their white, unbrushed tongues.

I will convert all venom into poison, all fangs into straws
that get thrown away because I don't use them,
rimming the germs of the slutty glass
with my puckered, buttery mouth.

I drink out of random half-full glasses
filled with flat, unchilled liquor in the bars—

I drink for free, and better than that, I risk pathogens.
My immune system is stronger
and declares martial law on my soma.
I wager my death on the leftovers of others with their earnings.
The best part
is that they get me drunk unconsciously,
for they cannot see the chance of their actions,
cannot see their actions' worldliness.

Mourning is just personalized melancholia,
but melancholia cannot arise except out of mourning—
the way morning breath cannot arise
without waking.

317. Severed nerve of death

The fountain of youth
uses electricity to circulate the water
to give it the appearance of freshness
and origin.

As someone else's rock, you never grow.
As your own rock, you die by growth
and by the force that deposits you.

318. dirty dancing

The bodies grind against one another on the dance floor
and grind on the job.
The teeth grind in the sleep and at the gym.

Love_Is_An_Anonymous_Cyberbully

The gears are ground
like corn added to everything.

The tips of her hair drip with sweat,
like icicles thawing from a hot earth
whose overall warming causes greater swings in hot and cold.
Her hairs fall off nervously as we shower
like edges of the glacier,
when it's impossible to tell whether the slow death of a life
is self-created
or a fate.
She cuts her fingernails
like iron bars cut by thieves' blowtorches,
stealing from me the pleasure of having them dig into my back
and leaving tracks of our animalism
that I can trace later to the kill.

The Ouroboros is a donut
accreted from primordial slime that God uses as an inner-tube
in a viscous, crystalline ocean
of pure feeling without content
until God crawls out of that sea like mating reptiles
and swings it around God's acephalous neck,
down to the knees and back up the Tripartite body
in snakelike gyrations.

The earth spits us out and sucks us back in
like a juvenile slurping up a stalactitic filament of saliva
still attached to its mouth.
That attachment is our Love.
We bungie jump into existence
from a bridge between ape and man—
pointless thrill-seekers that *pay* for experience
one way or another.

The commodification of everything
makes alienation *total*
(and un-partializable, that is, unapproachable)
so that transcendence is a useless fad—
the unrepression of a bodily transcendence
that is a mere cooptation of alienation—
cooptation being the mode of capital—
as the final last-ditch of progressive thought.
Partial alienation is bondage—it is sexual.
Total alienation is zero,
where zero is the ovular equivalent of infinity—
our patterned rotation around bodies.

319. Ode on the Avalon Shopping Center/Neighborhood

It is beautiful and cinematographic
like the rest of American cultural tourism.
It is an anagram for Lady Liberty,
and its soundlessness even sounds
like a Woody Guthrie song must've sounded
echoing through Dust Bowl country
or everywhere that isn't a national park.
It says better than anyone else ever could
"This land is your land."

The shopping center/community
is the largest commercial/residential construction project
at the moment in the US,
and only phase 1 of 3 has been executed.
It's fifteen minutes of fame
appears permanent *now*

Love_Is_An_Anonymous_Cyberbully

and death lags here
in the hyperspeed of shopping
for no apparent reason, unnecessarily.
It is settled atop a plateau—
and you cannot tell if it began as a natural plateau
or is one made by bulldozers,
and for some reason it doesn't matter which
because it is pleasant and functions nonetheless.
It is poetic—it exterminates value and authority,
but only terminates character.
And *reasonably*, life is better that way—
because without God you're flat upon yourself
and too much a burden to yourself,
too much of a devotee to yourself to function
(who they created through established needs).
Shopping is poetic
because a life could have been written by anyone
and there are no powers determining your fate—
not yourself
not a superstructure
not God
Mickey
kings
presidents
bosses
families
spouses
or Fate—
nothing but products simple and perfect in their availability.
It is a totally circular movement of the cosmos
spiraling down to the real feeling of goodness.
It's always preferable
that no one determines anything,
rather than one or few determining everything.

And no matter what capitalism would have you believe
with its huge wealth gap,
it has achieved this accidentally
and potentially fulfills its own reversal like a quota,
that is, with itself not only intact
but saving itself from itself
in the discharge of meeting requirements.

When I go there, I lose all philosophy
and become an American consumer instead of a European intellectual
and feel beautiful again.
Though still I can feel the eeriness of a 'place'
that feels like a pop-up base in Afghanistan
or movie set from an old Western
that was abandoned and discovered later as a *real* ghost town
or like an old abandoned amusement park as pretty as Pompeii,
smelling purely of the Unconscious
and its pleasure of simultaneous amnesia and residue—
like the Grecian Urn,
that ode to ambiguity, death and superficiality.

The death of philosophy feels *incredibly* sexy,
and the miracles of Life and Creation
suddenly *become real again.*
In this *shopping community*,
the visible needn't cover over the invisible
and the invisible needn't leave behind the visible—
the two are left *stranded* here,
spiraling around one another the way God intended,
the Spirit being the void around which staved-death orbits extraneously.
All progressive history—the history of technology—
is based on the eternal return of a tendentious error.

Love_Is_An_Anonymous_Cyberbully

Shopping is good because you can't go wrong—
just shy of good and evil.

The relation between shopper and shopper and employee and customer
feels different here—
more real than those of analyst-patient
priest-prayer
teacher-student or God-man.
The roles are exchanged and circulate.
My former lover persistently called me "dude" or "man."
She would even say things
like "I'm so in love with you, dude,"
the implication being she could relate to me as a mate
and as a stranger.
The name is a terror proportionate to the gaze
the face
the body in its totality that reproduces the totality of the world—
signifying too much
and yet still growing for no apparent reason
except to increase money,
which would increase perfectly fine without humanity.
Shopping eliminates that, *in deadly fashion.*

From the perspective of the '60s or postmodernism,
the community is a façade.
But things are different with simulation.
The pretended goodness *becomes* real, reproducible goodness.
The model not only becomes but supersedes the real thing.
And having abolished all paradigmatic thought and humanism,
the model is better off that way
without inefficiency of sorrow
that is only ever considered an illusion
or internally staged phenomenon.

Critical Leisure, Book III, Volume VI

An outdoor mall— the mall liberated from the design limitations
of airport terminals
cathedrals
and hospitals.
The liberation of shopping in a 'green-space'
that has internalized hygiene.
Even here, in this free-range sarcophagus
to which you can bring your pets,
you can't literally shop 'til you drop even if you reside here—
they have measures for that.

I am here in this beautiful town/mall,
and I *know* that I am alive
(the question has a final solution: shopping).
And I know that something I cannot speak anymore of
has driven me here.
I have never seen anyone die, so I come here.
And of all the places I could be
that may make me more an Academic than a Poet,
I am here witnessing the wonder
of a place that, had I been logged into any moral virtue
or high culture,
or truly any former locution or methodology,
I would have abstained from *checking into*
(since you cannot *check out*, i.e., lose interest and thus disappear).
Things that are stupid can be beautiful,
and the excellent is only that tautology of a creature or thing
that is what it is—
to which I can only resign myself
and be *with*, never *for* or *against*.

I can laugh at this place and these people
as a superior being,
but I also sit on my ass as they do.

Love_Is_An_Anonymous_Cyberbully

The difference is they act as if they do not.
In truth, this place beautifies them
with looks that kill and fashion to die for—
an avatar of purpose.
It is filled with Mana.
It offers a safe death and a safe sex
and a cheap preview of God's private show on His webcam.
It is not a conspiracy.

There is no authenticity,
and that lack is all that can seduce us into Life.

There is no longer alienation
and no longer an unhappy consciousness
because the distance between the biologic and the symbolic
has been abolished by *a life that is but a screen within a screen*,
where the Sistine Chapel is not preferable to Coca Cola
and the morgue no more preferable to Redbox.

320. stationery magic

Responsibility is nothing
but the ability to respond to the demands of the order of
production.
Responsibility means employability,
readability, i.e., the readiness to be interviewed at any given
moment—
this *on the spot*, spotless flexibility
and accessibility, that is, shallow, spiel.

Commenting is not free speech.
(And what can you 'do'

when freedom (anti-ideology) is an ideology?)

The defiance of death is insignificant.
The body is consciousness and thus worthless,
void of all symbolic value in its functionality.
Defiance is a symbolic rectitude,
and the rectal itself is an exam.
Honesty is a complete (finished) waste of time.

Suicide cannot be rationalized
because death is precisely the destruction of the ratio.
The suicidal cannot be reasoned with
and must be destroyed by happiness no matter what the cost—
the sort of happiness that is good for you
precisely because it is against your will,
like the happiness the police give you
in their politeness during your arrest.

I will not kill myself, because I lack value.
I will not kill myself, because my death matters
to the dishonesty of my friends and family.
But *I am the only person for whom my death does not matter—*
so the suicidal in me
has not been detained by the policeman in me
but banished by a shamanic laziness and silence.

I seek death in others—
a festive, communitarian suspension of rules
at my sacrifice.

Love_Is_An_Anonymous_Cyberbully

321. compensation, a sensation

Someone (me)
thought that I accumulated words to make up for a lack of possessions,
that being a 'master over language',
i.e., a master over appearances,
was compensation for not being a master over objects,
acquiring them and—by acquiring them—
predicting and pre-supposing happiness.
All this to become more charming towards women.
But if I am anything,
it's a woman amongst women
and an object in the presence of objects.
And objects cannot acquire, only send away.

The people who accuse me of 'poetry',
of the wealth of words,
the space for which is necessitated
the negation of objective acquisition—
only *they* believe in the power of words.

For me, words please no one…not me at least.
Why would I acquire something that formally obstructs its function—
where acquisition is aimed at the pleasure of another?

Words, as soon as they bud from the tongue and acquire taste,
turn to bumper stickers.
Whatever I say is dead—
if not dead already, ruined by the many,
by *listeners* (who are indistinct from *viewers*).

If anything,

by accumulating words I hit negative wealth—
I go into a debt I will not have nearly paid off
upon death.

With interest (concern), value deflates.

322. clean me with your sandpaper tongue, Leo

You hunt for the Pack of humanity like a pack of batteries—
a future defense lawyer for White Collar crime,
then Politician.

You consumed me like the placenta off your healthy young—
like the unfit one.

When you licked my tiny head, it moved a little—
but then back to its proper place
like a buoy pushed over by the wake of a lifestyle,
an expensive yacht full of models
artists
architects...
those barnacles on your coated, bitchy face.

There exists a barrier between us,
but it is a Great Barrier Reef
whose micro-organismic brilliance looks like unwashed Play-Doh
shared by kindergarteners for a whole school year
from space.

You cut me down like hedges at the Playboy mansion—
the heart that has pursued you like glitter—
and I will grow again

fuller
richer
and a lighter shade of green for the next woman
until my insides grow dark
because the new coat of leaves has stolen all the sunlight.

323. Her plastic network of love: arranged a(r)mour, aimless love

They are searching for a designer love,
one that they can ask a question and get a final answer—
a love of messages and a follow-back,
whose structured liberality they feel responsible for.
A functional love without secrets
without mysteries
without a beyond—
seamless
streaming
and clear.
Not the patriarchal love that asked of its partners to be "in line"
but a modern love that constantly checks
to see if its participants are online.
A lover's whole discourse determined by a network of lovers—
favorited like tweets.
Love, the basic (one-dimensional) unit of modern living,
virally imposing its structure on language—
where the noun has become the verb.
This perfect circulation of messages without interiors
without room
without color or vanishing point—
this anal love of control
manipulation

and trade.
This bio-engineered love of cells
whose nuclei are 'improved' via a molecular injection of gold dust.
This cybernetic love of feedback loops
and 'personal growth' through the transfer of information...
this technically-perfected love
of problem-solving and never taste,
an algorithmic love that 'knows you better than you',
begging the question "Why not trust the system?"

we were fucking other people,
and she would tell me about her encounters as she was having them,
as if I could validate her
in her perfect hypochondria about the social order
and obsessive arrangement of her affections.
"Are you trying to make me jealous?" I asked.
"You don't care who I fuck," she replied.
She was right, I didn't—
because I was in love with her
and knew that I would have to take her *as she came*,
that nihilistic love-for-love's-sake that traverses pros and cons,
that certain-uncertain love that doesn't transcend time
but doesn't assimilate it either.
I hated her too *if that means anything*.

I told her jealousy is not the same as possessiveness.
But I couldn't help but state timidly "I wonder what I am to you."
Curiosity resists the trickery of the MMORPG of love
(with *in-app purposes*),
that love-become-political that kills seduction.

"You are my favorite for now," she responded.

Love_Is_An_Anonymous_Cyberbully

Either she was testing me
or being totally, systematically honest,
the clarity of which allowed her total immunity
from how her actions affected me—
either way, she wasn't playing.
I was in her network.
She was an Intelligence Agency
monitoring me like a potential recruit,
one that could gain security clearance into the depths of her soul
with each gain in experience or 'right move'.
Each piece in her free, open network
intercommunicated with the other.
I got my meaning only in tandem—
never in succession—
with the other objects in her plastic network of love.
Without uniqueness, she kept me in her network—
as her favorite—only via my difference…
difference-for-differences'-sake.
And though I couldn't delete her immediately
without reducing my 'natural' love to its technical double,
I could hide her in the recycling bin
of fast distance.

324. Her needless love

She trapped me like chance,
an atrophying calf she chained to the wall
to make chewing unnecessary.
I spoke her, too much.
Some words she liked, some she didn't.
What suited her, flattering or not, she acquired.
What didn't fancy her, she consumed like water,

meaningless water,
after running intensively.
Nevertheless, fancied or not,
there is nothing that enters the body that does not leave.
(Although, like shit, it doesn't leave *because of* effort.)

I wanted her, unfortunately.
Her words bounced off my words.
My words accomplished nothing,
but violated their intentions by interacting with hers.
There are many ways to reach one stationary outcome—
infinite ways to play,
never having the same opponent,
an opponent that leaves the game with a new difference,
a new way in which they are other than you.

Men of effort almost always imagine themselves beating time.
To win a gal, they imagine that they move forward in time
while the woman stands still,
immovable but able to be pushed.
The man,
leading the conversation to the woman's moistness,
is already in bed with her, has already taken her home—
according to matchmakers
scientists
and Walt Disney,
imagining success and presupposing it in the actions themselves
is the most successful route to success.
If he is unsuccessful,
it's that she never caught up to him,
never approached the certain rest from timely anguish.
In this case, time isn't money but anguish,
where the money sign is a sinew cut vertically
that will cut you with *le fin* in its breathless agitation

Love_Is_An_Anonymous_Cyberbully

if you don't let it go like a fish—
that filthiness of the money that's been I know not where.
Chance is represented [by money] as a venereal disease.
It becomes safe
certain
and out of circulation
only when accounted for.

And so men play the inquisitor
and imagine that to lose isn't to also play.
They 'spit game'
like snakes whose venom is injected,
unlike poison (which is ingested).
They imagine that they beat the pussy up
because they sucker punched it.

I can't say that she played a better game with me.
If I imagine her having been strategic,
it's because I am,
and if I imagine that she was being honest,
it's out of rancid hope.
I must go on what she says,
but part of what she says is that she is master over appearances.
If I go on what she says, I am seduced—
and just as "everyone loves her," so will I.
If I read into what she 'really' means,
I will have invented someone more comfortable for me.
Either way, my private opinions make no difference—
they make me agitated
but still mean nothing even to me.

Chance has stricken me with her—
a beautiful luck like a clean shit that doesn't demand a wipe
or the death of someone you don't care for,

like a clean cut that deepened without the pain to yell "Stop!"
A divine luck of chips
that can't be kept even if the cards are constantly folded,
since the blind increases as the night tornadoes from the eye of the jack.
The luck against which experience and technique
can't predict bluffing from 'a tell'.

She told me she didn't need love.
It sounded like a challenge.
It sounded gross
hot
aristocratic
feigned
new.
She hooked me—because I was in decline
and experienced the wonder of a half-pipe,
disgusting in its simplicity and aerodynamics.

I didn't see her as a sudden challenge—
that was a common reaction.
Reverse psychology is the genius of children.
And I am not yet as sickly and generous as a parent.
I have as yet kept no pictures of myself,
no proof that I existed before now/was born/grew.
I don't see why I'd need to burn my image into her,
not at least without causing her pain—
but I didn't want her pain.
She has her own—the pain *that she is*—
and what could any I could offer do to add to that—
if anything, she'd subtract me to keep the pain.

Because she was so estranged,
holding her hand was something I wanted to do.

Love_Is_An_Anonymous_Cyberbully

It was common
wretched
dragging a dangling leg like a roach.
I didn't hate holding hands
like I didn't hate roaches—
and the two enter the world
with the same thoughtless expurgation of an absence
and both will outlast the apocalypse.

Holding her hand—
she could float away in rapture
at any future time,
while I am left behind to another future;
left forward, left for ward.

Her love is needless.
She not only creates it in a space opened for it
by her
by me
by nothing at all—
she wastes it on me.

What luck there is *by chance*,
that there is some spring in the board,
so that I might dive into my death
rather than tiptoeing to forestall contact with the edge,
at the mercy of the tips of blades—begging.

Slavery is a behavior.
And I have given nothing yet gotten everything—
with no moral worth or a promise.

Her needless love is less rational than God's,
which, like mom's, is disgusting

because it is in itself involved.

325. Startup company

Corporations join the fight against terrorism
because Twitter is no different than Lockheed Martin.

The banishing from Twitter of Terrorist Groups
is considered a legitimate Progress in the War on Terrorism.

But @JamesFrancoTV has a small, overpopulated country of followers,
and that is OK.

Everything is going to be alright.
The Office is on Netflix.
The Bachelor Crashes Viewing Parties in his home-state of Iowa.

Everything is going to be OK, but just OK [Original Kitsch,
the new iOS (or Original Sin)].
Missy Elliot is making a comeback.

Everything is going to be Good.
State Parks are still generating revenue.
Culture is still a mark of distinction.

Everything is going to be Fuckin' A (Fuckin' Assimilation).
We will rebuild the Towers they destroyed
with even nicer interiors & Apple Pay.

Everything is going to be Swell.
The Boom will be a Bust.

Love_Is_An_Anonymous_Cyberbully

And shopping and Marathons will Not be interrupted
by teenage Terrorists.

Everything will proceed Effortlessly.
Whole towns will not be shut down because one former ROTC member
is hiding under a rock with Tuna cans.

The stores will be open on Christmas.
There will not be 7 cops responding to
and pointing their guns
tasers
and chest-cams
at petty thieves.

Neiman Marcus will come to a mall-near-you.
And Iran will not be allowed to have Nuclear missiles
because everyone needs a Villain to believe in their own
Responsibility.

Lockheed Martin will foster 'Community Relations'
and produce sleek aircrafts
called "Raptor"
"Orion"
"Hercules"
"Superfortress"
"Galaxy"
and "Starlifter."

The poetry will be better than ever,
precisely by becoming impossible.
And TMZ will colonize your disgust
and remind you You are 'More Real' than the Stars.

The Terrorists will produce Viral Videos
and their fashion with be anti-fashion,
and there will always be something to Overcome politically,
something to Do socially.

The Occupy movements will keep the Masses occupied
like a unisex, one-person bathroom.

326. a transition, Love

I don't want to be part of a series,
but I don't want to be a model either.
Holding out for the model, you end up with no one.
Giving into the series, the trials of the search for the model,
you end up with many—
that profuse equivalent of no one.
Like a Bachelor faced with a pre-screened, selected cast
of *real* love interests
(as through a promotional contest, that magical competition of
lotteries)
that only have personalities insofar as they are *cast-members*,
we begin with an absurd overabundance of choices
to the extent that we desire advertising to relieve us of choosing.
And the further we go about eliminating options,
the more we realize
the arbitrariness of our default freedom and our choices.

Searching for the singular, you get only the Name
the backstory
the differential connotation
the status.
Searching for the distinctiveness of the Name,

Love_Is_An_Anonymous_Cyberbully

you get only she him them man dude or baby…
in short, the Human—
the new humanism of consumption.

We are disillusioned when we try to make contact with the soul,
that thing beyond the flesh but not merely inside,
and get only the tongue
the vagina
the anus
or the guts.
We seek the cause, the will in its abstract freedom—
that supposed Universal aspect of the Person—
and only the flesh-rocket is launched into the Cosmic Her,
who submits to our categories only in appearance,
rejecting us through a curtsying complicity
with our introjections...
white rocket with racing stripes
and a number on the side like an old Dodge.
O how you dodge the question with a pre-conception
(a contraception)!

Are we truly destined or meant to love each other,
the two of us—white—
in the maternal void of a household
in which we can only strafe miraculously at both ends of a square
to stymie a little white dot of our agnostic affections
that we counter and volley with greater rapidity
until it is lost to one of us?

Was it not just a mistake?
Could a flippant remark out of the frustration of language—
of the instantaneous sort levies on your unsorted thoughts—
really erase the past…
stretch the immediate past into the distant

like glass plastically dripping,
expanding yet not increasing in size or coming apart?
Is it not that eraser on mass produced #2 pencils
that leaves a streak or rips the wide-ruled paper
pressed with the intensity of love,
the clammy hands of which press diamonds from without?
The cheap graphite is never fully erased,
the eraser never soft and supple enough,
so, though the words cannot be made out,
it's obvious that something was written before
and shoddily erased.

327. One genius and talented millions

Bukowski was a poet and he knew it,
only writing books to pay bills and debts,
but the books didn't pay until later—
while they continue to pay the bills of NBA fans
and App-developers.
And publishing functions like drug dealing in the suburbs,
when the 'dealers' are just rich kids with an allowance
making %100 profit.

A leader is a leader sometimes,
not because they ask for the reins,
but because a million inferiors recognize them
as their only hope to escape themselves.
A million inferiors Give of Power
and some think they receive a little in return,
so don't punish the Ones—
some are not as manipulative as you might think
and Artists are consumed less by their art

Love_Is_An_Anonymous_Cyberbully

than by consumers.
Although they are generally too weak
to dispense of their power,
the receivers are so weak they would imagine
they receive it in equivalent measure—
they are more like receptionists.

Sure, in hand-to-hand combat
a 'leader' might say "You better fucking recognize,"
but some would rather be nobody—
because that's how they began—
than weighed in as the catch of the day by aliens
that look at them like Brooke Shields lengthening her eyelashes.

No quote was ever made by anyone who said it,
but by the unimaginative cancer
blogging about their lives via references—
and even comedians do not steal jokes,
that ultra-comic expression of the times.
People send memes and shit Christmas cards.

Get booze on drunk,
not the cheers of people who wear headphones
or carry planners
or check off calendars
because their ignorance and detachment are more alert.
And they look at you out of the corner of their eye
out of fear
and cool (same thing).

"A riot is a last-resort for the unheard."
That is what MLK Jr. said,
and he never saw the riots of fashion
or internet comments

or punk rock coke bars.

There are people from *that* past who are long dead,
but were smart enough to understand the present times quickly
in their backwards lexicons.

Whether you look at it from above or below
or right or left or future or past,
it is shit.

Bukowski was a poet
and poets hate everything, love it and do nothing about it—
because poetry can turn the Nile into a short piss stream,
and inside every poet there is a walrus on a rock.

Bukowski wrote novels out of contingent compulsion,
and that's all.
After all, he said
"AVOID THOSE THAT ARE ALWAYS READING BOOKS"
which necessarily includes *his* readers.
I will never write books. I am not Bukowski.
I don't enjoy reading novels
because they are full of filler, always.
(I only have redundant things to say about them.)
I will always prefer the summary,
and that is not my fault or the fault of the writers.
I would have read them, but only out of social pressure—
never personal gain (two sides of one dick).

Pynchon or DeLillo or Ballard or Danielewski—
they do not understand poetry
and are like Pharaohs constructing pyramids.
The poets were always slaves—not even masons.
Their poems were the pleasure of waste, the inalienable,

Love_Is_An_Anonymous_Cyberbully

what cannot be stolen because it isn't wanted—
because expenditure always comes from luxury.
Their poems are hara-kiri,
burnt money,
guns that only smoke.

Poems give less than novels...
and make fun of themselves without authority to do so.
Novels are full of psychological depth
and detail
and the law of non-contradiction
and precision—
even the precision of obscurity—
even if during the whole masterwork, they only portrayed one
Idea.
Novels are also all so full of plans
sketches
and technics—
but the poetry flows like shit
piss
and whale fat.
Novels like Moby Dick or the Bros Karamazov
were designed for a time when people had leisure
and immense boredom and dread.
But I can watch 10 films in a day
or read 150 poems or 1000 tweets—
each as silent as a Sports Illustrated Swimsuit Ed. page
and as superfluous as the bios.

I don't care what your protagonist had for breakfast;
I don't care about their back story—
I have my own, and it's already WAY too LONG,
and it's out of respect for others like me that I don't repeat it.

Poems are slim peasants
who have the appetite of loggers and the metabolism of women.
They are not wasteful out of utility.
They are a bruised shin peeking out of a red-carpet dress
sexier than the 21-year-old ass cheeks hanging out of mom-jean
cut-offs.

After Bukowski the novelist:
a million shit 'comedy' novels
and a movie directed by James Franco that got canned,
when it's unclear what comes first—the thing or the image.
Apparently even the accursed can be made sexy.
Bukowski's corpse was happier,
more beautiful than he was
and advised better than Socrates' death "Withdraw your effort."

Our best specimens inspire the worst among us
to do the stupidest things.
A redneck family kills the biggest crocodile in recorded history
with a starter rifle they bought from Bass Pro Shop—
because if you are in your prime,
you'll fall prey to a million lay-idiots.
So why write at all?

328. snapchat

I sat next to you at the bar
like a car parked too close to the white line,
and I couldn't open the door to my mind
without scratching yours.
Your hair flowed frozen dead down your body
like a shirt on a hanger that leaves stretch-marks on the shoulders.

Love_Is_An_Anonymous_Cyberbully

Your skin, an off-white—yellowish like an aged electrical outlet.

You played trivia on your phone with your brother.
You were either nervous
distracted
bored
or not interested in what I had to say—
but it was you who asked if you could see me.
I am a display unit only.

The lights were dull in the bar,
and the ambience was filtered—
the mood was technical, auto-fixed.

You said that you didn't like to leave traces,
that you liked my poems more when they were not about you,
that you grew furious when you read them when they were.
I am not the one
who decided that your image be beyond your control.
That was decided before you were born,
but God did not speak it.
You said you can only have relationships that mean nothing.
You were safe—
but safe like a person who lost their fortune
and found shelter and love among Christian churches
whose only functions are to grow the numbers.
You said your relationships with men
have nothing to do with you,
and you like to keep it that way.

When variety and freedom have exhausted you
like a stake-less footrace whose only pleasure is that of a test,
it seems ignoble to have an opinion.

Critical Leisure, Book III, Volume VI

The libido can be reduced to a squib kick,
oozing like toothpaste,
when all the holes gape and preclude friction—
peaceful coexistence.
You think sex is a stupid social dance, and I don't disagree.
The wonder cannot withstand
the vivisection of a curious consciousness
for which nothing is not suspect.
Things that kill passion:
baseball and allegiance to the American flag.
Passion wilts like cellophane melted to enclose drugs,
the only passions we're allowed.

'Writer's block' is a fantasy invented by Homo-oeconomicus.
It turns out, communication may have originated as an ideology.
The ability to chat *in a snap*
is what invented the awkward silence that irrupts in shooting the shit—
the cuticle of killing time.

There is a vertiginous panic in our fun.
We rock autistically, only socially
and thus despairingly,
cradling a lost loved one *we killed*.
The object is gone—
but the joy remains in the form of laughter
and perpetuates the sorrow,
albeit videoed by a camera hidden by you
like porno outtakes and gag reels.
Hedonism, a failure. Utilitarianism, a failure. Asceticism, a failure.
Nihilism, a possibility—
short (or ahead) of a success or a failure.
The cock we offered Asclepius is limp,
but krumps headlessly.

329. There Is No Natural High

We lock the door.
Not to Actually keep out the Badies.
The 'locked door' is not a real, effective means of deterrence.
The 'locked door' is a *sign* intended to ward off Evil,
to magically Display security,
a discourse intended for ourselves,
a rabbit's foot on a key chain like a pocket-book can of mace.
"No one has broken in
because we keep our doors locked," we say—
never having been subjected to a break in.
Our securities are miraculous.
It's Hope and Insurance that kill Faith.

Our securities are sacrifices given to God
the Sun
the Light Without Objects, the Total Medium.
We are vampires living off the patented *blood-drink* of Christ—
where Sanguine is a red Jell-O
molded into the shape of whatever apparatus it is chilled in.

The trees,
plotted in rows in islands that separate the Two lanes of the streets,
gawk at us
like Fundamentalists outside of the abortion clinic.
We hang like towels
draped over aluminum rods coated in sterling silver,
free to eat pizza in bed.

There is no Natural High.

We are all Woman (simplified).

Critical Leisure, Book III, Volume VI

330. the rapid pelvic thrust of anality

We know longer believe in sex.
And what is left? Play?
But no, the play is preceded by a copy,
the vivre by a model whose anality can only loop joy,
fearfully mastered to a dull panic.
The future is spun into a series of days,
whose certain vertigo
blurs their limits to a fascinating hue,
to that gaze without a focus, without a periphery—
a stare whose interruption is without daydream
as if an invisible seizure…
the future expropriated by a flip-book consciousness—
that, while certain to the vague extent of an irritable perfection
that configures its own contents to a mix-and-match, arbitrary precision,
must constantly prove to itself
that something happened before and after something else
with the jargon of now.

To simulate sex, which we no longer *want* or believe in,
we *demand* technique—
and when mere technique cannot keep with the demand of simulation,
the market economy of equipment—
wrongfully called 'toys' (which would still be related to play)—
comes into the bedroom
with the speedy angle change of the camera
hidden by the discontinuity of television commercials.

For the eye, too, has grown bored of the cinema
and must be locked in
by constant undeniable movement.

Love_Is_An_Anonymous_Cyberbully

And no one will ever get this far
in this book.

331. fetish-conscious fetishizers

I considered the classroom
through a window in the door,
and the floor was padded with wrestling mats.
The room was filled with naked people.
None of them were touching one another,
but the men were erect, and the women were moaning,
flaring their nostrils
as their irises bounced around in their eye sockets
like puppets on stage.
The people were moving rather oddly,
still mechanically, technically—
not dancing, since dancing is sensual
free
and improvised
(the limbs do not obey the dictates of formality).

The room was a total medium,
and the bodies in it were not bodies.
They were messages.
The space between them was thickened,
quickened by their movements,
but not infected by their gestures.
The longer I watched the proceedings therein,
the more familiar the gestures became.
Two familiar words: "thrusting" and "riding."

The people attending this workshop,

as I came to understand it,
were there to experiment.
They were pedagogically receptive
to some brand of technical instruction.
It had nothing to do with application—
it was a code of conduct.
The bodies were not conductive,
as touch is what electrifies the body.
The body was without current, without currency—
and it was not an object
a commodity
or even mere material.
It was info
data
code.

Erect penises stabbed the lurid air
like Chinese Opera—
but without grace since grace still implies an aura.
The vaginas dripped
and the drops slung around the room
as if they were waiting for slow-motion cameras.
The ejaculate couldn't be distinguished from the sweat—
that is the secret of work,
which these people are proving really *is* a demand.

It became clear to me,
what these people were 'doing' was fucking air,
the fetish to end all fetishes.
Not touching a body, but not even looking at a body—
not even looking at the body as a linear porno.
These people were fucking air
humping it
cumming to it.

Love_Is_An_Anonymous_Cyberbully

They weren't looking at one another—
like people in cars stuck in traffic.
They weren't saying anything to one another—
sort of like people watching television.
Their orgasms had no trajectory,
but popped up like ads
in this space no different from ad-space sidereal the site content
and yet primary to the site.

These people didn't mutilate the body by using it.
Nor did they mutilate its image by jerking off to it.
Nor did they reduce it to one of its fragments
by partializing and fetishizing it.
They *preserved* the body *by not touching it.*
They preserved sexuality by taking the sex out of it.
By fucking air, they proliferated sex
with no concern for a natural whole or an artificial part.

By making it a farce, they gave it a future.

332. I prefer the dead to you, hero

Almost all my friends are dead.
They are no longer even decomposing
but are the shit particles of mites
sold
but not labelled for individual sale at Home Depot—
incorporated into plants programmed to die shortly thereafter.

They cannot pester me.
They cannot sit too closely to me on the couch.
They cannot bother me by putting things too close to my face.

They cannot offend me by comparing me to other people.
They cannot ask me "Where do you want to go eat?"
They demand nothing of me:
no decision-making
and nothing to live up to
entertain
or reciprocate.
Our nebulous friendship is more beautiful than the dark,
and their presence is less terrifying than the Beatles.
I see the Beatles like I saw beetles under damp logs
within the despotism of childhood curiosity
that pulls things apart and makes them other than what they
were—
where wristwatches taped to batteries
become bombs
that don't require understanding of their mechanisms.

They are good friends in their silence.
If I met them they'd disappoint me,
but that disappointment would be their lesson
and their gift.

If my partner ever met Jesus,
who said "It's too much to text, but Elvis is a metaphor for myself
a prophet of God
my father
my brother
my best friend
and really the only way I relate to being alive.
Elvis is everything to me,"
she'd belch him from her bowels
cramp up
throw up

and brush her teeth, pull out her hair and become a new human being—
new and blemished by neither Elvis or her former self.
His glitter would be glaucous
like the castles littering Europe, abandoned but maintained,
with all the blood that formerly soaked them—
and made them exceptionally common—
pressure-washed away.
Europe and South America get their fertility from sacrifice alone,
and they do not prefer human blood
to carapaces drained by spiders.
American soil, like Elvis, is too productive and bloodless
to sustain us for too long—
but like Elvis, it will consume us in our starvation
and *become richer without us.*

Mostly, if people met Jesus they'd find him annoying—
like progressive, democratic lesbians who use organic toilet paper.
Jesus is too pretty in his pictures—
but that is *his message*,
since he was made a god the same way children enter the world—
covered in shit and piss that lubricate the exit
out of a ripped visible organ.

333. Born second

She came out after me
like the urine that follows the shit,
that infantile orgasm of excrescence,
bladder of the world depressurized by its own bowels.

I am the billiard balls left on the table after the 8 ball has been sunk

that the losers will sink for practice
with a cue ball in place of the will,
an investment or competitiveness.

I finger her digestively
like the villi over which the shit crowd surfs in the colon.

She eyes me with numerous looks that hook into my back
and travel with me,
as plentiful and painless for her as the quills of the porcupine,
whose number I can't estimate without creating a margin of difference
like a bell curve smaller than her breasts.
I am suspended from the dungeon slab ceiling,
her hooks digging into my back fastened to chains—
Goldie Locks opening Bastille like Walmart on Black Friday,
but a day earlier to beat the competition.

I see her Ferris-wheeling eyes, drunk,
giving the Plebs access to the skyline
and the condo condescension
that comes with the vapid return to Google street-view.
The dermal layer of my brain bleeds away menially
from our synthetic chemistry,
but rebounds like fingernails
hair
teeth
and the stuff of tumors.

My head throbs—Remembering—like my member.
She dismembers me,
throws my giblets in a lake,
but returns panicked for my head
when she notices the black garbage bags floating

to forestall the investigation.

Nothing impresses either of us.

334. The light in the oven

They put a light in the oven
as if you need to watch it cook,
an extension of the rotating pleasure of the microwave,
the vision of which will give you brain cancer.
The useless addition of the inner vision,
the banal certainty of the ultrasound,
the in vitro preparation,
the pantomimic radiology of the X-Ray,
when the sun is irradiated
and skin only shines a cloudy, dirty martini olive.
They will make ovens that live-stream the cooking on your smart phone
and in utero monitors to live-stream the development of the fetus.

We want to watch 'our' Unconscious develop.

335. font

When the wind is absent so that the trees look dead
or when the leaves are dead so that the wind looks invisible
or when the wind is rapey
and the leafless trees finger the sky like tickle-fetish erotica,
trees doing a drunken jig
and spitting from cigarettes that last too little or too long...

when the will is like an AK47
that still loads and fires with the sand
the water
and the sun
like sex on the beach that signifies but is unenjoyable,
and when the love takes all your clothes in the cafeteria,
and the fear is a couch with no ottoman,
and the work-ethic is firewood for sale in the front lawn
that expects a trustworthy knock on the door,
and the beauty is women in sweat suits
at the psychologist's office
school
or the supermarket...

the focus groups are anarchists,
the sex partners enter one another like shopping carts,
the apartments stack into one another like unclouded plastic containers,
the truth scratches off
like lottery tickets that pay out enough to buy another ticket
and the folly is freemium.

336. On agon, Off agon – le cirque de logique

When you arrive early to Anywhere,
babysit a bottle of wine as you wait for another to arrive
like Christ's arrival as a crusader,
Hitler's return from the center of a hollow, Tootsie Pop earth
in a yellow submarine,
Dionysus' return to gendered being
or a return

Love_Is_An_Anonymous_Cyberbully

to indifference that dismisses differential fitness,
to health as accumulation of life and antibiotics,
to no one.

Can you eat pizza like an American machine—
the opposite of a vending machine—
taking the junk and spitting up the cash.
Drunk ON wine,
ON the media creating 'fake' wars,
each resembling one another like the blades of a fan,
with only a flash of a Scud shot down by a Patriot
replayed 1756 times in a row,
until you can really feel the whistling Scud limit your data usage
and AC
as the girl from down the street arrives crated somewhere—
bartered/auctioned/created/displayed
like a retina display that improves on the eye,
which cannot look away
to the extent that it becomes a useless function,
seduced by the movement of things that have already disappeared.

The reenactment is a re-run
before the event has had time to take place or finish,
the movie already in the works
as what demarcates the war from a fraud,
the real proved by the anti-real.

A war cannot be a war any longer.
The *agon* is retained only in the furtive passings of everyday
scoffs.

Express remorse when the punk girl of 19
says you really scare her drunk, while you're being polite,
that she's afraid you *might* do something fucked up

so is already upset with you,
but feel the triumph of intimidation intimately
like a fortune unearned.

There is a WAY, an American way—
a police waypoint—
that makes you anticipate (in a useless attempt to prevent) events.
The interim between consumptions and expulsions.
Is it as unbearable as the time of wine,
alone in a cock-sucking pizza parlor
supposed to be more authentic
more original
more romantic
radical [rooted in reality]
than a papa john's?
But I like the skin-like flappy crust dangling like a horrid cunt
or a limp baby found in a hospital toilet,
saturated in a plasti-cheese like the fat
off a TV screen more alive and more loved than you or me.

It will make you enjoyably sick
like the man spreading AIDS as if he were the Nuke himself;
like the homeless man selling postcards he calls "prints of his artwork,"
saying that he will make more paintings in the winter
when he will be spending more time indoors.

He will give you the shocker
as he rolls up in his 2013 Camaro, *fully loaded*,
with a trunk-full of acrylics
installation art
and the women of the block.

When the girl of 19 arrives,

Love_Is_An_Anonymous_Cyberbully

looks at you more forcefully than a TV screen
but equally as provocatively and says "You scare the shit outta me,"
it will make you feel the ecstasy
of a copy of a copy.
You ought to express your gratitude to her
because when life gives you the spins,
you must de-form yourself *out of* habit—*out of* gratitude.

So, when you go home drunk OFF wine
and your roommate owes you 47$,
punch a door off the hinges
and express remorse the next day by cleaning it up without speaking
because the only passion greater than misanthropy
is magnanimity.

337. Youth, get a Life

She told me to 'get a life'.
That means I need to live truly and not falsely
(insofar as the true is simply the actual).
But if I were to draw that distinction between truth and lie
I would only be swearing allegiance to ancestors
and an immature mentality of humanity.
Before art there was just work,
and the liar was just the unproductive consumer
cheating by saying his output was greater than it was.

And where would I have drawn the line?
I would have to be a Heideggerian Nazi of authenticity.
And I would only be able to find the Majestic

in part of the world,
the part that supposedly is good and true.
I would have had no choice but to be a naturalist
in the pathetic sense (in the sense that to live is 'instinctual').
I would have had to live off the land somewhere
in the Blue Ridge Mountains,
but we know those folks *only* exist to entertain us on Reality TV.

I tried out many ways of being.
I tried spiritual religiosity and analytic scientificity.
I tried Republicanism and Liberalism
and their "neo-" evolutions.
I tried to be an Anarchist.
I have even been a Fascist for a little while
and watched Nazi documentaries
and shaved my head without ever acting on my pretenses.
I tried to be moral
thoughtful
and pure,
and I tried to listen only to the body and reduce everything to a
body.
I tried abstinent asexuality and licentious sexuality.
I tried sadomasochism
and shy politeness
and non-aggressive, intimate love-making.
I tried all sorts of philosophies
goals
rules
hairstyles
and manners of dressing.
I tried to love and to give myself,
and I tried to hate everyone and stay uninfected.
I tried to be classy and to be a thrifty hippie.
I thought once maybe I was crazy,

Love_Is_An_Anonymous_Cyberbully

and I thought once maybe my parents screwed me up,
and I thought another time I was to blame for everything.

I thought once I would only date older women.
And I thought when I got older I'd only date women 25 or younger,
but fuuuuuck that.
I once believed in true love and soulmates,
and once I believed love is just a word or a narcotic.

I once believed in selfishness,
another time in altruism
and another time in the enlightened self-interest of society.

I believed in social contracts,
in nihilism,
in Jung
and in Freud,
in Hegel
and in Marx.

I've been a romantic
a skeptic
an existentialist
a post-modern
a critical theorist
a socialite
hermit
and imbecile.

All in all,
I've been an alien moving from Heavenly Body to Heavenly Body,
mining each to exhaustion
and gathering only enough fuel to move to the next one.

I suppose you are familiar more with the layman, Don Quixote,
moving from mirage to mirage
and dragging his friend through the whole *trip*,
really *laying* it on him.

My problem is not that I have no life,
but that I've tried so hard to procure one (a future)
that I have come to realize through my experience
the *active apathy*
that's above all an avoidance of a single question, "How to live,"
in the manic construction of a ground wire
before the circuit is even closed.
And now with her words as the mark,
it's time to die—
to live presently, destroyed.

338. save a troll, ride a toll-road

Things always seem to work out for me—the good and the bad,
the bad so long the good nearly burns out
(in a donut, or an accelerated turn while the brakes are still on).
It gets better and it gets worse.
My luck is bound to run out. I'd rather have fate.
Probably because it always eludes me.

I promise you you're more alone than you think.
You think your parents love you,
but get into some real trouble and see if they stick around,
and you're poisoned by their blood, anyway.
(I don't always keep my promises.)

You think you've got friends,

Love_Is_An_Anonymous_Cyberbully

but the only reason they care about you
is because you've got something they desire or need,
and if they really hate you they will satisfy you
only to the extent that they are not alone,
never alone………………………….
and get to tell one more person EVERYTHING about them.

If you're as lonesome as people are theorized to be,
then you'll find someone—your own personal WD-40—
and two lonesome doves will be cured like pepperoni.
And maybe he'll get up one morning
and the apartment will be emptied—
no note, not even the TP she paid for.
Or maybe he'll push her into the oven
or leave her things on her front steps and quote Christopher McCandless
because he found some photographs…
who cares? I don't right now.

You can go around thinking about the world,
engaging in things
affairs
everyone and everything—
whether it's sitting in silence for 673 straight minutes
with dead strangers
or trying to sleep next to a coyote or Toucan Sam
or too much teeth for 47 years.
You can be sure of it, I promise you
(YOU TRUST ME RIGHT?!),
community is for the birds,
and you can huddle together for warmth all winter
and try to hatch your perfect continuance if you'd like,
but it will catch up to you.

Because one thing is reliable if you're depressed:
people are dirt.
And having so little care, they don't care.
And having no one to talk to, they don't let you talk.
and if they stand nothing to gain, you will lose them,
middle finger up your ass to aerate your abject isolation.

Hold fast to the nobodies.
Because only the loner understands
and respects you enough to let you be,
and everything is cool and understood, and who cares?
They don't anymore.

It's better that way.
When they love you, they disappear with you
before the somebodies vanish.

339. If I don't disappear

If I keep writing
I'll be the only person who isn't a singer.

If I keep writing
I'll be closer to my dream of doing nothing.

If I keep writing I won't disappear
because I won't be doing just nothing.

If I keep writing
it's because I think I'm better than Rilke
Neruda
or Jenny McCarthy.

Love_Is_An_Anonymous_Cyberbully

If I keep writing
it's because I'm watching
the nightly local and/or entertainment news.

If I keep writing
I'm still lying about quitting writing
and getting attention that doesn't matter because I created it.

If I keep writing
it's because I'm afraid of doing nothing.

If I keep writing,
it's because I'm in denial of writer's block.

If I keep writing
it's out of habit and military-style routine.

If I keep writing
it's because I have trouble concentrating.

If I keep writing
it's foreplay with Death
whose swollen feet make his dick seem like it'll be bigger.

If I keep writing
I have taken a break from learning.

If I keep writing
something else didn't pan out (including writing).

If I keep writing
I'll leave other promises unfulfilled.

If I keep writing nothing will change.

If I keep writing
I'll improve my brain with the science of neuroplasticity.

If I keep writing
I'll forget I wrote *this* piece of shit.

If I keep writing
it's for the "The Women Tell All" special.

If I quit writing—
which I have already done by now (editing)—
I exhausted the poetic and had to shut up
or had to lay low after a Ponzi scheme called *being an author*.

340. Poetry is no longer itself

Poetry is no longer itself.
Poetry believed in as labor power (revolutionary)
and *read* out loud in public spaces
is for degenerates—
poetry become a spectacle only because it's dead
and known to be so,
like family photos that leave no room unpenetrated
by the disgusting happiness of the lifeless.

Poetry realized become a function
a blog
a newspaper column
a university publication
a contest

Love_Is_An_Anonymous_Cyberbully

a *reading*
like music become 'a show'—
all these desperate significations and circulations
that 'express' like Descartes, sickeningly,
that "poetry MATTERS *because it exists*
is still produced
is still shared," express nothing...
they SIGNIFY nostalgia for a dead husband
by a wife that no longer has a purpose
because her life was dedicated to him.

'Poets' are only those beings who cannot let go,
who even if they have rejected transcendence
by now have done so only in favor of ironic participation—
in favor of a metaphysic-begetting immanence.
They are Warhol, whose speech asked for no verification
but lacked the awareness of itself as such.

Either this "dumb blonde" poetry or that of the New Yorker—
all reactionary measures and policed deterrence.
They defend poetry.
They defend poetry like their right to a fair trial.
They defend poetry like they defend beautification of urban areas.

Poetry, like Bukowski, is dead.
Poetry, like Bukowski, can only placate mechanics
and baristas
and servers.
Poetry is not subversive. Neither is it waste.
It isn't transcendence or immanence or depth or superficiality.
It referees nothing.
Not the relation between appearance and reality,
or between the individual and society,
or between being and nothingness.

It doesn't produce. It doesn't even seduce.
Poets are like the people
paid to dance and hold up signs—
since there is absolutely no reason for a human being to hold a sign,
which could be pinned to a telephone poll
or sent in an email
or posted on the news feed,
other than the need to give people jobs.

The anarchist poets cling to life
to meaning
justice
queer theory
feminism
philosophy
to Poetry
and history
to representation
and the breakdown of representation.
And that's because *there is none of that.*
They are backwards neurotics
when discontentments have become exchangeable signs
that lead to success.

Poems can offer nothing but a combination of messages,
whose content is different
only because they all share the same form.
That's because poetry is 'written' on the computer,
and if it's hand-written on paper
that's because of the *aforementioned nostalgia.*
So you might as well get an MFA
and go fuck yourself (by telling people about it).

Love_Is_An_Anonymous_Cyberbully

Poetry (or what I'd rather call 'Broetry')
can be nothing but a montaged collage of combinatorial signs.
It cannot hurl disparate images at one another—it cannot *seduce*
culture.
It has lost exoticism—no East and West in the global.
It has no culture.
And cultured poets kneel in fealty to the guillotine.
It doesn't even have the hallucinatory fever
of solitary confinement or darkness—
no cave and no allegory.
It is pure light without negation.
It has presents no criticism, only commentary,
because it's identical to the system.
Poetry is not even stripped bare.

Poetry, as a fragment of the system, can only reproduce the
system—
because it, like a hologram,
can reproduce itself from every fragment
like how DNA can reproduce any whole organism.
It is useless to revert to thought experiments
about whether the clone is identical to the organism—
that's just a hope for the meaning of personal experience.
Poetry is a sign (and at the level of signs, *all things are*
equivalent).

Broetry is not the acceleration of Poetry's demise—
destructivist thought imagines some living thing to kill
and thus perpetuates the 'victim',
but poetry is no longer a thing.
Do not reify it.
Neither is Poetry to be given up for 'lived poetry',
whatever that means.

I am caught between the unwillingness to reject
and the unwillingness to participate.
It is a somewhere I know not where,
an impasse and stupid utopia (in which I do not believe).
I'll hate nothing—because I do not believe in anything.
But my lack of hatred is not a Yes.

I offer future 'writers' nothing—
no footholds and nothing to be rejected or overcome…

because to overcome me
would be to think I am something,
but I am not even nothing.

341. "Be together, not the same," said the marketer to Wallace Stevens

The King of Burgers
and Romeo harking at his incompatible lover
through the drive-through microphone, gag-gift of convenience.

The willy-nilly as the Daring Willing,
the whatever as Right—
Hamlet, ghost-hunter, interfering subjectively with the Tape.

The Receipt w/ a cutoff Coupon with Code,
the colonoscopy of the Ratio—
Candide Wwoofing as Christmas farms rope off Blue Ridge.

Morals will not Save you with the Inflation.
Bonds appreciate in deposit boxes like friendship,
which pits two against the Social.

Love_Is_An_Anonymous_Cyberbully

Unroll socks like sod into Silicon strips
when truth is a dancer who grinds on your lap,
touches you,
but who you can't touch back and must pay.

342. Blistery night

I cannot get off on love or lubricity.
I need blisters, tight holes that grip me like calloused hands.

The female orgasm
makes no sense to the Rationale of Human Productivity,
more akin to an automated workforce
of robots owned by the elites.

The female orgasm has nothing to do with love
or childbearing or function.

The female orgasm is a superfluity,
never reached
never understood
only witnessed in its effects—
unconscious to the Spirit of capitalism.

The female orgasm is easy faked
easily simulated
easily exaggerated
and demands skepticism
apathy
and comparison.

I cannot get off on pleasing the Other,
on other-directedness or the auto-didact.

I cannot get off on the moan
the full-body
the squirt
or the placement of cum into speech.

I fuck her hard, hardly thinking of her,
questioning if she is consenting, hoping to rub her raw
myself raw
and cause *her pain* pleasure.

I hope to drain her lubricity,
but she keeps reproducing it and I never cum.
If I cum, her thighs are pressed together, extending her cunt,
or her sphincter squeezes me and chokes my dick to its last breath—
spitting up its life like its lunch money,
rejecting its content like a baby 'fucking with' its concerned parents.

If she cums it is secondary
subsidiary
a detour.

I grip the life right out of her.
I fuck her until she can take no more, not even primitively.
With no need for foreplay
thought
visibility
or play.

It's not rapey—just hard fucking,

Love_Is_An_Anonymous_Cyberbully

exposing the lack of necessity for positivity,
the needlessness of anything other than brute, base matter.

She gets off, I get off—
a mongrel who rolls over after release,
cuddling tightly after
with the same closeness I try to break through
by ramming myself into her,
beating the head of my dick against her vaginal walls.

I don't need to blindfold her
whip her
fondle her
suck her
call her a slut
or cum on her face—I don't care what she asks for.

I hope she stays silent
cold
with no signs of pleasure—
I'll fuck her harder if she does all that and she knows it,
takes advantage of it.
We compete.

We compete not through mutual technique,
trying to better the other.
We compete through our coldness, our distance—
proving the other is nothing to each
(because they are everything).

In that way we are equals—made for each other.
Strong.
The pubescent strength that detaches itself from the parents
but still takes from them

in their need and 'pathetic' attachment.

343. a tree, you can't move me

I lean against the bank at the ATM,
making a withdrawal—from myself—
so others can't read my PIN number,
the four-digit number *I* came up with all by myself…
the freedom the bank gives me.

I lean over the bank
with my branches dipping into the water
like the antlers of a great buck stopping for a drink,
my newest limbs bent by its movement but not broken.

In the faces of the poor, you can see a life—
our wrinkles resemble the fields in their fertile Pandemonium—
a Life exhausted by Providence, not the other.

With all your Money
and Beauty
and Prestige—
you have no purchase on the living values,
no Poetry,
but the tutelage of a refining mask and chemical peel of society—

that impermanent simulacrum of Being.

344. Burnout

They say burnout is apathy—
they focus on its subjective
dysfunctional
irrational aspect.
They do not treat its objectivity.

Burnout is a mechanical, *technical* failure,
a product of functional objects themselves.
The will pushes beyond the capabilities of the machine.
The wheels are spinning at their rapidest,
but the vehicle—
an apparatus intended to throw you forward
with minimal effort on your part—
goes nowhere.

Burnout is a psychophysical phenomenon
attached to the monopolization of gestures by technology

…and they tell us a kindness will increase the release of serotonin
and reduce burnout—
so we crowdfund modern technologies.

345. under the hood of the vagina

I can never understand Her.
If I could I could control Her.

I can but experience Her,
become experienced in Her—
(always her impermanence and mood swings)

but as that happens, she changes.

I must love her uncertainly
or live in constant paranoia.

346. Slim-picking

I could never have you
(and you were a piece of Life's pie),
could only receive you as a gift to circulate...
what property cannot do.
You were a bounty,
a gift that keeps on giving
because the motive of gift exchange *is to give*
and the reception of the gift is the vulgarization of gifting.
You were a bounty on my head,
my face marring the aimless snuffing out of the familiar
in hopes of its breakage.
A bounty turned apple resting on my head, the apple of sin,
as the jester throws knives at me like cards
like rappers throwing singles at strippers.

It's as if the world was overwhelmed by itself, by its own richness,
and had to extend itself through us,
its tears in joy and in agony.
God became so agitated by his secretions without end
that he excreted us,
the finite, accidentally, to return to a state of lack.

You looked at me with the same incandescence
with which you looked at all creatures—

me, this arbitrary fragment of things, a severed organ,
this criminal transgression of perfection, the Absolute.
This body is a sliver of your pickings from the rotting corpse of
Life.
Life violates itself to emerge at all.
Life, with no control over its limbs, flailing to be picked up.
Life projects itself through us—the world thinks us.
It thinks "Shit + gold = 0."

You looked at me *generally*, beyond me.
Through me, I emerged as an apparition passing through other
bodies.
I was a shadow that left the floor
and at a perfectly right angle encroached up the wall
(a broken stalk headed by a flower still dying brilliantly).
You spoke through me:
'Horizontal is at some point vertical'.

"At some point you end and I begin."
That attitude is wrong if not inevitable.
You have made a circle out of us.
We have together destroyed each of us.
We have made the satisfied vulnerable to the never mind.
There is a Mobian way once we are stripped,
upon which we walk together forever—
when forwards and backwards dissolve
in a simple twist of fate…You.

You knew you could never have artfully drawn me like a bath
without having traced another, previous image of me
someone else created.
To have drawn me in clearly defined outlines,
you'd have reduced yourself to operator.
You were not a critic.

Critical Leisure, Book III, Volume VI

Criticism is but the application of something dead
the moment it explains everything.
Critics use thought as a readymade.
They enjoy the fruits of others' labor,
use language like an employee
and subordinate the future to the *former*
(as in both the past and the one who forms).
How Western thought is that of children poking at dead bodies!
Bodies of knowledge are no less
thrown under the communal bus than 'real' bodies.
You and I both know words are not our property,
that we are not our property— being creatures of language.
Arguments are antibodies
that without pathogens generate cancers—
they, like antibodies, are not employees of the bodies.
They become autonomous if they are not being used.
Their function is to destroy
and *cannot but pervert their aims to fulfill their function.*
The function is that which works *for itself for another.*

You and I and no clearly defined earth.
You and I without demarcation, without previous markings.
You and I, incomplete towards death.
You and I, lush with previous destructions.
You and I, and there are no masses—just matter.
You and I, realizing neither of us is God and weeping.
You and I, inhaling Life and holding it in
until only a noticeably degraded smoke returns to the atmosphere.
You and I, undertaking unknowing feats.
You and I, round table without executors.
You and I, trouble and insufficient for one another.
You and I, sawing one another in half,
living
and fooling the audience.

Love_Is_An_Anonymous_Cyberbully

You and I, ravenous pit of despair.
You and I, uninhabitable ravine training the eye,
making nautical exploration conspicuous.

Humanity—
shit that won't drip from the sphincter to the water below,
afraid to take a dive
(to lose on purpose,
to let go of the urge to win to leave richer).

347. the Dada, doubling and annulling the phoneme

I analyze the cityscape as a graph
plotted to model the mass extinctions throughout geologic time.
I watch the moving pictures
as images right out of Lascaux or La Magdaleine—
both now off-limits to me and everyone else, I'm sure of it.
I see an Asian woman surrounded by black men
shoving their enormous dicks
into every one of her *tiny little* holes.
She gasps for air and chokes on her own spit.
I see the ithyphallic buildings throbbing for terroristic insertions
and I get horny as hell.
The first cities—where length and girth converged.
I think of where she might be.
The images in my head turn,
and I see her reaching down a man's pants—
I cringe as she whips out a chubby clit-dick.
I become so depressed I think I'm having an anal orgasm.
I've heard that's how they do it at the bank when you're dry.
I think of who she's with

and think she might be swallowing some tiny amount of cum
oozing out
and gasping for air.
I think of holding her hand through these rectilinear avenues
as fellow men eye up her ass and we both ignore them all.
I want to squeeze her hand more and more tightly
until she acknowledges the pain—
that would be creative.
I think of her creeping fingers
skulking up the inside of my shorts,
grabbing the head like a Ritz cracker
as others are there in the room eating finger foods.

Today, I can't discriminate the fabricated memories
from the real ones—memory is liberated! —
but in both cases, they are sexy/horrible.

348. scrying

As I spill my guts to her, my girl taps on her phone
like a monkey-man tapping on the glass to the sharks in an
aquarium
while eating slider burgers.
The damned witch can't put that thing down,
her crystal ball.
She carries it with her everywhere like a repressed memory.
The only time she doesn't have it
is when I try to communicate with her through it.
It cross-cuts our intimacy—there is no *through it*,
no more private distillation of the public,
but the public interruption of the private,
which always existed as a hermeneutical foothold

Love_Is_An_Anonymous_Cyberbully

to analyze public coercion.

I tell her I love her.
She says she only wishes to go to sleep.
That's why she's leaving me: I keep her awake!

Well, girl, sleep off the hangover Life's given you
in your well-lit coffin with built-in charger…

but you'll wake exhausted from over-sleeping.

349. how to make out in this economy without making it out *of* this economy

Read Bukowski
and write like Bukowski
but deny having ever read him.
And if you can, turn his style against his stupidity.
Repeat for Freud and Marx and Nietzsche
and Baudelaire and Rimbaud and Dylan, et al.
And when people tell you they like Buk
tell them, all in all, you prefer Men's Health,
and laugh out loud when people raise their hand in class
or at a conference
or during the press release.
And when they notify you they've been published
or fucked
or that they made an A
or a Baby
say you plan on dropping out with one more credit to go—
and you like unrehabilitated, molested things.
Take a class on Sartre

and have a nervous breakdown during the discussion of Nausea,
and say Celine is better
and that Rimbaud would have fought for the Nazis
just because of the senseless delirium of the Holocaust.
And when you get kicked out, call the professor a hypocrite.
Seduce your first cousin
and tell your mother
you did anal with the lady two houses down last night
and that you hate all people equally, including yourself.
Don't ever tell a beautiful woman she's beautiful,
and if she tells you you're pretty, say thank you and walk away.
And if there are uglier women in the room
go over and talk to them,
and if there are men in the room
look at them
only when you're trying to eye someone up and get away with it,
the men only temporary breaks between seductive glances.
But never stop smiling
like you know something they don't.
Do 40 mph on the highway,
but when people try to pass you, do 80 mph.
Don't go to ice cream socials
or discuss novels
politics
or premarital.
Don't ever take surveys
or vote
or run for office
and if you do fake everything except your victory speech
and give the masses all the free TV dinners they demand.
Don't ever let the doctor stick a tube up your ass
because if you do, they'll want more from you (a metaphor for love).
Realize a talkative woman merely wants to force out your secret

Love_Is_An_Anonymous_Cyberbully

as with everyone else.
You're best just to let them talk themselves into transparency.
Let them deepthroat their own miserable life story,
gagging but getting off.

350. A language

Without the TV guide, the shows and le chose.
Without the movie poster, the poster-child
or the news, the photo or neighborhood pool.
Without the graphic tee or degree in graphic design.
Without the KitchenAid or bistro or café.
Without the roundabout or the right of way.
Without the search engine or Steven King book.
Without the terrorism or shopping mall.
Without the crime or The Times or performance.
Without health or happenings or fad diets.
Without new theories or cures or car crashes.
Without fundraisers, BOGO or going green.
Without the celebrity or politics…

could we then even speak to one another?
But then, existence would just be existence.

I'd like to be a primitive…
fucking
sleeping
not talking
grinning as from an inside joke
according to which *Nature only exists in the White Man's mind*
and lying to him about my pre-history
picking nuts and berries whenever I feel like it, naked.

351. The sacrifice of plasticity or the plasticity of sacrifice

Was love really a record
that when you first purchased and listened to it
was so good you thought you would listen to it forever,
so you listened to it repeatedly, so much so that you got sick of it—
sick of it like the playlist that recycles in the establishment you work at?
Was it an obscure lo-fi album you never grew tired of
because you never quite understood the lyrics—
even if it was a single line that always eluded you?
Or was it pop album you knew all the lyrics to
and so could sing along to whenever any of its songs played—
the hit song everyone knew the words to at the bar,
that everyone just *had* to dance to?
Likewise, was love a cult film everyone in the theater could recite
and laugh at collectively?
Or was it a classic film in whose intimacy you could re-watch
and discover something new in with each additional watch,
depending on your circumstance?
That is, is love anything other than a cultural connotation,
a primal experience that never changes
but is relived like weekends—
or is it an intimate life-form,
a living being that has no essence because it exists in time?

The question of whether love is real or artificial—
or authentic or inauthentic—
is as useless as the comparison
of 'natural' substances like wood to 'artificial' ones like concrete,
even if to the chemist
some things are more structured (i.e., bonded) than others.

Love_Is_An_Anonymous_Cyberbully

The question is
can love remain love—can love *be*.
If it *is*, it dies.
The question becomes whether love lasts—
how long
and to what extent.
Does love grow into great love
and persist by maintaining relevance,
obliterating its form via sudden structural changes?
Or does love regress to a functional relationship?
A plastic love filled with sacrifices
or a rigid love that is preserved—simulated—
by sacrificing the plasticity of those joined by it…
a love that's a rhetorical question
or a love that is a multiple choice…
hot love or cold love.

We love one another,
and by loving one another, always-already love many—
two histories of otherness
contained in the cryptic, violent contradictoriness
of a single gaze between two pairs of eyes…
the 'instinctual' totality of two bodies refracted through space-time.
Can our promises change meaning
and remain what they are?

Is there acrobatic agility
or mere prestidigitation in our love?

Critical Leisure, Book III, Volume VI

352. Let us be satellites without love

Let us be satellites hovering indefinitely
in the constant pull of the object.
Let us orbit the object and take in its data
only to reflect it back at it.
It will implode by its accumulation of the energy we do not let escape.
But we will still be here,
looking up at its absence with the memory of its presence.
We will always be the other's immediate past.

One believes in the truth of nihilism.
I believe in a different truth.
I'd be lying, however, if I left out
even the sun makes me angry.
And I am not even an epileptic.

If joy weren't rare,
always turning itself over into new fashion,
we would be embarrassed to wear it
or would wear nothing.
No one wants to look at the sun,
and if they do it's only because it obscures itself through clarity—
like Hegel.
People would prefer its collapse if only it looked different—
but no one wants a hand-me-down happiness,
even though they cannot be sustained
by a completely new one.

Same channels
same sun
same penis and indifference—
an indifference we neither admire nor despair of

Love_Is_An_Anonymous_Cyberbully

but blink at as if staring into the sun.

Only humans can value even indifference—
creatures that can equally ignore it
(which is still a relation to what would then be a phenomena).

353. My 'goal'

I will become what they have called me:
a "piece of shit," an oxymoron (since shit it holistic).
Though I enter the world in pieces
I am made to disappear.
Yet in my disappearance, I link up to shit proper—
no longer a piece, just shit.
Out of view, my poetry accelerates the bio-degradation of paper.
Let me sell many copies and lay waste to the planet.

As shit, I can *be produced*.
As shit, I am useless.
As shit, I am produced *by consumption*.
As shit, I cannot be consumed.
As shit, I disgust you and remind you of death
and the destiny of all nourishment
taste
and enjoyment.
As shit, I make you laugh, strain.
As shit, you look at me curiously and narcissistically
before you flush me.
As shit, I make you think "That's not me."
As shit, I have multiple consistencies
and exit strategies.

354. I am also disgusted by my morals

When human relations will kill you,
wipe you out in their cleanliness
their order
their rationality
their programming,
one day the atom bomb will be an inefficient means of mass death.
We slow down for 'children at play' signs
as the children are in cramped spaces linked up to cyberspace,
not outdoors,
unless (*or even*) in 'poor areas'—
if we can differentiate those
from a general impoverishment of everyday life
and a fatigue of forced projects or a forced self.

We don't care about the good or are unsure what it is,
but we know 'Thou shalt not look bad
and shalt show all the signs of goodness'.
The premise is still valid.

When we see a beautiful person, we look at her.
We eye up ugly people as well.
We eye up everything stealthily in logically constructed patterns
like a rotating security camera on a schedule—
although with the transience of an oscillating fan
blowing in all directions, inflating egos that wait in complicity.
We don't go up and talk to them.
Eyeing them up is enough.
We've already downloaded the data.
We'll upload later.
In any case, looking is enough—in fact, it is better.
It is cleaner.
Yet it still offers a visceral experience.

Shock and awe—the feeling of being a terminal of information.
The doors of perception are clean.
Everything appears infinite because everything is based on a model and reproduced to infinity.

We treat possibilities like words and things.

355. Tres Equis Especial and the Most Uninteresting Man in the World

The trees do not look special.
The architecture does not look special.
And the fields
flowers
mountains
do not look special.

The sky does not look particularly special.
The ocean does not look particularly special.
And the moon
the sun
the stars
do not look particularly special.

The animals do not look spectacular.
The children do not look spectacular.
And Man
Nature
the Cosmos
 God
do not look or feel spectacular.

The music does not give me ecstasy.
The poetry does not give me voluptuous pleasure.
And drugs
sex
BDSM do not give me ecstasy,
but they are sort of enjoyable.
Yes, Not can be *done*.

The image in the mirror does not satisfy me.
The look of a beloved does not satisfy me
yet exhausts my life in its apogee.
And me, I do not satisfy me.

I have left Everything behind.

I have left Art Philosophy Love Culture Knowledge Work Wealth
and Science behind.
And what am I left *with*?
Myself?
No, I have left Myself behind—
entangled by all those things that deprived it from arising—
like the future, when it's interesting, leaves behind the dead—
a residue.

I have left it all in the dust, but I have not gotten Ahead.

The Guillotine moves faster than a head can.

The Pendulum swings too quickly to be isolated.

The Gallows take Effort.

The Cross I carry is light
because it is made of particle board

Love_Is_An_Anonymous_Cyberbully

and my backpack is posture-pedic.

The Dreams are not Lucid.
They are Vivid but forgettable, and I do not interpret them.

I am so deep that I am superficial, skin-deep like Beauty—a Wound.

I will laterally find the single unnoticeable Feature
that cuts through your beauty like the Gordian Knot
and make you into my Torment.

I will telescope your Flaws by cutting and pasting you
and making a million copies of you, rendering you Base and Disgusting.

356. first impressions

"I appreciate that my androgynous stature
is becoming more like the accepted norm of masculinity
…
women are bringing out that more affirmative, assertive style…
yea, I love that."

He kept talking about a male dominated world,
powerful women
and dating.

"I meditate, I exercise, I cook, I clean, I go to school, I always go
to class, I work, I pay my car payments,
I trim my pubes, I mean…

women don't want all those problems solved,
or else the two of you have nothing to do together."

He went on about a simulation of an enjoyable time.
Apparently drinking is of this kind of simulation.
(But not talking.
Definitely NOT *what he's doing—words* are meaningful.
Yes, relationships are *so* meaningful
and like all meaningful things, *must* be founded.
Harmony. L-O-V-E. Compatibility scores. Compatriotism.)

He said something about his friends—
lesser evolved creatures who got the dick for free
but not the expensive brain—
not understanding why he doesn't have sex.
(I felt an explanation would follow.
It might have.
I mean, pretty much anything counts as one when truth is a demand.)

His mother taught him he's not a white man from America
but a human being from planet Earth—
by the time he got to "Earth," he was speaking Ebonics.

He told her *that* before asking her out on a date.

Instead of saying yes, she just kept talking.
I wonder if he noticed.

Of course he noticed.

Anyways, they had something else to talk about:
how race is not an issue.

Love_Is_An_Anonymous_Cyberbully

(I wonder how many interracial couples
begin with this very conversation.)

"I feel like people only know how to compliment white women
[but not me]."

This part, the racial part of the convo,
lasted for way too long,
so long it expressed a fundamental wane
in the conversational.

I felt like I was on a television network
that played nothing but documentaries—
95% of them about Africa/India/South America/Asia,
the other 5% commercials.

I have sat through worse for a little nookie,
only getting it afterwards
because I complained the whole way through,
if necessary.
Tom Sawyer was a pesky rascal
who might have even been called "a pimp"
if he went to my middle school
(even kids take pleasure in violating seduction
by linking it to exchange).
Like the kids, this guy totally misses the point—
and he and his like
taint all the women they touch
by dulling their sense of taste.
And thankfully,
for the better among them learn what is distasteful
in this sociality and politics,
like a thoroughbred spitting out a toad
that has pissed in its mouth.

I'm not saying love is unreal and thus unfree
and thus unworthy of pursuit,
only that it is *unnecessary*.
I was a little more honest than he was.
And he didn't even sleep with her
after all that castrating
(though *he* even sees *that* as a victory).

357. The beauty of appearances

The men are always about to cum.
The women are always cumming.
The 'man' has a future, lacks cunning.
The 'woman', in the present, *isn't one*.

The 'true' beauty of appearances
is that you need not believe in beauty,
but can let others believe in it
while performing the *label* 'cutie'.

She can only cum out of her mind—
only leaves her mind when cumming.
She has no nature. It's assigned—
not alienated, just becoming.

358. Beauty is secretive

What is this Thing that buries its face and looks only at me
when I am not looking, metonymous and irradiated…

Love_Is_An_Anonymous_Cyberbully

even if I probably have invented it?

The evocative is revoked vocally—
the beauty is thick,
singling me out and belittling me to an irreducible participant,
a player—
who could leave the game at any moment
but never break its rules.

A gentleness breaks through the script
and generates a secret that *recurs ahistorically*.
A halo is more beautiful than a ring
because you cannot place a finger on it.

I speak the chicanery of thrown anticipation, the madness of the made—
handmaid to my procurements
insofar as they are already presentations to others.
I ignore myself like a master but fail pitiably yet irresponsibly.

Accolades are narcotic.
I lie on my side next to you facing you
so I don't choke on my own vomit—
I feel calm with you, Empty,
the sweaty purity of having just expurgated
what has nourished and poisoned me.
I am nothing, not even a mirror image,
behind questions and responses…
a little forgetful and in need of reminders.

Without you, I dry heave reality.

359. Slippery when wet, she was

She would have preferred to be daft—
dead
resigned
immediate.
She is a prokaryote that absorbs eukaryotes with anguish—
drifting and changing course
only by being both deflective and soft,
without impermeable boundaries (amiable).

Of great mind, she is exorbitant—unreasonable.
Seductive, I let her win—always.
I willingly take on a disadvantage.
I am without desire—*out of desire*—ever deferring judgment.
I don't care about the future of humanity—alien to me—
why should I care about my own?
I hope she is in it, and I abhor that grotesque unlikelihood
(a sickening pessimism that defends against nihilism).

There is some point, I know not which, where I turn into her.
Reasons locate that point
but in so doing obscure passage from one to the other.
There is some point at which I cease to love her particularly
and begin loving her generally—
as totally distinct from others
yet without qualities per se.
There is some point at which implosion passes into irruption—
where she brings out the possible in me
through destroying me by our effusive contiguity
(our fusion).

She is "loved by everyone," and I hate when she says that.
At one moment she 'is' self-conscious

Love_Is_An_Anonymous_Cyberbully

about her arms
her ass
her gestures
her walk
her ears
her mouth.
At other moments, she's "hot" and she "knows it."
Each of her moments cannot be added up to a whole.
And neither do they spring from an essence.
They thus constitute neither oscillations nor juxtapositions.
Only the movement of aimless negativity
whose goal is health
can destroy the law of non-contradiction,
since it does not merely 'disobey' it (i.e., legitimize it).
Her negativity comes in contents and that's not enough—
the diluvial rush
comes without the memory of droplets.

She is nervous in my presence,
"can hardly look in my direction" she says as she looks me in the eye.
I tell her she is beautiful.
She says "thank you."
I say that beauty only means something
to those who lack it
and defend it like California against desertion—
whose attention demands the abandon of the Colorado
and its erosive properties.
They cannot see beauty in the effluvium—
that muck generated by power not exchanged with the human.
Their beauty is trimmed and pruned—
but the beauty of horror and flow returns perennially,
forever.
A beauty that does not incorporate putrefaction

weakens aesthetics,
which can only defer totality to modifications
and their conglomeration.
I would not have fully appreciated her
were it not for the ingrown hairs on her legs
her tiny mouth
her deformed pinky fingers
her gelato triceps
her bulbous twat
her double chin—
all those isolated elements
with which came present-at-hand assertions of her unease.
The body is not the sum of its parts—the body has no parts—
but becomes feasible only in its dismemberment.
It becomes sacred with further desecration.
Worse, it secretes.
Beauty is the impotence of the body,
and nothing else for it is possible.

She thinks vaginas are hideous.
The vagina is the dog's mouth of the human body—
safe in its putrescence, runny and open.
I fuck her until I feel exhausted but don't stop there.
Cramped, I work myself to death.
Like Earth, I sweat most of the water from my body,
become a desert across which appropriately named beetles
roll shit-balls.
She says she hates eye contact during sex.
She gazes into my eyes in the dark—
the intermediary that mediates by negating each and privileging
none.
Our brown eyes gaze at one another like pipes expelling shit,
the view through which night enters or leaves the underground.
Sight cannot inhabit it, only the feelers of roaches and maggots.

Love_Is_An_Anonymous_Cyberbully

We embrace one another so tightly while she is on top of me
that we bruise.
Reminiscent of death, welcome mat of maggots, the bruise
contaminates
and its browning—like our eyes—
reaches the inedible joys of chewing gum.
She doesn't cum. Neither do I.
But the sex is incredible without the credibility of an *end*.

She has removed me from the crib of the past,
and thereby from the causa sui of the future.
I have to doubt whether I have been in love.
I thought I had.
I was not wrong exactly—but now lack an answer.
Our proximity abandons our correspondence via letters—
all anticipation destroyed by experience, not vice versa.
She keeps records of conversations she has had.
I forget everything—not necessarily by choice.
It isn't exactly luck. But something like it? Maybe.
If I can say one *thing* about myself,
it's that I don't think what I say is important,
including that previous utterance.
My words are attempts and nothing more.
I am as fallible as the Devil,
sometimes immediately Other, fleshly,
losing the feeling of movement through the incomplete Chaos.
I sacrifice the clarity of memory
for acute sensitivity to the present—never ready for it.
She is here now and will be gone soon.
I try to accommodate that with mental phenomena,
but it's useless.
I am already missing her as I watch her playing with her phone.
She is gutting me of my content(ment)
with the most insignificant of habits I take personally *out of habit*.

She is an accident. I am disfigured.
I can't anticipate her future presence in my life
like I cannot anticipate death.
She is killing me with life.
The accident is what cannot be entered into net gains—
that which is less than a loss.
I am risking myself
her
in winnings re-rolled.

Knowing that she cannot grasp me,
that surest position achievable by the beloved,
she is slowly realizing the only thing that can be grasped
is that which already holds you in its grasp.
She is a lapse in my clutched, phallic identity—
that fucks me by *letting me* piss out the fire of my life,
making me feel powerful and cold, illusively.

O how servility and appropriation can reverse!
How I want to hold her and yet send her away!
How I want to free her *from me* and have her too!

How absurd! To think that I could lose her!

For that would require I have her in the first place—
but my desire for her is different than that.
Were I to have her, my desire for her would cease to exist.
As far as objects are concerned, desire dies.
But there is second order desire,
that in desiring to desire, desires lack—
only there is it infinite.

As an object, she's not identical with my desire.

Love_Is_An_Anonymous_Cyberbully

This other,
she dissolves its channel and it floods
and soaks into various vascular systems from which it sweats.
A portion of her exceeds what I have become familiar with
and breaks out to my excitement
with each new moment we have together.
She surprises herself even.

We both *undergo* a singular embrace together—
and our bodies,
by setting up touch as a limit to be transgressed,
set up the infinitude of our affection
(and infinity amounts to zero).

360. Indifference, hatred, seduction

Her body felt emaciated
like a sharp instrument or a piece of modern furniture.
She had little muscle and no fat, a perfect vegan.
She didn't shower,
but she didn't stink like me because I sweat toxins,
while she sweats in perfect attunement with the water cycle.
Still, her body felt like Christ's:
sharp and jagged—abandoned and obsessed over.
Her piss was clearer than mine,
and her mind was too.

Her whole body was like a giant vulva,
and when I touched her breasts lightly,
she quivered and exhaled abruptly
like she felt so much pleasure that it hurt her.
The tendons on her neck were two clitorises

and felt equally organic and muscular.
She experiences a decentered
deterritorialized
primitive pleasure.
An explosive pleasure—amputative—
that overloads and destroys pleasure in its violent dispersion.
Pleasure does not take pleasure in itself.
She had no erogenous zones,
just a central nervous system—a decentralized psychic system.
She would touch me close to my genitals,
linger and stagnate,
and while I would get impatient and revolt,
she'd extinguish my rebellion for my own good—
a rule beyond principle.

I don't know what she wants with me.
She is too good for me.
She cannot resist me for some reason.
If I knew it, I could accentuate and develop it.
That's why she will keep it a secret—
perhaps it's my not needing to know.

I wanted to show the world in its glorious waste…
when it's already too late—
and thus a waste of time—to do so.
I wanted to disclose the sign in all its artificial destruction,
thought in its realistic simplification.

361. Don't take my *word* for *it*

I have always been content to keep silent
wherever there has been an overabundance of words—

Love_Is_An_Anonymous_Cyberbully

to let talkers talk, without exactly listening,
but better, letting them believe that I am listening,
that 'them' that they place within me like a card swallowed by an ATM,
disappearing only to be spit back out along with the withheld money.

You should not listen to me.
If you do, it is not my fault—like the Devil.

Tending is the Accidental, the ineffable,
a predilection to curtail the delectable.
Pre-tending is training for work,
a subordinate activity given categorically to children
by adults whose language has grown too exact
to understand irony or play.

362. The leap is not a fall

I was the garbage bin she landed in (like one 'lands' a job interview)
after she jumped from the balcony—
cushioning her fall by transferring the lingering smell of a piss sauna,
the sweat beneath hooker tits,
Bruce Jenner's Adam's apple in a pickle jar,
Madonna's Spanx unwashed
and pressed with cornstarch, crack and meatball subs.

I am hard and soft like sand
snow
water

or trash—
such is friendship.

If you leap, I will catch you, Other.
If you fall, you're on your own, Same.
If I fall, let me, Lover.
If I leap friend, observe the rules silently. Game.

363. reification through anti-reification

Art pour l'art is still an art project,
and we illuminate Night with epilepsy
like a nervous prison guard puts the hood over the hangman's head
(which will remain alive for 6 minutes
after his body is already dead *to him*).

364. Baby, you are a K-hole (from what I understand).

Her inane grace,
her warmth of insanity
and the solicitude of her endogenous gaze
were too well-chiseled—
the vertigo of the pluperfect, the masculine—
to not have been abrupt.
I had a cerebral feeling she was a Trojan horse
left anonymously outside the gates of my knowledge
by God, herself.
Absorbing her, I inherit the unassimilable diffused
and am fractured by seduction—
which God achieves on luck alone, unintentionally.

Love_Is_An_Anonymous_Cyberbully

The wound is sealed and replaced by new tissue,
fresher, uglier.
I vomit then hallucinate.
Anyone with enough experience becomes a hypocrite.

Sometimes God isn't paying attention to me
because He is watching the miraculous in Real Housewives,
in which what is portrayed
is objective reality with all human ends removed from it—base matter.
When He isn't listening I ask him for his credit card;
he says yes unwittingly, and I spend spend spend.
He is only my sugar daddy when He's distracted.
He is angered when he sees the bill,
but that always comes *later*.

Fate can only show itself in chance.

365. Lorem Ipsum

Time doesn't billow backwards.
Neither does it force you forward.
It fakes you into your freedom.
It doesn't go anywhere, but it can't stand still.

They put meat-like soy on the baby
to look freshly made for the movie.
Time spins on surfaces like bottles—
pauses on the person you pessimistically kiss.

And how many idealized lovers
came to symbolize death for their failures—

desires that exceed existence
and tastes develop that we cannot defend.

A presence pries open all your atoms
that made you look away before it did.
Curiosity *curates*. Uncertainty culls—
demands you address her then deepens your shame.

You desire to be appreciated,
but no one's around to see it.
You rely on a small group of people,
and eventually they all make you disappear.

You package your gifts in a worldview
intended for all who're beyond you,
given to a future you can't presuppose
that'll misinterpret everything you made.

366. Jerking off

I jerk off for quick relief
and search for jobs that will be brief
and full of shame, spunk and blisters
think I'll never be somebody's Mr.

As affectionate as the pejorative ass,
disinclined to take my pain with class
and without heart attack during the free fall,
I hope for death but peddle and stall.

I butt-chug to bypass metabolizing life
that mixes rectally with my blood rife—

Love_Is_An_Anonymous_Cyberbully

my introversion interpreted as a keg-stand
around which others chant then disband.

Like Disney put the Jiminy in hegemony
my auto-affective funds are hedged monistically.

367. I hate hating myself and wanting to die makes me want to die

A morbid fear of humiliation.
A solipsist who prevents with impatience.
Embarrassed for caring or for not,
for standing out or for fitting the slot.

Ashamed, my sufferings pale when compared.
And feeling singled out, my claims are unfair.
Hating myself for pain I might've invented
knowing candles aren't burned that aren't scented.

First-world problems have me crippled.
Hung up on what to others seems simple.
Guilt for not reaching my limits—potential—
a voice too monotonous to be Provençal.

"They must be laughing at me! Who else?"
That is the only way I have special felt.
Really, I'm an unbound coupon catalogue—
cut up during errand day without dialogue.

368. Mao Mix for House Cats

Whether I'm feigning illness or health,
I can't make sense of being-without-help—
I look back and see relativized
the past to lack of contact by the eyes.

From disaffiliation completed in a few days
to a general decomposition and malaise—
without even an event to place it,
making it impossible to efface it.

Become incapable of getting on the ball,
I'm disappeared or immeasurably small.
Dead inside and irrevocably irrational,
I've already missed my only curtain call.

After I've given up play with the 'me' I seek,
that me continues hiding and doesn't peek.
When, still attached, I move to other games—
it starves to death and hides its remains.

A thing of equivalence—not one of a kind—
with the feeling of being left behind
can no longer feel itself at stake,
apparently incapable of a double take.

I am touched by your dislike of touch,
traumatized by too little, not too much,
told that my sufferings are insufficient
to deserve treatment, care or attention.

Deflagrated by social structures
that reheat the coolness of the rupture,

Love_Is_An_Anonymous_Cyberbully

I never feel what others do: connection.
In the social mirror, I see no reflection—

an immortal mortal, an indifferent vampire
the more fully I withdraw from the empire,
without hope of renewal, with no former status,
with honeysuckle vines disjoining the lattice.

The darkness underneath my eyes—
explicated as sleep deprived—
plumes like a frostbitten limb
that, severed, leaves perception dimmed.

A pathogen thriving in a clean room,
a host whose party no one comes to,
I dawdle, and they faradize
to forcibly implant the glint in my eyes.

A senseless violence put on record
to certify a lossless past uncheckered
like a blind man blamed for running into,
you can't navigate the place you're sent to.

Told I'm dysfunctional for lack of dreams,
that I'm boring and exactly as I seem—
told exactly who I remind you of,
told that my suffering gives me a buzz.

Trying to determine how I created this,
I forget about the whole by making lists—
when it's cliché to be misunderstood,
when prescriptions are consumer goods—

left to my own devices that fail,

too introverted to accuse or to yell,
paradoxically deadened and an easy target,
without consent, a caught and released varmint.

369. Incompatibility

Some mixtures make sudden explosions
and eat flesh faster than piranha hordes.
The explosions exceed normal dosage.
The bursts alter what you can afford.

The paper trail and the pros and cons
and the expectations are unclear or gone—
people are always better, people say,
if they remain forever those who got away.

We leave the task—we die—unfinished,
and the sessions tend to end mid-sentence,
except that there is never again a next week
to resolve our complicities by freeing speech.

Left with the error without the trial
and always too having gone out of style.
Too organized, we find where we belong
when in doing right we go about it wrong.

When industry was too much, we ate death—
like how after we killed god we saw in life *a test*.
Now, with death in our bellies, in the drive,
we try to elude him but early arrive.

When love is made into an all-night buffet,

Love_Is_An_Anonymous_Cyberbully

some avoid it—dyspeptically anticipate.
But when love is made into a happy hour,
some drink it too fast and lose motor power.

You apologized for your cruelty & it was hard.
Especially for me since it was for your self-regard.
You broke it coolly into cause and effect—
a simplified ballot for the silent many to elect.

You made love into a stock, not a share—
a frame with cardboard enclosure cut to a small square.
You'll keep records, dead words to exhume
to convince yourself the killer isn't in the room.

The metadata of our brief exchange
will subsist within an accountable range,
yet even as you arrange neatly your past,
the future doesn't listen to your sass.

Trace the death of us to a beginning.
Mark it and learn it as a sign.
Abstract a cause, claim your winnings.
In the next attempt you'll be on time.

What to make of incompatibility
when love isn't energetic, has no plasticity?
What to make of your eerie feeling
that this has always been too revealing?

I'm not worth your disparaging cries.
I'm a poet full of shit, shame and lies.
You yell so spitefully at something so puny
that it may appear that you're the looney.

Critical Leisure, Book III, Volume VI

I gave you my truest love, I'm guilty.
It was imperfect and made you see me
as a little, disgusting animal breathing,
not as the foundation on which you built me.

I followed you too closely, scoped you out,
and you noticed, albeit behind the scene.
Then who was following who came into doubt—
like the sun beading off the mirror as a beam.

Give me your suffering like a sugar mint
to wash death out; I'm your fresh discontent.
Brush my whiteness from you swollen tongue
and gag from the tickle of the bulimic young.

I am still a stupid Babar, uncivilized—
murdered by disgraceful Christianity, chastised
then set ablaze as I hang my raised head—
all because of what I never said.

Trivializing your pain, that's your charge?
I'm guilty of the suddenness with which I barged.
It's too much to get attention without rehearsal,
or else I languidly found clever the commercial.

I hold up a mirror, and maybe you hate yourself.
Surely you hate me by extension, who else?
The painter of your unembellished portrait
who never finished it, this malingerer who's torpid.

What an explosive, traumatic, Mobïan twist!
You verbally grab and jerk me by the wrist—
humiliate me to a poor-man's supplication,
except morally with resentful condemnation.

Love_Is_An_Anonymous_Cyberbully

You quickly attack me in my essence
that can abruptly stumble, change its florescence,
that may destroy itself with your nasty words,
as defensive postures are for the rigid reserved.

For some, seduction is an attack.
From the start, they plan to get you back—
worse, get you off their backs with their terms,
until what they said about you wells up, yearns,

because seducing risks seduction.
Now, I beg naively for pain's reduction.
I could disappear with you when you go—
but fresh eyes cannot tell the *to* from the *fro*.

370. Trauma, what dreams are made of

After I have been dismantled,
I leave no trophy head on the mantle.
I will even have been deemed pathetic
for waking during surgery from the anesthetic.

Parents who'd rather I'd not have been born,
to no one will I be a memory mourned—
not even a subject of sleep paralysis,
and worst of all, I resist analysis.

With my social network effectively diminished
and with no suffering that I can handle,
I deserve no sympathy as a cynic.
There will be no vigil held with candles.

Critical Leisure, Book III, Volume VI

The writing may read "inferiority complex"
or may be dismissed as mere reflex
of someone incapable of discerning action—
reduced to a series of brute reactions.

The glue hasn't worked but sticks to my hands
like callouses without proving that I'm a man—
what has always been in question for me,
someone whose stays are called "attempts to flee."

I haven't left the material for a documentary
while remaining incautiously sedentary.
Somehow, the more abuse I continuously receive,
the more my responses take their leave.

They would have beat me in the military
because the more I'm pushed the more I'm weary.
When I'm rushed I move slower than a ferry,
and the more I must smile, the less I'm cheery.

When you're dead from apparently nothing at all,
others think you have a lot of gall.
The sublime is before you, you show no surprise.
Unspirited, you are what the healthy despise.

When the social doesn't get you excited,
it must be that everything for you was provided.
After death, you become like a spoiled child
who to keep silent has empty riches on him piled.

I can't even threaten myself with death.
For hostages I won't negotiate.
Even nothingness can't put hair on my chest.

Love_Is_An_Anonymous_Cyberbully

I'm someone who I can propitiate.

If asked "What, after all, do I have left,"
they'd prefer that I respond "Nothingness."
But that would be to retain some thing,
and I'm left with neither bite nor sting.

If the great man is the man of project
then your hate is logical—I'm the reject.
Worse than my lack of nerve in a pinch
is my willingness to sit on the bench.

The system of needs produces urgency
to the extent that dropout, death, is insurgency.
The unfolding of the self in material life—
what has seemed desperate *to me* is strife.

When identity becomes private property,
the return takes precedence over the offering,
and when you call all my gifts self-interested—
with inconsistencies I appear an invalid.

In all my attempts at goodness I'm naïve,
and thought, always too late, makes me grieve.
My mouth is too close to the microphone.
The airbag powder in my eyes, nose, mouth is thrown.

When I want to travel inside me,
I use the satellite image—forget the territory.
When words fail to appear, I become a curse.
"Fucking piece of cunt shit" comes to mind first.

On paper, I am a fine specimen of individual.
Why I've nothing to show perplexes others.

Critical Leisure, Book III, Volume VI

I search for trauma to make it communicable,
find nothing but sexual terminology—truffle butter.

No! I am held together by serial trauma,
whether it's the war of all against all,
being cast in others' melodramas
or being cut for not being on the ball.

371. narcissistic withdrawal

The body is a ready-made
and b/w the ears is a secret—
the Unconscious, a secret glade
for the needy who can keep it.

An aging woman's skinny neck
that crumbles with her speech
disappoints with its little death—
mudslide on a Californian beach.

Pore-less faces of news anchors
reflect our hopeless renditions.
With all from self-tanner to oil-tankers
we acupuncture human frissons.

372. Endless material for theory

I become an experience—sudden,
without a quotient or a lesson...
singular, in one place at a time.

Love_Is_An_Anonymous_Cyberbully

A profile makes *from me* what I am not,
something omnipresent for many at once—
being everywhere for everyone by my being nowhere and no one.
I am not representation—a double—
but a clone,
a scission with no fatherly relation to me at all,
a separation,
a cut off organ become a thing that surpasses and undermines me
like Phineas Gage by the railroad spike.
Accordingly, as experience, I am constantly being destroyed.
To prevent shock, i.e., my existence,
I am never allowed to appear—
the description, like an ad, always pre-establishes and silences me.
They always talk over *me*.
My profile *precedes me* as a simulacrum that masks my absence
and yet bears no resemblance to any reality whatsoever.
I no longer belief in myself—show myself no affection.
I die senselessly.
Actual me is the alibi of a profile.

I am constantly diffused
dissolved
avoided through the detour of language
endlessly deferred
desecrated.
I reach laughter.
Dismemberment tickles me with feathers plucked from chickens
whose steroid-produced muscles crushed their hearts.
I never even *show up*.
I am halted by militant guards that introject fantasies and symbols
and drag me by the balls like mistresses
into the screen and a system of ambient equivalences.

There will always be a better offer.

If I'm a gamble, it's considerable risk and low gain.
The consequences outweigh the initial enjoyment—
the scales of Justice are flaying me alive,
either making me suddenly drop from my own weight
or tossing me suddenly into the air from my lightness.

I suffer it as from a neighbor
in a familiar basement where no one will ever find me.

373. The paparazzo poet

With information—and *reality*, that cybernetic buzzword—
poetry has left aesthetics, and perhaps even the 'daily news',
to favor paparazzi.
Like the 'stars' of reality television,
and because poetry is a form of photography
(written, as it is, on computers),
the entrance of the cameraman-poet into the lives of its subjects
affects their behavior, for better or for worse.

Over-sharing and consent,
which nevertheless nullify one another
as pathologically as the life and death drives,
seem to increase *with* one another.
The security industry grows along with the general insecurity
of being filmed at any moment without one's knowing it.
Still, such an insecurity exists alongside a general demand
to snap
share
and tag anyone anywhere, always.

The bother of poetry today

Love_Is_An_Anonymous_Cyberbully

is the shame of the seduced who take mirror-selfies
without their having managed it themselves.
Neither candid nor choreographed,
they see their photographs as surfaceable without consent
and without the right
to blame the poet who captured their *innate performance*.

What comes to their surprise
Is a sudden realization of their weakness—
their possessiveness towards their 'private information'.
They would share the utmost banalities of their 'moments',
including the 'historical moments'
of the culture whose 'happenings' found their whole discourse.
They would share the banalities of their opinions
their wishes
sufferings
joys—
their purchases that give them a purchase and new lease on life.
But when the poet exposes
their innermost, most apparent, most negligible banalities—
be it the unconscious quirks of their mannerisms
or their most calculatedly guarded secrets—
they feel embarrassed and thus wronged
by who they perceive as a thief of their secrets...*of their identity!*

And the Law will not be too far behind them...
so that it will uphold their right to privacy,
that is, *to lies*,
precisely when secrecy is no longer considered a virtue.

Most importantly,
by exposing the unmentionable in the citizen (the micro-celebrity),
poetry risks itself
in the very uselessness of its readership.

If it says one thing after this loss of its wisdom
(as other than a diversion),
it says: "by all means,
like a person speaking to an automated message
that forces one to repeat one's responses with clearer annunciation,
feel ashamed for having participated in this book.
You spill *your* guts here, not I."

374. Is there a from death, not an out of death?

She sent me flowers of the sort she would place on Elvis's grave,
only I was still alive, i.e., dead in life to life.
Beyond her sudden disallowance
of any future writing about her pain—
its commodification, only worse,
since its writing was utterly disoriented
uncoordinated
unprofitable—
her hatred of me broke through the indifference
within which I formerly analyzed her.
It said, "Look at me…recognize me."
She loved with the ferocity with which she hated.
I saw her, beyond all matter-of-factness, affected—affectionate.
She was a dialectician.

Her traumas,
about which I will no longer speak because she spoke them,
repeat without yielding the slightest pleasure—
neither sadist nor masochist nor both.
She had a lustrous resilience—

Love_Is_An_Anonymous_Cyberbully

a brilliance beyond her resistance to me, a resistance beyond strike—
like a diamond that can be cut only by what it normally reflects
when it is concentrated into a singular beam
(a hypercathexis beyond the panoptic possibility of death).

Seeing her speak herself, the trauma of herself,
seduced the seduction I had devised
as the last option to which she left me.
In that intimate moment,
the strategies of desire were seduced
of which we were both masters.
It constituted the singular event of my unfinished life —
the only experience that deserved the name—
a truly boundless moment
in which all bound energy gave way
and flooded the basement where all the linens were normally washed.
Only there was a *way* placed within *my history,*
the free-floating energy of my indifference.

I trivialized her pain,
as with the same insectoid scientificity with which she treated it.
Only the impersonality of the author
(against the ritual investment of the poet,
who perishes *with* his object so that nothing remains)
could produce the depersonalization-effect of its subjects,
the scission between the form of writing and its contented participants,
between lover and beloved—
the synthetic (and deathly) embrace
given way to the insectoid, curious gaze.
The writer, once the work of writing has given way to the virtual

and the written (of the visual order) has given way to the operated
upon,
has lost all relation to her subject—the subject of writing—
in the manner with which a scientist
checks the sum of particles on a monitor.
A form of writing akin to integral calculus—
the tendency to list,
to constantly interrupt in the excessive chatter of its nervousness
and get distracted.
The senseless
depoliticized
dehistoricized violence
that accompanies a deplasticized, *plastered* form of writing.
A writing preceding from a matter-of-factness
that precludes the would-be destructive experience of its subjects.

I challenged her to appear
by writing of her as if in her absence.
She challenged me to take a leave of absence from my absence—
to make me *disappear from invisibility*.
Our challenges were entangled.
In a single movement,
we drew out the reactions—as actions—
each of us wanted (but neither expected) from the other,
that the expected withdrawal of each of us
could no longer be drawn out in the process of repetition.
She burst into presence from my writing about her absence.
I burst out of absence from her suspicion of my integral presence
or narcissistic projection onto her.
But we cannot *speak* of the '*moment*'
in a form of language that makes one cause the other,
that gives one or the other temporal priority.

Can there be a compassion in the writing of indifference,

a solidarity that begins from a form of writing
that portrays in its very existence
the breakdown of the intimate in the sociable?

Can what begins from the sterile phobia, or virtual expropriation,
of touch be touching?

Can the fear of seduction seduce?

From death, can we synthesize?

(What if that's doomsday?)

375. To whom is what is given up given?

In giving, are individual things given?
Or is it exchange, the form of the gift itself, that is given?
Is kinship a product of the gift exchange,
or is what is exchanged kinship itself?
The generation of the general in generosity
(as opposed to the Universal),
of the given (as opposed to the True) in the gift—
are not the form (the relation) of exchange and the act of the gift
equi-primordial?

I will give you my life by giving you my death.
No longer 'me'
but *an* offering extant only in *the* offering—
we existed before 'you' or 'I',
and so never was there a breakdown of defenses,
never a coming-together,
only the preeminence of us.

No desires—which can only be fulfilled, never given,
which only exist without *us* as little bits or units—
only love.
Desires break up time
and so reify a time when there was just 'you and I',
that inclusive disjunction,
to the extent that our separation is preserved
in a dialectical, illusive (and elusive) 'partnership'.

Now, (which isn't to say 'currently'),
it's that I never existed—a separate unity—
but only have become initiated from *life/death* to *life-death*
in the shared dissolution and reversibility of us.
It's not that before I lacked sense.
It's not that you returned to me what is 'mine'.
It's that we died together, and lived therefrom—
we were not merely altered upon the alter
(that religious chopping block
that severs partnership to join two individuals),
we were simply nothing apart.
Apart from ourselves, we were everything together.
We have always been together.
Only 'reality' has separated us.
And were we without enjoyment,
it's that we took pleasure in each other.
But *we* cannot be extracted, only given and received—
where the latter lacks the temporal linearity of sex and the orgasm,
as a love that cycles through eternity.

Promises are mistaken to refer to a future.
They are fulfilled, kept, not given (not givens).
Now, forever,
I promise not to replace our love with my discourse,
that is, my psychobabble.

Love_Is_An_Anonymous_Cyberbully

I will give that up to your destructiveness…

The End

www.ingramcontent.com/pod-product-compliance
Lightning Source LLC
Chambersburg PA
CBHW071640160426
43195CB00012B/1313